NATIONAL GEOGRAPHIC

TRAVELER
India

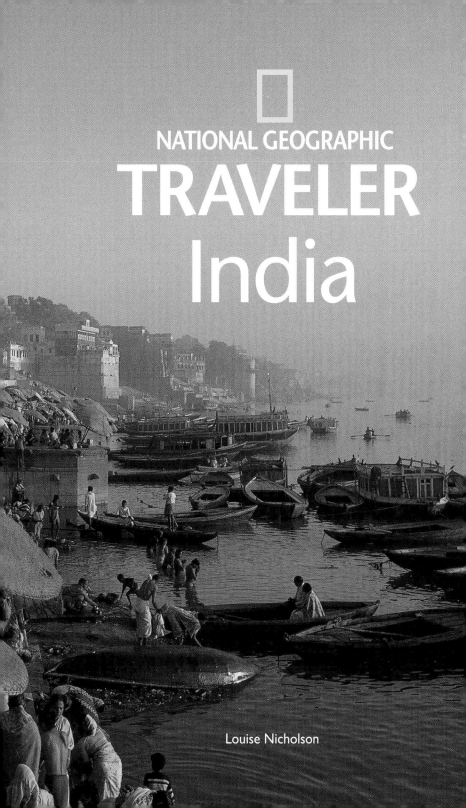

NATIONAL GEOGRAPHIC

TRAVELER
India

Louise Nicholson

Contents

How to use this guide 6–7 About the author 8
The regions 61–334 Travelwise 335–385
Index 386–97 Credits 398–99

Page 1: Carving on
Madurai's Minakshi
Sundareshvara Temple
Pages 2–3: *Brahmans*
and pilgrims at
Dashashwamedha Ghat,
Varanasi
Left: Film poster
suspended over a busy
Mumbai street

How to use this guide

See back flap for keys to text and map symbols.

The *National Geographic Traveler* brings you the best of India in text, pictures, and maps. Divided into three main sections, the guide begins with an overview of history and culture. Following are nine regional chapters with featured sites selected by the author for their particular interest. Each chapter opens with its own contents list.

The regions and sites within the regions are arranged geographically. A map introduces each region, highlighting the featured sites. Walks, drives, and boat rides, plotted on their own maps, suggest routes for discovering an area. Features and sidebars give intriguing detail on history, culture, or contemporary life.

The final section, Travelwise, lists essential information for the traveler—pretrip planning, special events, getting around, emergencies, and a glossary—plus a selection of hotels, restaurants, stores, and entertainment.

To the best of our knowledge, all information is accurate as of the press date. However, it's always advisable to call ahead when possible.

In India, travel is generally by public transportation or by car and driver. Directions are included to allow you to plan your trip, but detailed driving directions are therefore not included in this guide, as your driver should know the best way to get to the sites you wish to visit.

Color coding
Each region is color coded for easy reference. Find the region you want on the map on the front flap, and look for the color flash at the top of the pages of the relevant chapter. Information in **Travelwise** is also color coded to each region.

Taj Mahal	
Ⓜ	95 C4
✉	Tajganj
☎	0562-330498
🕐	Closed Fri.
💲	$

Visitor information
Practical information for most sites is given in the side column (see key to symbols on back flap). The map reference gives the page number of the map and grid reference. Other details are address, telephone number, days closed, and entrance charge in a range from $ (under $4) to $$$$$ (over $25). Other sites have information in italics and parentheses in the text.

TRAVELWISE

Hotel & restaurant prices
An explanation of the price bands used in entries is given in the Hotels & Restaurants section (see p. 343).

REGIONAL MAPS

- A locator map accompanies each regional map and shows the location of that region in the country.
- Adjacent regions are shown, each with a page reference.

WALKING TOURS

- An information box gives the starting and ending points, time and length of walk, and places not to be missed along the route.
- Where two walks are marked on the map, the second route is shown in orange.

DRIVING TOURS

- An information box provides details including starting and finishing points, time and length of drive, and places not to be missed along the route, or tips on terrain.

NATIONAL GEOGRAPHIC

TRAVELER

India

About the author

Louise Nicholson, a trained art historian living in London, catalogued Indian art at the auctioneers Christie's before spending her honeymoon in India in 1980. Since then she has returned more than 120 times.

Louise finds all aspects of the country endlessly fascinating, from the buildings, traditions, and colorful festivals to the exotic bird life, weaving traditions, and contemporary culture. She has traveled to all parts to lecture and do research for books and journalism—most of her 25 books are about India or London—and was Associate Director for the acclaimed six-part TV series "The Great Mughals." Louise shares her considerable knowledge and practical experience of India by leading lecture tours, advising private travelers, and taking her young family on exciting Indian adventures.

History & culture

A pink-powdered boy celebrates the Ganpati festival in Mumbai.

India today

INDIA HAS ALWAYS INTRIGUED FOREIGNERS. BACK IN THE FOURTH century B.C., Alexander the Great's men were amazed by the elephants. Later, William Shakespeare (1564–1616), who never visited India, alluded to its exotic trading wealth in his play *A Midsummer Night's Dream*. More recently, in 1897 the well-traveled writer Mark Twain (1835–1910) called India "…the one land that all men desire to see, and having seen once, by even a glimpse, would not give that glimpse for the shows of all the rest of the globe combined." Today, India continues to fascinate with equal force, all the more so because much of life is lived in public.

LAND OF CONTRASTS

India is a land of sharp contrasts where history and tradition go hand in hand with the dynamic present. It is second only to the United States in information technology, yet home life remains traditional and families eat together, enjoying laboriously prepared fresh dishes rather than convenience fast foods. Examples of this contrast abound throughout the whole of this vast country: A highly skilled silk-weaver from a village near Chennai will confirm his orders by cellular phone, while young students of international law at Delhi University volunteer to have their marriages arranged by their families; in a Rajasthan village a group of women swathed in magenta and saffron saris sits on the ground selling their vegetables next to an Internet café.

Contrasts are obvious from the moment you arrive. On a busy stretch of road outside the capital, New Delhi, you could see a camel, a bullock cart, a bicycle, a herd of goats, a Harley-Davidson motorcycle, an elaborately hand-painted truck, the latest model Mercedes car, a wandering cow, a streamlined, air-conditioned bus, and even a dancing bear or an elephant—all somehow getting along together with remarkably few accidents.

And the contrasts extend to huge differences in material wealth. The appalling poverty that was so vividly publicized by Mother Theresa and continues to be a living horror, exists alongside India's less well-known vast wealth in natural resources, wildlife, culture, crafts and skills, and personal affluence. India has more millionaires than the United States, and real estate prices are among the world's highest. And there are regular displays of outrageous extravagance. At some Hindu festivals, intricate images of the gods that take a full year to make are paraded once and then cast into the sea, where they disintegrate in moments. During the wedding season, thousands of families fall into debt in their efforts to put on an impressive show.

From the point of view of the visitor, India assaults the senses, stretching them further than you may have thought possible. You may hear calming religious music, see women dressed in vivid colors, and taste new flavors—not all of them spicy. You will smell fresh coconut milk and jasmine blossoms, and feel the smooth stones of temple floors beneath your bare feet.

India can make you laugh for joy and catch your breath in wonder; it can turn your ideas upside-down and introduce whole new subjects to think about—and, occasionally, it may well make you lose your patience.

People talk of seeing "the real India," when they have taken a local bus or spent time living in a village. This is indeed India, but there is more to it than that. To get anywhere near the real India, you should take advantage of every opportunity available to experience as many different sides as possible of this immensely rich, varied, and stimulating land.

INDIA'S DEMOCRACY: COHERENCE & DIVERSITY

The government of India is, in many ways, a daily miracle in the way that it administers a vast area, inhabited by a vast population. This huge land is home to more than a billion people (only China has a larger population), making India the world's largest democracy. It has

Tradition clashes with modernity in India. Here, a mother swathed in a sari sits proudly with her fashion model daughter.

a president as head of state, a prime minister as head of government, and a two-house parliament elected by universal suffrage—Lok Sabha (House of the People, 552 seats) and Rajya Sabha (Council of States, 250 seats). Based on the British Parliament, the political structure also draws on the United States' system and incorporates a bill of rights.

The country is divided into 25 states and 6 union territories, with the northern city of Delhi, the capital since 1911, in a separate category of its own due to its large population. Because the states were created after independence (see p. 50) on broadly historical and linguistic criteria, each has its own distinct character, culture, achievements, and disadvantages, and many have their own language. Looking at the political map of India on the inside back cover of this book, you can see how the states vary in size, from huge Madhya Pradesh to tiny Goa. Their populations vary too: Uttar Pradesh contains more than

Bangalore, India's most international city after Mumbai (Bombay), displays a mixture of the traditional and the contemporary.

139 million people, while remote Sikkim's has about 400,000.

As each state sends its members of parliament to Delhi, so Delhi sends a governor to each state. Each state also has its own administration, called the Legislative Assembly, and elects its own representatives, who can keep in touch with local needs—Delhi can be far away, in thought and culture as well as miles.

Government at all levels is cumbersome. Although India has two national languages, Hindi (written in Devanagari script) and English, there are 16 more, many with their own script. As you travel, you hear Bengali in West Bengal, Malayalam in Kerala, Tamil in Tamil Nadu, and Marathi in Maharashtra. Imagine the complexities of a Lok Sabha debate between MPs from several states.

A BILLION PEOPLE

With such a huge population, it's no wonder that the government struggles. The statistics reflect the extent of some of the country's complexities. With more than a billion people, India has 16 percent of the world's population living on 2.42 percent of the world's total area. The population explosion after independence, when it stood at 350 million, was mainly caused by increased longevity thanks to a better diet, control of famines, and treatment of diseases such as malaria, smallpox, and cholera. The average life expectancy has risen from less than 40 years to 63 years. Population growth is now being curbed by successful family planning programs: India's growth rate has been reduced from 2.5 percent in the 1960s to a current rate of 1.6 percent.

Women are playing a leading role in this effort and in India's impressive literacy campaign, especially in the south. Kerala's literacy is around 93 percent, Tamil Nadu's

65 percent, but in the north, tourist-popular Rajasthan's is only 38.5 percent, and there only 20 percent of women are literate. However, overall, between 1990 and 2000 India's literacy rate rose from 52 percent to 62 percent, a huge improvement from the 18 percent at independence in 1947.

Other major changes have come about since independence: Until recently, India's people lived in a mainly rural land; fewer than 10 percent lived in cities. Today, migration and

Seen from afar at night, Mumbai's high-rises, streetlights, and sweeping seafront combine to evoke a Western coastal city.

increases in numbers have pushed the urban population up to 27 percent, straining cities to their limits—12.6 million live in Mumbai (Bombay), 11 million in Kolkata (Calcutta), and 10 million in the capital. In the country's ten largest cities the average population density is 6,888 per 2.5 square miles (1 sq km).

The liberalization of India's economy in the 1990s has turned India from an inward-looking, highly regulated country into one that has taken its part in the global economy. It sustains 24 stock exchanges, from Mumbai to Bhubaneshwar, from Delhi to Chennai.

While India has made huge strides in many areas in recent years—the "green revolution" helped make the country self-sufficient in food with some produce left over to export—some problems persist. Officials calculate that 35 percent of the population still lives below the poverty line (a reduction from 54 percent in the 1970s). This is most acute in the states of Bihar, Madhya Pradesh, and Orissa, hit by the cyclone of 1999. Health problems persist, too. The government, in partnership with thousands of nongovernment and charity organizations, is currently focusing on providing clean water and sanitation to more rural areas and on tackling the persistent presence of malaria, leprosy, AIDS, and tuberculosis.

VISITORS IN INDIA

It is important for visitors to be aware that India plays a minor role in world tourism, even though, from the opposite point of view, tourism is India's third largest export industry (after gems and jewelry, and ready-made garments). Tourist activity (and therefore spending) in India is concentrated in the Golden Triangle formed by Delhi, Agra, and Jaipur, and in the increasingly popular towns of Rajasthan. Elsewhere, with exceptions such as

India has a population of more than a billion and huge crowds are commonplace. Hindi has special words to describe crowds.

Ajanta's caves and Varanasi, the more adventurous traveler will find most of India refreshingly quiet.

Traveling around the country is easy. There are good road, railroad, and air networks, and Indian people are particularly helpful and friendly. It is easy to observe and take part in

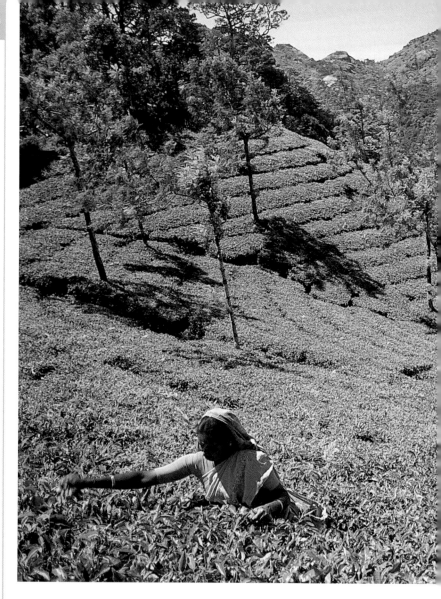

local life. The host of major festivals (see pp. 379–82) is augmented by thousands of smaller, equally charming ones. You can stop to join in the celebrations of a village deity, inspect the goats at an agricultural fair, and watch the lively wedding processions that dance their way through the streets.

In villages you can find craftsmen practicing ancient skills—making gold jewelry, weaving silk saris, or casting in bronze. The village elementary school usually welcomes a spontaneous visit and an exchange of songs. In the fields you can see the traditional irrigation methods, the planting of wheat and paddy, the gathering in of harvests of cotton, chilies, oil seeds, tea, rubber, lentils, and more—70 percent of Indians depend on agriculture for their livelihood. You will be welcomed into temples, *gurudwaras*, and mosques to observe the faithful and their rituals.

Cities are places for finding top-quality cultural performances, seeing one of India's

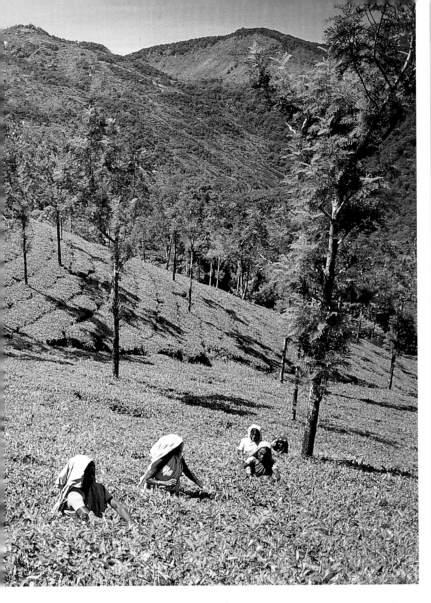

"Bollywood" movies (the name is a pun on the idea of Hollywood in Bombay), visiting the large markets and high-quality stores, and obtaining information on the surrounding area from the visitor information office.

To find out what is important to Indians now, pick up a copy of the periodical *India Today* or a local newspaper: Of India's 41,000 or so dailies, 338 are published in English and give insight into local concerns. For a glimpse into sophisticated high society, take a look at

Tea production in India has doubled since independence in 1947. Women nip out the shoots while men work in the factory.

Verve magazine, India's equivalent of *Vogue*.
Gone are the days when travelers had to compromise on their accustomed comforts. India's affluence means that in most metropolitan areas cars are comfortable, hotels efficient, communications streamlined, and stores stocked with international goods. ■

Land & landscape

INDIA IS VAST. IT STRETCHES FROM 8° TO 36° LATITUDE NORTH AND FROM 68° TO 97° longitude. The country's diverse landscape of rivers, fields, forests, mountains, and deserts is shaped like a large diamond. To the north, it is cut off from the rest of Asia by the Himalayan mountain range. To the south, the 2,000 miles (3,218 km) of coastline are washed by the Arabian Sea in the west, the Indian Ocean in the south, and the Bay of Bengal to the east.

These mountains and seas separate India from surrounding countries. Pakistan and Bangladesh, which shared India's history until 1947, are the exceptions. Historically, the mountains have been India's natural defense, and only the most determined invaders have penetrated them. The coast, on the other hand, benefited from the east–west sea trade routes and is dotted with ancient trading posts, especially on the Konkani, Malabar, and Coromandel stretches.

Modern India occupies a strategic position in Asia, looking westward to Arabia and Africa and eastward to Malaysia and the Indonesian Archipelago. Its borders meet, from west to east, Pakistan, Afghanistan, China's Sinkiang Province, Tibet, Nepal, Bhutan, Myanmar (Burma), and Bangladesh. The long strip of the Andaman and Nicobar Islands in the Bay of Bengal and the Lakshadweep Islands in the Arabian Sea are also part of the Republic.

India claims part of the great Himalayan range, the world's highest mountain system and one of its youngest, created when the drifting Indian plate collided with the Tibetan plate of south Asia about 50 million years ago. Mountains, including Everest and 95 other peaks rising above 24,600 feet (7,500 m), were formed well after that, by later movement of the continental plates. Today much of India's forest, which covers 20 percent of the land, is in this region.

India's lesser mountain ranges include the Aravallis, one of the world's oldest mountain systems, in southern Rajasthan, west of which lies the Thar Desert. Here is some of India's mineral wealth, in copper ore, lead-zinc complexes, and rock phosphate. The Vindhya and Satpura Mountains cross central India, a barrier to invaders' southern progress. They rise to the Deccan and Mysore Plateaus, from which the Sahyadris (Western Ghats) drop

sharply to the west coast and the gentler Eastern Ghats to the east coast. Iron ore mined here—in the states of Goa, Karnataka, and Madhya Pradesh—and in Orissa and Bihar make India the world's largest producer of that metal. Gold and diamonds are mined farther south, and rubies and other gems are mined in Kerala.

All of India's mountains help gather the country's precious waters from its two mosoons. The great southwest monsoon begins in Kerala in June and sweeps up north across India through July, August, and September, dumping its final gallons in the Himalayan mountains. The smaller southeast monsoon drenches the east coast intermittently in October and November, enabling Tamil Nadu farmers to harvest three rice crops annually, but sometimes bringing cyclones and destruction, as in Orissa in 1999. After this, the weather is at its best throughout most of India until April, when the heat arrives and the mountains become cool retreats.

Rivers originating from these mountain watersheds nourish India's soil. From the Himalayan mountains you can trace the path of the great Indus, the Ganga (Ganges), and, in the east, the Brahmaputra. The Indus waters the Punjab, India's wheat bowl. The Ganga, Hindus' holiest river, rises near the Gangotri glacier, and with its tributaries, flows through the heartland of rice-growing ancient India to the Bay of Bengal, creating India's largest river basin, which covers 25 percent of the country.

Most of the great rivers of peninsular India meander through flat valleys to the Bay of Bengal. The Brahmani and Mahanadi irrigate Orissa; the Godavari and Krishna flow off the

Coconut palms shade fishing villages here on the Andaman Islands and along India's southern coastline.

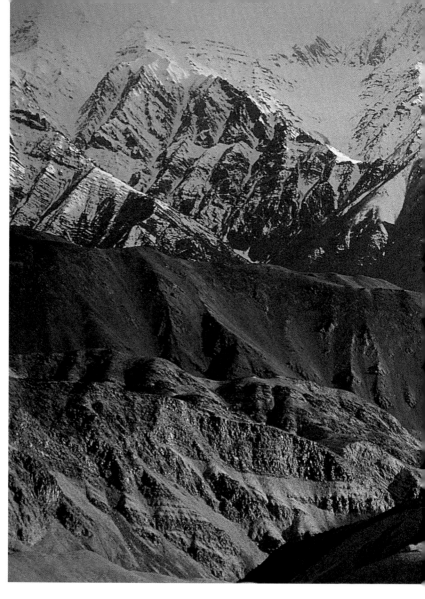

Deccan Plateau and the Penner, and the Kaveri (Cauvery) flow from the Mysore Plateau. The great Kaveri benefits from two monsoons and is southern India's holiest river, but siphoning off its waters for irrigation is a contentious issue between Karnataka and Tamil Nadu states. The Narmada—with its controversial dam that threatens to permanently alter the ecology and cultural balance of the area—and Tapti Rivers flow down from the Vindhya and Satpura ranges to the Arabian Sea.

This rhythm of life can, however, go wrong. India's landmass, surrounded by warm oceans, straddles the Tropic of Cancer and is at one of the Earth's major plate junctions. This means that periodically it suffers from violent natural events that may leave disaster in their wake. Tropical cyclones are frequent in the Bay of Bengal, while the relative youth of the Himalaya means that this is a major earthquake region, as exemplified by the devastating earthquake that hit Gujarat in 2001.

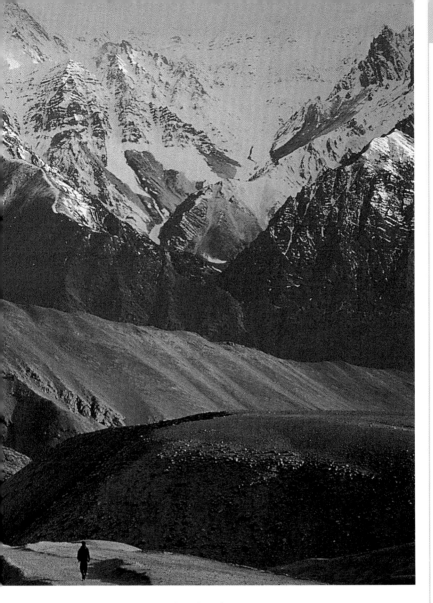

Monsoons are relied upon throughout the country to provide water for growing crops. Heavy monsoons, however, can bring floods that often have a high death toll. These floods have been exacerbated by deforestation of the hills for industrial and agricultural purposes. The balance between having plenty of water to flood the rice fields and having too much so that crops, homes, and even lives are lost is a fine one. The alternative to the floods may be famines. However, India's infrastructure can

Barren, beautiful Ladakh is believed to have been inhabited first by herdsmen from Tibet, then by early Buddhist monks.

now deal successfully with these: When the monsoon fails in one area, the army is able to move supplies to the drought-stricken area. As a result of this organization, few lives were lost in the Maharashtra famines of 1965–66 and 1974–75, while more than two million people died in the Bengal famine of 1943. ∎

Food & drink

CLIMATE, GEOGRAPHY, RELIGION, AND TRADITION HAVE SHAPED THE MANY cuisines of India. There is a huge variety of foods to eat, from the simple to the extravagantly rich. One of the delights of traveling is to sample the dishes of different communities. Even the staple southern Indian meal of rice and *dhal* (pulse—peas, beans, and lentils) varies subtly from town to town; indeed, so many kinds of pulse are grown in India that the financial papers give the pulses stock exchange prices a special section of their own.

India is traditionally associated with spicy food such as curries. The word curry itself has confusing connotations. For many people it implies a highly spiced and rich meat casserole that may well be difficult to digest. In fact, the word comes from Tamil, a southern Indian language: *Kari* simply means "to eat by biting." But curry has for centuries referred to a savory sauce of meat, fish, fruit, or vegetables cooked with a *masala,* a blend of locally available bruised or ground spices. This was traditionally added to the rather bland staple food of grain, either flour, baked into unleavened bread (in the north), or boiled rice (in the east and south). Thus, *karis* gave interest and variety—one fifth-century text describes the hero taking "rice dressed in butter, with its full accompaniment of curries." Today, India's vast array of curries fulfills the same function.

India's sheer size and geographical diversity mean that most foods are produced somewhere in the country. To visit the vast wholesale market outside Delhi is to be at the crossroads of a countrywide food-trading network. Here you see up to 20 kinds of bananas from the south, oranges from the Lower Himalaya, rice from Bengal and Tamil Nadu, and sackfuls of spices.

If you travel to the north, try the breads— *naan, chapatti, roti, paratha,* and the paper-thin *romali roti* (handkerchief bread). They go well with mildly spiced lamb or chicken barbecued on skewers in a tandoor (clay oven). In Rajasthan, too, you will find the food is quite gentle, but watch out for the chili peppers. Meat, dhal, and *sabzi* (vegetables) are scooped up with pieces of nutty-textured breads made from maize, millet, or gram. A spoonful of spice-hot *brinjal* (aubergine) or *nimbu* (lime) pickle completes the meal.

In contrast, the dishes inspired by the Islamic courts of Agra, Delhi, Lucknow. and Hyderabad are rich and complicated. Meat is cooked very slowly with cream, almonds, and dried fruits until it is very soft. Vegetables are just as rich, be they *okra* (edible seed pods), *sag* (spinach), *mattar* (peas), or *aloo* (potato). Even the essential dhal has added cream, and breads are sometimes stuffed. So it is essential to have plenty of rice to balance the meal— and to wait until your body is acclimatized before enjoying this kind of feast. Should you wish for some wine with such a meal, India now has vineyards up on the Deccan Plateau. Otherwise, do as the Indians do: Stick to the light local beers and bottled water.

Along the coast, you can relax in the shade over grilled giant shrimp or a pomfret fish cooked with plenty of coconut, which helps to balance the fire-hot spices. As the sun sets in Goa, you might like a glass of *feni*—or a fruit juice, such as mango, papaya, or watermelon. Other thirst-quenching drinks found all over India are *lassi* (thin yogurt drink) and fresh lime juice with either sparkling or still water. The ubiquitous *chai* (tea) is drunk strong with milk and sugar, a surprisingly reviving drink.

Vegetables are popular throughout the country, but it is in the mostly vegetarian south that the vegetable is the star. The best way to sample the variety is to order a *thali* (platter). This circular plate has six or more *katoris* (little dishes) around the edge, each containing a different vegetable or pulse. There will also be *dahi* (yogurt), chutney, and *mighai* (sweet pudding). Start with the *rasam* (clear soup) and work round, mixing boiled rice from the center of the platter into each dish. A thali is utterly delicious, healthy, and always a little bit different to the last one. ∎

In Old Delhi's spice market, you can buy dried chilis, powdered turmeric, cinnamon bark, and other aromatic products.

History & culture

INDIA'S HISTORY STRETCHES BACK SEVERAL MILLENNIA, THROUGH THE RISE and fall of warring states and empires, invasions and conquests. Foreign rulers have pillaged, destroyed, and rebuilt, while rival religions, imported and homegrown, have clashed and merged. Traders from over the mountains and seas have brought their own languages and cultures. But India always remains and retains its uniqueness.

PREHISTORY TO THE CLASSICAL AGE

The subcontinent abounds in uncharted archaeological remains and, therefore, much archaeological activity. The result is that scholars are still reassessing India's early history. The most spectacular group of inhabited rock shelters yet found are the thousand or so strung along a ridge at Bhimbetka (see p. 115), near Bhopal. Half of them are decorated with paintings. Discovered only in 1957, no exact date can be given for these paintings, but estimates of their age range from 10,000 to 40,000 years. Vestiges of human life on the subcontinent go back some 400,000 years. Crudely sharpened stones dating from the period of the Himalayan glaciations (Pleistocene) have been found in India. Stone hammers from the Upper Paleolithic (up to 30,000 years ago) have been found at Pushkar, in Rajasthan, where quartz, agate, and carnelian have been used and arrowheads carved to a beauty and precision far beyond their practical demands.

During these early times, the Upper Paleolithic and Mesolithic periods, early settlements displayed evidence of various lifestyles—fishing, hunting, gathering, simple agriculture and husbandry, and organized trading. Paintings from this era show foreign visitors, and activities such as dancing, hunting, and ambushing. In the Indus Valley, barley and wheat were cultivated; sheep and goats were domesticated; and by 5000 B.C. the familiar humped Indian cattle were the most common domesticated animals. The potter's wheel appeared around 3500 B.C., ushering in mass production, as did grain storehouses built of mud bricks, which are evidence of large, organized communities. Major excavation sites include Banavali and Mitathal (Haryana) and Surkotada (Kachchh). Meanwhile, the Ganga plains reveal evidence of similar but independent developments.

Indus Valley Civilization

Within this widespread cultural network, with its increased use of the floodplains for more productive farming, arose the urbanized Indus Valley Civilization, also known as the Mature Harappan culture, which peaked around 2500 B.C. Its best known cities, Moenjodaro and Harappa, are in Pakistan, but India's sites include fascinating Lothal port (see p. 152) and the spectacular fortress city of Dholavira, both in Gujarat, and Kalibangan in Rajasthan.

These and other cities of this sophisticated civilization were much advanced in comparison with earlier ones. They usually had a clear city plan focused on a high mound, probably a religious-political center. There were special areas for craftspeople, housing for the wealthy, and workers' accommodations. There were large granaries, efficient water and drainage systems, and evidence of international trading.

This intriguing, unified social and political organization extended over present-day Pakistan and much of northern India. Yet two mysteries about the culture remain. Its tantalizing stone seals have not yet been deciphered, and the cause of its final decline around 1700 B.C. is in question. Was it invasion, famine, over-farming, or something else? Whatever the answer, much of the culture was passed down to later Indian society.

Vedic Age: 1500–1000 B.C.

During this period, the Hindu religion and a specific social order known as the caste system (see p. 29) began to be formed—two powerful, cohesive forces that would endure as empires rose and fell over the next 3,000 years.

The gradual migration of Aryan tribes from the Iranian plateau over the mountains

The riotous carvings on the soaring roofs and gateways of Hindu temples can be enjoyed by the faithful outside.

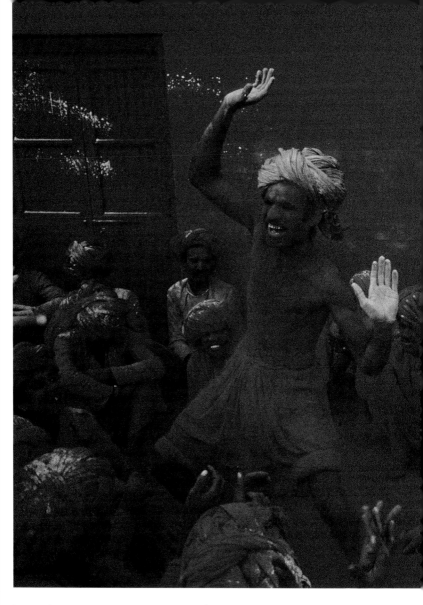

into northern India began between 1500 and 1300 B.C. These seminomadic tribes were pastoralists who formed simple, settled farming village communities quite different from the sophisticated Harappan cities. Each had a warrior chief, called a *raja,* who received tribute in return for being the villagers' protector. Cattle were the main form of wealth, and thus a main reason for war.

The raja's status was confirmed by his priests, called *brahmans,* who compiled the great hymns and verses in Vedic Sanskrit, at first handed down orally but later written down; the *Rig Veda* is the best known. These and other texts, such as the *Upanishads,* the epic *Mahabharata,* and the *Puranas* tell us about Vedic history, life, and thought; the abstract doctrine of *karma* has its roots in Vedic philosophy. The Vedic religion centered on the worship of personified forces of nature and abstract divinities. It emphasized ritual, sacrifice, chanting of hymns, and the

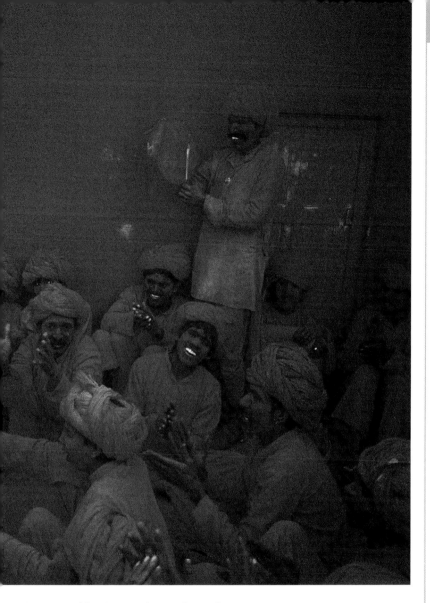

importance of the priest as mediator, and it became the basis of what is known as Hinduism (see pp. 54–57).

As tribal identity became territorial, so royal power was symbolized with coronation and sacrifice, the old tribute became a tax, and trade and agriculture flourished.

Most important of all, a new social order of caste hierarchy emerged, the *varna*. Varna means color, and at first the distinction was between the pale Aryan immigrants and

A group of men sing and dance to celebrate Holi, the arrival of spring, in Jodhpur, western Rajasthan.

darker non-Aryan people of India. The Aryans were divided into priests and teachers *(brahmans)*, warriors and rulers *(kshatriyas)*, and merchants and cultivators *(vaishyas)*, while the non-Aryans and other economically low groups formed the *shudras*, whose purpose was to serve the three superior castes. Ritual

While the caste system officially no longer exists today, it is still exceptional that K. Ramaswamy, born an untouchable, could rise to become a justice of India's Supreme Court.

status and subcastes called *jatis* soon evolved, as did the idea of purity of caste and its opposing pollution. This brought two results: strict caste rules pervading social life, and a fifth caste, the untouchables, whose occupations were considered impure. Mahatma Gandhi later attempted to give these people status by renaming them *harijans* (children of God).

Gradually, Aryan and non-Aryan cultures fused in northern India, creating an Indo-Aryan society whose language groups are the roots of 74 percent of the Indian population today; they include Hindi, Punjabi, Rajasthani, and Bengali. Meanwhile, in southern India, the Dravidian culture remained isolated from Aryan culture, as reflected in its main languages, which predate Indo-Aryan ones: Telegu, Tamil, Kannada, and Malayalam. India never had a common language, but Sanskrit, the most highly developed Indo-Aryan language, remained the language of the educated people until English usurped it during the Raj and became the lingua franca, still used.

Early empires, new faiths

In all, India was unified by its trade routes and by its traders, who enjoyed unprecedented status, patronized the arts, and encouraged the growth of towns. By about 600 B.C., trading had stimulated the rise of port towns (called *puras*) along the rivers, such as Varanasi and Vaishali, marking the start of India's second widespread urbanization, this time in the Ganga Valley.

Economic developments followed, including a common script, coinage, and banking. Meanwhile, invasions from the northwest by the Persian Achaemenid emperor Cyrus in 530 B.C. created a Persian cultural and trading bridge. In this post-Vedic world of republics, monarchies, and powerful traders, the strictures of Vedic Hinduism came into question, and two princes of northern India founded Buddhism and Jainism, instantly successful back-to-basics religions whose practicality and equality appealed especially to the increasingly powerful trading castes.

The kingdom that eventually emerged preeminent was Magadha, whose rulers Bimbisara (543–491 B.C.) and Ajatashatru (491–461 B.C.) founded Rajagriha (Rajgir, near Patna), then Pataliputra (Patna). By the late fourth century, however, the kingdom was in trouble, embroiled in a dispute over succession. The decline of the Magadhan kingdom coincided with the arrival of the Greek general

The magnificent eastern gate of Sanchi's great stupa, carved in the first century B.C., testifies to the attraction of Buddhism for wealthy traders trapped in the Hindu caste system.

Alexander the Great, who invaded the Punjab in 327 B.C. He left garrisons and governors behind when he departed two years later, but his death in 323 B.C. rendered the fledgling Greek province dangerously unstable.

Astute strategist Chandragupta Maurya, who had already taken over the weakened Magadhan throne in 381 B.C., lost no time in throwing the Greeks out of northeast India: The powerful Mauryan empire (321–104 B.C.) was born. This, the first of India's many great empires, stretched from Assam to Afghanistan, from Kashmir to Mysore. Its legendary capital was at Pataliputra (Patna). Chandragupta, a Jain, abdicated to join a Jain community in southern India and died by *sallekhana* (slow starvation). His grandson was the greatest Mauryan ruler, Ashoka *(R.269–232 B.C.)*. Ashoka converted to Buddhism and promoted its concept of *dharma*—social responsibility to maintain human dignity and socio-religious harmony. He had his edicts on social values and behavior engraved onto rocks and columns across his empire, usually using Brahmi script and the Pankrit language.

The Shungas and Kanvas succeeded the Mauryas before the focus moved to the northwest. Here the Bactrian Greeks invaded from Afghanistan in 190 B.C. and ruled Gandhara (in modern Pakistan); at its peak their kingdom stretched to Mathura, south of Delhi, only to be supplanted by the Scythians in the first century B.C. and then the Parthians, both central Asian tribes.

India's second important kingdom was the Kushana, which flourished from the first century B.C. to the third century A.D. Its borders encompassed central Asia and northern India, stretching to Varanasi and Vaishali (near Bhopal); its capitals were at Peshawar (now in Pakistan) and Mathura. Under its greatest ruler, the Buddhist convert Kanishka *(R.100–120 A.D.)*, sculpture and other arts flourished, heavily influenced by the Hellenistic art of the Roman Empire. At this time the impressive Buddhist monastery and *stupas* at Sanchi (see p. 116) were built, financed by the traders of nearby Vaishali.

Meanwhile, among the kingdoms of the Deccan (now made up of the states of Karnataka and Andhra Pradesh), the Satavahanas rose in the first century B.C. to enjoy four centuries of preeminence. They maintained a careful mix of Vedic principles, Mauryan political philosophy, and tolerance toward the powerful Buddhist traders. Their

India timeline

B.C.

ca 2,500 Probable peak of Indus Valley Civilization.

327 Alexander the Great of Greece invades.

ca 269–232 Ashoka rules Mauryan empire

190 Greeks from Bactria invade.

A.D.

ca 100–120 Kanishka rules Kushana empire.

ca 335–415 Chandragupta II rules Gupta empire.

ca 600–630 Mahendravarman I rules Pallava empire in southern India.

8th century on Rajputs rise to power in northern India.

805–1278 Chola Empire dominates Tamil Nadu.

1192 Qutb-ud-din-Aibak takes Delhi; in 1206 establishes Slave Sultanate, India's first Muslim kingdom.

1206–1596 The Delhi sultanates: Slave, Khilji, Tughlaq, Sayyid, and Lodi.

1398 Timur (Tamburlaine) sacks Delhi.

1336–1565 Vijayanaga Empire unites southern India.

1509 Alfonso de Alburquerque takes Goa, makes it capital of Portugal's maritime empire.

1516 Babur invades, takes Agra, initiates Mogul empire, crushes Rajput confederacy the next year.

1527–1707 Height of Mogul empire under Emperors Babur, Akbar, Jahangir, Shah Jahan, and Aurangzeb.

1562 Akbar's first Rajput alliance, with Amer (Jaipur).

1616 on Sir Thomas Roe wins trading rights from Jahangir; Portuguese power wanes but English power rises under the East India Company.

1631 Mumtaz Mahal dies and Shah Jahan builds the Taj Mahal as her mausoleum.

1639 Madras founded as English trading headquarters.

1648 Shah Jahan brings the capital back to Delhi.

1772 British administrative capital moves from Madras to Calcutta.

1799 Arthur Wellesley defeats Tipu Sultan of Mysore; Ranjit Singh takes Lahore and establishes the first Sikh kingdom.

1815–1947 The British government leaves Calcutta for Shimla hill station for six months each year.

1840–1914 India is Britain's most important trading partner.

1857–58 Rebellion against the British at Delhi, Lucknow, and Kanpur. Delhi retaken; Bahadur Shah II deposed, ending Mogul Empire. British power, known as the Raj, is now direct from Westminster.

1869 Suez Canal opens.

1885 National Congress founded, to fight for India's freedom.

1906 All India Muslim League founded, to safeguard Indian Muslims' interests.

1911 King-Emperor George V announces British capital to move to Delhi.

1915 Gandhi returns from South Africa to fight for India's freedom.

1930 Gandhi leads the Salt March protesting against the British salt tax.

1931 Lutyens garden city of New Delhi inaugurated.

1947 Independence for India; Pakistan created.

1950 Republic of India inaugurated. Constitution adopted. Jawaharlal Nehru is India's first prime minister. Gandhi assassinated.

1966–77, 1980–84 Indira Gandhi prime minister.

1971 East Pakistan becomes Bangladesh.

1991–96 Narasimha Rao prime minister; major drive to open India to world market forces.

2001 On January 26, an earthquake devastates Gujarat. India's population reaches more than one billion.

patronage is evident in the rock-cut temples of Karla (see pp. 183-84) and Kanheri (see pp. 170–71), both on trade routes to the Konkan ports.

Farther south, the Chola, Chera, and Pandya chiefs were supreme. Their body of literature, called the *Sangam*, reveals a mainly non-Aryan society whose peasant communities developed ports that thrived. Until the fall of the Roman Empire, trade was brisk in jewels, ivory, fragrant woods, perfumes, and spices, the last an essential part of European culture. When the Visigoth Alaric sacked Rome in A.D. 410, his ransom was 3,000 pounds of Indian pepper, not gold. A Roman cohort was maintained at Calicut on the Malabar coast, and coins, pottery, and other objects testify to foreign trading communities in the coastal ports and at the commercial city of Madurai.

Chola period bronze of Shiva Nataraja

CLASSICAL AGE: A.D. 300–650

India's classical age was dominated by the Gupta dynasty (circa 319–circa 467) in northern India, while the Gangas were powerful in Orissa, the Kadambas in the Deccan, and the Pallavas (fourth to seventh centuries) in the deep south.

Chandragupta I (*R*.319–335) brought the Guptas to power, widening his empire's boundaries to the Indus in the west and the Bay of Bengal in the east. His principal cities were on the Ganga at Ayodhya and Allahabad. Their influence stretched southward to the Pallavas' territory around Kanchipuram. Thus, they dominated trade from coast to coast as well as to central Asia and to the old Silk Route between China and Bactria (Afghanistan).

Gupta rulers performed Vedic sacrifices (which sometimes involved animals) to legitimize their rule. They patronized the brahmans and senior courtiers by giving them land grants and privileges, and they supported Buddhism. During this period, essential elements of Hinduism emerged, such as *bhakti* (see p. 56) and image-worship. So, too, did the importance of the Mother Goddess, the temple as the center of social and religious life, and Vishnu and Shiva, whose complex myths and legends were written in the Purana texts.

Under the Gupta patronage of art and literature, especially under Chandragupta II (*R*.335–415), a new classical style emerged that became the aesthetic yardstick for subsequent artists and craftsmen. Sanskrit poetry reached its apogee in the works of Kalidasa, which include *Raghuvamsa* and *Kumarasambhava*.

Sculpture reached new heights of technique, spirituality, and three-dimensional expression. Architecture witnessed the formative phases of the Nagara and Dravida (see p. 262) temple styles. Coins had fine designs, and the paintings of Ajanta (see pp. 178–79) and Bhaja (see p. 184) influenced Buddhist art across Asia. Formal principles that were followed for centuries were laid down in treatises: Vastu for architecture, Shilpa for sculpture, and Chitra for painting. The 18th-century architect Vidyadhar Bhattacharya looked to these when he was planning Jaipur city (see pp. 131–32).

India was already at the forefront of studies in subjects such as astronomy and medicine. Now, under the Guptas, Aryabhata and Varahamihira pushed the study of astronomy further, while new ideas in mathematics, the cipher, and numerals were exported via the Arabs to Europe. Legal texts abounded, and covered every subject, from social problems to property rights. An almost humanist interest in the ideal citizen preoccupied the philosopher-writers of the time, and Vatsyayana wrote the sophisticated treatise on the art of love, the *Kamasutra*. Only when waves of Huns, then Gurjara, had succeeded in disrupting trade,

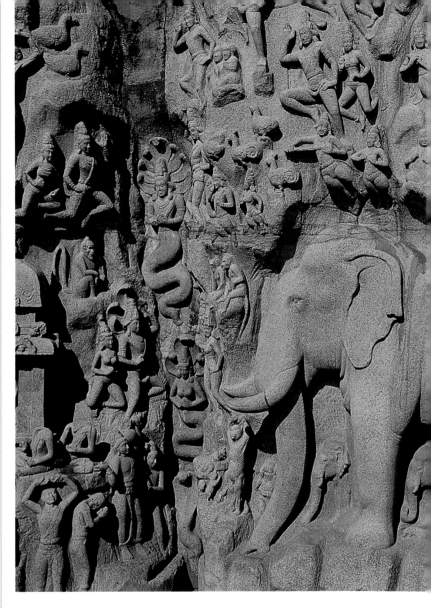

did Gupta power wane. Some of these invaders were ancestors of the Rajput clans of Rajasthan (see p. 37).

Down in southern India, most kingdoms of this period followed the Vedic rituals. Kingdoms usually concentrated their worship on either Shiva or Vishnu, and promoted royal-religious power in the Gupta style by giving land grants to both priests and temples. At this time that the temple became the central element in the government of what was an agrarian community, where rice was both the main crop and the standard bartering unit.

Temple architecture blossomed under the early Pallava rulers, who believed they were descended from Brahma. Much of their work survives at their capital, Kanchipuram, and their port, Mamallapuram (Mahabalipuram). Mahendravarman I (*R*. 600–630), was a dramatist and poet who converted from Jainism to Shaivism (the worship of Shiva), and under his patronage architecture, literature, and the applied arts began to acquire their distinct Dravidian character.

The Pallavas' arch enemies were the Chalukyas, who ruled in the Deccan, first from Aihole and later from Badami. During the post-Gupta disruptions in the north, Harsha Vadhana eventually lost his kingdom to the Chalukya king Pulakeshin II.

A classical Indian culture developed from the collective achievement of the many remarkable individuals of this period. Its wide

These elephants are part of a huge, lively, and complex relief sculpture cut into the rock at Mahabalipuram.

scope of learning pushed knowledge forward in a range of subjects, from the development of Sanskrit to the concept of a god-king, from Buddhist philosophy to the *Ramayana* stories. Traders carried this sophisticated culture into the east, where it profoundly influenced the other cultures that it came into contact with.

Seated Buddhas, painted in the fifth century with tremendous virtuosity, are just a fragment of the many vibrant, naturalistic frescoes that coat several caves at Ajanta.

FROM THE CLASSICAL AGE TO ISLAM'S ARRIVAL: 650–1206

Post-Gupta northern India saw the growth of regional states, while southern India rose to a new prominence. Here, artistic innovation flourished, as seen in the vigorous sculptures of Elephanta and Ajanta and in the creation of monumental stone temples such as those at Thanjavur, Chidambaram, and Gangakondacholapuram. These temples became a focus for all the arts, especially sculpture, bronze-casting, dance, music, and painting. Patronized by rulers, they played a vital role in endorsing royal power.

During these centuries, autonomous village government was established; it is still strong today. Indian merchants' guilds specializing in textiles, gems, and spices expanded to trade with the Jewish, Arab, and Chinese peoples. Sanskrit was the language of officials and high literature. As Buddhism and Jainism waned, Hinduism absorbed local cults to acquire regional characteristics.

In the north, the Ganga Valley and its main city, Kanauj, were under the control of first, the Pratiharas; then, the Palas; and finally the Rashtrakutas, the first Deccan dynasty to reach this area. To the east, the Somavamshis established their capital at Bhubaneshwar, whose fine temples survive.

In the Deccan and far south, wars were fought over the fertile valleys and lucrative trade routes, but in peacetime fine temples were built. The Chalukyas built theirs at Aihole, Pattadakal, and Badami, while the later Hoysalas left intricately carved temples in and around their capital, Halebid.

Farther south, the Pallava rulers, still at loggerheads with the Chalukyas, continued to build temples at their port of Mahabalipuram and their capital, Kanchipuram, one of the seven sacred cities for Hindus, and southern India's largest international textile center. They enjoyed lucrative maritime trade with Sri Lanka, Arabia, and southeast Asia.

In the mid-ninth century, the Cholas (850–1278), longtime chieftains in the area, created the most powerful southern state. Their greatest rulers—Rajaraja I (R. 984–1014), Rajendra (R. 1014–44), and Kulottunga I (R. 1070–1118)—expanded their territories to cover Tamil Nadu, southern Karnataka, southern Kerala, and northern Sri Lanka. From their principal port, Nagappattinam, at the mouth of the Kaveri River, Chola trading extended to China.

A sixth-century triple-headed carving of Shiva in the Elephanta Island cave temple dedicated to Shiva. The right head is feminine while that on the left is fiercely masculine.

Back in the north, Rajput clans were rising to power. These immigrant clans acquired kshatriya (see p. 29) status in the caste system and traced their lineage to the sun and moon. Some called themselves *Agni-kulu* (Fire Family) and claimed descent from a mythical figure that arose out of a vast sacrificial pit near Mount Abu. These clans included the Kachwahas (Jaipur) and Sisodias (Udaipur) of Rajasthan, as well as the Chandellas (Khajuraho) and the Tomars who founded Delhi around 736. They warred constantly. It was the great Chauhan hero Prithviraj III who took the Tomars' Delhi and managed to fight off an early Islamic invader, Mohammad of Ghor, in 1191.

But even Prithviraj could not stop Islam from taking hold. Arab Muhammad bin Qasim arrived in 711, by sea from Baghdad at a point east of Karachi. Mahmud of Ghazni, a Turk, made repeated raids between 1000 and 1026, his men crossing the Hindu Kush to plunder the northern plains and their rich temples; the Nagda temples near Udaipur are rare survivors (see p. 138). Then, in 1192, the Turkish invader Mohammad of Ghor's slave general, Qutb-ud-din-Aibak, defeated Prithviraj III and took Delhi. When

Mohammad of Ghor was assassinated in Lahore in 1206, Aibak assumed control, made Delhi the capital of India's first, if unstable, Muslim kingdom, and initiated the Delhi Sultanate that would be succeeded by the Moguls. Islam, not Hinduism, would now be the dominant political, social, and cultural force in northern India for six centuries. The capitals, Delhi and for a while Agra, saw the creation of a rich Indo-Islamic culture, much of which survives today in palaces, tombs, cuisine, inlaid marble, and in music and other arts.

THE DELHI SULTANATE: 1206–1526
Until Aibak's own lieutenant, Iltutmish, seized power in 1211, Delhi locals might have been expecting the Islamic presence to be temporary. Iltutmish, however, ruled for 25 years. He consolidated his empire, and his Slave dynasty (he was a Mamluk, a Turkish "slave") (1206–90) was the first of five successive sultanates to rule Delhi. There followed the Khiljis (1290–1320), Tughlaqs (1320–1413), Sayyids (1414–51), and Lodis (1451–1526).

Iltutmish benefited from dramatic events in Central Asia: Ghengis Khan and the Mongols swept through between 1219 and 1222, removing threats to India and ensuring

that Muslim India would carve its own history. The Slave usurper was able to annex Sind and Bengal, and his men (known as *mamluks)* provided the military leadership, provincial governors, and officers of court—a pattern that would be repeated in subsequent dynasties. His richly carved but surprisingly modest-size tomb still stands behind the mosque at Lal Kot.

The Mongols made repeated raids into northern India in the 13th and 14th centuries. Meanwhile, Delhi became the chosen refuge from the central Asian hotbed for many immigrant nobles, bureaucrats, and adventurers. One of these groups, the Turkish Khiljis, succeeded the Slave sultans. Their popular and capable ruler Ala-ud-din-Khilji (*R.*1296–1315) survived a Mongol siege in 1303, conquered wealthy Gujarat, took the great Rajput forts of Ranthambore and Chittaurgarh, and pushed his empire far southward to Daulatabad, near Aurangabad. His Delhi city, known as Siri, had a great reservoir and a fine university.

Having overstretched themselves, the Khiljis lost out to Ghiyas-ud-din-Tughlaq, a Turko-Mongol. His successor, Muhammad (*R.*1324–1351), was the most colorful and controversial sultan of all, a mixture of extreme generosity and brutality. He strengthened the Muslim administration by inviting Muslim immigrants to Delhi. One was a Moroccan, Ibn Battuta, who wrote a detailed account of 14th-century India. Muhammad then moved the capital from Delhi to Daulatabad in 1327 to encourage Muslim colonization of the south, only to relocate back to Delhi in around 1330 to maintain power in the north.

Muhammad's huge empire began to crack. Bengal became an independent sultanate (1335), as did Kashmir (1346) and the Deccan (1347), which went to the Bahmani sultans. Muhammad's impressive successor was the enlightened Feroz Shah Tughlaq (*R.*1351–1388), whose Delhi was renowned for its beauty, refinement, and intellectual life. Feroz Shah chose to be buried in a fortlike tomb beside Ala-ud-din-Khilji's reservoir. After his

death, the empire's disintegration sped up. The Asian conqueror Timur (Tamburlaine) sacked Delhi in 1398. In northern and central India, Jaunpur (1400), Malwa (1406), and Gujarat (1407) went independent, while the Rajput states of Marwar and Mewar emerged.

In the Deccan, the Bahmani state gradually broke up to form five competing sultanates: Gulbarga, Ahmednagar, Bidar, Bijapur, and finally Golconda. South of them lay the bulwark of the last great Hindu power of southern India, the Vijayanaga, which peaked under the rule of Krishnadevaraya (*R.*1509–1530). By uniting all smaller southern Hindu states, the Vijayanaga Empire (1336–1565) could remain powerful until four of the five sultanates, usually competing against each other, united. At the Battle of Talikota in 1565, the Vijayanaga forces were roundly defeated.

Thus, the territory ruled by Delhi's last two sultanates, the Sayyids and the Lodis, was reduced to just one of many Muslim states in India. In each, power lay with a minority of Muslims and was dependent upon raising land taxes and controlling trade routes and ports. There was relatively little conversion of the local, mostly Hindu, people. At the various courts, with their cosmopolitan mixtures of Muslims and Hindus, the rich Indo-Muslim cultures evolved. You can trace these in surviving buildings, sculptures, and metalwork in the Islamic remains of Delhi, Ahmadabad, Bijapur, Bidar, and a number of other medieval Muslim cities.

In 1502 Sikander Lodi left Delhi, moving his power base 122 miles (196 km) south to Agra. The once legendary capital became nothing but a necropolis surrounding the village of Nizamuddin, where the *durgarh* (shrine) of the Sufi saint Shaikh Nizam-ud-din Chishti (1236–1325) was maintained by the faithful. His royal devotees had included Muhammad and Feroz Shah Tughlaq, and would number several Mogul emperors.

MOGUL EMPIRE'S GREAT AGE: 1526–1707
Into this fragmented India, Babur, a Burlas Turk, arrived in 1526. He had failed three times in his great ambition to take the Timurid city of Samarkand. Now he looked beyond the Hindu

Hindu and Mogul styles blend in Jai Singh's refined 17th-century additions to Amer Fort, outside Jaipur.

Kush to India's wealth, encouraged by the invitation of disgruntled Afghan chiefs governing Ibrahim Lodi's Punjab territories. Victory over Ibrahim Lodi at Panipat was easy. But when the Rajput clans joined forces under the Sisodia ruler Rana Sanga of Mewar—the only time the quarrelsome Rajputs united under one flag—Babur faced a far greater test. To encourage his men, Babur promised unconquered territories to his own nobles, declared *jihad* (holy war in the name of sacred duty) on the Rajputs, renounced wine, and took a vow to fight to the death. Then, mustering his immense leadership skills and the superior war tactics of Central Asia, Babur crushed the Rajputs in March 1527.

The Moguls had arrived, and they would stay to become the greatest and the last of India's Islamic empires (1526–1858). The first six emperors, known as the Great Moguls (1526–1707), ruled from father to son: Babur, Humayun, Akbar, Jahangir, Shah Jahan, and Aurangzeb. All were great leaders, politicians, and soldiers. All were scholars and highly cultured; all were prone to weaknesses, such as alcohol, opium, or plain superstition; and all oscillated between religious tolerance and orthodoxy. Their diaries, disarmingly frank, reveal their relationship with India (Babur praised peacock meat but missed Persian gardens), their weaknesses (Jahangir has his drinking problem noted glass by glass), and the later stultifying court life (seen in Shah Jahan's opulent Padshahnameh manuscript).

Babur (R.1526–1530) celebrated his triumph with an international gathering and huge feast at Agra. But it was short-lived. After he had defeated a joint force of Afghans and Bengalis near Varanasi in 1529, his health failed. He returned to Agra, and then to Lahore, where he died in December 1530.

Humayun (R.1530–1540, deposed, then 1555–56) inherited an as yet unstable empire and made the decision to move the capital back to Delhi. This gifted soldier matched great his victories with equally great parties and indulgences, a combination which allowed the already superior military and political skills of Sher Shah Sur, the Afghan leader in eastern India, to flourish. Lacking his father's charisma, Humayun lost his supporters, was deposed in 1540, and fled westward

across Rajasthan and up to Shah Tahmasp's Persian court.

The brief rule of Sher Shah Sur (R.1540–45), whose handsome tomb lies east of Varanasi, was important for the future of the Moguls. Not only did he develop a strong central army but he also built roads and large travelers' lodgings, including the Grand Trunk Road that stretched from Kabul through Lahore and Delhi eventually to Kolkata. Sher Shah Sur also standardized weights and measures, regularized trade tariffs, and, maybe most important of all, created a tax revenue system that would be the blueprint for the next Mogul emperor, Akbar.

In the chaos that followed the death of Sher Shah Sur's son, Islam Shah (R.1545–1553), Humayun retook his throne in 1555, only to die in Delhi the following year. His teenage son, quickly brought to Delhi from the Punjab, would prove to be the successor to Sher Shah Sur's legacy.

The 14-year-old Akbar (R.1556–1605) first reconquered the Mogul empire, then expanded and consolidated it. Under the guidance of his regent, the able Bairam Khan, he retook most of central India and the Rajput states, including the great forts of Chittaurgarh and Ranthambore in 1567–68. These conquests he cemented with marriage alliances and employment in the Mogul army for the conquered people. In 1562, on his way to Ajmer, where a revered Sufi saint lay buried, Akbar met with Raja Bihar Mal of Amer (Jaipur's old capital). Akbar agreed to marry Bihar Mal's daughter and take his adopted grandson Man Singh into Mogul service—providing the basis of Jaipur's wealth. Only Mewar, under Rana Pratap and Amar Singh, refused to bow down to Mogul power.

With this stability and his new fort (1567–1575) underway, in 1571 Akbar began to create Fatehpur Sikri, a palace-city emulating the Timurid courts. It was from here that, in 1573, he left to conquer Gujarat, a rich land on the Muslim pilgrimage route to Mecca. To celebrate his victory, he built the Buland Darwaza, the great gate of Fatehpur Sikri's mosque. By 1576 Akbar had completed his victories in eastern India, and in the 1580s and 1590s he extended his empire to the trading cities of Kabul and Qandahar, and to the provinces of

Ghazna, Kashmir, Orissa, and Bengal, and to all the land down to the Godavari River.

Akbar now ruled over a large, centralized state defended by nobles of various ethnic and religious groups—Rajputs, Persians, Indians, Muslims, and others. He was a strong, non-sectarian ruler, a soldier and statesman, an art patron, and a liberal philosopher, all of which he used to strengthen his position as emperor.

The administrative framework created during Akbar's rule sustained the empire until the 18th century. It managed to keep the peasantry and nobility happy while filling the state coffers. Akbar was careful to keep close to the ruling Rajput clans and to display religious tolerance. He had Hindu advisers and kept discussions going with the resentful but powerful Muslim orthodoxy in the form of the *ulama* (learned men). Akbar's liberal views, which annoyed them, led him to lift the *jizya* (poll tax) on non-Muslims and to welcome the Portuguese missionary Father Monserrat for discussions at Fatehpur Sikri. His ideas on kingship, though, led him to initiate the Mogul tradition of the emperor showing himself to his people at sunrise, thus increasing his power by identifying himself with the ultimate source of energy and endowing himself with supernatural divinity.

From within this prevailing atmosphere of tolerance, India's last great new religion began to emerge. This was Sikhism (see p. 59), whose ten Gurus (teachers) span the 16th and 17th centuries. Their ideas were eventually formalized in 1699.

Akbar's son Salim, born to his Hindu wife from Amer, ascended the throne as Jahangir, or Siezer of the World (R.1605–1627). He was then 36 years old. At a personal level, his intense interest in painting, science, and coins lifted the Mogul court to new cultural heights, but it was matched by a life-long addiction to alcohol and opium. At a political and military level, he ended Mogul–Mewar conflict, expanded the empire into the Himalayan mountains and Kachchh, consolidated control of Bengal and Orissa, and campaigned down in the Deccan.

Ghiyas Beg, a Persian adventurer who had entered Akbar's court, became chief minister, or Itimad-ud-Daulah (Pillar of Government) on Jahangir's accession. His clever, ambitious

daughter married Jahangir in 1611 and was soon given the title Nur Jahan (Light of the World). She effectively ruled from behind the veil, even riding into battle carried in a litter slung between two elephants. Her daughter by an earlier marriage was married off to Jahangir's eldest son and heir, Khusrau. Meanwhile, Ghiyas Beg's equally clever and

Emperor Akbar passes the crown from his son Jahangir to his grandson Shah Jahan, to reinforce Mogul legitimacy.

ambitious son, Asaf Khan, had become deputy prime minister and in 1612 gave his daughter, Arjumand Banu, in marriage to Jahangir's third son, Khurram. The couple later rebelled against the emperor and sought refuge at the stoically anti-Mogul Mewar court at Udaipur. When Jahangir's cocktail of drink, drugs, and asthma finally killed him, Asaf Khan triumphed over his sister in the political fallout: Khurram became the next emperor, under the name Shah Jahan (Ruler of the World), and his wife took the title Mumtaz Mahal (Chosen One of the Palace).

For most of the rule of Shah Jahan

(R.1627–1658), political and economic stability were sustained throughout the ever expanding empire. The emperor and his vast army, which grew fourfold during his reign, secured Muslim territories in the Deccan, southern Hindu kingdoms, the eastern Assam border, and the northwest frontier to Kabul. Large, cosmopolitan cities emerged—Lahore, Agra, Ahmedabad—whose citizens traded with Asians and newly arrived Europeans, and were the patrons of sophisticated crafts and grand architecture. Meanwhile, land revenue from the now enormous empire sustained the the parasite Mogul nobles and the army; however, dependence on this income would eventually cause the breakup of the empire.

Shah Jahan's increasingly rich, ostentatious, and unwieldy Mogul court, weighed down with ritual and sheer size, no longer moved from place to place. When not on campaign, Shah Jahan revealed the extent of his grandfather Akbar's devoted attention to his education. At Lahore and Agra he and Mumtaz rebuilt the sandstone royal rooms and state audience halls in marble, showing a new refinement in their proportions and decorating them with floral patterns of semi-precious stone inlay, called *pietra dura* (meaning "hard stone" in Italian).

In June 1631 Mumtaz died giving birth to their 14th child at Burhampur in the Deccan, while on campaign with her husband. It was a watershed for Shah Jahan and his empire. With his rock gone, he first mourned for two years, giving up music, fine clothes, and celebrations. Then, ill-advisedly putting his campaigns into the hands of his four sons, he threw himself into ambitious building projects. At a personal level, he mixed rigorous orthodoxy with unashamed debauchery. The jizya tax was reinstated on non-Muslims, conversion was encouraged, and building of Hindu temples discouraged.

While Shah Jahan launched into building the Taj Mahal as the mausoleum for Mumtaz, he also began the marble Pearl Mosque in Agra Fort and promoted the building of mosques across his empire. He also laid out an entire new city at the traditional capital, Delhi, calling it Shahjahanabad, today's Old Delhi. The world's grandest emperor and his court

moved there in 1648. Today, the palace is forgotten but the walled city outside it buzzes with life, and the great Jama Masjid is the most important mosque for India's Muslim community.

Shah Jahan's sons, meanwhile, watched for their chance. It came in 1657, when the emperor became ill. In Mogul tradition, the sons began plotting and competing for the throne. After a series of false alliances, tricks, and murders, the third son, Aurangzeb, won.

The long rule of Aurangzeb (R.1658–1707) saw the empire stretch to its farthest limit and begin its collapse. Campaigns to keep the northwest and the Rajput princes in line led Aurangzeb unwisely to take control of Jodhpur and later demolish its temples. The result was his loss of all Rajput allies; not one Rajput chief fought for the Moguls in the later Sikh war.

Aurangzeb then turned his attention south. In 1681 he left Delhi for good. His ambition was to control all of peninsular India and to convert its people to Islam. He had already faced the newly strong Marathas of the Deccan, under their hero leader Shivaji (see p. 180). Jai Singh II, the Jaipur ruler who commanded a large Mogul force, captured Shivaji in 1666, but he escaped from Agra and later became king (1674–1680) of his followers. The Marathas would continue to wield their power and, in the 18th century, expand from their base in Pune right across southern India.

Aurangzeb's relentless campaigns, which in some years he unwisely continued through the monsoon, brought depression and illness to his soldiers. Eventually he nominally won almost the whole peninsula, but few of his gains were consolidated. Aurangzeb further weakened his position by doggedly reinforcing his orthodoxy. He called his campaigns jihad, enforced the jizya tax, and replaced Hindu administrators with Muslims.

Aurangzeb, the last of the six Great Moguls died devoutly and quietly in the Deccan. Unlike his predecessors, with their lavish and magnificent tombs at Delhi, Agra, and Lahore, Aurangzeb followed the Koran's demand for simplicity. His unadorned white stone slab lies

The Taj Mahal is the tomb of Shah Jahan's wife, Mumtaz Mahal, and a symbol of Mogul power and the might of Islam.

CALECHV MVM INDI

in the precincts of a modest mosque at Khuldabad, near Aurangabad.

EUROPEAN TRADERS ARRIVE: 1498–1858

While Delhi lost its control and whole tracts of the Mogul Empire became independent, from Bengal and Avadh in the north to Bijapur and Golconda in the south, Hindu rulers and landowners asserted their power. The Jats were able to raid Agra for some of its marble inlay to decorate their palace at Deeg; the Marathas took the wealthy central kingdom of Malwa and started menacing the Rajputs. The Persian despot Nadir Shah had little trouble sacking Delhi of her wealth in 1739. The Afghans sacked Delhi again in 1757. In the power vacuum, new centers of Mogul power emerged: Murshidabad in Bengal, Lucknow in Avadh, east of Delhi, and Hyderabad in the Deccan.

Into this complex readjusting of boundaries and centers of power, with its attendant conflicts, came the European traders.

Trade with the West was not new. In 327 B.C. Alexander the Great's expedition had opened up social and trading links over the

mountains. The Romans traded by land and sea, as did Arab and Jewish groups, who settled along the west coast.

The dramatic increase in European trade in the 16th century was stimulated by the desire to break the monopoly of the eastern trade held by Venice and the Levantine. The solution was to bypass Venice, using sea routes around Africa. The Portuguese led the way, spurred on by Prince Henry the Navigator and the Catholic Church's missionary zeal. In 1498 Vasco da Gama (1469–1524) rounded the Cape of Good Hope and sailed across the Indian Ocean to land at Calicut, in Kerala, where Christianity had been flourishing since St. Thomas the Apostle's arrival in A.D. 52.

The second Portuguese expedition arrived in 1503, led by Alfonso de Albuquerque, who built a church and fort at Cochin. In 1509 he came again and took thriving Goa city from the Bijapur rulers. Goa dorada ("golden Goa") was soon a wealthy entrepôt and capital of Europe's largest maritime empire, one that stretched along the coasts of Africa up to Hormuz and included Diu, Daman, Goa, and Cochin on the west coast of India and, on the east coast, Hooghly near modern Kolkata, and on to Malacca in Malaysia. By 1580 Goa's population was 60,000 (Lisbon's was then 110,000), excluding the vast numbers of clergy and slaves. Each year a flotilla of 300 ships laden with spices, gold, and other luxuries would leave Goa for Lisbon. At a social level, while intermarriage between the Portuguese and the Indians was encouraged, European intolerance revealed itself in the wanton destruction of Hindu temples.

The Portuguese had missionary ambitions, and in 1540 the ideology of the Counter-Reformation arrived in Goa, followed by Francis Xavier (1506–1552) and the Jesuits two years later. Mass conversions began. When Xavier died in China, his body was brought to Goa for burial; in 1560 the Inquisition arrived and not surprisingly banned all non-Christian teaching and ritual. Despite Portugal's position as suppliers of horses to the Vijayanaga empire and as naval auxiliaries of the Moguls, the Portuguese were regarded as cruel, untrustworthy, and intolerant by the Indians.

Furthermore, other European trading eyes were on India. The Dutch, Danes, French, and

View of Calicut (circa 1600). Vasco da Gama founded this Portuguese settlement on the Kerala coast in 1498.

finally the English set sail for India, each competing to establish factories and trading stations. Eventually, while the English expanded, the Dutch were reduced to Chinsura near Kolkata, and the Danes to nearby Serampore and down on the Tamil Nadu coast at Tranquebar (modern Tarangambadi). The French kept their main base on the same coast, at Pondicherry, with smaller stations at Mahe in Kerala and Chandernagore in West Bengal.

The British came to India looking for trading opportunities after they failed to break the Dutch trading monopoly in the East Indies. On December 31, 1600, Queen Elizabeth I (R.1558–1603) granted the East India Company its charter "…as much for the honour of this our realm of England as for the increase of our navigation and advancement of trade." A few years later English trade moved forward when Sir Thomas Roe, a senior diplomat, arrived in India from the court of James I (R.1603–1625). In January

1616 Roe finally met the Mogul emperor Jahangir when his itinerant court was at Ajmer. Here he sealed the relationship between England and India that would grow into the greatest trading partnership and cultural exchange the world has known.

Using diplomacy rather than force, the English had established 23 trading factories by 1647, of which Surat (1613) on the west coast and Madras (1639) on the east coast were the most important. However, in 1661 the company acquired the marshy, malarial islands of Bombay (Mumbai) as part of Portuguese princess Catherine of Braganza's dowry on her marriage to Charles II (R.1660–1685). A great cosmopolitan trading city was born under Gerald Aungier, the city's Governor (1672–77).

Already, forays north had led to Calcutta's founding by Job Charnock in 1690. But it was farther south on the east coast, where the climate was healthier, that English trading really flourished. Francis Day founded Madras (now Chennai) in 1639, well-placed for trading cotton. By 1700 its population was 300,000; by 1740 trade with India represented 10 percent of British revenue and much of it passed through Madras.

EAST INDIA COMPANY EXPANDS

British initiatives were gradually transformed into political power. Rivalry between the southern states enabled the two strong Europeans in the area, the British and the French, to play out their rivalry too, but supporting different sides. The young British soldier (later governor of Bengal) Robert Clive (1725–1774), supporting the Nawab of Arcot, defeated the French under the Marquis de Dupleix in 1751, and British supremacy in the south was confirmed nine years later at the Battle of Wandiwash. In the north, Clive's triumph at Plassey in 1757 was confirmed by Hector Munro's decisive victory at the Battle of Buxar in 1764 against the kings of Delhi and Oudh.

The result was a trade boom throughout eastern India. Madras expanded, Calcutta became the headquarters of the East India Company, and from 1774 a string of governors-general, later called viceroys, began with Warren Hastings (1732–1818). European and Indian traders made fortunes from gifts, monopolies, and looting. In the 1780s, with Calcutta's population at 250,000, land revenues and the system of district collectors were fixed, so that, despite famines, the company amassed four million dollars annually.

With its insatiable appetite for profits from trade and land revenue, the company's influence soon expanded across India. From small Benares (Varanasi) kingdom to vast Hyderabad state, the majority of Indian rulers found themselves in debt to the company as a result of trade agreements. There were exceptions. The clever Mysore ruler Haider Ali brought prosperity to the Deccan and wanted, like the British, to benefit from sea trade along their coast. But his son, Tipu Sultan, was finally defeated at Srirangapatnam (1799). In the northwest, the British made a pact with the Sikhs, whose hero king, Ranjit Singh, took Lahore (1799) and established the first Sikh state, which included all of verdant Punjab. The Maratha confederacy, supported by the French and including the Scindias of Gwalior, the Holkars of Indore, and the Gaekwads of Baroda, stretched from Agra down to Karnataka. But their raids on Rajput territories such as Jaipur (1803) and Udaipur (1803) only helped the British win control of major princely states, and during 1816–18 the British finally defeated the Marathas. In the mountains, the Gurkas were defeated (1818) and the rulers of potentially threatening Persia and Afghanistan were dissuaded from allying with the French or Russians.

The British expanded out of their forts and beyond the open space of the Maidan, then replaced simple houses with grand stucco mansions and public buildings, keeping rigidly to classical designs to satisfy their own aspirations and confirm symbolic order and government over their surroundings. Modifications were made for deeper verandas, or to create cross-drafts. New kinds of buildings appeared: churches, cemeteries, cantonments (military stations), bungalows (which originated in Bengal), and social clubs. This westernization was most evident in Calcutta and Madras, which became elegant neoclassic cities. Soon both Indian rulers and merchants were building hybrid houses

Col. Robert Clive meeting Mia Jafar, commander of the Nawab of Bengal's army, in 1757 (Francis Hayman, 1760)

mixing Hindu or Muslim traditions with European elements, initiating a new cross-fertilization of styles.

To escape the searing summer sun entirely, the British discovered India's hills. Between 1815 and 1947 the British built more than 80 hill stations (see pp. 278–79), from Shimla and Darjling in the Himalayan foothills to Mahabaleshwar in the Western Ghats above Bombay and Ootacamund in the Nilgiri Hills—the main hill station for Madras and known as "Snooty Ooty." Each was a nostalgic re-creation of British feudal society, whose informal buildings belied a strict social structure within which hunting, jam-making, dog shows, and amateur dramatics all played their part. From 1832 to 1947 the entire government and its hangers-on of families and Europeanized maharajas moved from Calcutta to Shimla annually, governing one fifth of the world's population from a quaint, isolated, hillside town for half the year.

Problems began in the 1830s when, among other things, sales of cotton and opium to China and indigo to Europe dropped, British-made cloth put Indian weavers out of jobs, and famines swept the countryside. Despite social reforms by William Bentinck (1774–1839) and William Macaulay, India was becoming dissatisfied with company rule. Furthermore, the British modernizing projects of the railroads (1853) and telegraph (1865), and the building of irrigation canals and roads, at first disturbed the conservative basis of Indian society. Small, uncoordinated revolts took place all over India, including grain riots in defiance of revenue payments.

Against this background, the Rebellion of 1857—also known as the Mutiny—is not such a surprise. It was sparked by the Bengal army's irritation at the loss of privileges, the introduction of lower castes, the high local land revenues demanded by the British, and the possible pollution from the pork and beef grease on the new Lee Enfield rifles' cartridges, which the soldiers had to break between their teeth. Starting with the mutiny of the garrison at Meerut on May 10, 1857, uprisings in Delhi, Lucknow, and Kanpur (Cawnpore) spread across Bengal. Although Delhi was retaken in November 1857, the British government was badly shaken. The East India Company was abolished in 1858, and the last Mogul king, Bahadur Shah II, who had encouraged the rebels, was deposed. From then on, the British Crown, and much of British law, administered India directly. The Raj had begun.

BRITISH IMPERIALISM TO INDIAN FREEDOM: 1858–1947

India was now part of the British Empire, with a viceroy as chief executive. Indians were subjects of Queen Victoria. From 1840 to 1914 India was Britain's most important trading partner. In Bombay, the economic boom was further boosted when, during the American Civil War, the Confederacy ports were blocked, temporarily diverting more cotton trade to India. It was during this time that Bombay's Parsee community rose in importance, including the Sassoon, Wadia, Readymoney, Jeejeebhoy, and Tata families, and Bombay acquired the world's grandest set of Victorian Gothic public buildings.

In making Queen Victoria the Empress of India in 1877, Britain saw itself as a grand feudal power controlling the vassals of India. Hence the string of royal visits that peaked in 1911 when the King-Emperor George V visited India. On December 12, he announced to 562 maharajas and other grandees that the capital would move from Calcutta to its traditional and strategic site, Delhi, where an entirely new city would be built. Designed by Edwin Lutyens, assisted by Herbert Baker, it reflected the size and power of the British Empire. At the city's inauguration on February 9, 1931, few people recognized the gathering storm clouds that would bring independence to India in just 16 years.

The pomp and ceremony of these British royal visits were intended to impress the Indian rulers on their own terms and ensure their loyalty in an India that increasingly questioned Britain's presence. The British administrators recognized an uncomfortable

link between empire and unequal trade. Their policies to bridge the gap included Indianizing government building styles, promoting English education, building universities and high courts, and including more Indians in government. But only after World War II did the British fully accept that independence was unavoidable and that foreign enterprise could not answer India's problems.

Growing Indian political awareness percolated down from the intelligentsia, who had benefited from the education opportunities, to the masses. Agitation began in the 1870s, seeking a national culture and interests. The Indian National Congress party was founded in 1885, and in 1905 British attempts to weaken the unified National Movement were answered by a countryside boycott of

British goods. The next year, Muslims who felt that Congress did not represent them formed the All India Muslim League. While Hindus demanded the recognition of the Hindi language written in Devanagari script, Muslims wanted Urdu in Perso-Arabic script.

India's struggle for freedom entered a new phase in 1915, when Mohandas Karamchand Gandhi (1869–1948)—later known as the Mahatma, or Great Soul—returned from South Africa, where he had experienced racial prejudice. He led a moral protest against oppression (the British presence). Known as civil disobedience, it involved defying laws peacefully and taking punishment willingly. In noncooperation, India had a truly national and popular political campaign for the first time, promoted by nationalist leaders includ-

The Khan of Kelat (seated center) leased the Bolan Pass, linking India with Afghanistan, to the British in the 1930s.

ing Bal Gangadhar Tilak, Sir Sayyid Ahmad Khan, C. Rajagopalachari, Sardar Vallabhbhai Patel, A. K. Azad, and M. A. Jinner.

Gandhi's second civil disobedience movement, in 1930, included his Salt March, protesting the British monopoly on salt production. In the same year Congress, with the young Jawaharlal Nehru as president, adopted the resolution for complete independence for India. The Government of India Act was passed in 1935, giving Indians who met stringent educational and property-owning requirements (about 14 percent of the population) the right to vote to elect representatives.

Congress swept the polls. Agitation continued, and in 1942 Congress called for the British to "Quit India." Meanwhile, the Muslim League demanded a separate state for Muslims, to be called Pakistan. Back in Britain, Prime Minister Clement Atlee (1883–1967) and the postwar Labour government encouraged independence.

Nehru and Gandhi at the Indian National Congress committee meeting in Bombay in 1930, when Nehru became its president

In 1947 independence and partition came simultaneously. On August 14 the last viceroy, Lord Louis Mountbatten, witnessed the creation of Pakistan—in two parts, 1,200 miles (1,931 km) apart, to be called West and East Pakistan. East Pakistan became the independent country of Bangladesh in 1971. At midnight on August 14–15, 1947, in front of the Red Fort in Old Delhi, Mountbatten formally transferred British power to India's first Prime Minister, Pandit Jawaharlal Nehru (1889–1964), and India's saffron, white, and green flag was flown for the first time. Later, the two leaders toasted each other in Viceroy's House, soon to be renamed Rastrapati Bhavan. Meanwhile, hundreds of thousands of people fled their homelands: Hindus from Pakistan, now a Muslim state, into India; Muslims from what they believed would be a Hindu state, into Pakistan. It is estimated that two million died in communal massacres during this mass cross-migration. Gandhi wept over the violence, the loss of a single India, and the new hatred. On January 30, 1948, he was assassinated by a fundamentalist Hindu.

A YOUNG NATION STEEPED IN HISTORY: 1947–PRESENT

At independence about two-fifths of India, containing about a quarter of the population of 350 million people, belonged not to the Indian government but to the Indian princes. These states—representing Jat, Rajput, Maratha, Hindu, Sikh, and Muslim people— were scattered across the country and ranged in size from Hyderabad's 82,000 square miles (212,380 sq km) and 14 million population to tiny Kathiawar's less than half a square mile (1 sq km) and 200 inhabitants. But the autocratic rule and preference for traditional lifestyles displayed by most princes were at odds with those building a new, modern country. Gradually, the princes were absorbed into the new states—which loosely followed geographical, cultural, and linguistic boundaries—and the majority of their lands, palaces, villages, personal wealth, titles, and honors were officially removed. The state of Rajasthan was not completely formed until 1956, nor was Andhra Pradesh, which contains much of former Hyderabad. Today, only a handful of the former rulers and their families maintain their feudal customs and they take their consequent responsibilities seriously.

This is just one example of the massive reorganization that faced the government of

Students prepare cotton yarn at Gujarat Vidyapith, a school founded by Gandhi in 1920 to produce *khadi,* homespun cloth.

Asia's new and huge democracy in 1947. For this, the guiding principle was to maintain national unity and integrity against all potential internal and external threats.

Gandhi's leadership was the model; India's people who had struggled for freedom were its motivation. There was a need to balance modernization with India's strong traditions. Thus, political and judicial equality, a secular state, and improved farming methods were matched with tolerance for all religious

In Mumbai, space is at a premium: Here, four cobblers sit cross-legged in a cubby-hole that opens onto the street, while the client has his shoes resoled.

practices and some religious law, and recognition of the existing social order, including caste. The ancient custom of Indian rulers holding morning and evening audiences with the people was adopted by the democratically elected politicians—it was at one of these audiences that Prime Minister Indira Gandhi (1917–1984) was assassinated by two of her own guards. At the same time, the new country benefited from some of the practical legacies of British rule—the system of law and administration, the civil service, the railroads, roads and irrigation systems, a nonpolitical army, a free press, and a ready-made capital city. There was also the concept of India as a single country with, most importantly, a unifying language: English.

On January 26, 1950, the Republic of India was inaugurated and the Constitution adopted, an event now celebrated annually with a public holiday and grand parades through Delhi. In the face of major north–south controversies and independence bids from the Punjab, Kashmir, Assam, and other areas, there were two distinct visions of a unified India: Gandhi's decentralized village system and the new leaders' centralized, state-controlled system. The second vision won, modified by the first.

Pandit Jawaharlal Nehru was prime minister from 1947 until his death in 1964, during which time his National Congress Party remained unchallenged. His ideology and ambitions for a country as diverse as India were practical and realistic, and they set the tone for the next 50 years. They incorporated a gentle socialism, a secular state (India has no state religion), state-directed economic progress, and nonalignment in foreign affairs.

To these ends, India operated a closed economy until the 1990s, promoting its own industries and products. At the same time, India's high-quality hand loom-weaving and other handicrafts were revived and encouraged, with prestigious national awards and government-run stores to control quality. In food production, India achieved self-sufficiency with some to spare for export. Today, India's principal crops are rice, wheat, other cereals, pulses, oil seeds, cotton, and sugarcane—helped by a gradual doubling of irrigated land. In foreign affairs, India's sheer

In Bangalore, traditions are broken as men and women work together for national and international companies at the cutting edge of information technology.

size and strategic position have forced it to play a sensitive role with its smaller neighbors; internationally, it has maintained its non-aligned position and keeps a careful balance of friendship with China, Russia, and the West.

Nehru can be seen as the head of what, with a few interruptions, has been virtually a dynastic rule over independent India, albeit a democratically elected one. Indira Gandhi, Jawaharlal's daughter and no relation to the Mahatma, dominated Indian politics after her father's death. Prime minister for 15 years, 1966–1977 and 1980–84, she governed in a highly personalized and centralized way, which became dictatorial during the Emergency (1975–77); yet, after a spell out of office, she was reelected. On her assassination, her son, Rajiv, was reluctantly hurled into the job and began to open up India economically before he, too, was assassinated by a suicide bomber in 1991. His widow, Sonia, and his children are now on the political scene.

Meanwhile, Narasimha Rao (prime minister 1991–96) and his successors have had little effect on the unstoppable tide of modernization and the increased determination by individual states to choose their own destinies. This drive for self-improvement is especially true of the southern states (Maharashtra, Karnataka, Andhra Pradesh, Tamil Nadu, and Kerala). Here, progress and prosperity are evident in the cities and villages, in manufacturing and transportation, in education and health. This new wealth is reflected in the increased donations by the faithful to their religious institutions.

This means that, for the visitor, India is as diverse as it always was. But this diversity—in ancient cultures, in religions, in societies, in landscape, in cities, and in villages—has a new dynamism. The rise of Bangalore, capital of the southern state of Karnataka, to become the world's third most important information technology center, after Silicon Valley and Israel, has produced a city skyline mixing high-rises with colonial neoclassic buildings, medieval palace remains, and ancient stone temples. Hyderabad, capital of neighboring Andhra Pradesh, is following Bangalore's lead. In the north, however, picturesque Rajasthan looks to quixotic tourism for income, transforming every last palace into a hotel. ■

India: Land of many faiths

IF INDIA'S HISTORY SEEMS COMPLEX, THE SPIRITUAL LIVES OF ITS PEOPLE are equally baffling for first-time visitors. India has no state religion, but religion is a vital element in today's India, and integral to its history, monuments, and arts. Hinduism is practiced by the majority of Indians. Out of it were born Buddhism, Jainism, and, much later, Sikhism. With the diaspora of Indians and Indian ideas, all these faiths are now practiced worldwide. India has also absorbed religions—Judaism, Christianity, Zoroastrianism, Islam—whose Indian adherents have given each a regional distinctiveness. In addition, modern movements range from hedonistic ashrams (religious communities) to quasi-political groups. Meanwhile, nature worship and other very ancient practices continue.

To visit India is to encounter several of these faiths, which generally thrive peacefully side by side. A typical fishing village has room for temple, mosque, and church. Pausing to observe the rituals in urban and rural places of worship, or to talk to local people about their faith, is almost always welcome provided customs such as removing shoes are observed. Contact like this can illuminate the various philosophies and dispel preconceptions.

FAITHS THAT EVOLVED IN INDIA
Hinduism
Some 820 million people in India are Hindu—about 82 percent. Yet for all its popularity Hinduism is an elusive religion, and difficult for non-Hindus even to begin to understand. Hinduism has no single sacred text, no dogma, no single prophet, and it demands no formal congregational worship; nor does it oblige the faithful to go to the temple, to tackle its abstract philosophy, to follow specific rituals, or to know its sacred language, Sanskrit. Ideas of rebirth and a plethora of deities add to the confusion.

The beginnings of worship on the subcontinent predate the Indus Valley Civilization and suggest a reverence for natural elements. These were given definition by the pastoral Aryans (see pp. 26–28) who worshiped the sun as "Surya," and introduced ideas of a distinct religion that included precise rituals, sacrifice, and priests (brahmans) to mediate between the people and their gods. These ideas were set out in the four Vedic texts, composed in early Sanskrit, sung by heart and passed down through generations orally; writing seems to have begun only about 500 B.C.

Later texts such as the Upanishads (philosophical treatises on the soul) and the Brahmanas (on ritual) reflect important new ideas: spiritual karma and increased temporal brahman power. Karma may be understood to be the power of each person's good or bad thoughts and actions to affect the spirit's movement across generations. The spirit thus endures a series of rebirths with varying degrees of suffering and desire, as the soul progresses or regresses in response to past deeds. The soul makes its final escape either through nirvana, when personal identity is extinguished, or through moksha, the final release from the cycle of rebirth. Meanwhile, as these ideas became more abstract, ritual more convoluted, and Sanskrit more refined and unintelligible, so brahman power increased. Ordinary people felt excluded and were attracted to new, back-to-basics religions; of these, Buddhism (see p. 58) and Jainism (see pp. 58–59) were the most long-lasting and won merchant and royal patronage.

During and after the classical Gupta period (see p. 33) local spirits, gods, and heroes were absorbed into the central pantheon of gods. Gradually, Hindus began to focus their worship on one of these, with a passionate devotion known as bhakti. This encouraged elaborate ritual and the final, very long forms of the great epics (see p. 76): the Ramayana and the Mahabharata. This last includes the Bhagavad Gita, a discussion between Krishna and Arjuna on the essence of Hindu philoso-

A Hindu sadhu (holy man) who follows Shiva, god of creative and destructive energy, performs puja (worship) at Varanasi.

phy: the theory of karma and the human struggle for love, light, and redemption.

Over the centuries, Hindu philosophy, ritual, and myth have permeated almost every aspect of the believer's life. Hindus live, for the most part, in the grip of the caste system (see p. 29), even if modern social and business life seems to deny this. Marriage is usually arranged within the same caste, and dowries require ever spiraling debt as motorcycles and freezers are added to silks and jewelry.

Pilgrimages are the most popular form of Indian tourism, often undertaken in busloads, with much singing and souvenir shopping. The destination may be one of the seven Sacred Cities (see p. 385), or the temple of the believers' chosen deity. This deity is likely to be one form, or aspect, of what may be seen as the extended family of Hindu gods, whose presiding trinity are Brahma (the Creator), Shiva (the Energy, the Destroyer), and Vishnu (the Preserver). The faithful may do *puja*

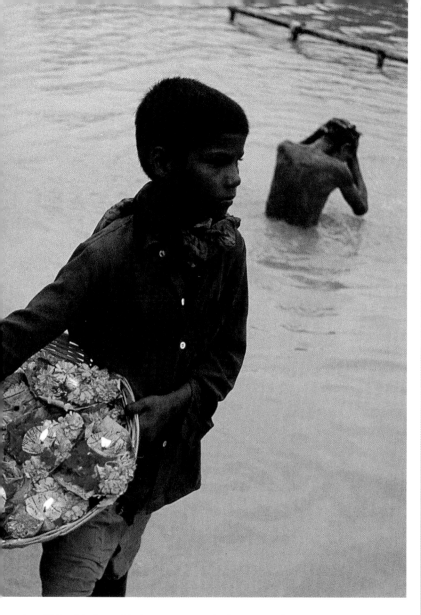

(worship) to this chosen deity in a corner at home or at the local temple, whose plan follows the ancient *shastras* (treatises). The priest, who receives the worshiper's offering, holds his position by inheritance and ensures the temple receives a steady flow of donations.

For all its vagueness in definition, Hinduism provides a clear pattern for life. There are four stages: childhood and learning, marriage and rearing a family, celibacy and meditation, and finally a renunciation of all

Children sell flowers and tiny oil lamps made of dried leaves for pilgrims to float as tributes on the Ganga at Varanasi.

worldly possessions in the hope of achieving nirvana or moksha. Throughout, the Hindu has four supreme aims: *dharma* (virtue, living the right way), *artha* (wealth achieved in the right way), karma (giving and receiving love and friendship), and, if these three are correctly followed, moksha.

Traditional dancing and music form a key part of Buddhist festivals such as the Ladakh Festival, held in Leh in early August.

Buddhism

India has just eight million Buddhists, yet this is the birthplace of Buddha (Awakened One).

The conventional dates for Buddha's life are 563–483 B.C., but recent research suggests about 450–350 B.C. or even later. A prince of the *kshatriya* caste (see p. 29), Buddha lived at Lumbini, now in Nepal. At the age of about 30, he questioned the point of Hindu austerity and asceticism, renounced his privileged life, and left home. Five years later Buddha attained *bodhi* (enlightenment) after meditating under a pipal (bodhi) tree at Bodh Gaya (see p. 301).

Offering insight rather than divine revelation, Buddha began his lifelong missionary work with his "Setting in Motion the Wheel of Righteousness" sermon preached at Sarnath. It presented life's overwhelming problem—desire—and its solution, The Middle Path (moderation) and dharma (faith as seen in the true nature of the world, human nature, and spiritual attainment). These, with *sangha* (monasticism for men and women), could lead to the goal, nirvana.

Reacting to Hinduism's inaccessibility, Buddha preached a rational, simple philosophy in the vernacular. His dogma was popular, especially among the merchants who, together with rulers from Ashoka Maurya to the Guptas (see pp. 31–35), patronized India's first substantial stone buildings *(stupas)* and sculpture, mostly sited along trade routes. Followers formed monasteries (*sanghas*), some with adjoining universities such as at Nalanda.

After Buddha's death, the sanghas continued his teachings. Then came the schism. The Hinayana (Lesser Vehicle) sect saw Buddha as the Great Master and spread its ideas to Ceylon, Burma, and Siam. The Mahayana (Great Vehicle) sect considered Buddha to be God and spread its ideas to China, Japan, Tibet, and Mongolia. Buddhism was India's dominant religion for several centuries, but lost out to reformed Hinduism in the seventh century and continued to decline.

Today, India has a growing group of neo-Buddhists, mostly farmers from Maharashtra inspired by the Buddhist convert Dr. Bhim Rao Ambedkar. Dharamsala is home to the Dalai Lama, the head of Tibetan Buddhism and leader of the exiled Tibetan people.

Jainism

India's four million Jains tend to live in the west, near their sacred hills, to which regular pilgrimage is required.

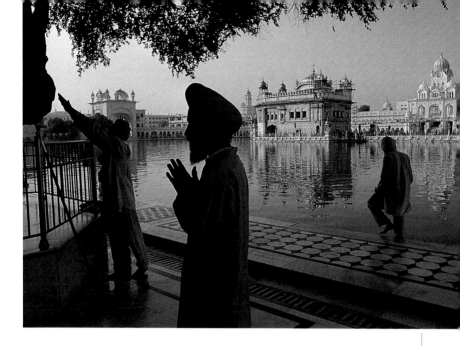

Hari Mandir (Golden Temple)—the Sikhs' most holy *gurudwara*, temple—rises from the Amrit Sarovar at Amritsar. The Sikhs' holy text, *Adi Granth*, is read here daily.

Their founder, Mahavira (Great Hero), is thought to have lived in the sixth century B.C. A religious reformer, like Buddha, he left his birthplace, Patna, to live as a naked ascetic until he achieved spiritual knowledge. He became a *jina* (conqueror), and his followers were known as Jains.

Mahavira taught his followers that the universe is infinite, not created, and that *jivas* (souls) are present in everything. Hence, Jains believe in *ahimsa* (reverence for all life), which demands strict vegetarianism. Adherence to ahimsa, together with the practice of a strict code of behavior can lead to moksha—like Hindus and Buddhists, Jains believe in both reincarnation and salvation. They also reject sacrifice and oppose the caste system, but they do permit *sallekhana* (death by fasting and meditation).

There are two Jain sects. The rigorous "sky-clad" sect, or Digambaras, have no possessions and believe that only men are able to achieve moksha. The white-clad sect, Shvetambaras, are less strict. In today's India Jains are mostly Shvetambaras, who are often commercially successful and may be substantial donors to hospitals, schools, and libraries (see also Ranakpur, p. 138).

Sikhism

Most of India's 20 million Sikhs live in the Punjab and Delhi area and are distinguished by their smoothly wrapped turbans.

Sikhs follow a philosophy founded by Guru Nanak (1469–1539), who was born near Lahore in today's Pakistan. One of several Hindu Sants (poet-philosophers) who introduced Islamic elements into Hinduism, he advocated a single God who is *sat* (truth) and reveals himself through his *gurus* (teachers). He promoted meditation and equality while opposing caste, ritual, superstition, astrology, and sex discrimination.

Nine more gurus consolidated Nanak's teachings. The tenth, Gobind Singh (1666–1708), formalized the new religion in 1699. He began the *gurpurb* (baptism) ceremony, which removed Hindu caste names, and he insisted men adopt the five *kakkars*: *kesh* (uncut hair), *kangha* (comb), *kachha* (shorts), *kara* (steel bracelet), and *kirpan* (sword). He also encouraged military prowess, forbade tobacco-smoking, and declared that henceforth guruship would rest in the Guru Granth Sahib (Sikhs' sacred texts). The most revered copy is kept in the *gurudwara* (temple) at Amritsar (see p. 123).

FAITHS BROUGHT TO INDIA
Islam

India's 120 million Muslims form the country's second largest religious community and the world's second largest Muslim community, after Indonesia's.

The Prophet Muhammad (circa 570–632) preached Islam (submission to God): one God and one community whose *jihad* (sacred duty) is to spread the word, if necessary by war. He proclaimed Mecca to be Islam's pilgrimage center and its Ka'ba (cube-shaped building housing a stone believed to have been given by Gabriel to Abraham) its most sacred shrine. Just 80 years later, Islam reached India, the first of many Islamic incursions that would end with that of the Moguls (see p. 37).

An early doctrinal split over the Prophet's successor created two sects, Sunni and Shia. Most Indian Muslims are Sunni. Many also follow the Sufi path, a mystical thread in Islamic thought that arose in the tenth century in opposition to the militaristic and orthodox mainstream, and whose spiritualism, asceticism, and indulgence of festivals and singing suited Hindu converts.

Muslims believe fatalistically in total surrender to the will of Allah (God) and in equality in life and death—reasons for Islam's early popularity with lower social groups. The Koran, Islam's sacred book, records the Prophet's revelations, much of it similar to the Old Testament. A Muslim has five duties: belief in one God with Muhammad as his Prophet; showing humility by praying five times daily; fasting from dawn to dusk during Ramadan, the month Muhammad received his revelation; doing charitable work; and going on *hajj* (pilgrimage) to Mecca at least once. To avoid the danger of idolatry, no images of Allah are permitted, so *masjids* (places of prostration, mosques) have no figural decoration.

Christianity

India's 25 million Christians belong to a variety of denominations introduced down the centuries.

The Syrian Christians of Kerala, still a powerful force locally, trace their conversion to St. Thomas the Apostle, who landed at Kodungallur (Cranganore) in A.D. 52 and later died at Chennai (Madras) (see p. 258).

The Portuguese traders of the 16th century (see pp. 44–45) brought Roman Catholicism to India, in particular to Goa. Locals underwent mass conversion and, from 1542, received the zeal of St. Francis Xavier (see p. 193), whose Jesuits brought the first printing press to India. Conversion from Hinduism, although often nominal, brought with it the attractive promises of one life and equality in death.

By the 18th century India had congregations of most denominations, from Anglicans and Methodists to Baptists, and these still thrive today.

Judaism

Jewish people have played a significant role in India's past. Refugees arrived Kerala after the fall of Jerusalem in 587 B.C. Jewish and Arab traders later carried shiploads of spices and luxury goods from India's western ports to the Roman Empire. A Jewish community lived for centuries at Cranganore (Kodungallur), then Cochin, where three synagogues still stand, although only one is used. "White Jews," who did not intermarry with locals, enjoyed high status; "Black Jews," who did, had less status.

During the British period, India had large Jewish communities: Bene Israel, Baghdadis, and Malayalam-speaking Jewish people from Cochin. Most have emigrated to Israel; fewer than 5,000, mostly elderly people, remain.

Zoroastrianism

India's Zoroastrians are better known as Parsees, an elite community that played a key role in building up Bombay.

Zoroastrianism was founded in Iran by the Persian philosopher Zarathustra (Golden Light) sometime between 6000 B.C. and 1500 B.C. Its dual philosophy focuses on the opposing powers of good and evil—the good found in the sacred elements (earth, water, sky, and fire), animals, and plants; the bad in decaying and dead matter. Bodies of the dead are left for the flesh to be eaten by vultures and the bones to be cleansed by the sun and wind, rather than allowed to pollute sacred fire or earth.

Fleeing the Arab Islamic conquests, some Parsees arrived in Gujarat in A.D. 936. Later, in 19th-century Bombay, they shared in the phenomenal business and trading success of the British, whose lifestyles they mimicked. ∎

The capital of the world's largest democracy sprawls across the plains, expanding greedily and unstoppably around the ancient monuments that testify to the attraction of this site for Hindu, Muslim, and British rulers.

Delhi

Independence was declared at Delhi's Red Fort in 1947.

Chandni Chowk, the bustling thoroughfare that runs through the heart of Old Delhi

Delhi

THE CITY OF DELHI IS THE POLITICAL NERVE CENTER OF ALL INDIA AND THE largest commercial hub in northern India. Most of its ten million inhabitants live in the sprawling 580 square miles (1,500 sq km) that surround the historic seven successive cities. Delhi is its own political unit, whose administration has to cope with an alarming recent growth rate and a dry climate with intensely hot summers and cold winters.

There are more than a thousand historic buildings in Delhi, down backstreets, in people's backyards, on golf courses. The flat plain enabled successive conquerors simply to abandon one city and build a fresh one. In theory all monuments are protected, but most are left to take their chances amidst Delhi's burden of humanity. Keeping your eyes open, you can make your very own discoveries in this supremely historic city.

By studying the map opposite you can trace an instant history of Delhi. Begin in the south, at Lal Kot, where tantalizing remains of the Tomar and Chauhan Rajputs' 11th- and 12th-century temples were used by Delhi's first Muslim conqueror, Qutb-ud-din-Aibak, to build his great mosque, begun in 1193. Here, too, is the Qutab Minar, Delhi's landmark tower. Scant remains of Siri, Delhi's second major city, lie to the north. Next came the three Tughlaq cities. Tughlaqabad's rarely visited fort is 5 miles (8 km) east of Lal Kot, while the remains of Sultan Muhammad's never-completed

Jahapanah are near Siri. The citadel of the last and grandest of the Tughlaq cities, Feroz Shah Kotla, stands east of Connaught Place and once overlooked the Yamuna, Delhi's almost forgotten river, which flows on down to Agra and joins the Ganga above Varanasi.

Delhi's sixth city, Purana Qila, was founded by the Mogul emperor Humayun in 1533 and enlarged by his usurper Sher Shah Sur, and it is today the focus of New Delhi's processional route, Raj Path. Farther upstream, Humayun's great-grandson Shah Jahan entered his vibrant Shahjahanabad (Old Delhi) in 1648.

Finally, after Delhi had languished as a backwater for a century or so, the British moved their headquarters here from Calcutta. On February 9, 1931, the British viceroy inaugurated New Delhi, designed by Sir Edwin Lutyens and Herbert Baker to allow for infinite expansion and to encompass all previous Delhi remains without destruction.

Remember that traveling across Delhi takes time. Traffic congestion during the rush hours and at midday slows down all movement. ■

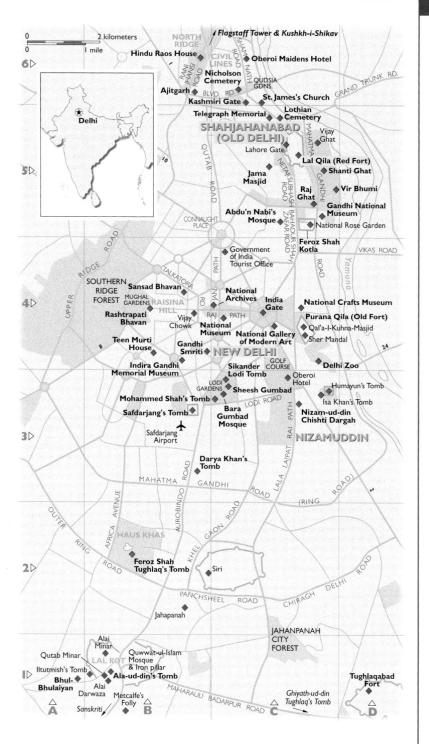

Flagstaff Tower & Kushkh-i-Shikav

NORTH RIDGE

Hindu Raos House

CIVIL LINES

Oberoi Maidens Hotel

SHAMNATH ROAD

RANI JHANSI ROAD

Nicholson Cemetery

QUDSIA GDNS.

Ajitgarh

BLVD. RD.

St. James's Church

GRAND TRUNK RD.

Kashmiri Gate

Telegraph Memorial

Lothian Cemetery

SHAHJAHANABAD (OLD DELHI)

Vijay Ghat

MAHATMA

Lahore Gate

Lal Qila (Red Fort)

Shanti Ghat

QUTAB ROAD

Jama Masjid

NETAJI SUBHASH ROAD

Raj Ghat

Vir Bhumi

GANDHI

CONNAUGHT PLACE

Abdu'n Nabi's Mosque

BAHADUR SHAH ZAFAR ROAD

Gandhi National Museum

National Rose Garden

Government of India Tourist Office

Feroz Shah Kotla

VIKAS ROAD

RIDGE ROAD

SOUTHERN RIDGE FOREST

TALKATORA

Sansad Bhavan

MUGHAL GARDENS

RAISINA HILL

JAN PATH

National Archives

India Gate

National Crafts Museum

Yamuna

UPPER

Rashtrapati Bhavan

Vijay Chowk

RAJ PATH

National Museum

National Gallery of Modern Art

Purana Qila (Old Fort)

Qal'a-I-Kuhna-Masjid

Sher Mandal

Teen Murti House

Gandhi Smriti

NEW DELHI

Indira Gandhi Memorial Museum

GOLF COURSE

Sikander Lodi Tomb

Oberoi Hotel

Delhi Zoo

LODI GARDENS

Sheesh Gumbad

Humayun's Tomb

Mohammed Shah's Tomb

LODI ROAD

Isa Khan's Tomb

Safdarjang's Tomb

Bara Gumbad Mosque

Nizam-ud-din Chishti Dargah

LALA LAJPAT RAI PATH

NIZAMUDDIN

Safdarjang Airport

Darya Khan's Tomb

MAHATMA

AUROBINDO ROAD

GANDHI ROAD

(RING ROAD)

OUTER RING ROAD

AFRICA AVENUE

HAUS KHAS

KHEL GAON ROAD

Feroz Shah Tughlaq's Tomb

Siri

DELHI ROAD

PANCHSHEEL ROAD

CHIRAGH DELHI ROAD

Jahapanah

JAHANPANAH CITY FOREST

Alai Minar

Qutab Minar

LAL KOT

Quwwat-ul-Islam Mosque & Iron pillar

Iltutmish's Tomb

Ala-ud-din's Tomb

Bhul-Bhulaiyan

Alai Darwaza

Metcalfe's Folly

Tughlaqabad Fort

MAHARAULI BADARPUR ROAD

Ghiyath-ud-din Tughlaq's Tomb

Sanskriti

A   B   C   D

0   2 kilometers
0   1 mile

Delhi

6

5

4

3

2

1

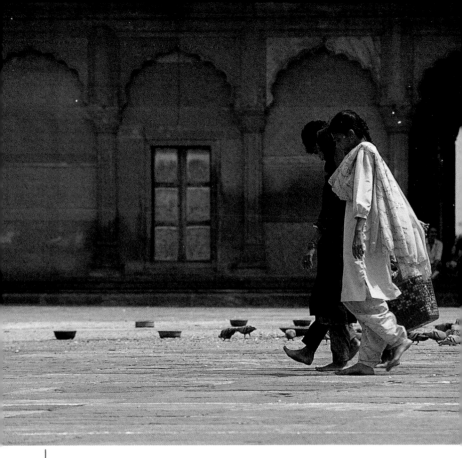

Shahjahanabad

WANDERING THROUGH THE BACK LANES OF BUSTLING Old Delhi, it is easy to imagine the great Muslim city built by the powerful Mogul emperor Shah Jahan to be the new capital of his secure, vast, and extremely wealthy empire. The lifeless, languishing Lal Qila, or Red Fort, once its centerpiece, is less convincing.

Shahjahanabad
🅰 63 C4

Government of India Tourist Office
✉ 88 Janpath, New Delhi
☎ 011-332 0005
e-mail rdnorth@ndf.vsnl.net.in

In 1638, Shah Jahan's fort at Agra, in need of maintenance and unsuitable for the now extensive court ritual, was spilling over with courtiers. The court was no longer itinerant and it needed more space. So with the Taj Mahal (see pp. 100–103) well under way, the now more orthodox widower was drawn back to Delhi. This was the traditional power base in northern India; it was also the burial place of Shaikh Nizam-ud-din Chishti (see p. 70), a Sufi saint revered by the Moguls. Shah Jahan intended to associate himself with previous rulers and holy men, while totally outshining them with his new city, Shahjahanabad. If the Taj Mahal was to be one symbol of imperial Mogul power, this specially built city was to be another, even more impressive one.

To enjoy Shah Jahan's masterpiece, it is best first to visit the old city and its impressive mosque opposite the fort, the **Jama**

In 1639 the foundation stone was laid for the great sandstone walls. Fort and city were divided only after the British created an open space that is now a roaring highway.

The fort's great bastion is an addition by Emperor Aurangzeb. Here, Jawaharlal Nehru addressed the people on India's independence day, August 15, 1947, and here the Indian flag was first raised.

Shah Jahan's building begins with **Chatta Chowk,** a covered market that still thrives today and has some interesting art stores at one end. Beyond it, you must use your imagination, as the British destroyed most of the buildings in 1858 (see p. 82).

The **Naqqar-khana** (royal drum house) stands straight ahead, where musicians heralded important arrivals through this official entrance into the **Diwan-i-Am** (public audience hall). The emperor would sit on the magnificent inlaid marble throne for the crowded daily *durbar* (audience). This consisted of music, displays of gifts, dancing, news from the empire, and the meting out of justice.

Only the most favored reached the inner palaces. These lay through high-walled courtyards and gardens that are today just empty lawns. To visit them, start at the right end with **Mumtaz Mahal** (Mumtaz Palace), now the fort's museum. Next comes **Rang Mahal,** the queens' palace, where the cooling Nahar-I-Bahisht (Stream of Paradise) flowing through the palaces broadened out into a marble pool. **Khas Mahal** (private palace) follows: Its modest rooms were where Shah Jahan slept, worshiped, ate, and at sunrise appeared to his people on the balcony.

The **Diwan-i-Khas** (private audience hall) was where favored diplomats and merchants were called before the emperor. ∎

Masjid (see p. 66). This is India's largest mosque, and was finished in 1656. You can see thousands of Muslims offering prayers there today, just as they did in Shah Jahan's time. It is surrounded by busy stores and restaurants, good for souvenirs and exotic food.

LAL QILA

Using his administrative skills, wealth, aesthetic sense, and knowledge of architecture, Shah Jahan laid out a new fort to suit his needs. Its Lahore Gate opened into the main street of a carefully planned adjoining city that thrives almost unchanged four centuries later, and which contains the Jama Masjid.

The site was north of previous cities and beside the Yamuna River, which has since changed its course.

Jama Masjid
- 63 C5
- Off Netaji Subhash Marg
- Closed to non-Muslims during prayer

Lal Qila
- 63 C5
- Chandni Chowk
- 011-327 3703
- Son-et-lumière times vary

A rickshaw ride around Old Delhi

The best days to enjoy the fun of a rickshaw ride are Monday to Thursday; Jama Masjid (the mosque) is very crowded on Friday. Agree on a price before you start, pay only on completion, and add a tip if appropriate. The driver will wait while you make visits.

Leaving **Lal Qila** ❶ (see p. 65) behind you, cross the very busy Netaji Subhash Marg into Chandni Chowk, Old Delhi's main street, which used to run right up to the fort. There are three landmarks on the left. First is the **Digamber Jain Temple** and **Bird Hospital** ❷ *(Donation).* The Bird Hospital, located within the precincts of the temple, is where injured birds can be brought for free treatment. Next, behind the busy flower stalls, is **Sisganj Gurdwara** ❸, a Sikh temple dedicated to the ninth guru, Tegh Bahadur. Finally, you come to **Sonehri Masjid** (Golden Mosque) where in 1739 Nadir Shah stood watching the destruction of Delhi and thousands of its inhabitants.

Turn left on **Dariba Kalan,** a narrow street lined with silver and gold shops that locals use as a kind of savings bank.

At the intersection, turn right and follow the road around to the left, past art stores and fireworks suppliers, to the **Jama Masjid** ❹,

well worth visiting. At the top of the great steps, leave your shoes, and borrow a cotton overcoat to cover you if your arms or legs are exposed; pay a modest tip afterward. Shah Jahan's last building (1656) proclaims Islam's power and is still India's principal mosque. Designed by Ustad Khlil on Delhi's only mound, it uses glowing red sandstone inlaid with marble and brass, and it has excellent views of the Red Fort from the courtyard. The mosque design, inspired by the Prophet's house at Medina, is simple: a large courtyard with a vaulted hall at one end. The faithful wash ritually in the courtyard's pool, then pray facing the central *mihrab* (niche) of the hall, which indicates the direction of Mecca. The *mimbar* (pulpit) is for the sermon at midday communal prayers on Friday, the Muslims' holy day; the minaret (slender tower) is where the *muezzin* summons the faithful to prayer.

Ride back into Dariba Kalan and turn left for **Kinari Bazar,** Old Delhi's wedding

Old Delhi Station

SHYAMA PRASAD MUKHERJI ROAD

MAHATMA GANDHI PARK

Old Delhi Town Hall ❼

KHARI BAOLI

CHANDNI CHOWK Sonehri Masjid

Sisganj Gurdwara

START

Moti Mahal

Diwan-I-Khas

Khas Mahal

Gadodia Bazar ❻ ❺ Naya Bazar

NAI SARAK

PARATHA WALAN

KINARI BAZAR

BAZAR KALAN

DARIBA

Digamber Jain Temple and Bird Hospital ❸ ❷ Lal Qila (Red Fort) ❶ 1 2 3 3

Rang Mahal

SITARAM BAZAR

SUBHASH

CHAWRI BAZAR

Jama Masjid ❹

NETAJI SUBHASH PARK

Mumtaz Mahal

DARYA GANJ ROAD

0 500 meters
0 500 yards

1. Chatta Chowk
2. Naqqar-khana
3. Diwan-I-Am

equipment street. Tiny, boxlike stores are filled from floor to ceiling with glittering braids, gold lamé grooms' turbans, currency note garlands, plumes, and tinsel. In October, they also stock the papier-mâché masks for the Ram Lila festival. Almost at the end, bear left along Paratha Walan and Nai Sarak. Turn right, passing stores piled with stationery, books, and saris.

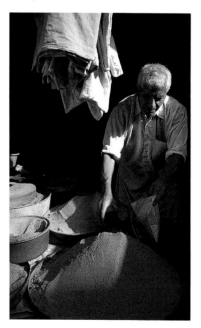

🅜 See area map page 63
➤ Outside the Red Fort
⬌ About 2 miles
🕐 1–2 hours
➤ Outside the Red Fort

NOT TO BE MISSED
• Jama Masjid
• Kinari Bazar
• Gadodia Bazar

Turn left on Chandni Chowk. At the end, turn right, then left on Khari Baoli. Here is **Naya Bazar** ❺, the market selling spices, dried fruit, and nuts from Kashmir and Afghanistan. You can taste before buying. The wholesale spice market, **Gadodia Bazar** ❻, is farther along Khari Baoli, through an arch on the left. Sackfuls of tamarind, ginger, turmeric, and chilis are weighed out on huge iron scales, then humped around by coolies who shout loudly if you are in their way.

Return along Chandni Chowk; the statue in front of **Old Delhi Town Hall** (1860) ❼ is of the liberal nationalist hero, Swami Shraddhanand, who, like Gandhi (see p. 150), was murdered by a fanatic. ∎

Rickshaws are a convenient way of getting around the busy streets (far left), and the markets, where you may see spices (left).

Women & marriage

It may be surprising to learn that for some years India's more privileged women have formed a greater percentage of leading company directors, surgeons, movie directors, and members of parliament than they do in most European countries. This results from a form of backroom emancipation, reinforced by the extended family support system where grandparents and other relatives of a working woman keep house and care for her children.

Indian brides wear a traditional red sari, gold jewelry, plenty of red bangles, and *mehndi* **(henna) patterns on their hands.**

But life for the vast majority of Indian women is different, full of inequality and deprivation. Even in India's more emancipated urban areas, tradition remains strong.

This starts at birth—even before birth. The use of illegal prebirth sex-testing in such wealthy states as the Punjab has been linked to the high numbers of private (and illegal) abortions by women carrying healthy female fetuses. After birth, India's children's homes find more unwanted baby girls than boys on their doorsteps. During childhood, girls are often kept back from school to help with the housework, or they drop out altogether. Despite government programs and energetic women's movements, all too often daughters' health, schooling, literacy, and training lag substantially behind their brothers'.

The only incentive parents have to educate a daughter is to improve her marriage prospects. In essence, most Indian parents consider a daughter a burden, who should be married off as soon and as well as possible to remove her as a mouth to be fed and as a responsibility. Unlike sons, who stay at home, a daughter goes to live with her husband's family. Marriage in India is usually more of a contract between two families than a love match. This is clear from the frank advertisements in the Sunday newspapers: Questions of caste, skin color, healthiness, job prospects, virginity, and social standing are paramount.

Most marriages are still arranged, even if more enlightened parents give the couple the right of veto. A teenage village girl may be married to a man she has never met; she moves to his village or town, keeps his mother's house clean, does manual labor in the fields, and bears and raises his children. She has no property rights; divorce is rare; and there is no social security for divorcées or widows. A middle-class woman's lot is not much better, and if she fails to live up to expectations, primarily to produce a healthy son, she may suffer. One of the worst atrocities in India today, despite being outlawed, is "bride-burning"—that is, a "kitchen accident" in which a woman dies from burns caused by flaming "spilled" kerosene.

In almost all cases, marriage is sealed with negotiations over the dowry. To the traditional silks, saris, and jewels, the husband's family may now add demands for such luxuries as freezers, VCRs, and even a car. The wedding, paid for by the bride's family, is usually a spectacular string of processions and parties.

Although apparently invisible, the women in a household wield considerable power in all decisionmaking, from investments and harvesting to the choice of bridegrooms for their own daughters. ∎

This child bride from a traditional area of western India endures lengthy Hindu wedding ceremonies and will visit her husband's family home for a few days. She will then return to her own home to live until she reaches puberty.

The exotic bangles and gaily colored saris only emphasize the fate of thousands of women who work as laborers for very low wages in terrible conditions of filth, dust, and heat.

East & North Delhi

DOWN THE CENTURIES, THE YAMUNA RIVER HAS BEEN Delhi's highway and local water source. Its western banks are thus the sites of major ancient monuments and, happily, are being rediscovered. A day spent moving northward along the river takes in a variety of top sights. There should be something to suit every interest: Simply skip the ones that do not appeal.

NIZAMUDDIN TO PURANA QILA

The streets behind the deluxe Oberoi Hotel have a medieval air about them. They form the village of **Nizamuddin,** whose heart is the *dargah* (shrine) of the Sufi saint Shaikh Nizam-ud-din Chishti (1238–1325). One of the great

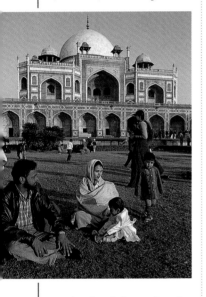

mystic orders, Sufism was brought to India by Khwaja Muin-ud-din Chishti, who settled in Ajmer (see p. 133). It has been said that the Sufis, whose devotion, piety, asceticism, and tolerance were so attractive to Hindus, were the true missionaries of Islam to India. The Chishti order's influential followers included many of the Sultanate rulers and Mogul royal families.

To visit the **dargah,** follow the streets past stores and stalls selling everything from the Koran to cassettes of *qawwalis,* gentle devotional songs. The shrine itself is surrounded by royal tombs, including those of two Tughlaq rulers and Shah Jahan's daughter, Jahanara (see p. 97) Here, too, lies Amir Khusrau (died 1325), whose poetry includes this couplet: "If there is a paradise on earth, it is this, it is this, it is this"—possibly referring to Shah Jahan's Diwan-i-Am building in the Red Fort (see p. 65). He also wrote qawwalis that you might hear in the daily singing there. All these tombs benefit from the spiritual strength of the saint's presence.

This is why the Mogul emperor Humayun is buried nearby. His is the most magnificent of Delhi's tombs, and it is an essential stop if you are intending to visit the Taj Mahal later, for this is its forerunner. **Humayun's tomb** was built in 1565 by his wife, Bega Begum. She employed the Persian architect Mirak Mirza Ghiyas to design the first great Mogul garden tomb. With his knowledge of monumental Timurid tombs, he created something new using local sandstone, marble, and stonemasons.

Once inside, the visitor moves along through a series of walls pierced by gateways. Inside the first, turn right to Isa Khan's sturdy tomb (1547), already adopting Hindu details such as projecting eaves and domed kiosks. The final wall surrounds a formal *char bagh*

The dargah of Shaikh Nizam-ud-din Chishti (above) is the focus of a Muslim burial ground for nobility, including the emperor Humayun, whose tomb (left) stands in a char bagh.

(four gardens) that reflects the Koran's description of paradise. Look at the great tomb on its high platform from here, the double dome making possible a soaring exterior and well-proportioned interior. Through the newly restored gardens, steep steps lead onto the platform to see the emperor's cenotaph (monument) in the mausoleum, and those of his son

Dara Shukoh and other Mogul royals. In accordance with Islamic custom, their bodies lie buried at ground level. Before leaving, see if you can spot Purana Qila fort, the next stop.

Delhi Zoo lies between Humayun's tomb and Purana Qila, India's biggest and most important zoo, established in 1959. Through poor management the potentially

Nizamuddin

🚇 63 C3

✉ W of Mathura Rd.

Humayun's tomb

🚇 63 C3

✉ Off Mathura Rd.

☎ 011-462 5275

💲 $

Delhi Zoo

🅰 63 C4

✉ Mathura Rd.

☎ 011-461 9825

🕐 Closed Fri.

fascinating collection, which includes the one-horned rhinoceros from Assam, the Asiatic lion from Gujarat, and other examples of India's rich wildlife, is not always a joy to visit. Better conditions for the animals would greatly enhance this zoo.

A Gujarat basketmaker displays her skills at the National Crafts Museum.

Purana Qila

🅰 63 C4

✉ Mathura Rd.

☎ 011-460 4260

🕐 Son-et-lumière times vary

Purana Qila (Old Fort) rises above it. Archaeologists say this spot may have been where Arjuna, one of the five Pandava hero brothers, founded the sacred site of Indraprastha (City of Indra) as recounted in the epic *Mahabharata* (see p. 76). More certainly, the second Mogul emperor, Humayun, brought the capital back here from Agra and in 1533 founded Dinpanah (Shelter of the Faith). The soaring walls and their three gates are his, but his usurper, Sher Shah Sur (see p. 40), erected the two buildings inside: the **Qala-I-Kuhna-Masjid,** with its five great arches and proto-Mogul decora-

tion, and the **Sher Mandal.** It was from the roof of this building that Humayun, having regained his throne in 1555, fell down the stairs and died in 1556.

NATIONAL CRAFTS MUSEUM

Sited in the shadow of the Purana Qila, this is arguably one of the finest museums of its kind and a must for anyone interested in the huge range of fine craftsmanship to be seen all over India. Jyotindra Jain, the museum's inspiration and its director since 1984, constantly commissions pieces and adds to the several thousand quality examples already displayed in a congenial, unstuffy atmosphere.

This is a museum that is guaranteed to bring smiles. A warren of courtyards and rooms designed by Charles Correa houses the primary collection. Do not miss the life-size carved wooden cows and horses, a model of a whole village, tribal metalwork animals of all shapes, and rooms covered with folk paintings. Giant storage pots, plastered walls, a temple chariot, and a carved wooden dovecote lead to the dazzling fabric collection upstairs.

Outside, there are sacred terracotta horses, a group of vernacular painted huts, a good gift shop, and a café. The highlight is watching craftsmen from all over India brought here to spend a three-month period making their own goods. You may find a weaver from Assam, a painter of miniatures from Jodhpur, or a potter from Tamil Nadu. You can buy direct from them; the museum often does.

FEROZ SHAH KOTLA & SURROUNDINGS

The centerpiece of this group of sites north of Purana Qila is Feroz Shah Kotla, entered from Bahadur Shah Zafar Marg road. It is the ruined citadel of a vast city that, in its heyday under Feroz Shah Tughlaq (*R.*1351–1388), stretched from North Ridge down to Lal Kot and was famed for its palaces, reservoirs, hunting lodges, mosques, and intellectual life. Then, in 1398, Timur (Tamburlaine) sacked it and

Within the complex lies the **National Rose Garden,** usually glorious in February and March. Across the main road you can see **Abdu'n Nabi's Mosque** (1575–76), built by Akbar's ecclesiastical registrar, who, failing to account for money that he had

National Crafts Museum

▲ 63 C4

✉ Pragati Maidan
(enter on Bhairion)

☎ 011-331764

🕐 Closed Mon., &
July–Sept.

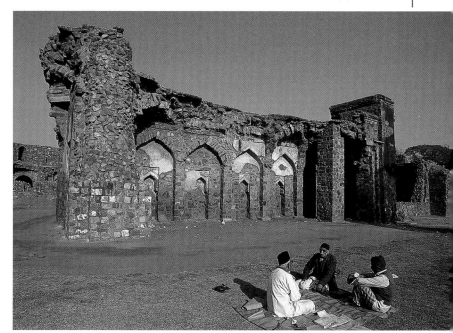

carried off its treasures. His descendant, Babur, later invaded India and founded the Mogul dynasty (see pp. 39–40). Imagine this as you wander the lawns around a ruined mosque, palace, and *baoli* (step-well).

Feroz Shah, a weak ruler but a great builder, intellectual, and antique collector, brought the mysterious carved pillar here from Meerut (and brought another to North Ridge), believing the inscriptions to be a magic charm. In fact, when the scholar James Princep unraveled the pillar's Brahmi script in 1837, it was discovered that the inscriptions were Ashoka's edicts (see p. 31) promoting *dharma.*

supposedly taken to the poor in Mecca, was summarily murdered.

MEMORIALS TO MAHATMA & OTHERS

The land left behind by the Yamuna when its course altered is now an undulating park devoted to the memory of India's modern heroes. Planted with fine trees and well kept, this is a tranquil and pleasant place for a walk in winter or during cool summer hours.

The first and most visited memorial is **Raj Ghat.** A platform marks the spot where Mahatma Gandhi (see p. 150) was cremated after his assassination on January

The scant but evocative ruins of Feroz Shah Kotla include Feroz Shah's own palace, a mosque, and a baoli (step-well).

Feroz Shah Kotla

▲ 63 C4

✉ Bahadur Shah Zafar
Marg

Raj Ghat

▲ 63 C5

✉ Mahatma Gandhi
Rd.

A statue of Mahatma Gandhi in contemplation, wreathed with marigold garlands

Gandhi National Museum

🅰 63 C5

✉ Opposite Raj Ghat, Mahatma Gandhi Rd.

☎ 011-331 1793

🕐 Closed Mon.

Vir Bhumi

🅰 63 C5

Shanti Van & Vijay Ghat

🅰 63 C5

✉ Mahatma Gandhi Rd.

30, 1948. It was then made into an oasis of peace using Vanu G. Bhuta's design of a walled, square garden entered through a simple arch. For Indians and others, this is a place of pilgrimage. If you wish to know more, you can visit the modest but informative **Gandhi National Museum** across the main road, where photographs, quotes, descriptions, and sometimes documentaries pay tribute to the Mahatma; literature is on sale at the gift shop.

Tragedy was to strike Indian leaders again after 1948. Just north of here, in a less formal setting, a string of memorials begins with **Vir Bhumi,** where Rajiv Gandhi (assassinated May 21, 1991) was cremated. The memorial to his brother Sanjay Gandhi (died in a plane accident, June 1980) is nearby. Their mother, Indira (assassinated October 31, 1984), was cremated at **Shanti Ghat** (Forest of Peace), as was her father, India's first prime minister, Jawaharlal Nehru (died May 27, 1964). Finally, **Vijay Ghat** remembers Lal Bahadur Shashtri, India's second prime minister (died January 11, 1966). If you get this far, you can enjoy views of Shah Jahan's riverside palaces.

CIVIL LINES & NORTH RIDGE

As historians gain a better perspective on the British period in India's history, so opinions are revised in the light of greater knowledge and objectivity. For those interested, a short trip into the rarely visited area that was British Delhi from the 18th century until New Delhi was built brings fascinating rewards. (See also Lucknow, pp. 310–313.)

On up Mahatma Gandhi Road and into Lothian Road, the tumble-down **Lothian Cemetery** is on the right, just before an arched ruin midroad. The ruin is the remains of the British Magazine, a huge ammunition storehouse. It was deliberately blown up by the British on May 11, 1857, to prevent the freedom fighters—Indian soldiers in the British Army who had mutinied in Meerut the previous day—from seizing it. The bang was said to have been heard in Meerut, 31 miles (50 km) away. Just beyond, the gray obelisk is the **Telegraph Memorial,** from which the Anglo-Indian operator warned the British Army of the mutineers' approach. On the right, the dilapidated, columned building dates from an earlier time: In 1803 it became Delhi's first **British Residency.**

The distinctive yellow-plastered and domed **St. James's** (consecrated 1836), Delhi's first church, merits a stop. It was built by Col. James Skinner (circa 1778–1841), the son of a Scotsman and a Rajput, who founded Skinner's Horse, crack cavalry regiments distinguished by their yellow uniforms. Skinner family tombs stand in the churchyard. Inside the church, the family pew is at the front, Skinner's tomb is by the altar, and there are monuments to other British men.

Lothian Road now passes a lone survivor of Shah Jahan's many-gated city (see p. 64): **Kashmiri Gate,** so called because the Mogul emperors and their court would leave Delhi's searing summer heat through this gate on their way to the cool Kashmir hills. In September 1857, 5,000 British troops swarmed down from the Ridge, breached the walls, confronted up to 20,000 rebelling Indians and, after six days of fighting, retook Delhi. Brig.-Gen. John Nicholson, who died at the gate, is buried in **Nicholson Cemetery** up the road on the left, across from Qudsia Gardens, now a pale memory of its lush former days.

Here Lothian Road is called Sham Nath Marg. On the right, the spacious and delightful **Oberoi Maidens Hotel** (see p. 347), built in 1900, may be just the place for some refreshment; Sir Edwin Lutyens lived here while his New Delhi was being built.

From here follow Underhill Road, which passes forgotten grand colonial houses set on large, leafy grounds. At the end turn left on Rajpur Road, then left again at the top on Rani Jhansi Marg. This takes you to North Ridge, from which British troops poured down to retake Delhi. **Flagstaff Tower,** on its crest, is where the British women and children gathered five months earlier, before fleeing to Karnal as the mutineers approached.

Near here you can find odds and ends from Delhi's history: first, the remains of one of Feroz Shah Tughlaq's hunting palaces, **Kushkh-i-shikav** (1356), on the right; then, William Fraser's country retreat, on the same side, called **Hindu Raos House** (1830). Fraser, who had six or seven wives, fathered uncounted children, and knew India better than most Europeans, was Resident of Delhi until his murder in 1835.

On the way down from the ridge you can see the small, tapering Gothic tower of the Mutiny Memorial. Built to remember the British dead, it is now renamed **Ajitgarh** and remembers Indian martyrs who died fighting colonial rule. A left turn on Boulevard Road takes you back to Kashmiri Gate. ∎

Lothian Cemetery
△ 63 C5
✉ Lothian Rd.

St. James's Church
△ 63 C6
✉ Lothian Rd.
☎ 011-296 0873

Nicholson Cemetery
△ 63 C6
✉ Qudsia Rd.

Kushkh-i-shikav
△ 63 C6

Hindu Raos House
△ 63 B6

Ajitgarh
△ 63 B6

A good book

Indian literature—written by Indians and non-Indians—is a rich and unending feast of intimate diaries, romantic fiction, matter-of-fact reports, and golden prose. And it keeps on coming: Unknown texts are continually being rediscovered and newly published; familiar favorites such as Rudyard Kipling's *Kim* are reprinted; and new writing on India is as fresh as ever.

It is easy to find good reading material to suit every taste. Moreover, the bigger cities in India have well-stocked bookstores with much lower prices than in the West.

India's literature may be daunting. However, a child's edition, or the children's cartoon strip magazines that recount the main epics episodically, are easy ways of grasping the background stories and a knowledge of these can help you enjoy India's paintings, dance-drama, and sculpture. The *Mahabharata* is an epic poem recounting the civil war between the Pandavas, led by Arjuna, and the Kurus. In a later addition, the *Bhagavad Gita*, Krishna discusses with Arjuna the human struggle for love, light, and redemption. The other great epic is the *Ramayana*, in which good king Rama, helped by monkey and bear allies, rescues his wife, Sita, from Ravana, the multiheaded demon king of Sri Lanka. The ancient Puranas, meanwhile, include the popular stories of Vishnu's incarnation as the vivacious human, Krishna.

Early and classical devotional poetry can be read in sensitive full translations. Try the Penguin editions of *The Kural* by the Tamil writer Tiruvalluvar, or the Sanskrit lyrical poems of Bhartrihari and Bilhana.

The West first learned about India through written accounts. The diaries, travel writing, and letters of early travelers formed the basis of Western knowledge of India until relatively recently. Images of India only became common when the uncle-nephew team of Thomas and William Daniells began publishing series of prints of India in London in the 1790s.

Jawaharlal Nehru wrote *An Autobiography* and *Glimpses of World History*. His contemporaries, equally aware of India's changing state, included Mulk Raj Anand (*Untouchable, Coolie*), Nirad Chaudhuri (*The Autobiography of an Unknown Indian*), and S. H. Manto, whose short stories include *Toba Tek Singh*.

Among recent generations of Indian writers, some of whom live outside the country, are Vikram Seth, whose epic *A Suitable Boy* explores post-independent northern India; Anita Desai, whose novels (for example *Clear Light of Day*) keep mainly to her home city of Delhi, and R. K. Narayan, whose novels are set in the south. Salman Rushdie, best known for *Midnight's Children*, explores Kerala and Mumbai in *The Moor's Last Sigh*; screenwriter Arundhati Roy's first novel *The God of Small Things* is set against a background of political turbulence in Kerala; while Rohinton Mistry's *Such a Long Journey* and *A Fine Balance* have a broader base. Away from the novel, almost all of V. S. Naipaul's candid observations and predictions ring true, beginning with *An Area of Darkness*.

A good way to enjoy a range of writing is to read an anthology. Bruce Palling's *A Literary Companion: India* includes the reactions to India of the 4th-century Chinese Buddhist traveler Fa Hsien, the 19th-century Bishop Heber of Calcutta, and 20th-century English novelist Evelyn Waugh. It is surprising just how many people have written about India—American novelist Mark Twain (1835–1910), the humorist Edward Lear (1812–1888), the poet W. H. Auden (1907–1973), the photographer Sir Cecil Beaton (1904–1980), the explorer Sir Richard Burton (1821–1890), the novelist E. M. Forster (1879–1970)—and many more. ■

Arundhati Roy (right), author of the Booker prize-winning novel *The God of Small Things,* and an influential environmental activist, is an example of the literary talent that blossoms in India today. Voracious readers of books and newspapers in English as well as in their numerous native languages, educated Indians make full use of their local libraries, bookstores, and newstands (below).

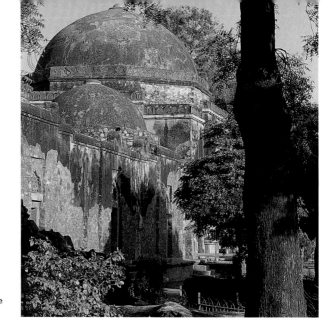

Feroz Shah Tughlaq's tomb looks to Afghan fort architecture for inspiration.

South Delhi

INTERESTING REMNANTS OF DELHI'S PRE-MOGUL CITIES are scattered over the large area of fashionable and increasingly built-up south Delhi. To use your time well, it is best to take a taxi or hire a car and driver for a long morning or, better still, a whole day. The following route works well; remember to take drinks and snacks.

Lodi Gardens
🅰 63 C3
✉ Lodi Road

Safdarjang's Tomb
🅰 63 B3
✉ Junction of Lodi Rd. & Sri Aurobindo Marg
💲 $

LODI GARDENS

A stroll through Lodi Gardens in the morning is a good start to the day; your driver will deliver you to one entrance and collect you from the other.

Lady Willingdon, whose husband was viceroy from 1931 to 1936, saved this group of majestic domed tombs from New Delhi developers in the 1930s, laying out lawns, shrubs, and shady trees around them. The tombs were built during the weak Sayyid and Lodi sultanates (see p. 39), whose rulers allowed noble power to grow. Neither dynasty built a great city, but both added many tombs and mosques to Delhi. After Sikander Lodi (R.1489–1517) moved to Agra in 1502, the forlorn former capital was nothing but a great necropolis.

If you enter from Lodi Road, you come first to the **tomb of Mohammad Shah,** the third Sayyid ruler. Built in 1450, its octagonal plan has sloping buttresses that contrast with the soft lotus patterns on the ceiling. Next comes the **Bara Gumbad Mosque** (1494), built during the reign of Sikander Lodi. In addition to the fine domed gateway, some of the best plaster decoration in India survives here; see the delicate filigree work and elaborate facade. The contemporary **Sheesh Gumbad** (glass dome), so-called because its dome used to have glazed blue tiles that glittered in the sun, stands on the hillock; the double-story room inside has wonderful stucco and painted decoration. The **tomb of Sikander Lodi** preserves its walled enclosure and adjoining mosque. Nearby is the **Athpula,** a seven-arched Mogul bridge built in the 16th century.

SOUTHWARD TO HAUS KHAS

South along Aurobindo Road toward Lal Kot, the first landmark building is the **tomb of Safdarjang,** the Nawab of Oudh (Avadh), a powerful minister to the dissipated, unpopular late Mogul ruler Ahmad Shah. Built in 1754, this is the last of the great Mogul garden tombs, keeping the formal layout of Humayun's (see pp. 70–71), but lacking its grace of style. Half a mile (1 km) farther down Sri Aurobindo Marg, a left turn to Kidwai Nagar reaches the grand tomb of **Darya Khan,** who served all the Lodi sultans.

The city of Siri, begun in 1304 by the popular and able Ala-ud-din Khilji (R.1296–1316), lay beyond here, but little remains. To get an idea of it, continue down Sri Aurobindo Marg and turn right into **Haus Khas village,** where many old houses have been renovated into upscale boutiques and restaurants (see p. 348). At the other end of the village street is a walled garden opening onto a huge sunken space. This was the *haus* (reservoir) that provided water for Siri's citizens. To the left are the steps, pavilions, and university buildings added by Feroz Shah Tughlaq in 1354. His austere **tomb** (1390) stands at the corner; its interior has fine plasterwork.

LAL KOT: THE EARLIEST DELHIS

About 7 miles (11km) south of Lodi Gardens down Aurobindo Road is the spot where historical Delhi began. Lal Kot was the Rajput citadel built by the Tomar king Anangpal in about 1060. Enlarged,

fortified, and given 13 gates by the Chauhan king Prithviraj III in 1080, this thriving city was captured by Qutb-ud-din-Aibak in 1192, marking the arrival of Islam in today's India (see p. 37). The next year Aibak began building a mosque, and six years later he began the Qutab Minar.

There is a lot to see in the complex. Through the arched entrance, remains of Ala-ud-din's southernmost Siri buildings survive on the right. Farther ahead, you find the base of **Alai Minar,** an unfinished tower he intended to be twice the size of the Qutab Minar (he died before much was built).

Aibak's mosque lies ahead: the **Quwwat-ul-Islam** (Might of Islam) mosque (1193–97), given additions by Iltutmish (1230) and Ala-ud-din (1315). Delicate stones taken from Hindu and Jain temples were used in the construction—you can see the ropes, bells, cows, and defaced figures on some. Cloisters lead to a courtyard and the monumental screen of the now vanished prayer hall, built by local Hindu masons. You can see how later parts of the magnificent, bold screen carving exchange floral and leaf motifs for more rigorously abstract Islamic arabesques and *suras* (verses) from the Koran. The Gupta **iron pillar** (fourth to fifth century), with its Sanskrit inscription, is a mystery in origins and casting, but legend says that those who encircle it with their arms behind their back will have their wish granted.

To the left of the screen, cross the ditch and turn right to find, at the end of the path, the modest **tomb of Iltutmish** (R.1210–1236), Aibak's son-in-law and successor. This is the earliest tomb of an Indian Islamic ruler, with beautifully carved walls. Back along the path, the ruins on the mound

Haus Khas village
63 B2
W off Sri Aurobindo Marg

Lal Kot
63 B1
Junction of Sri Aurobindo Marg & Mehrauli-Badapur Rd.

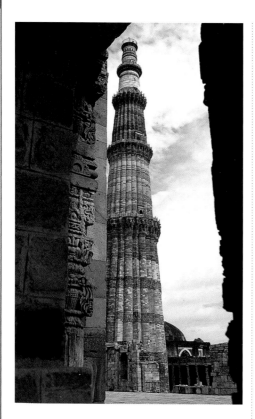

At Lal Kot, both the Qutab Minar (above) and the tomb of Iltutmish (opposite) used skilled craftsmen for their intricate carving.

Sanskriti
🗺 63 B1
✉ Anadgram, Mehrauli-Gurgaon Rd. (opposite radio station)
☎ 011-650 1125
🕑 Closed Mon.

Tughlaqabad
🗺 63 D1
✉ Off Mehrauli-Gurgaon Rd.

ahead are of Ala-ud-din's unfinished **tomb** and his **college** (university). Leaving them through an opening on the left, there are views over the whole complex, including Aibak's intricately carved, five-story **Qutab Minar** (the top two stories were rebuilt in marble by Feroz Shah), which served as a tower of victory and a minaret for calling the faithful to prayer. The stocky, square building to the right of it is **Alai Darwaza** (1311), the impressive entrance to Ala-ud-din's now-lost mosque extension. Its restrained bulk and large panels of low-relief carving make it the most Islamic building here. Beyond, the Gothic-style cupola added to the Qutab Minar by the British was so ridiculed that it now stands in a corner of the lawn.

OTHER SOUTH DELHI SITES

These real treats require a strong pair of walking shoes, curiosity, and determination to seek them out.

Take the street at the back of the Lal Kot parking lot onto the open plains dotted with Islamic monuments. Right ahead is **Metcalfe's Folly,** two ruined tombs bought by Sir Thomas Metcalfe, Delhi's British Resident from 1835 to 1853, and turned into a country retreat to which he would ride on horseback from Civil Lines (see p. 74). **Jamali-Kamali** (1528), the mosque and tombs of a poet-saint and his brother, lie beyond; you can walk or drive to them.

Next, head for Mehrauli village, half a mile (1 km) west of Lal Kot. Here you can find **Bhul-Bhulaiyan** (1562), the double tomb of Adham Khan and his powerful mother, Maham Anga, wet-nurse to the Mogul emperor Akbar. Just beyond it, a street on the left leads to a cluster of mosques, a *baoli* (step-well), and tombs of three late Mogul emperors.

If you enjoyed the National Crafts Museum (see p. 72), then it is well worth making reservations to visit **Sanskriti,** which lies south of Lal Kot. Here O. P. Jain, a collector and patron of Indian crafts, has a private arts foundation, whose collection of high-quality everyday objects is displayed in a peaceful garden bordered by artists' houses.

Finally, head eastward to **Tughlaqabad** to find the massive ruins of the city built by Ghiyath-ud-Din Tughlaq from 1321 to 1325. Here you can ramble over the fortifications, the palace precincts, and the citadel. Across the road stands Ghiyath-ud-Din's fortified tomb (circa 1325), once surrounded by a lake. As with the Sayyid and Lodi tombs, it contrasts with the garden tombs of the Moguls. ∎

The rediscovery of India

The British relationship with India's ancient sites and monuments was complicated. Progress in archaeology was pioneered by a few, such as Sir William Jones, who, with a group of fellow enthusiasts, founded the Asiatic Society in 1784. Discoveries were often by-products of military measures. This was true of the Survey of India, begun in 1800, which aimed to map the whole sub-continent from south to north. Teams of surveyors mapped the highest Himalayan peaks in the 1850s, naming the highest of all "Everest," after Sir George Everest, one of the project's superintendents. On this project and others, rediscoveries of overgrown, forgotten monuments abounded—the Chalukyan caves of Badami, the Buddhist *stupas* of Sanchi, the temples of Khajuraho, Ajanta's painted caves.

surveyor of India. Projects such as the restoration of Sanchi and Gwalior, and the publication of copies of the Ajanta frescoes, followed. Activity increased when Lord Curzon arrived as Viceroy in 1899 and recognized that India had "the most glorious galaxy of monuments in the world," whose maintenance was an imperial responsibility. He reorganized the Archaeological Survey, arranged funds for it, and in 1902 appointed 26-year-old Sir John Marshall as first director-general, a position he held for 29 years. Indian scholars were employed, excavations and drawings made, laws for the protection of ancient monuments passed. While the public's attention was most closely focused on Agra's Mogul buildings, the temples of Kanchipuram, mosques of Bijapur, and other monuments were also cleared, cleaned, and restored.

Ideas of restoration and conservation began in the mid-19th century. But the majority of British administrators still did not appreciate the significance of India's wealth of historical monuments. It took a piece of destruction of their own to kickstart the conservation movement. After Delhi was retaken, the British spent 1858 ransacking the city. They wantonly looted the imperial palaces and desecrated the mosques. Two-thirds of the Red Fort buildings were pulled down. Those remaining became the military garrison, and the area in front was cleared for security reasons. Suggestions for the fate of the Jama Masjid were that it be blown up, sold, turned into barracks or, worst of all, into a Hall of Remembrance to British victims of the war. This provoked an outcry among the enlightened. As the pioneering architectural historian James Fergusson argued, the military excuse for this destruction did not hold up.

The result was the appointment in 1861 of Sir Alexander Cunningham as archaeological

Since independence, this vast body of knowledge has continued to grow under the aegis of the Archaeological Survey of India. The headquarters is situated next to the National Museum, on Janpath, in Delhi; reliable publications (all too often out of print, sadly) are sold here and at many Archaeological Survey sites.

A more recent conservation group, the Indian National Trust for Art and Cultural Heritage (INTACH), was founded in 1984. This nongovernment organization has area chapters spread right across India, whose enthusiastic, dedicated, and knowledgeable members have already achieved impressive results, including the restoration of Elephanta's cave, work on Jodhpur Fort, fixing some of Varanasi's *ghats*, and creating a heritage plan for Kochi (Cochin) and Mattancherry. For more information on INTACH's work, write to 71 Lodhi Estate, New Delhi 110003, or call tel 011-4692774. ∎

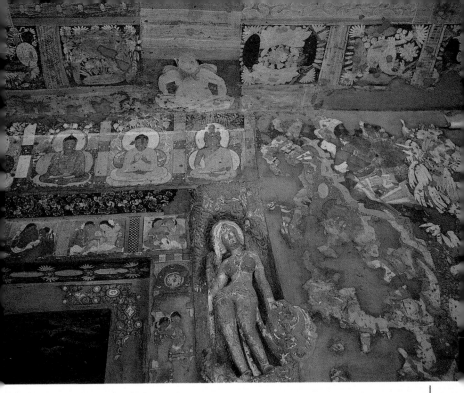

The British came to India as traders, but many were intrigued by the culture: They revealed India's wonders to the West, from Ajanta's murals (above) and Taj Mahal (below) to Khajuraho's sculptures (opposite).

The sun sets behind the Sanchi-inspired dome of Rastrapati Bhavan, while egrets sport on the lake.

New Delhi

THE BRITISH HAD THEIR HEADQUARTERS FIRST AT CHENNAI (Madras), then at Kolkata (Calcutta). Delhi, strategic as it had been for past rulers, was a backwater. Agra, not Delhi, was capital of the Northwest Provinces that stretched up to the Hindu Kush.

New Delhi
🔺 63 C4

Then, to everyone's surprise, during his royal visit to India in 1911, the King-Emperor George V announced that the capital of British India was to move from Calcutta back to Delhi. Delhi was to rise, phoenixlike, to be the specially built imperial capital of the sub-continent. The King-Emperor and Queen-Empress Mary then laid a foundation stone north of Old Delhi and went home.

In 1913 British architect Edwin Lutyens sailed for India. He and his Planning Commission—Sir Herbert Baker, J. A. Brodie, G. S. C. Swinton, and others—disliked the original site, so they rode around Delhi's scrubland on elephants and settled on another. One night they quietly dug up the foundation stone, put it on a bullock cart, and relaid it on Raisina Hill.

This uncompromising approach was typical of Lutyens, who was responsible for the overall design of

**Above, right:
The two majestic
Secretariat
buildings, North
Block and South
Block, face each
other on Raisina
Hill.**

the new capital, called New Delhi, Viceroy's House (Rastrapati Bhavan), and some designs along Raj Path. His team designed the rest—quantities of public buildings plus more than 4,000 flat-roofed, stuccoed brick bungalows.

To prepare, Lutyens toured northern India. Unimpressed by Mogul buildings (he thought Fatehpur Sikri "the work of monkeys"), he found Sanchi's Buddhist stupas inspiration for his domes. Then he got to work on his plan: classical buildings with Indian details, such as deep shading eaves, set in a gracious garden city capable of endless expansion. He described it as "an Englishman dressed for the climate."

More than 30,000 laborers were employed to transform the hilly, dry site. Glorious red sandstone was brought from Dholpur, as it had been for Shahjahanabad (see p. 64). William Robertson Mustoe, trained at London's Kew Gardens, advised on the planting of 10,000 trees. Costs soared, and the budget passed 15 billion pounds (21 billion dollars). Lutyens fought hard but plans were occasionally modified.

On February 15, 1931, New Delhi was inaugurated by the viceroy, Lord Irwin. Two weeks of festivities included a performance of *Madame Butterfly* in the Red Fort, Scottish dancing, a pageant of painted elephants, and a 21-gun salute to herald the unveiling of Baker's Ashokan columns.

Sixteen years later, New Delhi was one of the most useful, if unintended, legacies the British left to the newly independent India: a ready-made capital.

RAISINA HILL

This is the heart of New Delhi, and India's political center. A good way to see it is to walk from Vijay Chowk to Raisina Hill's controversial gradient: Lutyens accused Baker of making it too steep and blocking the view of his masterpiece, Viceroy's House.

Vijay Chowk is where the military parade known as Beating the Retreat is held each January, at sunset; to the north, the circular building is **Sansad Bhavan** (Parliament House). Moving up the hill, the first pavilion provides breathtaking views. Raj Path sweeps

An elaborate *sarpesh* (turban ornament) made in Jaipur in the 19th century.

down from this citadel of power, crossing Janpath, past India Gate and into the far distance. The grand parade on Republic Day, January 26, moves along here. The area on the right is a vast triangle of once

residential buildings; that to the left leads north to Connaught Place, now just one of Delhi's shopping centers.

The brow of Raisina Hill is unashamedly imperial. A wide avenue runs between Baker's **Secretariats,** their design a mixture of English baroque, Mogul doorways, and lotus-decorated domes, and leads to an ornate entrance screen. Beyond lies **Rastrapati Bhavan** (President's Palace, formerly Viceroy's House, *private*). Peer through the gates to see **Jaipur Column,** given by the Maharaja of Jaipur, a close British ally, standing in the courtyard. Behind, Lutyens' masterpiece has a facade 630 feet (192 m) wide and a

plan covering 200,000 square feet (18,580 sq m), making it larger than Versailles. It was here, behind the central steps and columns, that Britain's last viceroy, Lord Mountbatten, stood in the Durbar Hall to hand power over to India's first prime minister, Jawaharlal Nehru. Behind the house, President's Estate includes the spectacular **Moghul Gardens.** Inspired by the Moghul Gardens of Kashmir and Gertrude Jekyll's work in England, they are kept in shape by 150 gardeners and are open to the public each spring.

CIVIC NEW DELHI

To get a flavor of the city as it was, drive along Raj Path to **India Gate,** which remembers the 90,000 Indian soldiers who died in World War I and the Afghan War (1919). An eternal flame has been added to honor the Unknown Soldier. Farther along, the graceful sandstone pavilion beyond once held a statue of George V but now stands empty. A clutch of very grand former palaces surrounds it: Hyderabad, Baroda, Bikaner, and Jaipur Houses. The last is now the **National Gallery of Modern Art,** usually more rewarding for its Daniels and Bengali school pictures than for its contemporary shows.

Back along Raj Path, the intersection with Janpath was to have a collection of public buildings. It got just two. One is the **National Archives** building, whose exhibits include items from its collection of books and manuscripts on political, social, and economic history. The other is the

National Gallery of Modern Art
✉ Jaipur House, India Gate
☎ 011-338 2835
🕐 Closed Mon.

National Archives
✉ Janpath
☎ 011-338 9598
🕐 Closed Mon.

National Museum
✉ Janpath
☎ 011-301 9272
🕐 Closed Mon.

National Museum (1955–1960). Founded in 1949, its impressive collection makes a good introduction to Indian art. See especially the stone and bronze sculptures from Mathura, Bharhut, Sarnath, and Kausambi and southern India. They are exhibited in the entrance hall, corridors, and first-floor rooms and are some of India's most glorious artistic achievements. Upstairs are fine miniature paintings, musical instruments, and glittering jewelry.

THREE NEW DELHI HOUSES

Here is a fascinating insider's view of New Delhi. Ask your driver to take you first to the palatial **Teen Murti Museum** (1930) and its flower-filled garden, built for the commander-in-chief. This is where Nehru lived from 1948 until his death in 1964, and his desk, library, and bedroom are as he left them. Next is the contrasting **Indira Gandhi Memorial Museum,** a small bungalow in lush surroundings where Nehru's daughter lived. Photographs lining the walls recount the story of her leadership and the fates of her sons. On the grounds a sculpted river of glass marks the spot where, on October 31, 1984, she was assassinated.

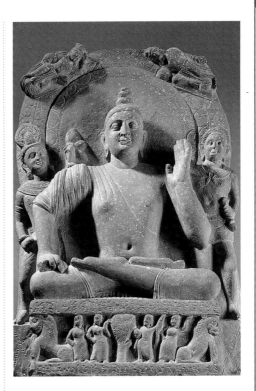

Gandhi Smriti (Birla House) is where, on January 30, 1948, Mahatma Gandhi was shot by a Hindu fanatic who believed he was too tolerant toward Muslims. ■

A seated Bodhisattva carved in the first century, found at Mathura, south of Delhi

The Gandhi factor

Politics can turn on a surname. When Indira Nehru, daughter of India's first prime minister, Jawaharlal Nehru, a Kashmiri of the brahman caste, married a Parsee man named Feroz Gandhi, she acquired arguably her most useful political tool.

The very name of Gandhi contained echoes of the greatness of the revered Mahatma, Mohandas Kamarchand Gandhi, although there was no blood connection. Even some Indians would be confused, and no Congress Party campaigners would risk losing votes by putting them right. The hero of the struggle for freedom would be allowed to radiate his influence to the benefit of all, even into the murky waters of politics. Rajiv Gandhi benefited, too, and today, as his daughter prepares to enter the political theater, people throughout India still speak not of the Nehru inheritance but of the Gandhi dynasty. ■

Teen Murti Museum
✉ Teen Murti Rd.
☎ 011-301 6350
🕐 Closed Mon.

Indira Gandhi Memorial Museum
✉ 1 Safdar Jang Rd.
☎ 011-301 0094
🕐 Closed Mon.

Gandhi Smriti Museum
✉ Hall of Nations Bldg., 5 Tees January Rd.

Creating a modern architecture

Though Le Corbusier's large-scale town plans were often rejected, his designs proved very influential.

When the French architect Le Corbusier (1887–1965) came to India in 1951, he was already 64 years old with a reputation as a brilliant, if controversial, architect and a semi-abstract painter, sculptor, and writer. He turned Indian architecture upside down, and it is only now beginning to find itself again.

Le Corbusier came at the invitation of the Punjab government to be architectural adviser for their new capital. Punjab had been sliced in half when it gained independence and Pakistan's section included the city of Lahore. The Frenchman was impressed by the grand scale of Lutyens' Delhi and by the abstract shapes of the Jantar Mantar there (see p. 92). These ideas he incorporated into his uncompromising designs for Chandigarh (see pp. 120–21), where he employed his modular system and *brises-soleil* (sunbreakers), and placed the emphasis on raw concrete.

Such a total break with the vernacular was welcomed; it underlined the new India's ambition and idealism. Le Corbusier picked up commissions from progressive patrons in Ahmedabad, capital of Gujarat state, where he built Shodhan House, Manorama Sarabhai's houses, and the Mill Owners Association building, all in the 1950s.

A posse of young Indian architects absorbed his tenets; anonymous concrete buildings sprang up all over India. Two exceptional architects were Balkrishna V. Doshi and Charles Correa. Both have early buildings in Ahmedabad, including Doshi's Tagore Hall and Correa's Sabarmati Ashram.

Correa's other public buildings, including arts complexes in Panaji (Goa), Bhopal (Madhya Pradesh), and, most recently, Jaipur (Rajasthan), show a slow return to Indian traditions but with modern interpretations.

The Jaipur project is the Jawahar Kala Kendra Museum, and it is just one of several major buildings in India that reflect a welcome change. As one writer put it, "Indian architecture is beginning to find its own way again."

The point of inspiration leaves Western philosophy and returns to an ancient Hindu concept, the *mandala*, a representation of the universe that can be used as the mathematical basis for architecture. Correa specifically takes a nine-square mandala, since Hindus believe nine to be the most spiritual and powerful number, which helps connect man to the universe. Two other Indian influences are at play: the Hindu temple design, where open and closed spaces flow in and out of each other, and Jaipur's Jantar Mantar, the giant abstract astrological instruments built by Jai Singh II.

Another powerful and vivid example of India returning to its own roots for inspiration is Satish Gujral's Belgian Embassy in Delhi. Like Correa, Gujral, a painter rather than a trained architect, looks back to the mandala. He also takes inspiration from Delhi's ancient tombs—the sweeping brick arches, the domes, the use of brick and granite. The whole building sits in a large sunken garden, echoing the Mogul emperor Humayun's Persian-inspired garden tomb.

The Jaipur and Delhi buildings are thoroughly modern but sing with the rich song of India's own culture. Furthermore, each has its own clear regional identity. India now has a growing number of architects who are similarly inspired. ■

Above: The vast Secretariat building (1958) in the modern, shared state capital of Chandigarh shows Le Corbusier's obsession with geometric shapes and emphasis on scale. Right: The simple house where Gandhi lived in Sabarmati Ashram, Ahmadabad. Below: The gleaming, white, unfurling lotus shape of the Baha'i Temple in South Delhi has been compared to the Sydney Opera House.

More places to visit in Delhi

ASHOKA'S ROCK EDICT

In 1966 another set of Ashoka's rock edicts (see p. 31) was discovered, this time on a rock in southeast Delhi, proving that a trading center or crossroads had existed in this area as early as Mauryan times.

✉ Off Shaheed Captain Gaur Marg, Srinavaspuri

BABA KHARAK SINGH MARG

This radial road at Connaught Place (see p. 91) is lined with the high-quality, fixed-price official stores of each Indian state, selling state specialties. Halfway along there is a good restaurant for hungry shoppers.

✉ Connaught Pl. 🕐 Closed Sun.

BAHA'I TEMPLE

The nine soaring white marble petals of this lotus-shaped temple make this a landmark in the south Delhi suburbs. There are guided tours of the spectacular central hall.

✉ Kalkaji District Park, Nehru Pl. ☎ 011-444029 🕐 Closed Mon., & services

CHANAKYAPURI

This is the diplomatic area of the city, where foreign nations were given plots of land at the time of independence. It became a showcase for each nation's contemporary architecture. Driving down its main avenue, Shanti Path, you can see the buildings and have fun guessing which style belongs to which country;

Well-stocked shops line the shaded colonnades of Connaught Place.

Pakistan's building is the one with the distinctive blue dome.

CHRISTIAN CATHEDRALS

Both the Anglican and Roman Catholic cathedrals in New Delhi are stunning landmarks, built to the winning designs of British architect H. A. N. Medd. The Anglican Church of the Redemption (1927–1935) is a dignified Palladio-inspired design. The Roman Catholic Church of the Sacred Heart (1930–34) is a bold, Italianate design close to North Avenue.

Church of the Redemption ✉ Church Rd.
Church of the Sacred Heart ✉ Bangla Sahib Rd.

CONNAUGHT PLACE

T. R. Russell's great amphitheater of stuccoed colonnades, which was named after George V's uncle, was originally compared with the city of Bath in England for its modern design, but it took time to win popularity. It eventually became, and has remained to the present day, the hub of Delhi's stores, modest hotels, and offices, even if the classy south Delhi colonies (as residential areas of the city are known) have their own commercial centers. If the combination of the eight radial roads running into the three concentric ones (see map p. 63) confuses you, just look for Janpath, which will lead you back to Raj Path.

🔼 63 C5

HAILEY'S BAOLI

This step-well (see p. 383) is thought to have been built during the Tughlaq sultanate and has a tiny mosque at the top of the steps. To find this forgotten relic, head northward up Kasturba Gandhi Marg, turn right on Hailey Road, then take the first lane on the left.

IMPERIAL HOTEL

The Imperial (see p. 345) was built between 1933 and 1935 by the Singh family and furnished with London silver and Italian marble. It is still owned by the same family today. Once the social center of New Delhi, with its majestic palm trees and expansive lawns, it has now been carefully restored.
✉ Janpath, Connaught Pl.

JANTAR MANTAR

Maharaja Jai Singh II of Jaipur was a noted astronomer. He built the first of his five outsize observatories here in 1724, although his principal one was in Jaipur

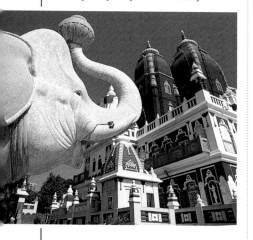

Ganesh, the elephant god, faces the eye-catching Lakshmi Narayan (Birla) Temple, funded by the Birla family in the 1930s.

(see pp. 131-32). These huge, pink stone, abstract-looking instruments were a gift from the Maharaja to the Mogul emperor Muhammad Shah, for whom he revised both the Muslim calendar and astronomical tables.
✉ Sansad Marg, Connaught Pl.

LAKSHMI NARAYAN MANDIR

Built by the prominent Birla merchant family, who were also patrons of Mahatma Gandhi, this ostentatious, tiered marble temple is appropriately dedicated to Lakshmi, goddess of wealth.
✉ Mandir Marg, W of Connaught Pl.

NATIONAL PHILATELIC MUSEUM

For philatelists, India is an especially interesting country. Yet this collection of rare stamps, first-day covers, and other treats is not easy to find: The best option is to go to the main post office on Sansad Marg, and once there, ask the head postmaster, who will happily direct you. Commemorative stamps are on sale at the main post office, too.
✉ Sansad Marg, Connaught Pl. ☎ 011-371 0154 🕐 Closed Sat.–Sun.

RAIL TRANSPORTATION MUSEUM

This is a railroad buff's delight, an open-air permanent home for some of the great engines and royal coaches that bring to life the great days of subcontinental railroad travel in India. The museum is home to about 30 engines and 20 rail cars, their interiors well-preserved. Those on display include the Maharaja of Baroda's gilt parlor car (1886) and the Maharaja of Mysore's teak car with ivory and gold trim. Here, too, is the car that was used by the Prince of Wales (later Edward VII) during his visit to India in 1876. Inside the museum building itself, you will find a model of India's first-ever train, the steam engine that chugged from Bombay to Thana on April 16, 1853, seen off with a 21-gun salute; there are also models of other famous engines and displays of old tickets.
✉ South end of Chanakyapuri
🕐 Closed Mon.

ST. MARTIN'S CHURCH

Looming over the cantonment (military) area, west of the Ridge, this was the British garrison church. It was designed by Arthur Shoosmith and was built between 1928 and 1930. St. Martin's Church is an extraordinary feat of German Expressionism in British New Delhi, a huge, gaunt monolith with a high, square tower, built using three million bricks. ∎

A rich choice of medieval forts and Buddhist *stupas*, riotous Hindu carving and tranquil Sikh temples, tiger country and exotic birds, not to mention the famous Taj Mahal, awaits those who want to escape from the steamy capital.

Around Delhi

Carved gateway at Sanchi

The Taj Mahal seen from Agra Fort, across a bend in the Yamuna River

Around Delhi

SLIPPING OUT OF DELHI FOR A FEW DAYS CAN BRING GREAT REWARDS. Tempting as it may be to head west to the better known Rajasthan, it is worth considering the riches lying in wait for you to the north and south of India's capital.

This map shows how you can follow the Yamuna as it flows south from Delhi through ancient Mathura to the royal Mogul buildings of Agra. Both cities are just inside Uttar Pradesh, a large state stretching up to the lower Himalayan mountains and eastward far beyond its capital, Lucknow (see pp. 310–13). The contrasting attractions of Fatehpur, Sikri's deserted royal city, and Bharatpur's wondrous bird sanctuary are nearby.

To the south is Madhya Pradesh, India's biggest state; it covers much of central India and has several notable wildlife parks—Panna, Bandhavgarh, and Kanha. Dramatic forest and rocky outcrops are the settings for the forts of Gwalior, Datia, and Orchha and, east of them, the isolated temples of Khajuraho. The capital of Madhya Pradesh is Bhopal, an excellent base for visiting Sanchi and other sites in the area before continuing to Indore and Mandu.

If the weather is hot, a trip north from Delhi might be more comfortable. The Grand Trunk Road runs through Haryana, a small state that takes Delhi's overflow and has the fastest growing economy of all states. It shares its capital, Le Corbusier's specially built Chandigarh (see pp. 120–21), with neighboring Punjab, whose western border meets Pakistan. The unspoiled towns of Patiala and Amritsar stand on either side of Punjab's lush landscape of almost continuous wheat fields.

North of Chandigarh, the cool beauty of the lower Himalayan mountains inspired the British to create their summer capital, Shimla (Simla), here. A trip northeast from Delhi can lead to other cool retreats, such as Mussoorie and Nainital, or join Hindu pilgrims at Hardwar and Rishikesh, ending with a visit to Corbett National Park.

Transportation is easy by car, train, and plane. The Shatabdi Express trains, running from Delhi through Agra, Gwalior, and Jhansi to Bhopal, make travel to this region particularly easy, as does the train up to Chandigarh. There are some particularly delightful hotels in the unspoiled provincial towns. ∎

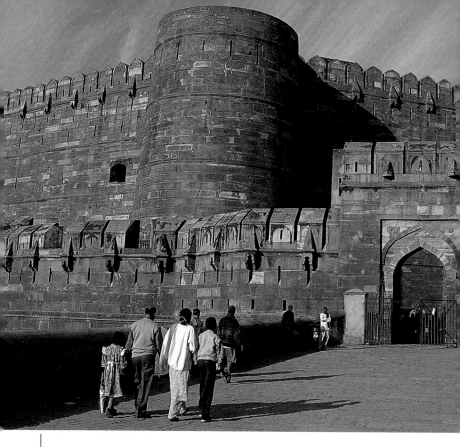

Agra & around

SIKANDER LODI MOVED THE CAPITAL FROM DELHI TO AGRA.
But the Mogul emperors transformed it into the dazzling, fairy-tale
court whose fame reached Europe, and one, Shah Jahan, built the Taj
Mahal here. Today the empty buildings need plenty of imagination to
bring them to life; looking at some jewel-like Indian miniature paintings of Mogul court scenes can help.

Agra
🅰 95 C4
**India Tourist
Office**
✉ 191 The Mall
☎ 0562-226378
e-mail goitoagr@nde.vsnl.
net.in

AGRA FORT
After Babur's brief rule, during
which he held a great celebratory
feast at Agra, Humayun took the
capital back to Delhi. But when
Akbar (R.1556–1605) built his fort
between 1565 and 1573, Agra burst
into life. Later, when his grandson
Shah Jahan returned to Delhi in
1648, the fort was left to plunderers
(see Dig, p. 133).

Grand fortifications
Cross the moat to reach the first
great gateway of one of India's
finest riverine forts: Akbar's magnificent double-walled fort beside
the Yamuna. Qasim Khan designed
it, using the glowing red sandstone
that distinguishes many great
Mogul buildings. With soaring fortifications and the Yamuna waters
lapping its walls, the treasury was

It is believed that Jahangir added the long, marble-inlaid facade of the building behind. Through the archway you find a fascinating suite of **Akbar's rooms.** Built by local craftsmen, they are not remotely Islamic. Instead, the stocky proportions, pillar-and-beam structure, and densely carved decoration give them the look of pure Hindu buildings, constructed in stone instead of wood. Look for the central courtyard's square arches, broad decorative brackets, and the Hindu motif of parrots in the carving.

From the courtyard ahead, Akbar watched his elephant fights, a sport only royals were permitted to take part in. Ever superstitious, in 1605 Akbar staged a fight between the elephants of his son Salim and his grandson Khusrau, to see whose would win and thus who would succeed. Salim's elephant won. Later, Jahangir lived in these and other, similar, rooms commissioning paintings and enriching the simple walls with gilt-painted stucco. You can also enjoy your first tantalizing view of the Taj Mahal from here.

Shah Jahan's marble additions

Moving on, the next rooms are a striking contrast. Sandstone is exchanged for white marble, stockiness for elegance. Shah Jahan (R.1627–1658) built them, living here with his beloved wife, Mumtaz Mahal, when not on campaign. After her death and his subsequent move to Delhi, the emperor was deposed by his third son, Aurangzeb, in 1658 and kept prisoner here, tended by his daughter Jahanara until he died in 1666. Shah Jahan's buildings are thus suffused with romance and sadness. **Khas Mahal** is his suite of private rooms, and **Mussaman Burj** is

State Tourist Office
✉ By Clarks Shiraz Hotel, 64 Taj Rd.
☎ 0562-223 4461

Festivals
Taj Mahotsava, Feb.: arts and crafts
Shardotsav, Oct.: dance and music

Agra Fort
🕐 Son-et-lumière 7:30 p.m.
💲 $

safe and the army, court, and citizens could withstand long sieges. Note the battlemented parapets with ramparts and loop-holed merlons. Today's Indian Army still occupies much of the fort. **Amar Singh Gate** comes next, and was built at right angles in order to deflect elephant charges.

Akbar & Jahangir's buildings
At the top of the ramp, a great **stone bath** stands in the gardens on the right, possibly a wedding present from Jahangir (R.1605–1627) to Nur Jahan in 1611. It is said that the rose petals used to scent her bathwater inspired her to develop *attar,* a type of pungent perfume, which is still sold in Indian bazaars; jasmine is one of the lighter ones to try.

decorated raised throne alcove, where the emperor gave his daily audience. As you leave through the arch on the left, imagine the citizens of Agra pouring in through the gate on the right to attend a royal *durbar,* a morning of pomp, ceremony, and entertainment.

AFTER THE MOGULS

Once the Moguls had moved to Delhi, Agra was occupied successively by the Jats, Marathas, and, from 1803 on, the British. The British cantonment area still has its wide avenues, elegant bungalows, and carefully sited public buildings. Try exploring Mall or Taj Roads, and look for **Queen Mary's Library** and **Central Post Office** at Sadar Bazar. Also, nearby stand handsome **St. George's** cantonment church (1826) and the **Havelock Memorial Church** (1873). In this commercial center, you will find upscale hotels, fine restaurants, and a busy shopping area with local handicrafts and fine leather goods. You may wish to sample some local dishes such as *petha* (pumpkin candy), *dalmoth* (fried chickpeas), and other delicious Mogul-inspired favorites.

North of old Agra city, go past **St. John's Church** the Roman Catholic cathedral with its landmark tower, and Sir Samuel Swinton Jacob's fine St. John's College, to find the **Roman Catholic cemetery** situated on the right. This is one of India's earliest Christian cemeteries. Christians who died in Lahore and Ajmer were brought here for burial. Its impressive monuments include the tomb of John Mildenhall (1614), envoy of Elizabeth I, and a miniature copy of the Taj Mahal built for the Dutchman General Hessing (1803), who was in charge of Agra Fort for the Marathas when the British took it.

Shah Jahan gave the old lanes of Agra this landmark mosque in 1648, the year he forsook the city for Delhi.

Itimud-ud-Daulah's tomb

✉ E bank of Yamuna River, 2 miles (4 km) upstream of Taj Mahal

$ $

the exquisite minipalace inlaid with *pietra dura,* built for Mumtaz. Upstairs, **Diwan-i-Khas** (public audience hall, 1628) is his most elegant building of all. In front of it stand two thrones; the black one was made for Jahangir when, a rebelling prince, he prematurely announced himself emperor in Allahabad in 1603. Underneath here was the treasury; the royal *hamams* (baths) were opposite, and the lawn was laid out with a formal pattern of water channels, fountains and flowerbeds.

Walk around the cloisters to find the tiny **Nagina Masjid** (gem mosque) and then, on the right, steep steps down to the **Diwan-i-Am.** Built by Shah Jahan to replace an earlier wooden version, it has elegant arches in front of a richly

ACROSS THE YAMUNA RIVER

It is worth every effort to visit the **tomb of Itimad-ud-Daulah** (see p. 41), built by his powerful daughter Nur Jahan, Jahangir's empress. The casketlike tomb (1622–28) has its walls coated with polychrome mosaic designs. Find delicate decorations inside, and outside enjoy serene gardens and delightful river views. On the same side of the Yamuna, there are substantial remains of **Ram Bagh** to the north, and **Babur's garden,** laid out in 1528; note the riverside pavilions and water channels. Between these two, the waterside tomb of Chini-ka-Rauza (1635) lies behind the market gardens. South of here and the railroad bridge, a stroll through Nagla Kachhpura village and then through the fields brings the reward of glorious views back across the Yamuna to the Taj.

AROUND AGRA

At **Sikandra,** 5 miles (8 km) northwest of Agra, visit Akbar's great garden mausoleum. He began it in 1602, on the site of Sikaner Lodi's fort, but after his death in 1605 Jahangir aggrandized it and swapped modest sandstone for marble; Akbar's mausoleum is on the roof. Akbar's huge entrance gateway is impressive; look for Jahangir's floral painted vaults. Beware of the black-faced monkeys, who are quite tame but expect handouts from visitors. East of the complex is Jahangir's fine Kanch Mahal. On the 5-mile (8 km) drive up here, visit the Roman Catholic cemetery (see p. 98); also, spot the *kos minars* (milestones) that guided Mogul travelers, and various tombs.

The ancient city of **Mathura** stands on the Yamuna 39 miles (62 km) northwest of Agra, at the center of the holy land of Braj, and in Hindu mythology was the birth-

Mowing the lawn Indian-style, here at Agra Fort

place of Krishna. As such, Mathura is one of the Hindus' Seven Sacred Cities. Its waterfront is lined with bathing ghats and temples: See especially Dwarkadhish Temple (1914), built by Seth Gokuldass of Gwalior; river trips leave from Vishram Ghat. The town's **Archaeological Museum** has a magnificent collection that reflects Mathura's place as a trading center under the Sunga, Kushana, and Gupta dynasties. It houses ravishing Buddhist and Jain stone sculptures, which often use the distinctive Mathura speckled red sandstone. The collection also includes sculptures made in Gandhara but found locally.

Vrindavan, the most important of a group of Braj villages sacred to Hindus and especially devotees of Krishna, lies about 6 miles (10 km) north of Mathura. Here, Krishna flirted with the milk-maids; at Mahaban, his foster father, Nanda, tended the young god; at Gokul, Krishna was raised in secrecy; at Barsana, his consort Radha was born; and Goverdhan is the hill Krishna lifted to protect the female cowherds from the god Indra's storms. Plan your visit to the villages to coincide with a big Hindu festival (see pp. 379–82). ■

Sikandra
✉ 5 miles (8 km) N of Agra, off NH2
💲 $. Free Fri.

Akbar's Mausoleum
☎ 0562-371230
💲 $

Mathura
✉ 39 miles (62 km) N of Agra on NH2

Archaeological Museum
✉ Dampier Park, Mathura
🕐 Closed Mon.

Vrindavan
✉ 42 miles (68 km) N of Agra off NH2

Taj Mahal

Taj Mahal

🅰 95 C4

✉ Tajganj

☎ 0562-330498

🕐 Closed Fri.

💲 $

SHAH JAHAN'S WIFE DIED IN JUNE 1631 (SEE P. 42) AFTER bearing their 14th child. Mumtaz (Chosen One of the Palace) had been the emperor's wife, companion, adviser, and support for 17 years. Channeling his despair into the creation of her mausoleum, Shah Jahan called a council of top architects and craftsmen and embarked upon his masterpiece. He chose Ustad Isa Khan Effendi, a Persian from Shiraz, as master builder, his pupil Ustad Ahmed for the detailed work, and Ismail Khan for the dome.

Enter through any of the three gates to the complex and you leave chaos for order. The great gate prepares you further for the serenity within, with its inlaid Koran quote known as Al-Fajr (daybreak), which ends: "O Soul that art at rest. Return to the Lord, at peace with Him and He at peace with you. So enter as one of His servants. And enter into His garden."

You then do just that, emerging into a **char bagh** (four gardens), which is how paradise is described in the Koran: a lush, well-planted, walled garden divided symmetrically by water channels. Pause to take it all in.

This **garden tomb** takes to ultimate refinement the Mogul garden tomb built for Humayun (see pp. 70–71). Here, the proportions

A villager fills his water pot from the Yamuna River, seemingly unaware of the reflection of the world-famous local monument, the Taj Mahal.

are more satisfying; luxurious marble is used instead of sandstone, and the whole platform and mausoleum building is pushed from the center of the garden to the end, to benefit from the river light and from being silhouetted against the sky. The dome shape is more elegant and, as close inspection will reveal, the inlay work is finer.

But this memorial is more than a symbol of paradise to reward the faithful. It also symbolizes the royal pleasure garden and a lush oasis in the dry desert heat. To this, Shah Jahan added another, political image: The Taj Mahal symbolizes the might of Islam embodied in the all-powerful Mogul rulers.

It took 22 years to build the Taj. Craftsmen and laborers came from Baghdad, Delhi, Samarkand, Turkey, and from elsewhere in Asia. The marble was from Makrana, near Jaipur; the precious and semi-precious stones from various places—jasper from the Punjab, jade from China, lapis lazuli from Afghanistan, agates from Yemen.

As you wander through the gardens, you see the white marble of the Taj through the contrasting dark green trees; you see it reflected in the long fountain pool. At the front of the platform, railings mark the spot where Mumtaz's body was buried while the Taj Mahal was being built. A **mosque** stands to the left of the Taj. Up on the platform, verses from the Koran, panels of low relief carving, and inlaid designs coat the exterior. Inside, cenotaphs for Mumtaz (central) and Shah Jahan lie surrounded by a finely decorated trellis screen (their real tombs lie in the now closed vault below).

The time of day that you first visit the Taj is important. The hard light of midday flattens it, whereas to enter the precincts midafternoon and slowly explore the gateway views and the lush gardens, ending at the platform as the sun ripens, is a near-perfect experience. You may find yourself inspired to return at sunrise to enjoy the magical and soft morning light. ■

Great Gateway

Char bagh (four gardens)

Above left and right: At the Taj Mahal, a family visits Mumtaz's cenotaph, while the nearby mosque is silent.

Marble inlay

Mogul patrons lifted the craft of *pietra dura* (hard stone) inlay decoration to new heights. The results are even more impressive if you know a little about this difficult, precise skill and see it being practiced.

Materials are supplied to the *ateliers* of Muslim craftsmen by Hindu merchants. The hard, nonporous white marble comes from Makrana, near Jaipur; coral and stones including turquoise, carnelian, and lapis lazuli come from all over the world. Once the design is agreed upon, a master craftsman draws it on the marble. The stones are selected, cut, and chiseled, then

the beds for each pattern gouged out. Each design is then fitted, fine-tuned, and stuck. Finally the whole surface is polished with fine emery.

Today, more than 5,000 pietra dura craftsmen are working in family-run ateliers in the Agra back lanes. To watch some more easily, visit Subhash Emporium on Gwalior Road. ∎

RULES & RESTRICTIONS

Ticket prices and security restrictions vary, and the Taj Mahal may close if government guests are visiting. Currently, video cameras are permitted no closer than just inside the great gate, after which they must be put in a locker.

Visitors leave the Taj Mahal gardens through the great gateway, symbolically leaving the garden of Paradise.

Masjid (mosque)

Main tomb

Mehmankhana (guest house)

Yamuna River

Fatehpur Sikri

Fatehpur Sikri
🅰 95 C4
✉ 25 miles (40 km)
SW of Agra on the
Jaipur road
☎ 0562-360517
$ $

FATEHPUR SIKRI IS A PERFECT GHOST CITY. THIS GROUP OF mysterious buildings is all that remains of the city conceived and built by Akbar as his ideal capital. Bursting into life in 1571, it was an instant success; just 14 years later it was virtually abandoned, partly because Akbar was called to defend the northwest frontier, partly because of inadequate water supplies.

Why did Akbar choose this spot? In 1568 the powerful 26-year-old emperor had consolidated his empire but, despite many marriage alliances, had no heir. After his annual pilgrimage to the Chishti tomb at Ajmer, on the way back to Agra he stopped here to visit a living Chishti saint, Shaikh Salim, who predicted that Akbar would soon have three sons. The next year, Akbar's Amber wife, Jadhai Bai, gave birth to a boy, who was named Salim after the saint. The following year Murad was born, and in 1572 Daniyal fulfilled the prediction.

After just two sons had been born, Akbar began to build a new city where the saint lived. He called it Fatehpur Sikri (City of Victory) and envisaged it as the cultural, commercial, and administrative center of his empire; most of his army and treasury stayed at Agra.

A good way to start visiting the buildings is to imagine the bazaars lining the road from inside the gateway up to the ticket office. Remember: There are no contemporary texts or plans, so each building's possible function is pure guesswork. Start by exploring the **Karkhana,** probably the royal workshops. Then see the so-called **Diwan-i-Am** (audience hall), whose built-in throne is decorated with *jali* work, and, behind here, the exquisite palace rooms, treasuries, and discussion halls. Beyond them, several palaces of what was probably the imperial harem have surviving painted decoration. Out

through the back gate, you have to run the gauntlet of peddlers to reach the Jami Masjid and see the saint's tomb, the prayer hall and the soaring Buland Darwaza (Gate of Magnificence) that celebrates Akbar's conquest of Gujarat (1573). ■

Visitor tips
To avoid heat and crowds, go early or in the late afternoon; take drinks and snacks.

The Buland Darwaza is a triumphal gateway that was built to celebrate Akbar's victories in Gujarat during 1573.

Shaikh Salim's tomb

Jami Masjid

Buland Darwaza

Shaikh Salim Chishti's tomb (above), with exquisite marble *jali* work, stands in the Jami Masjid's huge courtyard.

This intricate stonework in the Diwan-i-Khas has its inspiration in Gujarati wooden carving traditions.

Jadhai Bai's palace

Birbal's house

Maryam's house

Panch Mahal

Ankh Michauli

Diwan-i-Khas

Pachisi Court

Abdair Khana

entrance

Haran Sara complex

Khwabgah

Anoop Talao

Diwan-i Am

Huge, shaggy-feathered painted storks perch precariously high in the trees to nest.

Keoladeo Ghana National Park

TO SPEND A FEW HOURS WALKING IN SILENCE AND watching nature in this park (also known as Bharatpur Bird Sanctuary) is to escape the whirlwind of Agra sight-seeing. It quickly restores the soul.

Keoladeo Ghana National Park

🅰 95 B4

✉ 33 miles (53 km) W of Agra, 10 miles (16 km) W of Fatehpur Sikri

💲 $

🚲 No cars; visit by boat or walking, on rented bicycle or by cycle rickshaw

The variety of habitats and climates, and the traditional respect for birds in India, have made the country especially rich in bird life. More than 1,200 of the world's 8,650 species of birds are found here, with 2,000 subspecies among them. This makes India's checklist twice the size of those of North America and Europe. Moreover, the dramatic shapes and colors of many species make bird-watching easy and rewarding for the amateur. For once, patience is not essential, since the birds are everywhere. All you need are sharp eyes, a pair of binoculars, and a good reference book—Bikram Grewal's *A Photographic Guide to the Birds of India & Nepal* (Chelsea Green Pub. Co., 1998) has plenty of helpful

photographs. Using this, you will soon find that you are identifying plenty of birds on your own.

Keoladeo Ghana sanctuary takes its official name from the local temple dedicated to Keoladeo (Shiva). Established in 1956, it became a national park in 1981 and is today one of the world's most important sanctuaries for migratory birds and for herons. Although just inside Rajasthan, it is only an hour's drive from Agra, and is best visited from there.

The Maharaja of Bharatpur developed the 11 square miles (29 sq km) of freshwater swamp during the British period as the focus for his grand duck shoots. Viceroy Lord Curzon attended the first one in 1902; Viceroy Lord

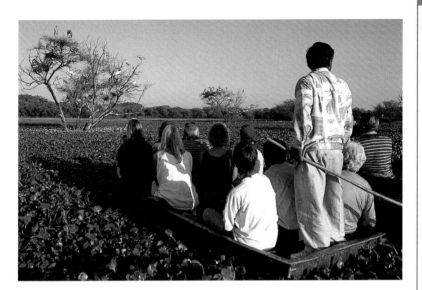

Linlithgow was there in 1938 when 4,273 birds were shot, the biggest "bag" ever.

With the guns now put down forever, energetic and enlightened conservation has brought results. There are sometimes more than 375 species of birds to be seen here in winter, when migrating birds arrive from all over Russia, central Asia, and other parts of the world, to join the 120 or so resident species. When the monsoon begins, so does the nest-building. Some 10,000 nests are constructed in the heronries of acacia trees by big birds such as painted and openbill storks, white ibises, spoonbills, and purple herons. Sleek black cormorants, dazzling white egrets, and the common and pond herons play their parts, too. Other species of waterfowl arrive from August to October. Late arrivals to the park include rosy pelicans and flamingos, and, during December and January only, the rare Siberian crane.

By the beginning of March, those chicks who have eluded the vultures and other birds of prey

and have become strong and fat begin to depart, bound for their summer homes.

As the land dries, terrestrial birds begin to breed, so even in April there is a rich assortment of birds to spot during a three-hour morning walk. At this time the park's animals—spotted deer, sambhar, blackbuck (small gazelles), mongoose, and others—can also be seen. So can large numbers of rock pythons, especially near the temple and main entrance.

Still, the best time to visit the park is in the morning from September to February. Take a rowboat (and a local ornithologist) out on the lake. As the mist lifts at sunrise, morning birdsong and flapping wings bring the islands of kadam trees alive. Metallic blue kingfishers eye potential breakfast from low branches, eagles glide through the still air, and large painted and black-necked storks stand up to stretch in their precariously balanced treetop nests. As the sun rises and the mist clears, the cacophony of sound rises to a climax: a magical experience. ■

On an early-morning cruise, the local ornithologist identifies each bird's call as it wakes up and welcomes the day with song.

Visitor tips
Best visited at sunrise or sunset; several nearby hotels. Binoculars and a field guide recommended, as is hiring one of the excellent local ornithologists, which your hotel can arrange for you.

Trains

E ver since the first steam train puffed out of Bombay's Victoria Terminus station to a 21-gun salute on April 16, 1853, the Indian railways have had their own special character. For many British arrivals at Bombay port, their first experience of India was a three-day train ride to their final destination. Soot from the belching smoke blackened the travelers' clothes, there were unaccountable stops between stations, and locals sold their wares at every possible opportunity.

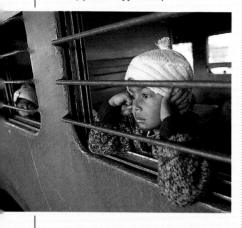

A child traveling by train in Rajasthan in the winter needs a warm pullover and a snug hat.

That first train carried just 400 people along 21 miles (34 km) of track in 75 minutes. Railroads were soon being built by the British to carry valuable trading goods to India's ports, and by the Indian princes to amuse themselves in their princely states: The Gwalior train still runs. Since then, India's railroad system has played a vital role in its economic, industrial, and social development.

Today India is one of the few countries in the world that is expanding its railroad system. The figures are impressive. A fleet of almost 7,000 engines, 34,000 coaches, and 300,000 wagons uses the 39,147 miles (63,000 km) of railroad track, which is punctuated by 7,068 stations. The longest route is Guwahati–Trivandrum, which carries passengers 2,469 miles (3,974 km) from the mountainous northeast to the steamy south. Each year, freight trains carry in excess of a million tons of goods; each day more than 7,500 passenger trains carry 11 million passengers (plus more riding ticketless on the roof). So all-pervading is the railroad that mobile eye hospitals reach isolated rural areas by train, not road.

The Indian railroad employs more than 1.1 million people, making it one of the country's largest employers. At large junctions, such as at Hubli in Karnataka, the workers live in neatly laid-out model towns, each with its houses, stores, churches (many railroad families are Christian), cricket ground, schools, and other public buildings. In India, one can be a railroad man from birth to death.

Gone are the steam engines, except for tourist enjoyment, and the delightful complexities of broad, meter, and narrow gauge are being simplified into broad gauge only. But some trains retain their romantic names—*Himalayan Queen, Pink City Express*, and *Grand Trunk Express*. And buying a ticket and catching a train in India is still a ritual that balances the apparent chaos of the Indian railroad station with the laboriously meticulous requirements of the ticket-selling staff. The process of buying a ticket, reserving a seat, understanding the departures board, and then finding the train and your seat demands plenty of time and possibly some new skills.

Grand new projects are at hand. The fast, reliable, Shatabdi Express train was introduced in the 1980s; its first route was Delhi to Bhopal. The Delhi–Agra stretch takes just over two hours compared to a driving time of four. As India's labyrinth of tracks is simplified and modernized, these trains connect most major cities. The great feat, however, has been the construction of the Konkan Railroad, which runs from Mumbai southward down the west coast to Mangalore (see p. 204). Next on the agenda is a line along Gujarat's long coast. ■

Steam trains are now very rare in India. This one, which does not carry passengers, awaits its signal outside Agra.

One of the greatest Rajput forts, Gwalior's palace rooms and great outer walls impressed even the fort-weary emperor Akbar.

Gwalior
🅐 95 C3

State Tourist Office
✉ Hotel Tansen
☎ 0751-342606

Gwalior Fort
✉ Gwalior
💲 $

Archaeological Museum
✉ Gwalior Fort
🕐 Closed Fri.
💲 $

Jai Vilas
✉ S of fort, Gwalior
💲 $

Gwalior, Datia, & Orchha

THIS TRIANGLE OF ELEGANT ARCHITECTURAL SITES SET IN a wooded landscape south of Agra (see map p. 95) is easy to enjoy, provided clambering up and down stone steps is not a problem.

GWALIOR

Once the capital of the prestigious princely state of the same name, whose ruler had the title the Scindia, this large town is still dominated by its imposing fort built on top of a huge natural sandstone bluff.

The city's history starts up at **Gwalior Fort,** reached through a series of spectacular fortified gateways. Turn right at the top and you pass two ornate **Sasbahu temples** (tenth century), possibly built by the Kachwaha Rajputs, who founded the fort. **Man Mandir** (1486–1517), built by the Tomar ruler Man Singh, is the fort's centerpiece and one of India's finest early Hindu forts. Note the two courtyards surrounded by suites of rooms, the bold decoration, the variety of roofs, and the glazed tiles on the exterior.

The Tomar Rajputs had seized the fort from Delhi's Slave sultan in 1398 and held it until 1516. After the Tomars, the fort passed successively to the Moguls, Marathas, and Jats, and it was the scene of fierce fighting in 1858 between the British, led by Sir Hugh Rose, and the freedom fighters led by a legendary woman, the Rani of Jhansi. Wife of the Raja of Jhansi, she held Jhansi fort against the British with the help of her personal bodyguard when her husband sided with the British in the "Mutiny." When the fort finally fell, she joined the main rebel force at Gwalior, rode into battle dressed as a man with her baby strapped to her back, and was killed. In 1886, Gwalior was ceded to The Scindia.

This brief history helps explain the variety of other monuments here. In the fort, four lesser

palaces lie beyond Man Mandir (two Hindu, two Muslim). On the way down, look for the Jain statues (7th to 15th centuries, defaced by Babur) cut into the rock, and enjoy the excellent, if informally arranged, Hindu and Jain sculptures in the **Archaeological Museum.** In the city see the **Jami Masjid** (1661) and the grand **tombs** of Muhammad Ghaus (late 16th century)—a Muslim saint who helped Babur win the fort—and Tansen (early 17th century), Akbar's court musician, in whose honor a national music festival is held here annually *(Nov.–Dec.).*

For a flavor of the heights of extravagance reached by India's self-indulgent princes once they allied with the British, visit colossal **Jai Vilas** (1872–74), designed by Lieut.-Col. Sir Michael Filose and now partly a museum. Do not miss the silver model train on the dining room table here, nor the real local one chugging around town.

DATIA & ORCHHA

On the road south from Gwalior to Datia it's worth stopping at **Sonagiri,** a Jain pilgrimage center for the Digambar sect (see p. 59). Take a look at the mirror temple and the white shrines leading up to the hilltop temple.

At **Datia,** a street crosses a causeway and leads through the walled village to the surprising sight of soaring **Govind Mandir Palace** (1620). Inside, dark stairways and labyrinthine corridors rise level by level to reveal a design of such symmetrical clarity and stone carving of such precision and beauty as to make this one of the finest Rajput palaces.

Both this and the grandest of Orchha's palaces were built by Bir Singh Deo of Bundelkund, who sealed his future with Emperor Jahangir by assassinating Emperor Akbar's court historian, Abul Fazl, who disapproved of Jahangir's (then Prince Salim) behavior.

Orchha is a medieval palace city. Its island fort is composed of the **Raj Mahal,** with bright murals of Hindu myths, and the later **Jahangir Mahal** (Bir Singh Deo's addition for Jahangir's state visit). **Sheesh Mahal** stands between them, now a government-run hotel. Other treats include **Rai Praveen Mahal** palace, **Lakshmi Narayan** hilltop temple with its murals, and walks beside the Betwa river to see the royal *chhatris.*

From Orchha you can continue to Khajuraho (see p. 112), Panna (see p. 119), Shivpuri (see p. 119), or Bhopal (see p. 114). ■

Datia

🅐 95 C3

✉ 39 miles (63 km) S of Gwalior

Orchha

🅐 95 C3

✉ 10 miles (16 km) S of Datia

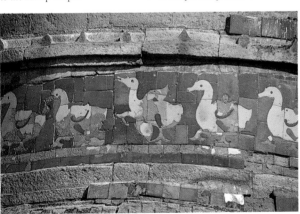

A frieze of ducks that enlivens Gwalior Fort's outer walls may have inspired the decoration on Agra Fort's inner gate.

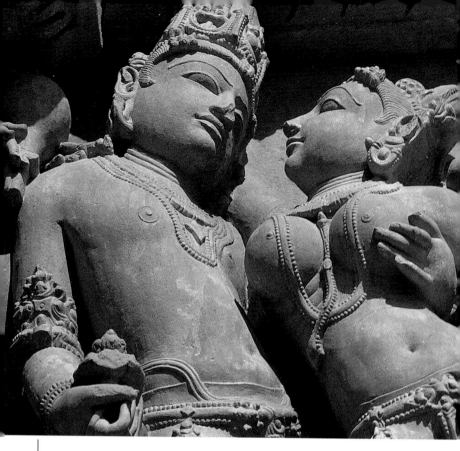

Khajuraho

📍 95 C3

Government of India Tourist Office

✉ By Western Group of temples

☎ 0768-617 2347

Festival

Maha Shivratri, Feb.– March: dance

Khajuraho

FORESTED ISOLATION PROTECTED KHAJURAHO'S CLUSTER of resplendent Hindu temples from Muslim destruction. Created between the 10th and the 12th centuries by the rulers of the Chandella dynasty, a Rajput clan who resisted Muslim invasion, they were then lost until 1819. Their rediscovery is a remarkable story.

In 1819 a British military surveyor spotted the temples in the dense jungle. His report map was unclear: Did the labels read "mines" or "ruins"? Twenty years later, Capt. T. S. Burt was traveling in the area by *palanquin,* heard rumor of the temples, and sought them out. He reported: "I found seven Hindoo temples, most beautifully and exquisitely carved as to workmanship, but the sculptor had at times allowed his subject to grow a little warmer than there was any absolute necessity for his doing."

The eroticism of the sculptures has been the attraction for visitors as much as their fine carving. But they are not a sex manual for voyeurs. New research reveals that Khajuraho was once known as Shivpuri (City of Shiva), and the sculptures decorating the temples recount and celebrate the marriage of Shiva, god of creative and destructive energy, to Parvati. Thus,

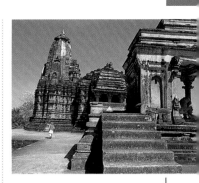

they portray the consummation of marriage and, at the same time, the highest spiritual experience achievable. According to Hindu theory, lovemaking demands that all the senses be given fully to achieve total physical and mental union.

The structure of each temple lends weight to this theory of marriage, consummation, and procreation. The *jangha* (body) of the temple, between the base and spire, is the celestial realm. Thus, the copulating couples are all the divine Shiva and Parvati, and the nymphs are expressing surprise that the god is attending the wedding party. Every Hindu temple mirrors the creation of life: The sanctum or *garbha griha* (womb), is where Shiva's *lingum* (phallus), representing potential creativity, is kept.

Khajuraho's 25 temples may have been part of a nonmonastic center of learning and religion. The most spectacular are in the Western Group, walkable from nearby hotels and the museum.

Today, the car or airplane has replaced the palanquin as the easiest way to reach Khajuraho. To go farther afield, either use a cycle rickshaw or rent a bicycle.

WESTERN GROUP

The added serenity of sunrise and sunset intensifies the surreal experience of seeing these temples. As all nine temples may be overwhelming, here are a few to look at closely.

Pass Varaha Temple, with its sandstone boar, to reach **Lakshamana Temple** (circa 950), the oldest of this group, whose riotous carvings of processions, domestic scenes, musicians, and dancers are full of vitality and movement. Next, visit the **Kandariya Mahadeva Temple** (constructed 1025–1050), possibly the finest of all the temples in its architecture, its rising silhouette, and its sublime and fluid

carving. An elaborate wedding garland at the entrance symbolizes the marriage gate; niches along the outside of the sanctum have carvings of the *Sapta Matrikas* (seven mothers) responsible for dressing the bridegroom, Shiva. Finally, pass the three temples of Mahadeva, Devi Jagadambi, and Chitragupta to find **Vishvanatha Temple,** built in 1002 by Dhangadeva *(R. 950–1002)*. Shiva's Nandi bull vehicle sits outside, while up on the jangha of the temple the sculptures of amorous couples, sensuous nymphs, and idealized women are especially delicate.

ELSEWHERE ON THE SITE

The simple, old **Matangesvara Temple** stands just outside this complex and is still in daily use. Near it, random Khajuraho artifacts are kept in the **Archaeological Museum,** including a frieze showing how the sandstone for the temples was dug from the Ken River, 20 miles (32 km) away, transported to this area of hard granite, and then cut and carved. The soft river stone then hardened; hence its crispness today. The eastern and southern groups are less spectacular, but nevertheless rewarding. In the first, the early **Parsvanatha Temple** is especially fine; in the second, the isolated **Duladeo Temple** (12th century) shows the Chandellas' decline. ■

Voluptuous Lakshmi nestles against her partner, Vishnu (above), in contrast to the simple shapes of Lakshamana Temple (right), set on a broad, high platform.

Archaeological Museum

✉ Near entrance to Western Group of temples

🕐 Closed Fri.

💲 $ (includes temples)

Bhopal & around

AS THE CAPITAL OF MADHYA PRADESH STATE, BHOPAL benefits from some impressive public buildings. By keeping its rampant modern expansion separate, it remains a delightful provincial town, only now bursting out of its preindependence mix of palaces, mosques, gardens, and lakes.

Bhopal
A 95 B2
State Tourist Office
✉ 4th floor, Gangotri Building, T. T. Nagar, New Market
☎ 0755-774340

Rashtriya Manava Sanghralaya (Tribal Habitat Museum of Man)
✉ Shamla Hills, overlooking Upper Lake
☎ 0755-661319
🕐 Closed Mon.

The Hindu ruler Raja Bhoj (1018–1085), a scholar of the Paramara dynasty, founded Bhopal in the 11th century. He sited it on a crescent-shaped ridge and created artificial lakes. But Bhopal's present character took shape only from the end of the 17th century. Dost Muhammed Khan, an opportunistic ex-general of the Mogul emperor Aurangzeb's army, took the by then deserted city and laid out a fresh one. Through consistent loyalty to the British, his descendants, including three city-improving *begums* (female Muslim rulers), became major Indian princes and princesses ruling over a happy mix of Hindu and Muslim cultures, a mix that continues today. Tragically, Bhopal's most recent fame came on December 3, 1984, when a lethal cloud of toxic chemicals escaped from a tank at the Union Carbide factory, resulting in death or chronic illness for thousands of local people. The factory is closed, and the site is a wasteland, but the effects continue to haunt locals.

Visitors can stay in Noor-us-Sabah, a delightful converted palace (see p. 350). The **Taj-ul-Masjid** (Mother of All Mosques), built by Shah Jahan Begum (*R.*1868–1901), is a good place to start exploring the city. The spaciousness of this and **Imam Square,** once the royal heart of Bhopal, contrasts with the smaller mosques and narrow streets of the **Old City,** where ladies wrapped up in *burqa* bargain for silver, silks (local Bilaspur and Chandheri examples are stunning), and jewelry.

Bhopal's museum collections are very impressive. Do not miss the stone sculptures in the **Birla Mandir Museum** *(Next to Birla Mandir, overlooking Lower Lake, closed Wed., $)* and, in the **Rashtriya Manava Sanghralaya** (Tribal Habitat Museum of Man), the tribal homes complete with murals and furnishings. Bhopal's impressive contemporary buildings include Charles Correa's 1982 multi-arts complex, **Bharat Bhavan** *(Lake Drive Rd., closed a.m. & Mon.),* always alive with exhibitions and performances, and his boldly majestic and colorful **State Assembly** (1999).

AROUND BHOPAL
Beyond the industrial suburbs south of Bhopal, a dirt road leads to **Bhimbetka** rocks. These are part of a 5-mile-long (8 km) ridge, where layers of pink, caramel, and cream sandstone have been weathered into fantastical shapes. Under some outcrops early humans left several hundred paintings, which were only rediscovered as recently as the 1950s. Most are line drawings in red or white. They show elephants, antelope, and wild boar, as well as people fishing, fighting, shooting arrows, dancing, and playing the drums. The paintings offer a glimpse of an ancient world dating back to between the second and tenth centuries B.C., possibly earlier. Beautiful and vulnerable, they as yet have no protection.

Best visited with Bhimbetka, **Bhojpur** is where Bhopal's founder dammed the Betwa River to make a reservoir, began his colossal Shiva Temple, and built the nearby Jain shrine with its stone image of Mahavira.

To see the beginnings of monumental Hindu sculpture, seek out the remarkable fifth-century rock-cut Gupta caves at **Udaigiri.**

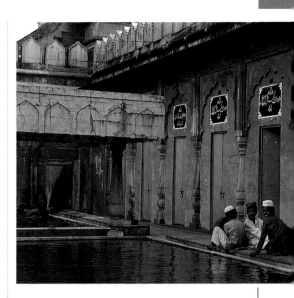

Fine *mihrab* patterns decorate a corner of Taj-ul-Masjid.

Climb up the steep steps in the rock face just before Udaigiri village; then stroll among the caves, ending at the best, Cave No. 5. Inside, the 13-foot-high (4 m) composition shows Varaha, Vishnu's boar incarnation, rescuing the earth goddess Bhudevi, possibly an allegory of the Gupta ruler Chandragupta II's unification of northern India.

Nearby at **Besnagar,** find a remarkable survivor: the Column of Heliodorus, a stone pillar erected in 113 B.C. and dedicated to Krishna's father by Heliodorus, a Greek envoy from Taxila, capital of Gandhara (see p. 31).

A marathon but rewarding journey for temple-lovers leads through sparsely populated countryside to the small village of **Udayapur,** clustered around the Udayeshvara Temple (1080). Its ambitious scale, rhythmic proportions, and rich sculpture proclaim its royal patronage, confirmed in an inscription. Its quality, style, dedication to Shiva, and an image of Parvati behind the *lingum* in the sanctum suggest a close relationship with Khajuraho's temples (see pp. 112–113). ■

Bhimbetka
🅰 95 C2
✉ 27 miles (43 km) SE of Bhopal

Bhojpur
✉ 10 miles (16 km) SE of Bhopal

Udaigiri Caves
🅰 95 C2
✉ 6 miles (10 km) N of Sanchi

Besnagar
✉ 4 miles (6 km) N of Sanchi

Udayapur
🅰 95 C2
✉ 82 miles (132 km) NE of Bhopal via Sanchi

Sanchi's stupa
itself represents
Buddha, as do the
wheel, trident,
footprint, empty
throne under the
bodhi tree, and
riderless horse.

Sanchi
🅰 95 C2

**Archaeological
Museum**
✉ Sanchi
🕐 Closed Fri.
💲 $

Refreshments
The state-run Tourist
Lodge (see p. 351) will
prepare food and drinks;
best to call in and order
before visiting the site.

Sanchi

SANCHI, WHOSE GREAT STUPA, WITH ITS FOUR SOARING
gateways embellished with intricate carvings, constitutes one of
India's oldest surviving stone buildings and is certainly its finest
surviving Buddhist monument.

Monuments spanning the third
century B.C. to the seventh century
A.D. crowd the hill rising above the
plain: *stupas* built to contain holy
relics, monastic buildings, elaborate
railings, columns, and temples. Yet,
despite the size and importance of
the site, there may well be so few
visitors that you can imagine how
General Taylor might have felt
when he rediscovered it, completely
overgrown, having acted on a tip-
off and trekked the 37 miles (60
km) out from Bhopal, in 1819.

Although Sanchi has no known
link with Buddha, there are relics
here of two of his disciples and of
later teachers. Inscriptions indicate
that merchants from nearby
Vidisha were donors.

It is best to begin with **Stupa 1**
(third to first century B.C. and fifth
century A.D.), whose relatively

complete preservation, including railings and gateway sculpture,
makes it the most important piece
of architecture and narrative art of
the Shunga era. The stupa itself is
120 feet (36 m) in diameter and
encases an earlier one. Its high
terrace makes a good viewing point
for the inside faces of the gateways.
The surrounding stone balustrade
and gateways imitate wood in their
structure, but their fully developed
motifs (flowers, animals, birds, etc.)
and sophisticated iconography nar-
rating the life of Buddha and the
Jataka tales (stories of his former
lives) may be derived from ivory
carving. On the stupa, Buddha is
never shown in human form (out
of respect), but is represented by a
wheel, trident, footprint, empty
throne beneath the bodhi tree, or
riderless horse. ∎

Mandu

THE ISOLATED AND EXTENSIVE REMAINS OF THE ONCE magnificent capital of the central Indian kingdom of Malwa make Mandu one of India's most magical forts to visit, especially during or after monsoon lushness. More than 70 handsome Muslim and Hindu monuments built between the 11th and 16th centuries stand amid farming villages on an extensive fortified hilltop, with the Vindhya Mountains as a backdrop.

The powerful Paramara ruler Raja Bhoj (see p. 114) fortified the hilltop, but in 1305 it fell to the Khilji sultans of Delhi. A later Afghan governor of Malwa declared independence from Delhi and moved the capital from Dhar to Mandu. His son, Hoshang Shah, gave Mandu some of its finest buildings (Jama Masjid and his own tomb). Having won the city back in 1436, the Khiljis added more buildings, distinguished for their elegant simplicity, mixing Gujarat and Delhi styles. The Moguls later restored some buildings and in 1617 Jahangir spent his birthday here.

Wandering the palaces, tombs, mosques, and tanks needs time. Here are a few highlights. Beside the modern fort entrance is Hoshang Shah's **Delhi Gate.** The village buildings surround the magnificent pink sandstone **Jama Masjid** and Hoshang Shah's white marble **tomb** (circa 1440), the earliest of its kind on the subcontinent. **Jahaz Mahal** (Ship Palace) is beautiful at sunset.

NEARBY SIGHTS

In contrast, nearby **Indore** (61 miles/97 km from Mandu) is Madhya Pradesh's second largest city and a major center for the steel and car industries. Forty-one miles (66 km) west is Malwa's ancient capital, **Dhar,** whose two mosques, Bhojshala and Lat Masjid, anticipate Mandu's triumphs. ∎

Rupmati, after whom these pavilions at Rewakund, to the south of the main site, are named, was the lover of Mandu's 16th-century ruler, Baz Bahadur.

Mandu
⬛ 95 B2
State Tourist Information
✉ Behind Ravindra Natya Griha Exhibition, Rabindranath Tagore Rd.
☎ 07292-63235

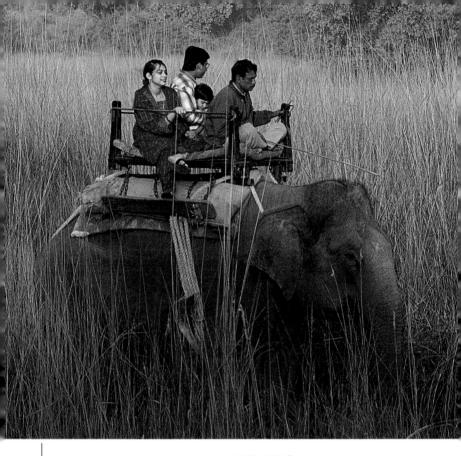

Wildlife parks
of Madhya Pradesh

**Bandhavgarh
National Park**

⛰ 95 D2

🕐 Closed July–Nov.

💲 $

✈ Nearest airports
Varanasi, Khajuraho;
stay at Tala

**Kanha National
Park**

⛰ 95 D2

🕐 Closed July–Oct.

💲 $

✈ Nearest airport
Nagpur; stay at or
near Khatia

THE WILDLIFE SANCTUARIES DEEP IN CENTRAL INDIA ARE
exceptional for their wild terrain and abundant animal and bird life,
so they are worth the effort needed to get there. Bandhavgarh and
Kanha have comfortable accommodations and, moreover, offer a
high chance of spotting a tiger.

BANDHAVGARH
NATIONAL PARK

The attractive combination of
trekking by elephant, the likelihood
of spotting a tiger, and the good
accommodations sited near the
park gates reward you for making
the journey. For those devoted to
elephants, there is the added bonus
of visiting their compound to see
them being bathed and fed and to
learn how they are reared and
trained, using methods unchanged
for centuries.

The park was established in
1968 and has since been enlarged.
Its 169 square miles (437 sq km) of
rugged and hilly landscape stretch
across the heart of the Vidhya
Mountains and currently harbor
the highest density tiger population
of any Indian park; next best are

Kanha and Ranthambore (see p. 133). Be on the lookout for tigers, langur, sloth bears, wild boar, *gaur* (wild ox), and porcupine. There are several kinds of deer: *chital* (spotted deer), *nilgai* (blue bull), *sambhar* (small barking deer), and *chowsingha* (four-horned antelope) amid the not too dense *sal* trees of the valleys and mixed foliage of the upper areas.

Serious ornithologists should arrange to watch the park's rich bird life—up to 150 species, including rare hornbills. From the old fort, you will need to hike up a temple-dotted hill.

KANHA NATIONAL PARK

This is one of India's largest and best parks, with more than 770 square miles (2,000 sq km) of land very rich in fauna and gently meandering rivers in the Banjar Valley. Rudyard Kipling's *The Jungle Book* (1894), made into a movie by Walt Disney, is set in this area and depicts the truly idyllic jungle life that you can still experience.

The park was established in 1955 as the start of a successful project to save the almost extinct hardground *barasingha* (Indian swamp deer). Some of the first serious research work was done on tigers here, by American big-cat expert George Schaller, in 1963–65. The park still carries out important Project Tiger work, which serves as a model for wildlife management.

As you travel through the beautiful landscape, you may spot the now flourishing barasingha, and chital deer, langur monkey, gaur, nilgai, wild boar, mouse deer, sambhar, and even the elusive leopard. If you can persuade your jeep driver to stay still long enough, you can glimpse rich bird life through your binoculars, including bee-eaters, black ibises, golden orioles, and serpent eagles.

PANNA NATIONAL PARK

Conveniently close to Khajuraho, this wilderness of valleys and gorges bordering the Ken River is glorious when monsoon rains have given it lushness and copious waterfalls. You may see nilgai, sloth bear, cheetah, sambhar, and *chinkara* (Indian gazelle) in the teak forest, and the rare gharial and mugger crocodiles in the Ken.

But the 210-square-mile (543 sq km) park is best known for its big cats. There is a good chance that patience will be rewarded with sightings of a tiger, leopard, or panther. A good place to wait for one is near the beautiful lake fed by Pandava Falls.

SHIVPURI NATIONAL PARK

This small park of deciduous plains forest was once the summer capital of The Scindias of Gwalior (see p. 110); their grand mausoleums were built in white marble for recent Gwalior royals, with idols lovingly tended by more than 150 people, and are well worth visiting. In the park, ornithologists can enjoy plenty of bird life, including sightings of demoiselle cranes. Animals to see include sambhar, chital, nilgai, and chinkara. ∎

Visitor tips

Accommodations tend to include in the price all meals, guides, jeep rides, and, if an option, elephant safaris; reserving in advance is essential.

Beware of temperature extremes: It's chilly at dawn and dusk in winter (there are sometimes frosts) but blisteringly hot after February. All parks offer good animal sightings, especially in the heat and dust between March and June. ∎

Riding an elephant through Bandhavgarh's wild landscape

Panna National Park
 95 D3
🕐 Closed July–Oct., best Oct.–April
💲 $
❌ Nearest airport Khajuraho; stay at Madla

Shivpuri National Park
95 C3
🕐 Open all year, best Feb.–June
❌ Nearest airport Gwalior

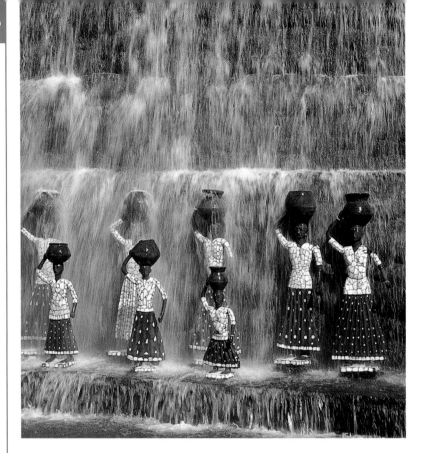

Nek Chand's Rock Garden is full of witty surprises, such as these women being drenched by a waterfall.

Chandigarh

THE FLAT, FERTILE, AND PROSPEROUS LAND STRETCHING from Delhi to the Indus was once all the Punjab. With independence, half was lost to Pakistan and since then further areas have formed two more Indian states: Haryana and Himachal Pradesh. The Green Revolution of the 1960s, introducing modern crop technology and improving on the already substantial British-built irrigation system, transformed the area into the breadbasket of India. A quarter of India's wheat and a third of its milk and dairy foods are produced in this area. Today, Haryana and Punjab share their capital, Chandigarh, a good base for some offbeat sight-seeing.

Chandigarh
🗺 95 B5
Himachal Pradesh Tourist Office
✉ Sector 22
☎ 0172-704570

Punjab Tourist Office
✉ Sector 22
☎ 0172-781138

Independent India's first planned city, conceived by Le Corbusier (see p. 88), was begun in 1952 and, with help from Maxwell Fry and Jane Drew, was completed ten years later. Today, its grid boulevards divided into blocks (called "sec-

tors"), and its grand civic buildings can be judged with some degree of historical perspective, although the initial dramatic effect has been softened by extensive planting.

Le Corbusier envisaged his ideal city as a living organism, with the

Capital Complex (*Guided tours, may be suspended for security reasons; call ahead*) as its "head" and the large green spaces as its "lungs." The capital is one of Le Corbusier's most innovative designs. Set against the Shivalik Hills, his monumental buildings for the High Court, Legislative Assembly, and Secretariat overlook the 1,300-foot-wide (400 m) square. Down the main avenue, Jan Marg, is the **Museum and Art Gallery** (*Sector 10, closed Mon.*), whose collection reflects the long, rich history and culture of the area, from Gandhara Buddhas to Sikh paintings.

On the city outskirts is the upbeat, witty artwork, the **Rock Garden**. This is retired road inspector Nek Chand's life work: The garden is composed of a succession of open-air rooms, each one individually decorated with colorful mosaics or surreal sculptures of animal and human figures.

AROUND CHANDIGARH

As you head north into the Shivalik Hills along the road to Shimla, **Pinjore** is well worth a stop to visit the walled **Yadavindra Gardens.** The Mogul emperor Aurangzeb's brother, Fidai Khan, reorganized the ancient gardens, giving them three pleasure palaces and broad terraced lawns; they're good for picnics. From **Kalka,** 2 miles (4 km) farther on, the *Himalayan Queen* and other trains leave for Shimla, a 5½ hour journey. Quaint **Nalagarh** is nearer—37 miles (60 km) from Chandigarh— and quieter, with good walking and the ruined **Ramgarh Fort.**

Southwest of Chandigarh lies **Patiala,** where tourists are hardly ever seen. In this charming, unspoiled city, once the capital of the Sikh state Patiala, do not miss the multistory **Motibagh Palace** with its many painted rooms, nor the busy street markets.

Farther up the Grand Trunk Road toward Amritsar, **Sirhind** has a cluster of Mogul and Sikh monuments you might visit. Then, bypass Ludhiana's wool factories and Jalandhar's bicycle industry to arrive at **Kapurthala,** a Paris-influenced model town and home to the Jalaukhana Palace, built in the 1890s by the French-educated ruler, Jagajit Singh Ahluwalia. ■

Government Museum and Art Gallery
- ✉ Sector 10, Capital Complex
- ☎ 0172-725568
- ⏲ Closed Mon.
- 💲 $

Rock Garden
- ✉ Behind High Court
- ⏲ Closed a.m. Oct.–March
- 💲 $

Pinjore
- 🅰 95 B5
- ✉ 13 miles (21 km) NE of Chandigarh on Kalka Rd.

Patiala
- 🅰 95 B5
- ✉ 42 miles (68 km) SW of Chandigarh

Motibagh Palace
- ✉ 1.8 miles (3 km) S of Patiala
- ⏲ May be closed to visitors

Sirhind
- 🅰 95 B5
- ✉ 30 miles (48 km) NW of Ambala

Kapurthala
- 🅰 95 B6
- ✉ 113 miles (180 km) W of Chandigargh

Grand Trunk Road

Made famous by Rudyard Kipling in his novel *Kim,* this is one of the world's great ancient roads. It stretches 1,200 miles (2,000 km) across the subcontinent, from mountainous Peshawar on the Pakistan-Afghanistan border to Kolkata on the Bay of Bengal.

Trade has been passing along this route since at least the fourth century B.C., when it was called the Uttar Path (high way). The Mauryan emperor Ashoka gave it paving stones, watchtowers, and some of his edict pillars (see p. 31); portions survive beside the current road. Sher Shah Sur carried out major maintenance work, built *serais* (medieval motels)—one survives at Sirhind, near Chandigarh—and employed spies at them to report rumor and discontent. The Moguls added wells; the British added asphalt and the present name.

Today, Kipling's "Backbone of all Hind" is India's National Highway 1 (NH1), nicknamed "G. T Road." Trucks, cars, bullock-carts, bicycles, and cows share this great road, perpetuating Kipling's "river of life." ■

Amritsar

Amritsar

📍 95 A6

State Tourist Information

✉ Mall Mandi, G. T. Rd.

☎ 0183-231452

THE OLD, WALLED CORE OF PUNJAB'S LARGEST CITY IS A network of bustling bazaars surrounding the beautiful Golden Temple and Jallianwalla Bagh (see box p. 123). These, the gems of Amritsar, are filled with an intense calm and peacefulness, despite their political associations.

Visitor tips

All are welcome at the Hari Mandir, but shoes must be removed and feet washed; no socks are to be worn, heads must be covered, and all tobacco and alcohol must be left outside the complex (there are lockers for this purpose).

Amritsar is the Sikhs' holy city. Every Sikh is required to visit it at least once, so there are usually thousands of pilgrims here. The fourth Guru, Ram Das, founded the trading town in 1577 and enlarged the Amrit Sarovar ("pool of nectar," hence Amritsar) to commemorate a crippled person being cured while bathing there. His son and successor, Arjan Dev, built the first temple (1589–1601) in the lake: the Hari Mandir (Golden Temple).

After multiple Afghan attacks and persecutions in the 18th century, Ranjit Singh led the Sikhs to victory in the Punjab and in 1830 gave 220 pounds (100 kg) of gold to gild the restored temple. In the 20th century, Sikhs saw their dream for Khalistan, an independent Sikh state based on the whole of Ranjit Singh's kingdom, shattered. Nehru made promises; Indira Gandhi offered a reduced version, then withdrew her offer. As a result of the ensuing conflicts, the Golden Temple was fortified, the Indian Army made an assault on it in June 1984, and Mrs. Gandhi was assassinated in the same year. Rajiv Gandhi drew up the Punjab Accord in July 1985, but the problem remains unresolved.

You need a couple of hours to visit the temple. Start by enjoying your first view of the shimmering **Amrit Sarovar,** on which the Hari Mandir temple appears to float. Then take a slow walk clockwise, right around the tank, following pilgrims as they pause at small shrines devoted to the founding gurus. Along this route, called the Parikrama, are four little booths where devotees take turns to maintain a continuous reading of the *Guru Granth Sahib,* the Sikhs' sacred book. On the east side, up to 6,000 pilgrims a day eat in the Guru-ka-langar (communal dining room) to remind themselves that all are equal.

The climax of your visit is on the west side. Here is the **Akal Takht,** the temple's second most sacred structure. Built by Guru Magolind to house the religious and political governing body of the

Pilgrims make their way along the Guru's Bridge (above) **to the Hari Mandir to listen to the continuous daytime reading from the Guru Granth Sahib** (right).

Sikhs, it has been immaculately rebuilt since the Indian Army destroyed it during the violent conflicts of 1984.

Before visiting it, worshipers collect their *prasad* (offering) and go along the Guru's Bridge to the highly decorated **Hari Mandir,** which houses a huge copy of the Guru Granth Sahib. You can go there, too, entering through one of its four open doors (symbolizing welcome to all four Hindu castes) to witness the continuous readings, chanting, and music. The book is set on a throne by day, but each evening, in a most moving ceremony, it is paraded to the Akal Takht to the sound of singing and the loud beating of drums. ■

Jallianwalla Bagh Massacre

On April 13, 1919, without warning, Gen. R. E. H. Dyer and his 150 troops fired continuously for 15 minutes on some 20,000 unarmed people gathered peacefully in a square hemmed in by buildings. The official death toll was 400, with 1,200 injuries. It was one of the worst atrocities perpetrated by the British in India.

The cause was the Rowlatt Act, which empowered the British to imprison without trial any Indian suspected of sedition. A series of one-day strikes in Amritsar escalated into looting, and Mahatma Gandhi called a mass demonstration for April 13 at Jallianwalla Bagh. No speech or aggressive action had been made when General Dyer ordered fire.

Today, the square is an extremely touching memorial park, reached through one of the original narrow alleys. A small gallery houses firsthand accounts, contemporary photographs, newspaper reports, and poet Rabindranath Tagore's moving letter, returning his British honors. ■

Delhi's hill stations

IF THE SEARING HEAT OF THE PLAINS IS UNBEARABLE, THE cooling comfort of the lower Himalayan mountains and their quaint British-founded hill stations (see p. 278) are near at hand. The climate and flowers are best in spring and fall.

SHIMLA (SIMLA), HIMACHAL PRADESH

The capital of modern India's mountainous Himachal Pradesh sustains its position as queen of India's hill stations. Set at an elevation of 7,260 feet (2,213 m) in the pine-forested Shivalik Hills, this was the summer capital of the British administration from 1864 to 1939. Each year, the huge machine of bureaucrats and papers, together with servants, coolies, packhorses, women, and children, made the long journey up here from Calcutta (and later Delhi) until the Kalka to Shimla Railway opened in 1903. From here, for more than half the year, amid the plays, games, dancing, hunting, and gossip, the British governed approximately one-fifth of the world's population.

Shimla's modern mix of mountains, imperial British buildings, Indian town, and wealthy Indian visitors makes it unlike anywhere else in India. To get the most out of it, be prepared to walk, as the center is restricted to pedestrians.

On **The Ridge,** in the town center beside Christ Church (which has fine stained-glass windows), there are splendid views over the surrounding hills. Walk along The Mall (the main street), past British buildings whose designs range between seaside flippancy and stoic Scottish baronial, past the lavishly refurbished Cecil Hotel, to find **Viceregal Lodge** (*Observatory Rd., partly open to the public, $*).

MUSSOORIE, UTTARANCHAL

At an elevation of 6,561 feet (2,000 m) and a mere 172 miles (277 km) from Delhi, this hill station makes for a good quick break. Discovered by the British in 1823, its popularity is sustained by its spectacular views of the Himalayas and the Dehra Dun valley.

As the town tends to be busy, peace is best found by walking in the beautiful surrounding countryside. **Childers Lodge,** situated above Landour, has the most exquisite views of all, while a walk out to **Tchenchen Choling** *gompa* (monastery) and its gardens is highly rewarding. If you would like to try a more ambitious trek, you can spend four days exploring the Harki Dun valley.

HARIDWAR & RISHIKESH, UTTARANCHAL

As one of the Seven Sacred Cities, **Haridwar** is a busy Hindu pilgrimage center. Here the sacred Ganga River leaves the rugged mountains for the flat plains, and Har-ki-Pairi *ghat* marks the exact spot. All day long the faithful visit the ghats, bridges, and islands; each

Shimla
- 95 B5
Tourist Office
- The Mall
- 0177-255279

Mussoorie
- 95 C5
Tourist Office
- The Mall
- 0135-632863

Haridwar
- 95 C5
Tourist Office
- Upper Rd.
- 0133-424240

Left: Shimla's British area recalls an English seaside town.

evening, hundreds gather for the Ganga Arati ceremony at dusk, when lights are floated down the river to the sound of gongs and music.

Rishikesh lies within sight, up the mountains of Garhwal. The Beatles put it on the hippie trail with their visit to the Maharishi in February 1968. Today, *ashrams* of all kinds abound, continuing and expanding the spot's ancient tradition as a Hindu pilgrimage stop. Those seriously interested in yoga should reserve in advance at the Shivananda Ashram *(The Divine Life Society, Shivananda Nagar, tel 01364-31140, fax 01364-31196, www.sivananda.org)*. For peace, go in winter and spring when the temples are shut and pilgrims fewer. Those wishing to follow the Ganga

to its source can journey on to Gangotri from here (see p. 321).

NAINITAL, UTTARANCHAL

Set in the Kumaun Hills at 6,358 feet (1,938 m), this town overlooking a large, natural lake has sustained its popularity since a sugar merchant, Mr. Barron, discovered its joys in 1841. Find action along The Mall, which runs the length of the lake from Mallital, the colonial area, to Tallital. Try boating on the lake, visiting a Tibetan market, the climbing ropeway to Snow View, and walking longer trails to Naina Peak and China Peak for more views. From Nainital you can visit Corbett National Park (see p. 126), with charming hotels along the route. ■

Shimla clings precariously to the mountainside.

Rishikesh
🄰 95 C5
Tourist Office
✉ Nehru Park, Railway Rd.
☎ 01364-430209

Nainital
🄰 95 C5
Tourist Office
✉ The Mall (Mallital end)
☎ 05942-35337

Corbett National Park

Corbett National Park

🗺 95 C5
✉ Ramnagar
☎ 05946-853189
🕐 Open mid-Nov.–mid-June, after which monsoons flood the riverbeds and cut off the roads
💲 $
✕ Nearest airport Pantnagar

ESTABLISHED IN 1936 BY JIM CORBETT (1875–1955), INDIA'S first wildlife sanctuary now preserves a rare expanse of sub-Himalayan wilderness. The dramatic scenery of the 201 square miles (521 sq km) of Kumaun hills, valleys, and rivers makes it particularly beautiful, and especially lush after the monsoon months (November to January), even if much of the core area of 127 square miles (330 sq km) is off-limits to visitors.

Jim Corbett, a hunter turned conservationist and author, was born in Nainital and knew the area intimately. Repeatedly called to save locals by killing man-eating tigers and leopards, Corbett was already concerned about threats to India's wildlife by the 1940s, when he began to champion the conservation awareness of Indians. It was appropriate, then, that in 1973 this

elephant, if you are riding one. Look in the rivers for snout-nosed gharial crocodiles, large mugger crocodiles, and river tortoises. On land, you may see wild boar, sambhar, Himalayan black bear, delicate *chital*, ugly hog deer, porcupine, and trees full of playful rhesus and common langur monkeys.

For ornithologists this park is a paradise, since it attracts an abun-

Lively and intelligent, rhesus monkeys are often seen in Corbett National Park. Watch for them as well in parks, woodland, and scrub throughout India.

Visitor tips
Stay outside the park at Ramnagar, on the Kosi River; the upscale hotels can arrange two- or three-night stays inside the park, taking their own staff and food. Government-run accommodations at Dikhala and elsewhere inside the park are very disappointing.

park was the first Project Tiger Reserve. Ironically, the project's success here has led to overpopulation, as each tiger needs 31 square miles (80 sq km), and there are now regular reports of the man-eating incidents that Corbett tackled.

The park's good infrastructure and its naturalists mean there is a fair chance of sighting the elusive tiger, possibly from the back of an

dance of both plains and hill birds. An hour in a *machan* will be richly rewarded—perhaps with sightings of black-necked stork, honey buzzard, crested serpent eagle, gray hornbill, scarlet minivet, and many different waterfowl, pigeons, parakeets, and kingfishers.

It is best to visit from November to March; after this it gets hotter, but elephant sightings increase. ■

With vivid colors glowing in the parched land, soaring forts telling of heroic legends, and fairy-tale palaces where, until recently, maharajas lived in untold luxury, this corner of India fulfills a visitor's most exotic dreams.

Rajasthan & Gujarat

A village woman carries her water supply home.

Rajasthan & Gujarat

THESE TWO DRY AND DUSTY STATES IN WESTERN INDIA EXTEND ACROSS THE punishing Great Indian Desert to the Pakistan border and the Arabian Sea, separated from the Ganga Basin by the Aravalli Mountains, and from peninsular India by the Vindhya and Satpura ranges. The annual monsoon is crucial: If it fails, the people suffer. Yet the location of both states has brought wealth through trade—a wealth increased in Gujarat because it lies on the pilgrimage route to Mecca used by northern India's Muslim rulers and their entourages.

Camels are the best form of transport through the dry Thar Desert.

Rajasthan is India's most popular area for visitors. It lies on the doorstep of Delhi and Agra; its former royals were quick to turn their palaces into hotels, and it offers classic romantic India, to be enjoyed easily without having to cope with much of India's complex history.

Most of the feuding Rajput rulers (see p. 37) turned to lives of pure pleasure once they accepted the mantle of British protection. A journey through Rajasthan gives you an idea of that life: visiting forts, shopping in colorful markets, riding painted elephants, spotting wildlife, and staying in one former palace after another.

But there are contrasts. The former states within Rajasthan have stoically held on to their individual characters and traditions. Jaipur, conceived as a commercial hub for the Jaipur princely state, is now the chaotic capital of all Rajasthan. Udaipur was and is distinguished for its lakes, beauty, and proudly defiant Mewar rulers, who poured their energy and vision into creating the most idyllic

Rajput city. Away in the west, Marwar's Jodhpur continues to feel like a royal frontier desert city. It would be no surprise if a camel train arrived in the shadow of the great fort.

Gujarat feels entirely different from Rajasthan. Its coastal trading and agricultural production were so lucrative that Emperor Akbar built the Buland Darwaza at Fatehpur Sikri (see pp. 104–105) when he finally conquered it. Today the many little preindependence kingdoms have metamorphosed into India's second wealthiest state—and one of the country's most enlightened. As an indicator, the literacy rate is 61 percent, compared with Rajasthan's 38 percent. Ahmedabad, its capital, offers a mixture of grand Islamic buildings, fine museums, and strong Gandhi associations: Gujarat was his home state. From Ahmedabad, you can make some journeys to see Harappan sites, Jain monuments, Hindu temples, art deco palaces, and rare wildlife. Hotels are often simple, visitors few, and the rewards considerable. ■

5 ▷

Ta

SAM SAND DUI
(DESERT NAT. PA.

4 ▷

Munabac

P A K I S T A N

3 ▷

Rann of Kachchh

• Lakhpat   Khavda

• Naliya   Bhuj

• Anjar

Gandhidham •

Mandvi •   • Mundra

Gulf of Kachchh

Okha

Jamnag

2 ▷   Dwarka

Kathiaw

△
A

Arabian   *S a*

Porbandar •   8B Je

Junagad

Sea

Somnath

1 ▷

△
B

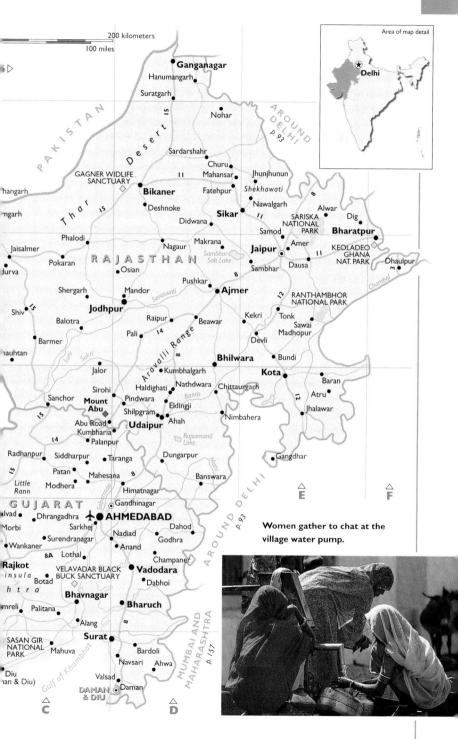

Women gather to chat at the village water pump.

Amer & Jaipur

Aesthete ruler Pratap Singh built the Hawa Mahal in Jaipur in 1799 as a grandstand for the palace women.

A VISIT TO AMER'S MEDIEVAL FORT AND THEN THE NEARBY walled town of Jaipur, each in turn the capital of the powerful Kachwaha clan, makes a good introduction to Rajasthan.

Of the 36 proud and warring Rajput clans, all *kshatriya* caste Hindus, the Kachwahas of Amer became one of the greatest. Legend traces their ancestry back to the sun, but their story enters recorded history from when they won Amer fort in the 12th century.

As waves of Muslim invaders swept through to nearby Delhi, Amer's hilltop site and surrounding mountains were not enough to protect it. Furthermore, it lay on the route to the popular Muslim Chishti shrine at Ajmer. Thus began a story of alliance and mutual benefit. Alliances began with the Chauhan rulers of Delhi and continued with the Moguls in 1562.

The Amer princess who sealed this alliance gave birth to Salim, later Emperor Jahangir (see p. 41).

The results were wealth, prestige, and the **Amer Fort** and palace complex you can now visit. Viewed from the road across Maota Lake, the left-hand section was built by Man Singh (*R*.1589–1614), who led Akbar's troops to repeated victories, while the right section, which emulates Mogul buildings at Agra and Fatehpur Sikri (see pp. 96–105), was built by Jai Singh I (*R*.1621–1667), who fought for three Mogul emperors.

The least tiring way to reach the palace is by elephant (*available to rent in Amer village*); once there,

Amer

🗺 129 E4

Amer Tourist Office

✉ Elephant Stand

☎ 0141-530264

RESERVED FOREST
Nahargarh Fort
Amer
Zorawarsingh Gate
Gangapol Gate
Tal Katora
GANGAURI BAZAR
Govinda Deva Temple
SIREDEORI BAZAR
Char Darwaja
Chandpol Gate
CHANDPOL BAZAR
City Palace
Jantar Mantar
Hawa Mahal
SANSAR CHANDRA ROAD
KISHANPOL BAZAR
TRIPOLIA BAZAR
BADI CHAUPAR
RAMGANJ BAZAR
SURAJPOL BAZAR
Jama Masjid
GOPALJI KA BAZAR
CHAT DARWAZA BAZAR
Surajpol Gate
Post Office
CHAURA RASTA
JOHARI BAZAR
Elephant Owner's Area
MIRZ ISMAIL ROAD
Ajmeri Gate
New Gate
Sanganer Gate
Ghat Gate
Ajmer
ASHOK ROAD
RAM NIWAS GARDENS
Central Museum
AGRA ROAD
Agra
PRITHVIRAJ ROAD
SAWAI RAMSINGH ROAD
JAWAHARLAL NEHRU ROAD
MOTIDUNGRI ROAD
ADARSH NAGAR RD.
GOVIND ROAD
BHAGWANDAS ROAD
Rambagh Palace
Airport
RESERVED FOREST
0 1 kilometer
0 1 mile

Right: Riding up to impressive Amer Fort on an elephant

don't miss the **Kali Mata Temple,** with Jai Singh's elaborately decorated suites (with good rooftop views) and the warren of Man Singh's simpler rooms.

JAIPUR

Fourth in succession after Jai Singh I, the precocious, 11-year-old Jai Singh II (R.1699–1743) came to the Kachwaha throne and was awarded the title Sawai (One-and-a-Quarter) to put him above his fellow Rajputs. Having shone on the battlefield, he indulged his love of science and the arts. In 1727 he began to lay out a model palace-city, Jaipur, employing a Bengali called Vidyadhar Bhattacharya as his architect.

Your visit could start with **City Palace** and its collections of fabrics, decorated weapons, paintings, and carpets; the one-and-a-quarter flag flies above. Nearby stands Jai Singh's Jantar Mantar (magical instrument), an intriguing

Jaipur
129 E4
India Tourist Office
State Hotel, Khasa Kothi
0141-372200

Rajasthan Tourist Information
Tourist Hotel
0141-365256

City Palace
0141-608055
$
Closed religious festival days
$. Free Wed.

A group of women picnic together on a Jaipur street.

Govinda Deva Temple
✉ Jaleb Chowk

Central Museum
✉ Ram Niwas Bagh
☎ 0141-565124
🕐 Closed Fri.
💲 $. Free Wed.

Rambagh Palace
✉ Bhawani Singh Rd.
☎ 0141-381919

Vidyadhar ka Bagh
✉ 4 miles (6 km) E of Jaipur on Agra Rd.

Sisodia Rani ka Bagh
✉ 4 miles (6 km) E of Jaipur on Agra Rd.
☎ 0141-64-0594
💲 $

set of outsize astronomical instruments, mostly designed to calculate time more precisely. Of the five sets he built, this is the biggest.

Outside the palace complex Jaipur's markets are a riot of color. Find bangles, shoes, puppets, and *attar* (perfume) at Badi Chaupar, in front of the landmark **Hawa Mahal** (Palace of the Winds), cotton cloth and jewelry along **Johari Bazar,** gems and jewels particularly down two lanes of it, Gopalji Ka Bazar, and Haldion Ka Rasta.

If the fervent worship in the Kali Mata temple at Amer (see p. 131) interested you, so will **Govinda Deva Temple.** Jai Singh brought the image of Krishna from Govinda; it is worshiped especially fervently at the 6 p.m. and 8 p.m. *pujas.*

South of the walled city, at the **Central Museum** a delightful collection of puppets, costumes, models, and Jaipur brasswork fills Sir Samuel Swinton Jacob's Albert Hall, begun in 1876 in the spacious lung of Ram Niwas Gardens. The Durbar Hall *(often closed)* contains spectacular carpets.

Farther south again is the **Rambagh Palace,** built by Maharaja Ram Singh II as a hunting lodge, which Madho Singh II transformed into a royal playground with extensive English gardens. It is now a hotel, but the public can enjoy the gardens, the Lalique fountains, and the Polo Bar of the lodge.

JAIPUR'S OUTSKIRTS
As you leave Jaipur on the road toward Agra, the walled garden **Vidyadhar ka Bagh,** on the right, remembers Jaipur's architect, Vidyadhar Bhattacharya. On the left, **Sisodia Rani ka Bagh** is the country palace built for Jai Singh II's Udaipur queen; there are lively murals and lush gardens. Behind it, troops of langur monkeys are fed daily at 4 p.m. at the **Hanuman Temple.**

On the left, along the Jaipur–Amer road at Gaitor, doors lead to the **Royal Cenotaphs.** Madho Singh II's is the largest; Jai Singh's, found at the back, has columns carved with mythological scenes supporting a marble dome. ■

Around Jaipur

IF THE CROWDED TOURIST HOT SPOTS OF AMER AND JAIPUR take their toll, seek out some of these quieter, often atmospheric places in the countryside around Jaipur.

Jaipur has a ring of protective forts, the most imposing of which is **Nahargarh,** reached either from the Amer road or by a brisk hike from the city's Nahargarh Fort Road. Sunset is marvelous, when Jaipur's city noises float up through the softening light.

An ideal detour after Amer, the spectacularly sited **Jaigarh** is where Man Singh and his successors stored their treasure. It was expanded by Jai Singh II in 1726, and you can see the great cannon, armory, gun foundry, and palace complex. In times of danger, Amer's royals retreated here.

Moving farther afield, the following sights are listed clockwise around Jaipur from the west. At **Ajmer** (112 miles/135 km from Jaipur) find the Dargarh Sharif (holy shrine) of the Sufi saint Khwajah Muin-ud-din Chisthti, who came to India in 1192 and died here (see p. 70); this is still a popular pilgrimage center, with regular *qawwali* singing. See also Akbar's fort-palace, the finely carved Arhai-din-ka-Jhonpra mosque (1193), and Shah Jahan's marble pavilions. In contrast, the quiet Hindu town of **Pushkar'**s draw is its sacred lake. (For the annual Pushkar Fair see p. 382.)

The rugged area of northeast Rajasthan known as **Shekhawati** is dotted with more than 360 villages. During the 19th and 20th centuries, Marwari families, such as the Birlas, Poddars, and Goenkas, made their money in commerce and then lavishly decorated their homes with lively frescoes inside and out. A trip to see these might include Fatehpur, Mahansar, Jhunjhunun, and Nawalgarh.

At Samode (26 miles/42 km NW of Jaipur), descendants of Jai Singh II's finance minister have energetically restored his isolated **Samode Palace,** whose rooms are covered with murals. Nearby, they have also brought the walled royal garden alive again, complete with working fountains.

The **Sariska National Park** (*64 miles/103 km NE of Jaipur*) is a Project Tiger reserve off the Delhi–Jaipur highway, sprawling over 300 square miles (800 sq km); dawn and dusk jeep rides may give sightings of a tiger but will certainly include good birds. **Alwar,** once capital of Alwar state, is dominated by Vinai Vilas (1840), the atmospheric city palace with a top-floor museum; see also the royal *chhatri* and Mogul tomb of Fateh Jung.

In the center of **Bharatpur** is the Jat kings' Lohargarh, which retains its decayed splendor. Part is now a museum. However, the evocative Bharatpur maharaja's summer palace at nearby **Dig** (circa 1750) survives intact: Wander its gardens, complete with marble swing, and explore the magnificent apartments, some decorated with marble booty from Agra Fort.

Another Project Tiger reserve is **Ranthambhor National Park,** 154 square miles (399 sq km) of deciduous forest rambling over the Aravalli and Vindhya Hills and around Ranthambore's great fort. It provides the ideal habitat for tigers and is popular and fashionable, so it's essential to reserve accommodations (see p. 356) in advance. ∎

Nahargarh
- ✉ 5 miles (9 km) NW of Jaipur on Amer Rd.
- ☎ 0141-320538
- 💲 $

Jaigarh
- ✉ N of Jaipur on Amer Rd.
- ☎ 0141-630848
- 💲 $

Bharatpur
- 🅰 129 F4
- ✉ 34 miles (55 km) W of Agra

Pushkar has many temples.

Dig
- 🅰 129 E5
- ✉ 61 miles (98 km) NW of Agra on NH2
- 💲 $

Ranthambhor National Park
- 🅰 129 E4
- ✉ 112 miles (180 km) SE of Jaipur

India's palace hotels

India is awash with palaces. There are thousands of them, huge and unnecessary in today's democratic India. Yet they are the core of every old city and dominate villages; they overlook lakes, perch on hills, and are found down the most unlikely mud lanes.

A stylish waiter looks out from the Rambagh Palace Hotel over its extensive lawns. Maharaja Madho Singh II transformed the hunting lodge into a royal playground.

Before independence, these were great households, often giving employment to several hundred people. They were places of patronage for painters, writers, musicians, and weavers. After 1947, the former rulers and nobles were obliged to give up some of their land, wealth, and properties. With them went the communities they headed. The grandest palaces and forts became landmarks open to the public, while others remained the ancestral homes of nobles, who found their upkeep increasingly difficult to finance. Hundreds more simply fell empty and silent, waiting quietly for their moment to come alive again.

Now, as visitors prefer palaces to high-rises to stay in, these buildings have their chance, encouraged by government tax breaks. All over India, they are being dusted down and opened up as hotels. Some are sensational, others less so; but all have a special charm that adds to a visit to India. The local staff, proud of their area, often ensure that guests have an especially memorable stay.

It was the Maharaja of Jaipur who first saw the potential of renting palace rooms to visitors. He opened the Rambagh Palace Hotel in Jaipur on December 8, 1957; tragically, while other hotels are being lovingly restored, its art deco suites have recently been ripped out. In 1961, Maharana Bhagwat Singh of Udaipur also recognized the end of an era and began to transform Jag Niwas Palace into the Lake Palace Hotel.

His energetic son, Arvind Singh, has continued his work with an attention to quality that is rare. Having restored his own palaces to create the Udaipur hotel cluster of Shiv Niwas, Fateh Prakash, and Dovecote, he now has a palace-hotel network stretching to Jodhpur, Jaisalmer, and Bikaner.

Heritage hotels, as they are known, are not restricted to Rajasthan. They extend from the Himalayan Mountains down to Tamil Nadu. Nalagarh Fort nestles in the Himalayan foothills near Chandigarh. In the west, there is Nilambagh Palace at Bhavnagar in Gujarat, Orchard Palace at Gondal in Saurashtra, and Hingolgadh Castle at Jasden. Central India has Jhira Bagh Palace and Ahilya Fort, both convenient for Mandu; Bhanwar Vilas Palace at Karauli; and Kawardha Palace—convenient for Kanha National Park. Down in the south, Mysore's Lalitha Mahal Palace Hotel is a gloriously extravagant Victorian palace hotel; and there are many more.

Such is the success of heritage hotels that enterprising Indians with flair have started to buy old properties and imbue them with their own, more democratic taste. The team of designer Aman Nath and businessman Francis Wacziac took on the challenge of restoring Neemrana Fort with some friends, then went solo to bring other forts, Raj bungalows, and even a French colonial house in Pondicherry to life. Lekha Poddar has taken the chaotic pile of Devigarh Fort outside Udaipur, stripped it back to its origins and, with immaculate taste, created an uncompromisingly contemporary world-class hotel. For details of these, and more suggestions, see the hotels and restaurants section of this guide on pp. 343–72. ∎

Famous for its school of miniature painting, family-run Deogarh Palace Hotel (above) at Devgarh has finely decorated rooms. The stunningly sited Lake Palace Hotel (below) at Udaipur, once a royal summer retreat, also has painted suites, some with their own swings. Like the Rambagh Palace, it is managed by the Taj Group.

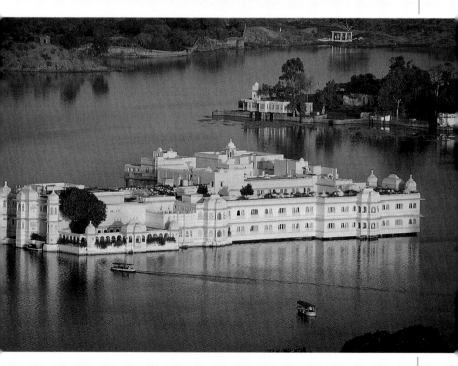

Udaipur

THIS IS RAJASTHAN'S MOST CONGENIAL AND ROMANTIC city, with its gentle light, shimmering lakes, compact center, bustling prosperity, and quantity of sensitively restored palaces. A far cry from the commercial aggressiveness and pollution of Jaipur, Udaipur is a perfect place for a relaxing day or two.

Once the capital of powerful Mewar state, Udaipur has Rajasthan's largest and best-maintained City Palace; it is more than half a mile long and still dominates the city.

Udaipur
🅜 129 D3
Udaipur Tourist Information
✉ Surajpole
☎ 0294-411535

Choose from a cluster of palace hotels and nobles' *havelis* to stay in; whichever you pick, you can visit the others for meals and drinks.

Start exploring the city by taking the evening boat ride from the main jetty around **Lake Pichola,** dug when Udai Singh fled Mogul danger at Chittaurgarh in 1567 and made this the capital of his state, Mewar. Udai Singh was head of the top Rajput clan, the Sisodias, descended directly from the sun via the god Rama. He and his successors built the huge and very Hindu City Palace. The boat chugs past the **Lake Palace Hotel** (1754, see pp. 134–35 and p. 356), built by Maharana Jagat Singh as a summer retreat, then stops at **Jag Mandir,** the island where Jahangir's son, the future Shah Jahan, sought refuge when he was a rebellious prince; his exquisite little palace (1622) antici-pates his later buildings.

On land, there is much to see. The fleet of gleaming royal cars is kept beside the **Garden Hotel** (delicious Gujarati food), opposite **Gulab Bagh** (rose garden). At the **City Palace** *(closed for religious festivals),* with its *jharokas* (project-ing balconies), maze of rooms, and wall decorations of inlaid glass, clamber up and down the narrow stairways of the Mardana (men's section), then see the recently restored **Zenana** (women's sec-tion). There is not a touch of Mogul influence here. Finally, visit the restored Durbar Hall and its Crystal Gallery in **Fateh Prakash Palace** *(Tel 0294-528016)* where a fabulous collection of British crystal is on display, including items from water basins to spitoons.

In the town, the main street leads downhill to the lively bazaars, passing Jagdish Temple and tiny shops selling cottons, wooden toys, and silver jewelry.

Fateh Sagar is an artificial lake. It was constructed in 1678 and Maharana Fateh Singh added the embankment (1889). The pretty shore road leads to well-kept **Saheliyon-ki-Bari** (Garden of Ladies); the island garden is **Nehru Park.** ■

The twinkling colored glass on this City Palace peacock (right) contrasts with the simple surrounding lanes and traditional houses with carved, overhanging _jharokas_ (balconies).

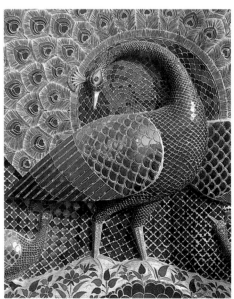

Around Udaipur

IF YOU CAN TEAR YOURSELF AWAY FROM THE RELAXING charm of Udaipur, there is a variety of outings, long and short, to suit all interests, out across the rugged Aravalli Mountains.

Shilpgram
- 129 D3
- 5 miles (8 km) W of Udaipur
- $

Monsoon Palace
- 9 miles (15 km) SW of Udaipur

Mount Abu
- 129 C3
- 116 miles (185 km) NW of Udaipur

Kumbhalgarh
- 129 D3
- 40 miles (64 km) N of Udaipur

Ranakpur
- 56 miles (90 km) N of Udaipur; 16 miles (25 km) SW of Kumbhalgarh

Nagda
- 14 miles (22 km) N of Udaipur

Eklingji
- 129 D3
- 14 miles (23 km) NE of Udaipur

Rajsamand Lake
- 129 D3
- 40 miles (65 km) NE of Udaipur

To the west of Udaipur you can visit the model crafts village of **Shilpgram,** founded to preserve western India's traditional architecture, music, and crafts. The houses include a carved wooden Gujarat building; you may see weavers, musicians, potters, and other craftsmen at work.

A hike up the hill from Udaipur to the abandoned **Monsoon Palace** (1880), now used by the local radio station, is rewarded with magical sunset and sunrise views.

To the north of the city are a number of sites within easy reach of one another. The rocky outcrops of **Mount Abu** provide Rajasthan's only cool retreat from the searing summer heat. Enjoy the walks, views, lakes, and the two sets of temples: the Jains' five finely carved marble Dilwara temples and the Hindus' temples at **Achalgarh** and **Guru Shikar.** See also the nearby Adhar Devi Temple, which lies at the top of an extremely long flight of steps; the views from the top are magnificent.

Also north of Udaipur, the spectacular 15th-century ghost fort-town of **Kumbhalgarh** rises from rugged countryside, the finest of 32 forts built by Maharana Kumbha. Inside the massive ramparts are Jain temples, cenotaphs, and the citadel, which can be climbed. Near the entrance, Aodhi Hotel provides sustenance.

At **Ranakpur,** one of India's finest Jain temples lies hidden in a wooded valley—hence its survival. The main temple (1439) is dedicated to Adinath, an enlightened Jain teacher, and built entirely of white marble, almost every surface of which is carved. Wander the 29 interconnecting halls and courtyards around the central sanctuary; two more small temples nestle among the nearby trees. For a final Jain temple visit, see Varkana's well-preserved **Parshvanatha Temple** (15th century).

Beside the lake at rural **Nagda,** the exquisite, intricately carved tenth-century **Sasbahu temples** bear witness to the scale of Hindu achievement in northern India and its destruction by Muslim invaders.

You can walk a good portion of Kumbhalgarh's massive walls, enjoying views of the **Aravalli Mountains.**

At **Eklingji** village, you can witness *puja* (worship) at two temples: Lakulisha (972) and Ekalinga (15th century), whose elaborately screened Shiva image is highly revered by all Sisodias; major pujas take place throughout the day on Mondays, the special day for Shiva.

Rajsamand Lake was created by Maharana Faj Singh to help prevent drought. Waterside pavilions (1660), carved with Krishna scenes, commemorate his marriage to a Kishangarh princess to save her from Mogul clutches. Enjoy the views from Digambara Jain temple.

Shri Nathji Temple at **Nathdwara** is a pilgrimage center for devotees of Krishna, whose image is from Mathura; there is an elaborate puja here at sunset. The *pitchwais* (cloth paintings) on sale have decorative value only. Nearby, **Haldighati** is where, in 1576, Udaipur's hero, Maharana Pratap Singh, denied the Moguls (led by the Jaipur ruler) their victory.

As you travel east from Udaipur, you come first to **Ahah,** the site of the ancient capital of Mewar. The Sisodias' royal cremation ground has elegant cenotaphs, especially that dedicated to Rana Amer Singh I (1621).

Rajasthan's most spectacular fort-city, **Chittaurgarh** was founded by Bappa Rawal in A.D. 728 on a wide, natural ridge rising from the plains. Three bloody sieges—by Ala-ud-din Khilji of Delhi in 1303, Bahadur Shah of Gujarat in 1535 and Akbar in 1567, when the capital was moved to Udaipur—caused thousands of soldiers' deaths and women's *johar* (ritual mass suicide), but they have only increased its Rajput romance. Inside the massive gateways, see the Palace of Rana Kumbha (1433–1468), the towers of Fame (12th century) and Victory (1457–1468), good temples, lakes, *sati* stones, and other buildings.

Sacred cows at Nathdwara's decorated fort

Until recently, **Bundi** seemed frozen in time. Visitors to the hilltop Taragarh Fort (1342), City Palace (begun 1580), Chatar Mahal palace (1660), and Raniji-ki-Baori step-well (1699) in the bazaar, all built by the Hara Chauhan Rajputs, can also see restored *havelis* along the main street, some now housing restaurants and crafts stores.

The thriving industrial town of **Kotah,** on the banks of the Chambal River, has a charming old quarter. City Palace (begun 1625) has remarkable murals and inlay work, and houses the Maharao Madho Singh Museum *(Closed Fri.),* which has a superb collection of deadly looking weapons and royal artifacts. The weaving village of **Kaithoon** and the temples of Jhalrapatan and Baroli are nearby. ∎

Nathdwara

🅰 129 D3

Haldighati

🅰 129 D3

Ahah

🅰 129 D3

✉ 2 miles (3 km) E of Udaipur

🕐 Closed Fri.

💲 $

Chittaurgarh

🅰 129 D3

✉ 80 miles (120 km) E of Udaipur

💲 $

A walk around Jodhpur

Rising up from the dusty desert, the great sandstone walls of Jodhpur city enclose a maze of bazaars and lanes crowded with people and camels that huddle around the base of a magnificent fort built on a soaring bluff. In 1549, Rao Jodha made this the capital of his powerful, ever warring Rathore clan's Marwar (Land of Death) state. Today, expanded Jodhpur is Rajasthan's second largest city, after Jaipur.

To explore its ancient core, begin by taking a rickshaw up to the old city and paying the driver's fee. Through **Nagauri Gate ❶**, one of seven in the 6-mile-long (10 km) city wall, a steep, zigzag path leads to the fort entrance. On the way, **Jaswant Thada ❷**, the royal cremation ground, is on the right; the white marble memorial (1899) is to Jaswant Singh II. As you pass through the sixth massive defense gateway, **Loha Pol ❸**, notice the handprints of royal wives who committed *sati* (self-immolation on their husband's funeral pyre).

Meherangarh Fort ❹ *(Closed 1–2:30 p.m.)* combines serious defense with refined courtly elegance. Beyond Suraj Pol is the palace area, now the Meherangarh Museum. From the interconnecting courtyards you can enjoy fairy-tale views of the sandstone walls, whose windows are carved into such delicate *jali* (lattice) work that they look like lace.

Inside, an organized route takes you through **Moti Mahal** (Pearl Palace, 1581–1595) and **Phool Mahal** (Flower Palace, 1730–1750, decorated 1873–1895), both of which have exquisite painted ceilings and walls, with dancing girls, deities, and proud Jodhpur rulers. **Moti Vilas** (1638–1678) houses the marble coronation seat on which all rulers except Jodha have

---

- 🅜 See area map pages 128–29
- ▶ Nagauri Gate
- ⬌ About 4 miles (6 km)
- 🕓 3–4 hours
- ▶ Umaid Bhawan Palace

NOT TO BE MISSED
- Meherangarh Fort
- Markets around the Clock Tower
- Umaid Bhawan Palace

Jodhpur's Meharangarh Fort, built on a natural bluff in the desert, glows in the evening sunlight and offers paternal protection, even today, to the thriving city outside its walls.

been (and continue to be) crowned. This and the adjacent *Zenana* (women's quarters) court have especially fine jali-work. In **Sheesh Mahal** (1707–1724) and **Rang Mahal,** see how inlay and mirrors are used in the decoration. The swords and shields in **Sileh Khana** (the armory) are more works of art than war implements. Finally, the sumptuous interior of **Takhat Vilas** (1843–1873) has jolly dancing-girl murals. Do not miss the splendid silk Mogul tent, booty from a raid on Delhi, nor the terrace with its ancient cannon and magnificent views.

To walk down into the city, take the path beside the painted building at the U-bend above the fort shops. At the bottom, wind your way through narrow alleys to the central Sardar Bazar and its landmark **Clock Tower** ❺—this is not a large area, and you will not get lost—to see street barbers, waterpot sellers, and **Tulahti Mahal** (1638–1681), a palace turned into a women's hospital.

A wide road leads straight to **Sojati Gate**

❻, where good locally made *bandhani* (tie-dye) cotton is sold. From here, take a rickshaw through the New City, pausing to enjoy the Victorian bric-a-brac in the **museum** ❼ in Umaid Gardens, and the crazy Anglo-Rajput style of the **Judicial Court** (1893–96). (Agree on a price with your rickshaw driver in advance, pay on completion, and add a tip if appropriate; he waits while you make visits.)

To end, sweep up the hill to the 347-room **Umaid Bhawan Palace** ❽ (1929–1944). Designed by H. V. Lanchester, it combines beaux-arts with art deco, Western lifestyles with strict *purdah*, and tempers high European 1930s style with Rajput royal taste. It is now divided into private palace, public museum, and deluxe hotel. The massive bronze front doors lead to a grand hall with sweeping marble stairway, circular basement swimming pool, and grand pillared hotel terrace, ideal for refreshment. The **museum** section includes the Durbar Hall, miniature paintings, armor, and fine clocks. ■

Around Jodhpur

Sandstone mansions coated in lacelike carving testify to wealth gleaned from the trade routes.

ACROSS THE DRY AND DUSTY THAR DESERT—WHICH CAN BE crossed by car, train, jeep, or camel safari—lie isolated towns whose buildings reflect past wealth accumulated by virtue of their position on one of the world's great east–west trading routes.

Mandor
🏔 129 D4
✉ 5 miles (8 km)
    N of Jodhpur

Osian
🏔 129 D4
✉ 40 miles (64 km)
    N of Jodhpur

Deshnoke
🏔 129 D5
✉ 125 miles (199 km)
    N of Jodhpur

Bikaner
🏔 129 D5
✉ 145 miles (231 km)
    N of Jodhpur

As you head north from Jodhpur, you soon arrive at **Mandor,** where the Parihar Rajputs ruled Marwar from the sixth century until the Rathores toppled them in 1381. The fort is gone, but Rathore royal cenotaphs stand in lush Mandor Gardens; one is dedicated to Maharaja Ajit Singh (1724), who also built the pleasure palace.

Rajasthan's largest group of early Jain and Brahmanical temples (8th–11th centuries) stands on the outskirts of **Osian**. Most temples stand on a platform, have a curved tower, and are very finely carved.

The Karni Mata Temple at **Deshnoke** may not be a first choice for sightseeing: It swarms with holy rats. Devotees believe departing souls can evade the wrath of Yama, god of death, by reincarnation as a rat. The temple is dedi-

cated to Bikaner's patron goddess, who is an incarnation of Durga.

To the far north of Jodhpur, reached across arid scrub and sand, **Bikaner** is less picturesque than Jodhpur and Jaisalmer (see p. 143) but just as interesting; it also has fewer visitors and a choice of palaces—hotels in town and lakeside at Gajner. Founded in 1488 by Bhika, sixth son of Rao Jodha of Jodhpur, it quickly benefited from the lucrative trade route. Junagarh Fort (1588–1593), built by Raja Rai Singh, one of Akbar's generals, protects beautiful, treasure-filled palaces: Chandra Mahal has Bhika's bed, exotic Anup Mahal the Coronation Hall enriched with ornamental lacquer work. Inside the Old City's pink sandstone wall, wander the lanes to find the piazza lined with merchants' houses and, in the southeast corner, two Jain temples with brightly colored murals. Don't miss the fine stone carvings at the **Ganga Golden Jubilee Museum** (*Closed Sun.*), or Sir Samuel Swinton Jacob's Anglo-Rajput **Lallgarh Palace,** begun in 1881 and now a hotel (see p. 352).

Northwest of Jodhpur, **Nagaur,** is a rich combination of grand mosques and painted palaces that reflect its Muslim and Hindu rulers. The town is the backdrop to a businesslike Cattle Fair (*Jan.–Feb.*), when thousands arrive to trade cattle, camels, and Nagaur's famously stout bullocks, with time off for dancing and racing.

Just west of Jodhpur, overlooking the artificial lake of Devi Kund Sagar, stand the magnificent, often domed, marble and sandstone royal **cenotaphs**. Farther out, a royal hunting ground is now preserved and protected as the **Gagner Wildlife Sanctuary**. Here you can see *nilgai,* black buck, antelope, wild boar, *chinkara,* gazelles, and in winter, important migratory birds such as the Siberian grouse.

To the west of Jodhpur, lying on the route to Jaisalmer, is **Barmer's** quiet crafts center. It leaps into life as thousands of Rajasthanis arrive for the annual Tilwara Cattle Fair (*Jan.*), the largest in Rajasthan and, so far, less commercialized than Pushkar's Camel Fair.

At **Pokaran,** a modest version of Jaisalmer (see below) with fewer visitors, you can explore the ornate, red-sandstone fort and its splendid *havelis* (mansions).

The fortified desert city of **Jaisalmer** is built of fragile, golden sandstone, often exquisitely carved. It has stood isolated in the Thar Desert since its founding by Rawal Jaisal, a Bhatti Rajput, in 1156. Despite its turbulent history, it thrived thanks to the lucrative trade routes from India to Persia, Arabia, Egypt, Africa, and Europe. More recently, when Western tourists discovered its romantic beauty, it was threatened, first with unsympathetic new buildings, then with an increased water consumption that has brought it to near collapse. Valiant work to save the city is being done by the British-based charity, Jaipur in Jeopardy. You can witness their efforts as you visit the fortifications, fort-palace, and several of the grand havelis. The colorful Desert Festival (*Jan.–Feb.*) is aimed at tourists.

A camel safari and sleeping under the desert stars around a campfire can be magical. Safaris last from one to four days and usually head out from Jaisalmer toward the **Sam Dunes,** Amar Sagar lake, and Lodurva's Jain temples or the magnificent royal cenotaphs at Bada Bagh; enthusiasts can ride to Bikaner or Jodhpur. Remember to bring high-factor sun lotion for days and warm woolens for nights.

On a village jeep safari you can learn about desert wildlife and the local Bishnoi tribe: See the tribes thatched huts, learn about their herbal remedies, and appreciate their crafts (often on sale). Trips can be arranged by your hotel. ■

Nagaur
🅰 129 D4
✉ 84 miles (135 km) N of Jodhpur

Gagner Wildlife Sanctuary
🅰 129 D5
✉ 164 miles (263 km) N of Jodhpur

Barmer
🅰 129 C4
✉ 146 miles (233 km) W of Jodhpur

Rajput cenotaphs near Devi Kund Sagar

Pokaran
🅰 129 C4
✉ 116 miles (185 km) NW of Jodhpur

Jaisalmer
🅰 129 C4
✉ 184 miles (295 km) NW of Jodhpur

Sam Dunes
🅰 129 B4
✉ 209 miles (335 km) NW of Jodhpur

The crafts & traditions of Rajasthan

Every town in Rajasthan has its markets, brimful with life, especially toward the end of the day when the heat is less oppressive. Walking through them is a treat, particularly to see all the different crafts on sale. Handsome men, their weatherworn faces framed by magenta turbans, bargain for handstitched leather shoes. Family expeditions choose the embroidered *pilo* (head veil), *choli* (blouse), and *ghaghra* (full skirt) for a bride-to-be. Gaggles of girls buy yet more lacquer bangles. Peek behind the shops and you see a silversmith or a painter; cast your eyes up and you see yards of tie-dye drying on the rooftops. As night falls, itinerant puppeteers set up their show, certain that they will lure children away from television for one night.

Tourism has helped revive several almost lost traditions. In Jaipur the art of block-printing on cotton, whose heyday was the 18th century, thrives once more. Recipes for natural dyes are being rediscovered, blocks of teak are being carved with new and traditional designs, and printers can barely keep up with demand. Another revival is Jaipur pottery, a softpaste pottery decorated with azure blue flowers and patterns.

In Jaipur and Bikaner, you find the best *meenakari* work, the art of enameling that used to depend upon court patronage. The best of these delicate patterns of birds and flowers in ruby red, deep green, and peacock blue often remain hidden on the reverse of gem-studded jewelry.

Jodhpur is known for its *bandhani*, the ancient Indian technique of tie-dyeing fabrics found throughout Rajasthan and Gujarat. Each community has its own designs. The merchant supplies the fabric to a family, usually Muslim. The father draws the pattern on the fabric using tiny dots. The women and children bind the cloth tightly, following the pattern, dye the fabric, then remove the strings. The process may be repeated with a darker color to build up the pattern. Jodhpur is also a center for wooden lacquer work, especially bangles and boxes.

Helped by some dynamic Delhi patrons, miniature-painting is reaching new peaks. Rajasthan's many painting schools declined in the 19th century, but artists are now practicing this very disciplined art using both traditional iconography and innovative designs.

Another joy of Rajasthan is the quantity of traditional entertainment still in evidence: Songs and stories are often so simple that mime is sufficient to explain them. In a land where evening entertainment is minimal, hotels often employ talented families of entertainers to put on a show for their guests. *Bhopas* (balladeers), originally from Marwar, have a visual aid, a *phad* (scroll-painting); while the father sings the story, the mother holds a lantern and they dance. Folk dances often relate to Holi, Gangaur, and other Rajasthan festivals: the *gingad* is accompanied by the big *chang* drum, the *teratali* is more like ritual acrobatics than dancing, and the *ghoomar-gair* is Rajasthan's version of the age-old stick dance. But the puppet show is always the favorite. *Kathputli*, as it is known, is performed by itinerant families. Drawing back the embroidered curtain known as the Taj Mahal, they back up the antics of their beautifully carved, painted, and costumed puppets with music, song, and high-pitched yelps. ■

Bold color and a strong sense of pattern distinguish this traditional Udaipur textile decorated with a row of regal Rajput warriors.

The rich red tones of this densely and laboriously worked cotton patchwork fabric from Jaisalmer (above), which may have been made for a dowry, contrasts with the simplicity of a street tailor from Fatehpur (right), who would be able to run up workaday cotton shirts and pants in a few hours. A group of Jodhpur men (below) swirl their long white robes as they take part in the stick dance, alternately crashing their sticks to the ground and against their partners' sticks.

Ahmedabad

THIS DYNAMIC CITY IS THE CAPITAL OF GUJARAT, A MODERN state with a very ancient history. It comprises three distinct geographical regions: hilly peninsula Saurashtra, barren Kachchh with its Rann (desert), and the central, fairly flat portion. As the country's prime producer of cotton and groundnut oil, and its second greatest producer of tobacco, Gujarat is India's wealthiest state. A visit to Ahmedabad's formidable and distinctive Islamic monuments, with their remarkably fine *jali*-work, and to its especially good museum, makes a perfect springboard for exploring this rarely visited state.

Ahmedabad

🗺 129 C2

Ahmedabad Tourist Office

✉ H. K. House, off Ashram Rd., S of Gandhi Bridge

☎ 079-6589172

THE OLD CITY

The city's ancient citadel, **Bhadra,** is a good place to start. When Ahmad Shah became Sultan of Gujarat in 1411, he moved the capital here from Patan (see p. 149) and built this solid, red stone citadel (not open to the public, but it is usually possible to climb the staircase inside the main gate to enjoy good views from the roof). Trade flourished, boosted by east–west trade to the ports, and the building of mosques followed. In this area, you can see Alif Shah's green-and-white mosque in front of the citadel

Akbar finally absorbed Gujarat into his vast empire in 1572 to benefit from its wealth and its location on the *hajj* (pilgrimage) route to Mecca. The mosque is isolated on a traffic island, but it is well worth risking the traffic to enjoy its ten magnificent, probably unequaled, *jali* (carved latticework) screens, especially those in the western wall (these can easily be seen from outside; the mosque itself is closed to women). Observe how local Hindu and Jain craftsmen have been permitted to carve heroes and animals from Hindu mythology.

Walk along Mahatma Gandhi Road to find more sites dating back to Ahmad Shah. First is his monumental **Teen Darwaja** (triple gateway) in Khas Bazar. Next is his magnificent **Jama Masjid** (completed 1424); go up the great steps with the faithful to see the courtyard, prayer hall (elaborate carving), and Zenana jali screens. Finally, his family **mausoleum** (1442, closed to women) and that of his wives stand in Manek Chowk among the streets of jewelers, dyers, and cloth merchants. See the Hindu styles and the fine inlay decoration.

To finish, take three short detours to Rani Sipri's very Hindu **mosque** (1514), the carved wooden **Swaminarayan Temple,** and surrounding traditional Guajarat *havelis.*

and Ahmad Shah's small, private mosque by Victoria Gardens, whose intricate *mihrabs* contrast with Sanskrit inscriptions on stones from an earlier Hindu temple.

Stay in this area to visit **Sidi Sayyid's Mosque** (1573), built shortly after the Mogul emperor

This charming mosaic of a pair of doves can be found in the Calico Museum of Textiles.

2001 earthquake

At 8:46 a.m. on January 26, 2001, western India experienced an earthquake that measured 7.7 on the Richter scale. Its epicenter was near Bhuj, a timeless, medieval walled town in the Kachchh (Kutch) region of Gujarat. Shock waves reached as far as Chennai and Nepal. Bhuj and more than 300 villages nearby were wiped out, and the whole state was affected. More than 20,000 people died, and many more were left homeless. In all, 1,016 villages and eight cities suffered substantial damage. In the capital, Ahmedabad, 179 buildings were affected. Plans have been made to rebuild Gujarat, transforming it from a medieval area into a modern one. ∎

Huge, finely tuned kites star in the annual kite festival.

Calico Museum of Textiles

- ✉ Sarabhai Foundation, Shahibagh
- 🕐 Closed Wed. Tours 10:30–11:30 a.m. & 2:45–3:45 p.m.

Shreyas Folk Art Museum

- ✉ Near Shreyas Railway Crossing
- 🕐 Closed Mon.
- 💲 $

Tribal Research Institute Museum

- ✉ Gujarat Vidyapith, Ashram Rd.
- 🕐 Closed Sun.

N.C. Mehta Gallery

- ✉ Indology Institute, Radhakrishnan Rd., near Gujarat University
- 🕐 Closed Mon.

Vishalla village

- ✉ Sarkhej Rd., Vasana

Gandhi Smarak

- ✉ Sabarmati Ashram, Ashram Rd.
- 💲 $

Sardar Patel Memorial Museum

- ✉ Near Shahibagh Rd.
- 🕐 Closed Mon.
- 💲 $

Adalaj Vav

- ✉ 11 miles (17 km) N of Ahmedabad on Ajmer Rd.

OTHER AHMEDABAD SIGHTS

After 1630, a run of famines, Marathas, and Muslims turned the city's fortunes. In 1817, under British influence, modern machinery made Ahmedabad the industrial powerhouse of the East. Mahatma Gandhi's arrival (see p. 150) further boosted its textile production and political power. Thus, of Ahmedabad's many museums, the most important is the **Calico Museum of Textiles,** where guides explain a dazzling variety and quality of weaving, embroidery, mirrorwork, tie-dye, printing, and skillful *ikat* weave, all collected by the Sarabhai textile magnates and kept in their foundation.

For other specialist interests, visit the **Shreyas Folk Art Museum,** displaying Gujarati crafts, the **Tribal Museum,** about the various peoples of Gujarat, the **Kite Museum,** and the **N. C. Mehta Gallery,** with its collection of top-quality Indian miniature paintings. Just outside town, specially built **Vishalla village** combines traditional huts, craftsmen (potters, weavers, etc.), a splendid museum of Gujarati metalware, and a superb restaurant. Le Corbusier enthusiasts can see several of his buildings here (see pp. 88–89).

Ahmedabad played a vital role in India's freedom movement (see p. 150). You can visit the Charles Correa-designed **Gandhi Smarak** in the gardens of Mahatma's Sabarmati Ashram, where Gandhi lived from 1917 to 1930; letters and photographs tell the freedom story, while a sound and light show recounts his life story. To complete the picture, the **Sardar Patel Memorial Museum** remembers the politician and freedom fighter who was deputy to Jawaharlal Nehru.

For a final taste of past Muslim glory and Hindu craftsmanship, Ahmedabad has three multi-layered, galleried, and elaborately carved step-wells called *vavs.* In town is **Dada Harini Vav** (1435), and nearby is **Mata Bhavani Vav** (11th century); on the road to Gandhinagar is the best of all, **Adalaj Vav** (1498). ■

North of Ahmedabad

DESPITE THE DEVASTATION OF THE 2001 EARTHQUAKE, LIFE goes bravely on. India's almost annual experience of natural disasters (flood, drought, famine, or cyclone) resulted in an admirably quick recovery of infrastructure, and there are still interesting places to visit.

Gandhinagar, named after the Mahatma, was India's second planned town and, like Chandigarh (see p. 120), was designed by Le Corbusier, assisted by B. V. Doshi. Greenery has considerably softened the impact of this *"cité idéale."*

Continuing farther, to the northwest of Ahmedabad, visit the Surya Temple at **Modhera,** begun in 1027 by Bhimdev I. It was an early achievement of the rich Solanki rulers (11th–13th centuries) and, despite its dilapidation after Mahmud of Ghazni's attack (see p. 37), remains one of Gujarat's great Hindu temples. It was financed by public subscription and built by voluntary labor, and its monumental conception is matched by rich ornamentation. From the huge tank with its double flights of steps, two *mandapas* (halls) lead to the sanctuary; here, note especially the carvings of Agni (south) and Surya (north). Enjoy these in the glow of sunset.

Still farther north you will come to **Anahilvada,** the Solanki capital sacked repeatedly by Muslim marauders, then abandoned for Ahmedabad. Among the remains of the fortifications, temples, and tank is the Solanki queen Udaimati's exquisite Ran-ki-vav (circa 1080), Gujarat's finest step-well. In the Sadvi Wada area of the bustling adjoining city of **Patan,** founded in 1796, watch the *ikat* weave being created in one of its finest forms, the *patola* silk sari; see also carved *havelis,* domes, and Jain temples.

Northeast of Ahmedabad, at **Taranga** you'll find a well-preserved Jain temple (1166), dedicated to Ajitanatha, the second Tirthankara, and built by the Solanki ruler Kumarapala. It's well worth the detour. Join Jain pilgrims for the hill climb. At **Kumbharia,** the five Solanki-period Jain temples (1062–1231) rival Mount Abu's; each is built entirely of marble and stands in its own court. ■

Gandhinagar
- 129 D2
- ✉ 14 miles (23 km) N of Ahmedabad

Modhera
- 129 C3
- ✉ 66 miles (105 km) NW of Ahmedabad

Anahilvada
- ✉ 106 miles (169 km) N of Ahmedabad

Patan
- 129 C3
- ✉ 106 miles (169 km) N of Ahmedabad

Taranga
- 129 C3
- ✉ 84 miles (135 km) NE of Ahmedabad

Kumbharia
- ✉ 118 miles (189 km) NE of Ahmedabad

A weaver creates the soft pattern of *ikat*-weave silk.

Mahatma Gandhi

One of the most influential men of the 20th century, Mohandas Karamchand Gandhi (1869–1948) was born in Porbandar (see p. 151) in western Gujarat, where his father and grandfather were *diwans* of the princely state. Having trained as a lawyer in London, he worked in South Africa, where his passive resistance against the government's color and race prejudice prompted Bengali poet Rabindranath Tagore (see p. 123) to give him the title Mahatma (Great Soul).

Simple in his lifestyle, Mahatma Gandhi sits cross-legged, wrapped in a shawl, to write.

Returning home in 1915, Gandhi joined India's struggle for freedom and founded the Sabarmati Ashram in Ahmedabad. Two years later he moved in.

Gandhi began a nonviolent moral protest against oppression, known to Indians as *satyagraha* (literally "grasping truth"), and to the British as civil disobedience. It meant peacefully defying laws and willingly taking punishment. Then, appalled by the atrocities at Amritsar generated by his peaceful, national, one-day strike in 1919 (see p. 123), he waged his Non-Cooperation Movement of 1920–22.

Gandhi's aim was to use *ahimsa* (nonviolence) and *satya* (truth) to achieve a united, independent India. When he spun cotton and wove the thread into cloth, it symbolized his vision of an autonomous, self-reliant India free of foreign domination. When he rejected

European clothes for the homespun cotton *dhoti* and shawl in 1921, his popularity soared with most Indians. Believing in the equality of all, he tried to give the untouchables dignity by renaming them *harijans* (children of God).

Gandhi had a strong, charismatic character matched by an austere code of living and huge ambitions for India. He campaigned relentlessly, fighting for *swadeshi*, the rejection of the imported cotton that had devastated India's weavers. He also supported the Congress Party president, Jawaharlal Nehru, when, on January 26, 1930, the resolution demanding complete independence was adopted.

That same year Gandhi launched a second civil disobedience campaign, given focus by the mass appeal of his Salt March, protesting against the British monopoly of salt production. On March 12, it left Ahmedabad amid Gandhi's rousing speeches for *swaraj* (freedom); a month later the protesters reached coastal Dandi, where they began to collect water and boil it to make illegal salt, thus expressing their objections to a system that touched every Indian household.

Salt was made illegally, saltworks were raided, government servants resigned, and on May 5 Gandhi was imprisoned. In January 1931, he and the British viceroy, Lord Irwin, signed a pact that led eventually to the Government of India Act of 1935.

During World War II, Gandhi introduced the "Quit India" slogan and worked to keep an undivided, free India. When Jinnah's call for "Direct Action" in 1946 provoked riots in Kolkata, Gandhi fasted until the violence had stopped. He again fasted for peace when, at partition, an estimated five million Hindus and Sikhs came into India, while the same number of Muslims left for Pakistan amid terrible bloodshed. On January 30, 1948, a Hindu extremist angered by Gandhi's tolerance toward Muslims assassinated him in Delhi. Ironically, this dreadful act had the effect of finally quelling the violence. ■

India's last viceroy, Viscount Mountbatten, and his wife flank Gandhi at a meeting at the Viceroy's House, New Delhi, in 1947.

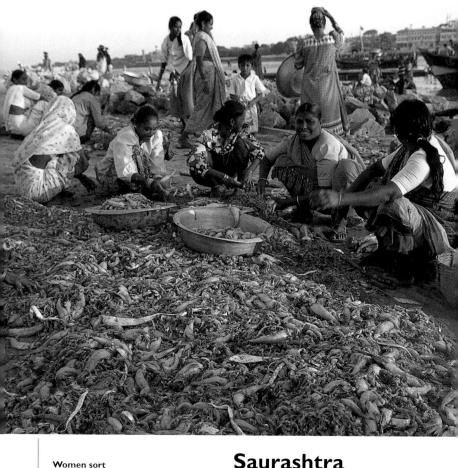

Saurashtra

THIS RURAL AREA OF GUJARAT FILLS THE KATHIAWAR
Peninsula bordered by the Gulf of Kachchh and Cambay and the
Arabian Sea. The ancient ports, forts, and temples recall occupants
of all faiths stretching back to the Harappans (see p. 26). In 1807 the
fragmented land of 220 petty states, many ruled by Rajputs, came
under British supremacy. The sights listed below are arranged in a
clockwise circle from Ahmedabad and are best visited in comfort
with a car and driver.

Saurashtra

⚑ 128 B2

**Ahmedabad
Tourist Office**

✉ H. K. House, Ashram
Rd., S of Gandhi
Bridge, Ahmedabad

☎ 079-6589172

SOUTHERN SAURASHTRA
On the road down toward Lothal,
you come first to **Sarkhej,** the site
of the tomb of Ahmad Shah's spiritual leader, Sheikh Ahmed Khattu
(1445). At Nal Sarovar Bird
Sanctuary you can see migrant
waterbirds *(Nov.–Feb.),* and at
Dholka (28 miles/44 km south of
Ahmedabad) there are three monu-

mental medieval mosques and a
beautiful wooden *haveli* temple to
visit. The remarkable and evocative
remains of **Lothal,** an excavated
Harappan port, include the dock
and the town's bazaars. The site
museum has jewelry, seals, and
weights and compasses.

At **Velavadar Black Buck
Sanctuary,** it's best to pay a guide

to learn more about the elegant Indian antelope (or black buck), traditionally protected by the Bishnoi tribe (see p. 143).

Founded in 1723 by Maharaja Bhavsinghji, the old city of **Bhavnagar,** a cotton-exporting port, has vibrant bazaars for silver, gold, cloth, and *bhandani* (tie-dyed fabrics). Exhibits at the Gandhi Smriti Museum range from Harappan terra-cottas to the story of Gandhi's life. From here you can visit **Palitana,** joining Jain pilgrims to climb their sacred hill of Shatrunjaya, dedicated to the saint Adinath; 900 little temples make its summit India's largest temple city.

The 8-mile-long (13 km) island of **Diu** was, with Goa and Daman, Portuguese until 1962. This is where to relax, enjoy the beaches and cafés, and rent a bicycle to see the old town and fort. Avoid holiday seasons, when Gujaratis flock here to enjoy unrestricted alcohol.

Sadly, there is more myth than reality at **Somnath Temple.** The early versions are part of Hindu mythology; the later ones were successively destroyed by marauding Muslims. Today's temple (1950) was built by Sardar Patel, keeping to the plan of the great Solanki temple at Modhera (see p. 149).

The last of the southern sites is **Sasan Gir National Park,** the final Indian refuge of the Asiatic lion, which roamed northern India's forests until the 1880s. About 300 lions (the numbers are rising) live in 100 square miles (260 sq km), together with panthers and the local Maldhari cattle breeders. It is best to visit from November to mid-June—the later the better for seeing lions.

WESTERN SAURASHTRA

From **Junagadh,** the ancient capital of Gujarat, Jain pilgrims climb their sacred Mount Girnar. Junagadh's old citadel, Uparkot, once a Maurya and Gupta stronghold, is reached through openings in solid rock—three gateways and massive walls; features inside include third- to fourth-century caves with richly carved columns, and two 11th-century *vavs* (stepwells). In town, the Junagadh rulers' mausoleums are some of Gujarat's finest. Out of town, on the way to Mount Girnar's 12th-century temples, a modern building encloses a boulder inscribed with Ashoka's edicts (see p. 31).

Porbandar, now renowned as the birthplace of Gandhi, is a port with ancient trading links to Africa

Sarkhej
- 129 C2
- 5 miles (8 km) SW of Ahmedabad

Nal Sarovar Bird Sanctuary
- 30 miles (48 km) SW of Ahmedabad

Lothal
- 129 C2
- 66 miles (105 km) S of Ahmedabad
- $

Velavadar Black Buck Sanctuary
- 129 C2
- 113 miles (181 km) S of Ahmedabad

Bhavnagar
- 129 C2
- 129 miles (204 km) S of Ahmedabad

Diu
- 129 C1

Somnath
- 128 B1

Sasan Gir National Park
- 129 C1
- Closed July–Oct.
- $

Porbandar
- 128 B2

Junagadh
- 128 B2

Climb the hill at Palitana for beautiful views like this one.

Daria Rajmahal
- ✉ 54 miles (95 km) from Diu Airport
- 🕐 Closed university holidays

Anut Nivas Khambala
- ✉ 15 miles (25 km) E of Porbandar

Kirti Mandir
- 🕐 Closed sunset to sunrise

Dwarka
- ▲ 128 B2

Jamnagar
- ▲ 128 B2
Lakhota Fort
- 🕐 Closed Wed.
- 💲 $

Rajkot
- ▲ 129 C2
Rajkot Tourist Office
- ✉ Off Jawahar Rd., N of Sanganwa Chowk
- ☎ 0281-234507

Kaba Gandhi no Delo
- ✉ Off Ghitake Rd., Rajkot

Watson Museum
- 🕐 Closed Wed., Sat.
- 💲 $

Morbi
- ▲ 129 C2
Dubargadh Waghaji
- 🕐 Courtyards only

New Palace
- ✉ New Palace, Morbi
- 🕐 Write to request a visit

and Arabia. Under British protection the port prospered. The fine stone was exported to Bombay and Karachi, and the city's rulers added two waterfront palaces: **Daria Rajmahal** and **Anut Nivas Khambala** (1927, museum in the Rajput Room). Gandhi's simple, unfurnished home, the **Kirti Mandir,** is where he lived until his family moved to Rajkot (see below). The neighboring temple, Kirti Mandir (1950), was constructed to commemorate him.

Devotees of Krishna believe he fled Mathura to make **Dwarka** his capital. Pilgrims flock here, especially for the Hindu festivals of Shivratri *(Feb.–March)* and Janmashtami *(Aug.–Sept.),* the latter of which celebrates Krishna's birthday.

Maharaja Ranjit Singh, who played cricket for England with W. G. Grace, gave **Jamnagar** city its first boost into modernity. Head for the old city built beside Ranmal Lake and protected by **Lakhota** and **Bhujia forts.** Inside the walls is Chandni Bazar, with its ancient *havelis* and spectacularly decorated Jain temples dedicated to Adinath and Shantinath; there are glorious murals inside. See also **Ratan Bai Mosque,** with its inlaid doors, Ranjit Singh's sweeping Willingdon Crescent at Chelmsford Market, and enjoy the excellent local *band-hana* work.

CENTRAL SAURASHTRA
The teeming industrial city of **Rajkot,** once the British headquarters of the Western States, is where Gandhi's family moved from Porbandar in 1881. Their home was the modest **Kaba Gandhi no Delo,** which can be found in the old city, among traditional wooden Gujarati houses with carved shutters and stained glass. In the **Watson Museum** (1988), there is

a variety of Harappan, medieval, and Rajput treasures, plus a splendid statue of Queen-Empress Victoria (1899) by Alfred Gilbert, creator of London's bronze statue "Eros." Other colonial buildings include Alfred High School (1875) and Rajkumar College (1870), designed to be Gujarat's equivalent of Eton.

Wankaner was the capital of the former state, where Gandhi's father was once *diwan* (chief minister) to the maharaja. Under British protection, Maharaja Amarshinghi *(R.1881–1948)* transformed the city into a model of self-reforming enterprise and helped the state engineer design his own palace, Ranjit Vilas (1907–1914). This is a landmark building, which manages to combine Victorian Gothic, Italianate, and Mogul styles. Inside is a remarkable marble double spiral staircase. You can stay in the palace's outer buildings.

In this area of Saurashtra, keep a look out for *pallias,* tombstones commemorating bravery. Various images are used to describe the manner of death: A carved hand records a *sati* (self-immolation); a mounted bard with spear indicates a poet who committed suicide because his master defaulted on a loan for which the poet was surety.

Dominating access to the Gujarat peninsula, tiny **Morbi** state was threatened until Thakur Sabhi Waghaji *(R.1897–1948)* gave it stability and modernization, with a streetcar line and railroad. He was also the man responsible for two palaces: **Dubargadh Waghaji** (1880), in Venetian Gothic style, and **New Palace** (1931–1944), a stunning art deco building with an immaculate interior. **Halvad** has a lakeside palace and plenty of pallias, while **Dhrangadhra** is home to herds of wild asses that also live in the Rann of Kachchh. ■

Kachchh

THE SALT FLATS OF THIS WILD, ARID, AND ISOLATED AREA dotted with villages are the world's largest breeding area for flamingoes, and a refuge for the prancing Asiatic wild asses. Up in the north, the marshy Great and Little Ranns of Kachchh (Kutch) flood completely in a good monsoon, making Kachchh an island; in the past they cut off would-be Muslim invaders. Although nominally part of various empires, the area has remained highly individual in its traditions and crafts—the women wear fantastic embroidered clothes—and highly independent in its maritime trading with Africa, the Gulf, and the Indian coast.

In Gujarat's Kachchh area, famous for its textiles, women wear stunning *bandhani* or embroidered shawls every day.

The wealth of Kachchh's second city, **Mandvi,** mostly came from its role as the port used by Moguls for their vast annual *hajj* expeditions to Mecca—more than 800 ships went in 1819, and the great *dhows* are still built here today. You can also see Vijay Vilas palace, and the grand, elaborately carved palaces of the great merchants including that of Ram Singh's with its later Dutch facade.

For the adventurous traveler, the rewards of visiting Kachchh's **villages** should easily compensate for basic accommodations. Taking a guide with you from the Bhuj Tourist Office (and a permit if you want to travel north), you might include **Mundra,** near the Jain temples of Bhadreswar, **Bhujodi,** with its weavers, or **Anjar,** with its bright embroideries. Along the way you can see various tribal communities, each with their distinctive dress: the pastoral Rabari, known for their embroidery, the Bharvad, who came from Mathura, the nomadic Ahir cattle-breeders, and the Charans, whose women are often worshiped for their association with the goddess Parvati. ∎

Bhuj

🅰 128 B2

Bhuj Tourist Office

✉ Aina Mahal

☎ (02832) 24910

🕐 Closed Thurs.

Festivals

Bhuj, Jan.–Feb.: five-day celebration of traditional Kachchh music, dance, and crafts.

Vadodara & area

Vadodara

⚠ 129 D2

Vadodara Tourist Information

✉ Train station

☎ 0265-329656

🕑 Closed Sun.

Lakshmi Vilas

✉ Nehru Rd.

🕑 Closed Mon.

💲 $

Maharaja Fateh Singh Museum

✉ On the grounds of Lakshmi Vilas

🕑 Closed Mon.

💲 $

THIS STRIP OF RARELY VISITED LAND, SO SIGNIFICANT WHEN the British established their first trading station at Surat in 1614, is now a backwater. However, there are several places that make interesting stops for intrepid, seasoned travelers on the way to Mumbai.

On the drive through lush country from Ahmedabad, the forgotten Muslim city of **Champaner** is a detour before Vadodara. After Muhammad Begada took the Chauhan Rajput stronghold in 1484, he spent 23 years building it up as his capital, then abandoned it. Having roamed the historic walls, gateways, mosques, and tombs, you can visit the Jains' sacred Pavagadh hill, rising behind.

Vadodara (Baroda) is an ever expanding industrial town,

Extravagant, expensive Lakshmi Vilas palace is a romantic cocktail of Rajput, Mogul, and Jain architecture, with a dash of Gothic and classical.

redeemed by the fine old *havelis* and bazaars in its old town and by the well-maintained parks, lakes, and public buildings added by Baroda state's enlightened and extravagant rulers known as Gaekwads ("protectors of cows"). Start with the palace, or the reforming Gaekwad Maharaja Sayajirao's **Lakshmi Vilas** (1880–1890), now a hotel, reputedly the most expensive

building constructed by a private individual in the 19th century. Designed by Major Charles Mant, who went insane, and completed by Robert Fellowes Chisholm, this mixture of all Indian styles also has London stained glass, Venetian mosaics, and a garden designed by experts from London's Kew Gardens. More practically for his subjects, this Gaekwad built roads, railways, and hospitals, outlawed child marriage, and made school compulsory. Nearby, the **Maharaja Fateh Singh Museum** houses European art. See, too, Pratap Vilas (circa 1910), Makarpura Palace, the Kalabahavan Technical Institute (1922), the Vadodara Museum and Art Gallery's sculptures and miniature paintings, and the university's sculptures from Vadaval and Buddhist monuments from Devnimori. Do not miss Naulakhi Baoli, the royal mausoleum of Kirti Mandir, or Tambekarwada, a four-story haveli coated in murals.

Drive past Bharuch (Broach) and Surat, once considerable trading towns, neither merits a stop. Speed on to relaxed, quiet **Daman** (131 miles/208 km north of Mumbai) but be sure to avoid public holidays (see p. 341) when, like Diu (see p. 153), it is besieged by locals for its freely available alcohol. Daman was Portuguese from 1531 until 1961, and south of the Damanganga River, in **Moti Daman,** you will find grand walls, Portuguese mansions, and some of the best preserved churches in Asia. Nani Daman, on the north bank, has hotels, markets, and docks. ∎

While Mumbai buzzes with talk of futures, mergers, and Bollywood movie budgets, some of India's most spectacular Buddhist caves, early Hindu temples, and historic forts lurk in Maharashtra's dramatic landscape.

Mumbai & Maharashtra

A huge movie poster backs a Mumbai man.

Mumbai & Maharashtra

MAHARASHTRA SWEEPS FROM THE Arabian Sea across the coastal paddy fields and coconut groves of the Konkan, up across the rugged Western Ghats (Sahyadris), and into the heart of peninsular India.

This vast state, India's third largest in size and population, nevertheless has a unity. Its Marathi-speaking people share a common history, enriched by cultures to the north and south. After a period when Marahashtra was part of the Mauryan Empire (321–185 B.C.), successive Hindu dynasties held power for a thousand years until 1294, when the Yadavas yielded to the first of a string of Muslim rulers. The great port city of Bombay, now renamed Mumbai, rose toward the end of the 17th century, just when the warrior hero Shivaji (see p. 180) was consolidating the Maratha people of the area into a powerful nation. Despite defeat by the British in 1817, Shivaji's inspiration lives on; notice the plethora of statues of modern Maharashtra's founding father in downtown areas.

   Visitors often rush through Mumbai and on to other areas of India. This is a shame. Mumbai is not just about trading: Its treasures include remarkable early Buddhist cave sculptures, a deserted Portuguese fort more atmospheric than anything to be found at Old Goa, and a group of world-class High Victorian Gothic public buildings.

   Away from the seething life of the city, whose humidity climbs sharply between April and October, the most important trip inland is to the cave temples of Ellora (see pp. 176–77) and Ajanta (see pp. 178–79), whose paintings and sculptures are often said to be some of the greatest achievements in world art. If these and the other Buddhist sites in Mumbai have intrigued you, there are more caves to visit at Karla, Bhaja, and Bedsa, cut into the rock of the Western Ghats (see p. 183). But if you seek Raj charm in the cool hills, take a short train ride up to Matheran, Mahabaleshwar, or Pune, British hill stations now much loved by local

Maharashtrans, set in the heart of what was once Shivaji's Maratha confederacy. For a more adventurous trip, the new Konkan railroad (see pp. 204–205) and the hovercraft crossing Mumbai's harbor make an adventure southward easy; you can go on down to Goa, and extend your journey into a coastal trip right down to Kochi (see p. 207).

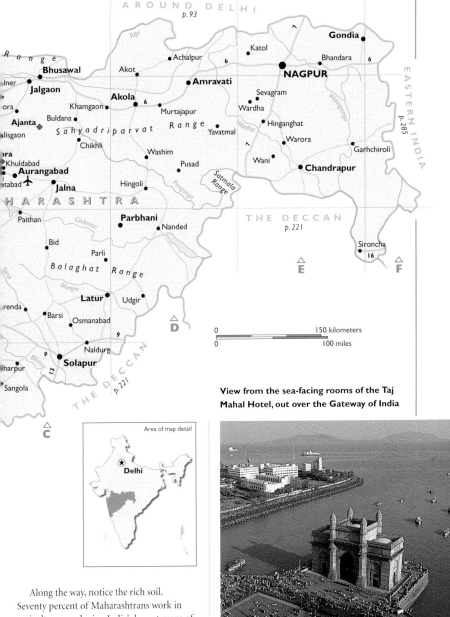

View from the sea-facing rooms of the Taj Mahal Hotel, out over the Gateway of India

Along the way, notice the rich soil. Seventy percent of Maharashtrans work in agriculture, producing India's largest crops of highly prized Alphonso mangoes, seedless grapes, Cavendish bananas, soft-seeded pomegranates, sugar, cashew nuts, and cotton. A convoy of bullock carts bringing in the cotton harvest at sunset is a memorable sight. ■

Mumbai's chief adornments are its billboard movie posters. They are often witty, sometimes hand-painted with great skill, occasionally three-dimensional.

Mumbai

Although Bombay's name was officially changed to Mumbai in 1995, to honor the goddess worshiped by early inhabitants here, the old name sticks. The first time you hear Mumbai used may well be after you arrive in this dynamic business capital of India. Mumbai, home to more than ten million people, houses the headquarters of almost all of India's major banks, financial institutions, insurance companies, and mutual funds. It has India's largest stock exchange, port, and movie industry (see box p. 161). Mumbai even has its own Manhattan-style high-rises, its own offshore oil fields, and *Verve*, its own answer to *Vanity Fair* magazine.

For a city that began as seven boggy, malarial islands, Mumbai has done well. The islands were part of the dowry of Portuguese Princess Catherine of Braganza when she married the English king Charles II, in 1662. In 1668 the British government leased them to the East India Company for £10 a year. The company, which had received its trading charter from Queen Elizabeth I in 1600, could make its own laws and collect all revenue of just under £3,000 per annum (the equivalent of about £300,000 or $480,000 today). Yet the climate was so unhealthy that of the 800 British living there in 1692, 700 died in that year.

fleeing Portuguese oppression in Goa, Arab traders, and others to settle in the city, so that by 1700 its population reached 120,000.

After the company lost its trade monopoly in 1813, the British presence increased. Trade boomed with China in cotton and opium, exchanged for the increasingly popular drink of tea. Fortunes were made. David Sassoon, whose Sephardic Jewish family eventually spread to Europe and America, arrived in 1833 and built up an international trading empire overseen by his eight sons, one of whom was knighted Sir Albert Sassoon of Kensington Gore in 1872.

Meanwhile, steamers brought out boatloads of single British women, known as the "fishing fleet," to supply the empire's men with wives. Bombay's railroad opened in 1853 (reaching the cotton-growing Deccan ten years later); the telegraph arrived in 1865, and the first cotton mill opened the following year. Sir Bartle Frere, governor 1862–67, gave Bombay its spacious streets and great Victorian buildings, and he began the land reclamation program that continues today. During this time the American Civil War closed the Confederacy ports in America, and Bombay traders quickly profited from this by supplying extra cotton to Britain.

When the Suez Canal opened in 1869, Bombay on the west coast became as important as Calcutta on the east. Today, this truly cosmopolitan city has moved with the times and held its position. It is India's most modern and international city, with the inevitable inequalities. Mumbai's rich are India's most ostentatiously rich; Mumbai's Dharavi area is India's largest and worst slum. ■

However, Bombay was soon the focus of India's west coast trade. Gerald Aungier, known as the "father of Bombay," was governor from 1672–77: He established the Courts of Justice and founded the company militia that became the East India Company Army. Most importantly, he actively encouraged Parsees from Gujarat, Banias (Hindu traders)

Bollywood—the Mumbai film industry

Mumbai's answer to Hollywood is the capital of the all-singing, all-dancing, all-shocking-color, not-much-plot Hindi movie. The huge, hand-painted advertising billboards all over India lure millions into the movie theaters every week to enjoy a sophisticated, slick, and perfectly timed mixture of heroism, romance, and fighting on wildly extravagant sets. Audiences may jeer at the villain, cheer the hero, and sing along with the songs.

Production is complex. Often, money is raised to fund just part of a movie then there is a pause while more financing is sought. Actors may be working concurrently on several movies. The essential music backing may be mimed by the beautiful star but sung by a favorite voice. To immerse yourself in India's foremost popular culture, go to a local movie theater. No one will mind if you do not watch all three hours of escapist entertainment. ■

This grand view of the Gateway of India and the Taj Mahal Hotel once greeted those arriving in India by ship.

Colaba & the Maidan

THIS IS NOT MUMBAI'S OLDEST AREA, BUT IT IS CERTAINLY its grandest, redolent of a vast British empire, with its public buildings the proud legacy of fortunes made from trade with East and West and of men steeped in the Victorian belief in civic pride and duty. The architects of these public buildings mingled Eastern and Western ideas to create some of India's finest Indo-Saracenic monuments.

Mumbai

⚠ 158 A3

India Tourist Office

✉ 123 Maharshi Karve Rd., opposite Churchgate Station

☎ 022-203 3144

e-mail mumbai@ tourismindia.com

🕐 Closed Sun.

Prince of Wales Museum

✉ 159–161 M.G. Rd.

☎ 022-284 4519

🕐 Closed Mon.

💲 $

The place to start is **Gateway of India** (1927). From the opening of the Suez Canal until the age of airplanes, this end of the Mumbai peninsula is where the ships arrived and passengers stepped ashore into India. George Wittet looked to Gujarat, specifically Ahmedabad (see pp. 146–48), for his honey-colored triumphal arch (1927) adorned with intricate carving, which commemorates the visit of George V and Queen Mary to India in 1911.

On February 28, 1948, after independence, the last British soldier left from here. Today, gaily painted fishing boats and ferries bob in the Arabian Sea, the old ferries ready to take visitors to Elephanta (see p. 169), the newer hovercraft heading for Mandve (see p. 186).

The red-domed **Taj Mahal Hotel** (1903) stands beside the Gateway of India, overlooking the harbor. Built by Jamshtji Nusserwanji Tata (1839–1904) and equipped with its own Turkish baths, it is still an institution among today's Mumbai rich. Tata, a Parsee trading tycoon, expanded his empire from cotton to include mills, hydroelectric plants, a shipping line, and this memorial to himself designed by Sir Charles Chambers (Tata's descendants went on to found what became Air India and to expand into tea, trucks, and scientific research). The lanes behind the hotel lead to Colaba Causeway, a quality shopping area always buzzing with action.

Wittet, again influenced by medieval Gujarati architecture, designed the **Prince of Wales Museum** (1905–1937), too. It commemorates globe-trotting George V's first visit to India in 1905, when he was Prince of Wales (heir to the throne). Statues of him and of his father, Edward VII, stand in the mature gardens. Inside, beneath the tiled concrete dome, the wide-ranging collection offers something for everyone. Choose from delicate Indian miniature paintings, embroidered Kashmir shawls, or Indian silver, glass, brass, and jade; there are also fine arms and armor, and Indian sculpture dating from the Harappan period to finely modeled 18th-century Christian ivory carvings from Goa.

But it is the extravaganza of High Victorian Gothic buildings strung along **Mayo Road** (K.B. Patil Marg), facing the open grass of the Maidan, that take the prize. Many were built of hard, beige Porbandar stone, and most were enriched with skillful, lively, even ebullient, local carving, inspired by Britain's arts and crafts movement. John Lockwood Kipling, Rudyard's father, who was an avid supporter of crafts and ran Mumbai's art school encouraged this unlikely source of inspiration.

Captain Wilkins' **Secretariat** (1874) is really a Venetian Gothic palace. It is 470 feet (143 m) long, with a central arched gable carrying the great staircase window and a soaring 170-foot-high (52 m) tower. Here, the Porbandar stone is enriched with blue and red basalt.

Sir George Gilbert Scott's buildings take a different inspiration. They were designed in England, built under the construction engineer Colonel James Fuller's

watchful eye, and financed by the Parsee benefactor Sir Cowasjee Jehangir Readymoney (his statue is in the gardens). The **University Convocation Hall** (1874) dresses up the 15th-century French decorated style for the tropics and adds some Victorian pomp. There is even a staircase modeled on the Château de Blois. The **University Library** and **Rajabai Tower** (1869–1878), next door, achieve the same success with 14th-century French and Italian Gothic, adding very delicate carving and stained-glass windows. The tower, based on Giotto's campanile in Florence, is decorated with figures representing the castes of western India. The clock used to cheer British residents with its chimes of *Home Sweet Home* and *God Save the Queen*.

Fuller designed the huge **High Court** (1871–79), with its steep, red tiles and skyline figures of Justice and Mercy (and beautiful Minton floor tiles inside). You now jump to the Venetian Gothic of Wilkins's **Public Works Office** (1869–1872), then to the Italianate **General Post Office** (1909), and end with the romantic oriental domes and polychrome stones of Stevens's Byzantine **Churchgate Station** (1894–96). ∎

Mumbai's Maidan is an informal cricket ground.

Visitor tips
Tourist offices and some hotels stock the useful fortnightly listings magazine, "What's On."

Secretariat
✉ Mayo Rd.
🕐 Closed Sat. & Sun.

University
✉ M.G. Rd., Fort
☎ 022-265 2832

High Court
✉ Bhaurao Patil Marg (entrance on Eldon Rd., off M.G. Rd.)

General Post Office
✉ St. George's Rd.
☎ 022-262 0956
🕐 Closed Sat. & Sun.

Churchgate Station
✉ Maharshi Karve Rd.
☎ 022-203 8016 (ext. 4577 for visitors)
💲 $

A drive through colonial Mumbai

The best days to look at Mumbai's remarkable legacy of classy colonial building are Saturday and Sunday, when there is less traffic and plenty of action on Chowpatty Beach. Tell your driver which places you would like to visit, and he will find the most logical way to reach each building. He will wait while you make visits to these British colonial sites.

The **Gateway of India ❶** (1927), built to commemorate the visit to India of the King-Emperor George V and Queen-Empress Queen Mary in 1911, overlooks the harbor at Apollo Bunder. Standing in front of it, you have a marvelous view of the **Taj Mahal Hotel** (see p. 162), one of the great hotels of the East, built by the Parsee industrialist J. N. Tata. To the right, a statue of Mumbai's hero, Shivaji (1961), stands in front of the former Yacht Club (1898) with its half-timbered gables.

Drive past the Yacht Club to Wellington Circle (1865). On your left, Phillip's Antiques is a delightful antiques curiosity shop; on your right, the Indo-Gothic Council Hall is the earliest of several Mumbai buildings designed by British architect F. W. Stevens (1870–76). The domed **Prince of Wales Museum ❷** (see p. 163) is straight ahead, set in lush gardens. Beautiful and evocative **Kenesseth Eliyahoo Synagogue** (see p. 168) is behind Rhythm House.

The next group of buildings to stop and admire is strung out along Mayo Road (K.B. Patil Marg), opposite the open Maidan. This is possibly the world's finest group of High Victorian Gothic public buildings. Their towering confidence and romantic skylines reflect the progressive age in which they were built. The first is Captain Wilkins's **Secretariat** (see p. 163); next is Sir George Gilbert Scott's **University Convocation Hall ❸** (see p. 163) with its spiral staircases, and his **University Library** and **Rajabai Clocktower** (see p. 163). The group ends with Colonel Fuller's **High Court** (see p. 163), Wilkins's **Public Works Office** (see p. 163), and in Veer Nariman Road (formerly Churchgate Street), James Trubshawe's **General Post Office**. Before leaving, you can enjoy a good view of F. W. Stevens's Byzantine-style **Churchgate Station,** where trains leave for Kanheri Caves and Bassein (see pp. 170–71).

Mumbai ladies stretch out at the Laughter Yoga Club on Marine Drive, with the high-rises of Malagar Hill in the distance.

Farther down Veer Nariman Road, you come to the brightly painted **Flora Fountain ❹** (1869), which gives its name to this area. There are charming period buildings. On the left, the domed one used to house the publishers Macmillan, and on the right, Handloom House was built as the mansion of the Parsee Sir Jamsetjee Jeejeebhoy. Mahatma Gandhi Road has more period buildings.

Behind **Horniman Circle** (1860) **❺**, with the Venetian palazzo of Elphinstone Buildings on the left, lies the old **Fort Area.** Here are two fascinating colonial buildings: the **St. Thomas's Cathedral** (begun 1672) and Col. Thomas Cowper's **Town Hall** (1820–23) **❻**, possibly the finest classical building in India, now the Asiatic Library.

From here, take Frere Road past old fort bastions and the Bijapur-inspired General Post Office (1909) to stop and explore Stevens' vast

Victoria Terminus (1878–1887, see p. 166) **⑦**, India's finest Gothic building. Stevens's colossal, domed Municipal Buildings (1893) stand opposite; the gable statue represents Urbs Prima in Indis (first city in India). Finally, cruise along Mahapalika and Carnac Roads past schools, hospitals, and colleges bearing the names of their Victorian benefactors. Stop at **Crawford Market ⑧** (1865–1871, see p. 167), where mangoes and chilies are sold in a French medieval-styled building. Then head for Marine Drive to take a stroll along **Chowpatty Beach ⑨**, which runs along beside the Arabian Sea, where locals gather to enjoy food stalls, street entertainers, and sand sculptors. ■

🗺 See area map pages 158–59
➤ Gateway of India
🔄 8 miles (13 km)
🕐 2–4 hours, depending on length of stops
➤ Chowpatty Beach

NOT TO BE MISSED

- Gateway of India
- University Convocation Hall and Library
- St. Thomas's Cathedral
- Victoria Terminus
- Chowpatty Beach

Victoria Terminus

✉ Dr. D. Naoroji Rd.,
Nagar Chowk

☎ 022-265 9512

💲 $

Victoria Terminus

THE VICTORIAN NOTION OF TRAINS AS A SYMBOL OF progress was exported to India. The British laid the first Indian train lines in Mumbai to help move goods to and from their trade capital. On April 16, 1853, the first train steamed off (see pp. 108–109). Its station was built later and is, with the Gateway of India, modern Mumbai's best-known landmark. Furthermore, it is India's finest Victorian Gothic building.

F.W. Stevens, a government architect, was commissioned in 1876 to build a new terminus for the Great Indian Peninsula Railway, the largest building project in India at that time. Stevens looked to George Gilbert Scott's St. Pancras Station in London for inspiration. What he achieved was a grander and more richly decorated, cathedral-like monument to the British empire's progress, symbolized by the railroad. Built in just nine years, 1878–1887, it cost the then-vast sum of £250,000 (about £15 million or $20 million in today's money).

If you stand at the great entrance, the effect is overwhelming. The huge facade has projecting wings crowned with a colossal, somewhat un-Gothic dome, on which a statue of Progress perches

Mumbai combines old and new: Here, an ox-cart shares the road with a public bus in front of the grand Gothic facade of Victoria Terminus.

proudly. Thomas Earp made this, as well as the helpfully labeled stone medallions of imperial worthies on the facade (see if you can find Sir Bartle Frere, governor of the city from 1862 to 1867), and the gorgeous symbolic imperial lion and Indian tiger on top of the gate piers. The whole building is a riot of various colored stones, decorative ironwork, marbles, inlaid tiles, and exuberant sculpture. Most of this ironwork and decorative sculpture was crafted by the Indian students of the Bombay School of Art.

Inside the reservations hall in the left-hand wing, built with pointed arches like a church nave, you can enjoy more glorious High Victorian decoration. The ceilings have gold stars on an azure background, the dado has glazed tiles with rich leaf designs, and the windows are of stained glass or ornamental iron grillwork to reduce the sun's glare. The fixtures are of local woods, the railings are of brass, the floor is tiled, and the stonework is carved with leaves, animals, and birds.

When the building opened, Indians and British alike must have been amazed. Even today, V.T., as it is fondly known locally, adds glamour to a train ride. Furthermore, the Mumbai municipality has honored this colonial building with a new name, albeit rarely used, that links it to the Maratha hero: Chatrapati Shivaji Terminus (C.S.T.). For a truly great Indian train journey, try taking the 24-hour ride on the Punjab Mail from here to Agra, or ride the new Konkan Railway line down to Goa (see pp. 204–205).

Following the success of V.T., Stevens received commissions to build Mumbai's ebullient municipal buildings (1888–1893) opposite the station. Combining Venetian Gothic with Indo-Saracenic styles and dressing them for the city climate, he managed to express imperial and civic pride at the zenith of the empire. Inventive, romantic, and resourceful, Stevens's final great Mumbai building was Churchgate Station. Here, to give a Byzantine character, he used the local red stone from Bassein (see p. 171) to contrast with the white and blue stones. The statue over the entrance, personifying Engineering, is holding symbols of progress—a locomotive and a wheel—in her hands. ■

Mumbai's markets

Mumbai is a rich trading city, great for shopping, either in the comfort of upscale hotel shops or—much more fun—on street after street of stores and stalls. Colaba Causeway, behind the Taj Mahal Hotel, is the place for international fashion, but you may want to be more adventurous. A good place to start is Crawford Market, where Lockwood Kipling's frieze and fountain are the setting for piles of exotic fruit, spices, and vegetables, and a crowded wholesale wing. Stay in the area and take a wander through the streets north of Carnac Road, whose backbone is Abdul Rehman Street. As usual in India, stores of one type tend to cluster together. Cloth can be found on Mangaldas Lane, jewelry in the Zaveri Bazar on Memon Street, near Mumbadevi Temple (dedicated to the titular goddess of Mumbai), and copper and brass on Baiduni Chowk. Farther afield, Mutton Road has stores full of old (and fake) curiosities (see also Bhuleshwar Market, p. 172). ■

Town Hall

✉ Horniman Circle

🕐 Closed Sat. & Sun.

Cathedral Church of St. Thomas

✉ Veer Nariman Rd.

☎ 022-283 9783

Kenesseth Eliyahoo Synagogue

✉ 68 Worli Hill Rd.

☎ 022-283 1502

F. W. Stevens's Municipal Buildings embody Victorian and imperial pride.

Fort

THE FORT AREA IN SOUTH MUMBAI IS WHERE EUROPEAN Mumbai began. Here today's crowded commercial streets were once a large walled fort facing Mumbai Harbor. The Portuguese struck a deal with Bahadur Shah of Gujarat to trade at Bombay and nearby Bassein (Vasai, see p. 171). When the Mumbai islands passed to the British and were leased to the East India Company, the British built great defensive walls and gates. Although these were mostly destroyed in 1862, you can trace their path along Mahatma Gandhi and Dr. Dadabhai Naoroji Roads. As you walk around, look up at the old facades, some of them dating from the 18th century.

Begin at the **Town Hall** (1833) at Horniman Circle, right by the docks, which were begun in 1860 by the Wadia family of Bombay. Here, the great East Indiamen ships were built of teak, which lasted five times as long as English oak. Col. Thomas Cowper's Town Hall, built overlooking a common, is India's finest neoclassic building. Mostly paid for by the East India Company, it reflects the confidence of the rising British Empire. The windows, with their wooden shutters and curving sunshades, are original. Go up the broad steps and past the fluted Doric columns shipped here from England to find a fine set of marble statues of Bombay governors in the lobby and stairwell, three of them by Sir Francis Chantrey. Today, the building is home to various learned societies.

On the other side of Horniman Circle, Gerald Aungier began the **Cathedral Church of St. Thomas** in 1672. Inside are some fascinating and beautiful funerary monuments to rival those in St. Mary's, Chennai (see p. 258). They include three by John Bacon: to Governor John Duncan, to Katharine Kirkpatrick, whose sons established British supremacy in Central India, and to Maj. Eldred Pottinger.

Down Apollo Street, past surviving old buildings, you find the simple neoclassic **St. Andrew's Kirk** (1819) on Marine Street. Nearby, behind Rhythm House, stands the 1884 **Kenesseth Eliyahoo Synagogue**. Funded by David Sassoon, this is the best of Mumbai's several once grand, but now forlorn, synagogues. The fine upstairs prayer hall is still in use. ■

Elephanta Island

Monumental
Hindu carvings at
Elephanta caves

A VISIT BY BOAT TO ONE OF INDIA'S MOST IMPORTANT early Hindu cave temples is a delight, thanks to the energy of the local branch of the conservation body INTACH (see p. 82). If the sea is calm, the journey itself is a joy, too.

The Portuguese renamed the island, originally called Gharapuri, after the carved elephant they found there (now in Mumbai's Dr. Bhau Daji Lad Museum, see p. 172). Climb up the steps past the souvenir stalls manned by people from the island's three villages, to find a helpful exhibition in the restored custodian's cottage.

The **cave temple** dedicated to Shiva is just beyond. It was probably the Kalachuri rulers who cut it out of a projecting chunk of the high basalt cliff in the sixth century, possibly with royal patronage. Enter the central opening into a simple, dark hall, whose columns have cushion-shaped capitals.

One spectacular, colossal stone carving of triple-headed Shiva in the center of the back wall dominates the several masterpieces showing the god's different aspects. Only just emerging out of the rock, it subtly combines ideas of male-female and husband-wife; the right head is softly feminine, the left side fiercely masculine. The panels on either side show an androgynous Shiva and his consort Parvati on the left, and Shiva helping the descent of the Ganga on the right.

Continue to the right, past the *lingum* sanctuary with its huge guardian figures, to find first the panel of Shiva's marriage with Parvati and then Shiva spearing Andhaka. Across the courtyard, the panels show Shiva as the Yogi and as Nataraja (Lord of the Dance).

Ahead you find another Yogi and Nataraja flanking the entrance, then two compositions of Shiva and Parvati on Mount Kailasha playing dice. ∎

Elephanta Island

- 🅰 158 A3
- 🕐 Closed Mon.
- 💲 $

Ferries

Ferries leave from the Gateway of India regularly from about 9 a.m. until about 2:30 p.m.; the journey takes one hour. Check on the time of the last boat back; if seas are choppy, change your plans. Those not wishing to climb the steps up to the temple can take a train to the site, or be carried in a thronelike chair. A nice restaurant awaits at the top.

Kanheri Caves & Bassein

KANHERI CAVES AND BASSEIN'S RUINED FORT EACH MAKE thoroughly rewarding days out of the teeming city and into two very rural settings going north up the coast. Avoid the long and tiresome drive through Mumbai's suburbs and, instead, take the local train. From Churchgate Station you slice up through the central Mumbai peninsula; the stations are mapped out above the doors of each railway car. Then take a taxi or rickshaw to the site.

Kanheri Caves

158 A3

Take the train to Borifili Station, then either a taxi or rickshaw to Sanjay Gandhi (Krishnagiri Upavan) National Park. From the north entrance it is 3 miles (5 km) to the caves.

$

KANHERI CAVES

At Kanheri, more than a hundred Buddhist monuments cut out of a granite outcrop overlook the Arabian Sea. For almost a thousand years, starting with the Satavahanas of the first century, this was an important Buddhist community that lay on trade routes connecting Nasik, Paithan, Ujjain, Aurangabad, and other cities to seaports such as nearby Sopara. As such, it benefited from donations from merchants, goldsmiths, and blacksmiths, as inscriptions reveal. It may also have been where traveling Buddhist monks stayed during the monsoon, when numbers swelled to several thousand. It was a sophisticated monastic community and may have included a university. The caves were used for study, for meditation, and as homes, and they reveal both Hinayana and Mahayana Buddhist occupation (see p. 58).

Caves nos. 2 and **3** are the most impressive: No. 2 is a *vihara* with two *stupas;* no. 3 (fifth to sixth century) is a *chaitya* with carvings of Buddha and bejeweled donor couples. Other fine caves abound, some with water cisterns, others with Buddha carvings (Cave no. 67) and ovens for cooking. **Cave no. 11** may have been an assembly hall; **no. 14** contains a carving of the 11-headed Padmapani Avalokiteshvara. At the top of the hill, **Caves nos. 84–87** seem to have been part of a burial ground.

There is a small café on the steep forested hill, where you can relax. The caves are popular with the locals on weekends.

BASSEIN (VASAI)

Spend a wonderful day at the most romantic and substantial Portuguese fort ruins in India, with massive walls and gateways, and soaring 16th- and 17th-century church and convent ruins, all completely overgrown. Rarely visited today, this large city—only Christians lived within its walls, while thousands of other people lived outside them—was Portuguese from 1534 until the Marathas took it in 1739; it was important enough to receive four visits from St. Francis Xavier (see p. 193). By 1818, when it became part of the British Bombay presidency, it was abandoned; today, local fishermen untangle their nets in the old citadel.

The sea gate, complete with its iron doors, is set into massive walls, and the bastions have cannon openings. Inside it, follow the path straight ahead to find the soaring triple-staged tower (1601) of the **Matriz of St. Joseph,** Bassein's cathedral. Next, the now empty **Citadel** on the right retains its stone gate, carved with the Portuguese coat of arms; a warren of rooms lies underground. A five-minute walk farther along the path are the **Church of St. Anthony** (1548), founded by St. Francis Xavier on his third visit, with a grand facade and, to the side, an atmospheric cloister. The climax is the **Church of St. Paul,** a Franciscan foundation whose grand columned portal leads to a vast nave, chancel, a gallery that you can climb up for good views, and a cloister; Portuguese tombstones are set into the floor.

To reach Bassein Fort, take the train to Vasai Station, then take a 20-minute auto-rickshaw journey to the sea entrance, where there is a café. Ask driver to wait, or agree on a time to meet at the other gate. ■

Bassein

▲ 158 A3

✉ 38 miles (61 km) N of Mumbai

$ $

An unadorned hemispherical stupa stands at the back of the elsewhere elaborately carved Cave no. 3 at Kanheri.

Ganpati Festival

Ganesh, the elephant-headed, sweet-toothed god of prosperity and good fortune, is loved by Mumbai's Hindu businessmen, who celebrate his September birthday with gusto. Huge, gaudy, pink-painted clay images of Ganesh, each with a morsel of last year's figure added to this year's clay mixture, are set up in factories, houses, and on street corners for ten days, decorated with garlands, flickering lights, and even working mini-fountains. On the day of the full moon, they are paraded through the streets to Chowpatty Beach amid music, dancing, and throwing of pink powder. Finally, they are immersed in the sea and bob on the waves until the images dissolve. ■

More places to visit in Mumbai

BHULESHWAR MARKET

This market is found along the streets to the south of C. P. Tank Road, toward Mumbadevi temple. Locals crowd the wonderful vegetable market on Kumbhar Tukda. There are also stores supplying Hindi movie costumes, others supplying idols to temples. Phool Galli ("flower lane") is where extravagant flower arrangements are made for temples and weddings.

BYCULLA

During the racing season, this area of Mumbai, north of the city center, provides a day's entertainment at **Mahalaxmi Race Course.** Established in 1878, it stimulated India's horse-breeding industry, which is still strong today. During the November to May season, stylish old men, flashy movie stars, and locals of all kinds come to watch the racing on most Wednesdays and weekends. If you have time to explore among the tall chimney stacks of Mumbai's 19th-century cotton mills, some still in use, you will see the David Sassoon-funded **Maghan Dawid Synagogue** (1861) on Sir Jamsetji Jeejeebhoy Road. North of it, **Dr. Bhau Daji Lad Museum** displays local crafts and Mumbai history in a delightful 1870s building. The Elephanta sculpture (see p. 169) is in the garden; David Sassoon gave the clocktower (1865).

Dr. Bhau Daji Lad Museum (Victoria and Albert Museum) ✉ Dr. Babasaheb Ambedkar Byculla ☎ 022-725799 🕐 Closed Wed.

KONDVITE

If you want to see more temples, you can take the train from Churchgate Station to Andheri. Here, 18 cave temples surround a hillock, of which the very early **Cave no. 9** (second century) imitates a thatched hut and **Cave no. 13** (fifth to sixth century) was once a monastery complete with cells and even beds cut out of the rock.

MARINE DRIVE & CHOWPATTY BEACH

Chowpatty Beach and the stretch of beach at the north end of Marine Drive (now called Netaji Subhash Chandra Road) are Mumbai's lung, a refuge from the city's punishing humidity for most of the year. Beside the sea, Mumbai's citizens promenade in the mornings and evenings, and children play cricket at all times of the day. Chowpatty Beach is the city's entertainment center, and is best enjoyed late in the afternoon. You can safely buy Mumbai *chaat* (snacks) from the stalls and wander among the sand sculptors, musicians, astrologers, and other entertainers. The beach is the focus of Mumbai's popular Ganpati Festival (see box above). ■

Karla's Cave no. 8, dating from the first century, has deeply cut columns with boldly carved capitals, mock roof beams, and a stupendous *stupa*.

Maharashtra

Despite its huge size, Maharashtra's principal sites conveniently fall into geographic groups, each with a city base offering good accommodations. To reach them, the most indulgent form of transport is to be driven; this way you can see the landscape, the farms, and the village life and markets. Alternatively, take a train—especially recommended for Matheran—or fly.

Aurangabad, where corporate majors have their industrial sites, has magnificent cave sculptures, and a 50,000-year-old meteorite crater. From here you can visit Daulatabad, Ellora, and, farther away, Ajanta.

Pune is the place to stay if you want to put on your hiking shoes and sun hat to explore the rugged Western Ghats with their spectacular forts associated with Shivaji (see p. 180). From Mahabaleshwar, you can take trips through rural switchback roads with breathtaking views of Shivaji's hill and coastal forts. To see the early Buddhist cave temples of Karla, Bhaja, and Bedsa, stay at the modest hill station of Lonavala.

The stretch between Mumbai and Goa is best visited in a progressive line. Until recently, Maharashtra's coast was among the least developed in India. With the new Konkan railroad and Mumbai–Mandve sea connections, this area is opening up. Accommodations are modest, except for the lovely, characterful hotel at Chiplun, with its lush terraced gardens, but the island fort of Janjira and the two coastal forts of Vijayadurg and Sindhudurg are well worth any discomfort. ■

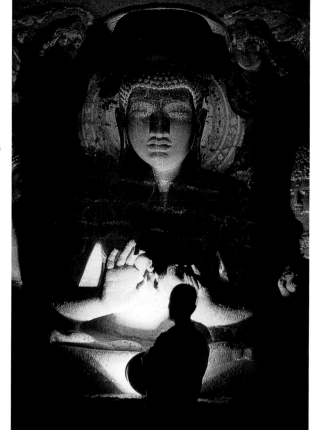

At Ajanta, locals help illuminate the breathtaking carvings and paintings in the rock-cut caves. In this case a large, serene Buddha sits preaching, sculpted in high relief in the sanctuary.

Aurangabad
🅰 159 C4
Aurangabad Tourist Office
✉ Krishna Villas, Station Rd.
☎ 0240-331217
🕐 Closed Sun.

State Tourist Office
✉ Holiday Resort Hotel
☎ 0240-331513

Purwar Museum
🕐 Closed Sun. & university holidays
💲 $

Buddhist Caves
💲 $

Daulatabad Fort
🅰 159 C4
💲 $

Aurangabad & around

TO VISIT THE SCULPTURED AND PAINTED CAVES OF Aurangabad, Ellora, and Ajanta is to see several wonders of the world. If your visit to India includes Mumbai, it is well worth flying to Aurangabad for two or three nights, making it your base for Ellora and Ajanta.

Despite its newfound business wealth, Aurangabad retains much of its Muslim past, and you can sometimes glimpse an earlier period when the city flourished at the crossroads of ancient trade routes. Malik Amber, a former Abyssinian minister for the Ahmednagar rulers, founded the city on the Khan River in 1610. He boosted trade enough for the Mogul emperor Shah Jahan to pillage it in 1621 and capture it in 1633. His son,

Prince Aurangzeb, headquartered here when he was governor of the Deccan (1652–58). He changed the city's name and built new walls. Later, as emperor, he moved the Mogul court here in 1682, making Aurangabad the imperial city until his death in 1707. It then languished as a provincial town in the vast Hyderabad kingdom.

To see a little of the town, visit the bazaar area of Malik Amber's city, where streets converge on

Gulmandi Square. Among the stores and mosques is the **Shah Ganj Masjid** (circa 1720), **Purwar Museum,** housed in a fine old *haveli;* and **Mogul tombs** such as Hazrat Qadar Auliya's, near Jaffa Gate. Out on the plain to the north of the city, the **Bibi-ka-Maqbara** (1679) mimics the Taj Mahal. It was built by Aurangzeb's son, Azam Shah, as the tomb for his mother, Begum Rabia Durani.

Aurangabad's glories are its **Buddhist caves,** built into the rock of the hills to the north and best visited in the afternoon. The groups are close together and date from the Vakataka and Kalachuri periods of the fifth and sixth centuries. The on-site guide lights up the sculptures, but take a flashlight.

Three caves are especially wonderful. In the west group, **Cave no. 3** (fifth century) has fine columns, capitals, and beams and, inside the sanctuary, a composition of devotees kneeling in front of a preaching Buddha. In the east group, **Cave no. 6** (sixth century) has a similar tableau plus traces of a painted ceiling. **Cave no. 7** (sixth century) has bold statues, including Panchika (pot-bellied guardian of the Earth's treasures) with his consort Hariti, plus Buddhas, goddesses, dwarfs, dancers, and musicians.

DAULATABAD

Maharashtra's most spectacular fort surrounds, sits on, and is cut into the huge Balakot rock northwest of Aurangabad, on the road to Ellora (see pp. 176–77). It began as Deogiri (Hill of the Gods), capital of the Yadavas, who lost it to the Khilji sultans of Delhi in 1294. Renamed Daulatabad (Abode of Prosperity), it was the Tughlaq capital from 1327 to 1347, the year the Bahmani governors declared independence. They later moved their capital to Gulbarga. Today's fort is a product of all these periods. One set of massive fortifications leads into **Ambarkot,** the outer fort; the battlements, bastions, guardrooms, and moat of the next set lead into **Kataka,** the inner fort. Through the huge gateways, a street leads between ruined buildings, including the **Jama Masjid** (1318) on the left, and a ruined **Mogul palace** on the right. Across from the Bahmani palace ruins, another imposing gate leads into **Balakot,** the citadel, where a succession of chambers, tunnels, blind alleys, and dark corners lead to the very top.

KHULDABAD

Aurangzeb, last of the six great Mogul emperors, was a religious man. He chose a simple burial in a village where Sufi teachers lived, and he rebuilt the village's walls and gates. If you go into the **Dargah of Hazrat Khaja Seyed Zainuddin** (died 1334), you will find Aurangzeb's tomb in a corner, surrounded by a marble screen added in 1921. ∎

Visitor tips
To visit the Aurangabad, Ellora, and Ajanta caves, you will need a minimum of two full days in Aurangabad, preferably more; the day-trip to Ajanta, where there is nowhere comfortable to stay, is long. Flights connect Aurangabad with Mumbai and Udaipur.

Khuldabad
🗺 159 C4

Visitors at Daulatabad inspect the six-yard-long (5.5 m) cannon before clambering up the edifice built into the granite outcrop.

Ellora

Ellora caves

⚠ 159 C4

✉ 18 miles (29 km) NW of Aurangabad

🕐 Closed Mon.

💲 $

ROCK-CUT ARCHITECTURE IN THE WESTERN GHATS reached its glorious last phase here at Ellora, with large-scale figure sculpture, complex compositions, and a wide range of iconographic schemes. In contrast to Ajanta, where aggressive peddlers and substandard guides try hard to get between you and the art, here you can wander the long, west-facing basalt escarpment, quietly soaking up the spirit of this place that has been sacred to Buddhists, Jains, and Hindus for many centuries.

Visitor tips

The caves face west, so afternoon visits are best; a simple but pleasant café is opposite Cave no. 16.

The caves span the sixth to the ninth centuries and divide into three groups: **Caves nos. 1–12,** at the southern end, are Buddhist; **Caves nos. 13–29,** in the middle, are Hindu, and **Caves nos. 30–33** are Jain. It is best to begin at the southern end, but be selective in your visits to avoid confusion. Try to reach **Cave no. 16** in the

mid-afternoon to see it at its best.

The Hindu **Caves nos. 21, 28,** and **29,** of the sixth-century Kalachuri era, predate the Buddhist **Caves nos. 10–12,** which were built by the Early Chalukyas of the seventh and eighth centuries. The Hindu **Caves nos. 15** and **16,** Ellora's pinnacle of achievement, were created under the

Rashtrakutas of the late eighth century to tenth century, as were the Jain **Caves nos. 30–33.**

Of the dozen Buddhist caves, the first nine are variations on a standard monastic form: columned verandah, central hall, cells to the sides, and a Buddha shrine at the rear. This is seen clearly in **Cave no. 2,** whose guardian figures flank the entrance. **Cave no. 10,** a very fine *chaitya* (worship) hall, is named Vishvakarma after the mythical architect of the gods. It can be found at the end of a courtyard, the two stories set on a basement carved with animals; steps on the left lead up to the richly sculptured gallery. **Cave no. 12** (Tin Thal) has three stories. The top floor (found up steps to the right) is a simple hall with colossal enthroned Buddhas on the side walls, plus rows of meditating and ground-touching Buddhas flanking the sanctum, inside which are goddesses seated on lotuses.

The Hindu group is even more impressive. **Cave no. 15,** named Dashavatara, is a Buddhist monastery later modified for Hindus and partly funded by the Rashtrakuta king Dantigurga *(R. circa 730–755).* Steps lead up to a *mandapa* (pillared hall) profusely sculptured with Shiva and Vishnu images. Moving clockwise, they begin with Shiva killing the demon and end with Vishnu as the man-lion Narasimha.

Cave no. 16, the Kailasha temple, is the spectacular centerpiece of Ellora: a monolithic temple to Shiva entirely sculpted out of the solid rock. In technique, decorative scheme, and quality of sculpture, it is unsurpassed. The Rashtrakuta king Krishna I *(R. 756–773)* began it; his successors continued the royal patronage. If you walk up the cliff on the right, you have a bird's-eye view of the whole complex:

entrance, Nandi pavilion, temple with pyramid-shaped tower, and surrounding courtyard with shrines. Then go down for a closer look. Guardians, the Ganga, and the Yamuna flank the entrance, setting the tone for bold, vibrant sculpture inside. Amid the profusion of decoration, note especially the temple's elephants gathering lotuses on the lower story, compositions from the *Ramayana* and *Mahabharata* on both sides of the steps, and a great Shiva composition in the center of the south side. And do not miss the small hall in the southeast corner,

with its almost three-dimensional figures lounging on a seat.

Finally, there are two late sixth-century Hindu caves, earlier than the others. **No. 21** has remarkably sensuous sculpture: See the female bracket figures on the veranda, the loving couples on the balcony wall, and the river gods Ganga and Yamuna. Interestingly, **Cave no. 29** has a layout and large Shiva wall panels that may be influenced by the cave at Elephanta (see p. 169).

It is a pleasant walk to the Jain group. The finest is **Cave no. 32,** called Indra Sabha. Make your way through the little courtyard, pausing to enjoy the delicate carving of Jina figures; then go upstairs to find exuberantly carved columns and large figures of Ambika (mother goddess) with a child, and Indra. ■

A large, carved, teaching Buddha lurks in Cave no. 10 at Ellora (right), while a walk on the uncut cliff surrounding Cave no. 16 (above) overlooks the Kailasha temple.

Ajanta

THE MIRACULOUSLY PRESERVED PAINTINGS AND sculptures that decorate 30 caves cut into the basalt rock of a beautiful crescent-shaped gorge provide the most extensive idea of early Buddhist artistic traditions in India. They are also the sources for iconography and styles found in later central Asian and Far Eastern Buddhist art.

Ajanta Caves

🅰 159 C4

✉ 64 miles (102 km) N of Aurangabad

🕐 Closed Mon.

💲 $

The caves date mostly from two periods: the second and first centuries B.C., then the late fifth century A.D., when the Vakataka rulers, especially Harishena (R. 460–478), were energetic patrons. These caves contain the most impressive sculptures, ranging from votive images to narrative tableaus with many figures and an elaborate decorative motifs.

These later caves also have India's only extensive series of Buddhist paintings of such virtuosity, quality, and wide range of subjects. They depict Buddha's life and the stories from the *Jataka* tales (former lives of Buddha). These are retold in huge, densely

Ajanta's caves are found in the rocky cliffs of a dramatic and beautiful gorge, fed by a waterfall.

filled compositions depicting contemporary fifth-century city, court, and forest life. Tempera was used to achieve the sinuous lines and harmonious, soft colors. The rock was primed, then given a layer of white

lime, on which the outline was sketched with red cinnabar. The artists then used lapis lazuli for blue, glauconite for green, soot for black, ocher for yellow, and kaolin chalk for white, thickening it with glue. Finally, the murals were polished with a smooth stone.

Abandoned in the seventh century and rediscovered in 1819, most caves are in fine condition. So, as with Ellora, selection is essential because you need time to drink in the detail. Here are eight to start you off: All except nos. 9 and 10 date from the late fifth century. They can be visited in any order, to avoid the crowds.

Cave no. 1 is one of the finest and deserves time. Elaborate sculpture includes flying couples on the column brackets and the great Buddha in the sanctum, preaching the first sermon at Sarnath, his wheel, deer, and monks on the pedestal. The murals are some of Ajanta's best. Two Bodhisattvas flank the sanctum: Padmapani (left) and Avalokiteshvara (right). *Jataka* tales fill the walls, while to the right of the outer doorway some foreigners with caps and beards offer gifts to a figure who is possibly Harishena, the Vakataka king and patron of the cave.

The sculpture of **Cave no. 2** is more profuse than that in cave no. 1; see the fat *yakshas* (demi-gods) and attendants in the left shrine on the rear walls. In the right shrine, there are paintings of processions of female devotees, a very richly

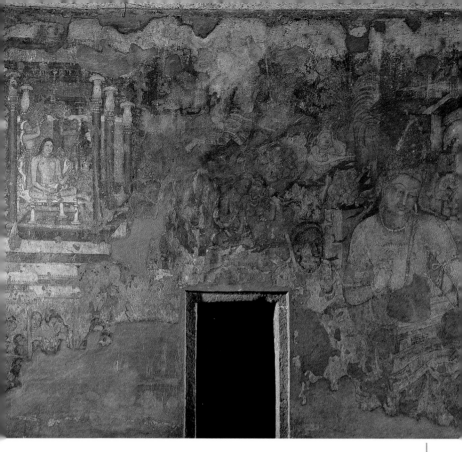

painted ceiling, and *Jataka* and life-of-Buddha stories on the walls.

Now for two early caves, nos. 9 and 10. **No. 9** (first century B.C.) is an elegant *chaitya* hall with plain octagonal columns and a curved vault; the *stupa* on its high drum is the devotional focus. Of the two layers of paintings on the walls, that underneath is contemporary with the building. **Cave no. 10** (second century B.C.) is similar but even earlier, with clearer layers of painting to see; on the left wall, a royal figure worships at a bodhi tree.

One of Ajanta's finest monasteries is **Cave no. 16,** with an inscription dating from Harishena's reign. Its ceiling is carved to imitate wood and there is an image of Buddha teaching. A mural on the left wall shows the conversion of Nanda, Buddha's cousin. **Cave no. 17** is similar, but the decoration of the shrine's doorway is particularly elaborate. Of the murals here, several are outstanding, including the seated Buddhas over the doorway, the wheel of life on the left of the verandah, and the *Jataka* tales on the inside walls.

Cave no. 19 is an almost perfect chaitya hall with restrained yet elaborate carving. Before entering, see the couple on the left wall; inside, the votive stupa, unusually, has a Buddha image on the front. Finally, wonderful sculpture occupies **Cave no. 26.** The large chaitya hall has a splendid Parinirvana: A 23-foot-long (7 m) Buddha reclines on a couch, his eyes closed in peaceful sleep, his disciples mourning him below. ■

Frescoes coat the walls of Cave no. 1: This one recounts a *Jataka* tale on the left and shows Padmapani displaying compassion on the right.

Visitor tips
Currently, the caves are closed on Mondays to help preserve them; these closings might increase. Take water and easily portable food such as bananas and cookies, because there is no good restaurant. Weekends are very busy.

Shivaji, the Maratha hero

This extraordinarily able and charismatic leader founded a Maratha polity that gave his people an identity, inspired later generations, and affected Indian history. It is a story worth telling.

Shivaji (1627–1680) was born into war-torn and famine-struck Maharashtra. In 1647, aged 20, Shivaji began sub-verting local Bijapur authori-ty. He stormed or tricked his way into forts of the *desh-muks* (landed nobles) to carve out an independent and Hindu Maratha zone around Pune, agitating the two powerful Muslim forces that dominated the area, Bijapur and Mogul.

Inspiring and dazzling his people, Shivaji used guerrilla tactics to annoy both enemies. Among his many exploits, in 1659 he killed Bijapur's top general at Pratapgarh Fort and then grabbed Panhala Fort and a tract of the Konkan coast between Mumbai and Goa, where he formed a navy. When Aurangzeb sent Mumtaz Mahal's brother, Shaista Khan, to deal with him in 1660, Shivaji lost many forts and his hometown, Pune, but recovered and promptly sacked Surat in 1664. Mogul pride was wounded. The next year Aurangzeb sent Jai Singh I of Jaipur with 15,000 men. At Purandhar, Shivaji agreed to give up 20 forts, and the next year arrived at Agra to do obei-sance to Aurangzeb. Unexpectedly put under house arrest, he promptly escaped to become the ultimate all-Indian hero.

In 1674 the rebel Shivaji underwent a succession of Brahmanical rituals, acquired the ancestry essential to Hindu kingship, and made himself king of the Marathas. Back on his campaigns, he took Vellure and Gingee Forts near Madras, before dying of dysentery in 1680.

The next year, his son Shambhaji gave refuge to Aurangzeb's rebel son, Akbar. This, together with the fear that the Marathas and Rajputs might ally against the Mogul throne, plus the desire to convert peninsular India to Islam, made Emperor Aurangzeb decide to move his entire court and administration—some 180,000 people—down to Aurangabad in 1682. Before his death in 1707, he had killed Shambhaji, besieged his brother-successor Ramjan at Gingee Fort for eight years, and taken and almost immediately lost countless Maratha forts.

It was at this time that the Maratha chiefs, inspired by Shivaji, began to strike out independently. Maratha raiders reached Malwa in central India and sacked the rich cities of Hyderabad and Masulipatnam to control almost the whole peninsula. Then, in 1714, Shambhaji's son made Kanhoji Angria, admiral of the Maratha fleet on the west coast, his *peshwa* (prime minister). Soon the pesh-was, not the royals, were ruling the Marathas from Pune.

The scene was set for the Maratha state to become the Maratha confederacy. As the Mogul empire devolved into provincial governments, so the Marathas concentrated on revenue rather than territory. Out of this opportunism emerged the great Maratha princely families of the 19th and 20th centuries: the Gaekwads of Baroda, the Scindias of Gwalior, the Holkars of Indore, the Bhonsles of Nagpur, and the Tarabais of Kolhapur.

Simultaneously, the romantic story of Shivaji inspired Bal Gangadhar Tilak and other nationalists to shake off the British yoke. Conceived in Pune, the first conference of the Indian National Congress was held in Mumbai in 1885. It was to be instrumental in India's winning independence. ■

Shivaji's hero image lives on down the centuries, in miniature paintings (opposite) and in a modern idealized statue (above).

SEVAGI.

Pune

Pune

◪ 158 B3

State Tourist Office

✉ 1 Block, Central Building

☎ 020-668867

🕐 Closed Sun.

Raja Dinkar Kelkar Museum

✉ 1378 Shukrawar Peth

☎ 0212-444466

🕐 Closed Jan. 26, Aug. 15

💲 $

Viddhant Bhavan

☎ 0212-565 3413

🕐 Closed Sat. & Sun.

Ohel David Synagogue

✉ 9 Dr. Anbedekan Rd.

☎ 0212-632048

Sassoon Hospital

🕐 Call at reception

Osho Commune International

✉ 17 Koregaon Park

☎ 0212-628561

🕐 Tours 10:30 a.m., 2:30 p.m.

💲 $

HIGH IN THE WESTERN GHATS, ON THE EDGE OF THE Deccan Plateau, thriving Pune is Maharashtra's second city and offers striking contrasts: an old city, the spacious British-built new one, and a controversial *ashram,* more classy resort than religious school.

Above: Devotees of Bhagwan Rajneesh, more often Western than Indian, share their emotional experience with each other.

It was not Shivaji but the later Peshwas who, from 1750, made Pune a center of Maratha power. The British took over in 1818, after the battle of Khadki (Kirkee). To see the best of Old Pune, find the remains of **Shanwar Wada Fort** and then wander the crowded lanes of traditional brick houses and many brightly painted Hindu temples to reach busy **Mahatma Phule Market** (1886), opposite Bel Bagh Temple. A few streets farther south, at **Raja Dinkar Kelkar Museum,** there is a vast collection of everyday arts and crafts amassed by the poet Kelkar (1896–1990) from all over India, displayed on three floors of his beautiful Peshwa-period mansion.

After 1818, the British, calling the city Poona, built southern India's largest cantonment and attracted commerce, Parsees, and Jewish people from Mumbai. From 1820 Pune was the summer retreat of the Mumbai Presidency. Today the Indian Army keeps the white colonial houses and their gardens spick and span. Along the broad, tree-shaded roads are **Viddhant Bhavan** (the former Council Hall, 1870) on Manekji Mehta Road and **St. Paul's Church** (1863) nearby. David Sassoon funded the **Ohel David Synagogue** (1863) on Laxmi Road, where he is buried; Sir Jacob Sassoon funded the **Sassoon Hospital,** built in the English Gothic style in 1867.

Pune is best known, however, for Bhagwan Rajneesh, or Osho (1931–1990), founder of the **Osho Commune International.** To the amazement of locals, thousands of foreign hippies flocked here to join the ashram he founded in 1974. Far from promoting the traditional Hindu ashram aims of nonmaterialism, peacefulness, and meditation, its bywords were sexual liberation, partying, and heady materialism—at least for the ashram. When the experiment of creating a utopian city called Rajneeshpuram in Oregon, U.S., failed, the Bhagwan returned to Pune, where he died. His ashram was likened to a spiritual Disneyland by the *Wall Street Journal,* and it claims more visitors than the Taj Mahal. ∎

The Western Ghats

Sunset at Porcupine Point, Matheran, a popular retreat from the summer heat of Mumbai

A HEADY COCKTAIL OF ROCK-CUT CAVES, FORTS, AND HILL stations excites interest in the rugged Sahyadri ranges of the Western Ghats that climb steeply from the Konkan coast up to the Deccan Plateau. The whole region is linked with the rise of the Marathas, led by their hero, Shivaji (see pp. 180–81). Stay in Pune and make a series of one-day trips.

Amarnath is a short detour from Kalyan. Ambaranatha Temple (circa 1060) has a curved tower and, inside, graceful female figures in recesses. Together with the temple at less accessible Sinnar (see p. 188), this is the best surviving monument of the Yadava period, which immediately preceded the Muslim arrival in the south.

People flock to **Matheran** on weekends to enjoy the fresh air, 2,460 feet (750 m) above sea level, at the closest hill station to Mumbai. A delightful way to arrive is by train, first on the Pune Express from Mumbai to Neral, then on the narrow-gauge train up the hill. Even if you go by car, it must be parked 3 miles (5 km) from the center, which does not permit

vehicles. Matheran was popularized by a certain Hugh Malet, who built the first European house here in 1851; Lord Elphinstone, governor of Mumbai, had a road built to his lodge in 1858, sealing its place in fashionable Mumbai society. This is a place to take walks for sensational views down to the plains from Panorama Point and Duke's Nose. For sunsets, try Porcupine Point. Walk to Louise Point for views across the plateau to the ruined hill forts of Prebal and Vishlagarh.

Visitors who like early Buddhist rock-cut temples can take in **Karla, Bhaja, and Bedsa,** found near the popular hill resort of Lonavala, which has plenty of restaurants. Avoid weekends, when crowds disturb the peace.

The "toy train" runs from Neral to Matheran around 281 switchbacks.

To see the temples chronologically, begin at Bhaja, where 20 caves date from the early Satavahana period of the second century B.C. **Cave no. 12,** possibly the earliest apsidal rock-cut *chaitya* hall in the western Deccan, once had a teak beam roof; **Cave no. 19** has exceptionally early figural compositions showing, possibly, Surya (left) and Indra (right). At Bedsa, about 6 miles (10 km) away, the chaitya hall of **Cave no. 7** (first century) has a richly carved exterior. Four miles (6 km) north of Bhaja, Karla's caves and cisterns surround the largest and most completely preserved early Buddhist chaitya hall in the area, known as **Cave no. 8.** Built during the brief Kshatrapa rule of the first century, a monolithic column topped with a capital of four lions stands in front of the doors, decorated with the six pairs of donors (the Buddha images were added later); the side walls have splendid elephant sculptures. Inside, see the magnificently carved columns and *stupa*.

If you are traveling on to Nasik (see p. 188), you can pause at **Rajgurunagar** (Khed) to see the mosque and tomb of Dilawar Khan (1613), who had his headquarters here when he commanded the Ahmednagar forces against the Moguls. Farther along the road, a detour left reaches **Junnar,** renowned as the birthplace of Shivaji, which has various 15th- and 16th-century fortifications, mosques, and tombs. Ancient Junnar's position on a trade route to the Gujarat coast brought patronage for a flourishing Buddhist center during the Satavahana and Kshatrapa periods (second century B.C. to third century A.D.). About 50 simple Buddhist caves are cut into **Shivneri Hill,** 11 more on **Tulja Hill,** 26 on **Lenyadri Hill,** and 50 on **Manmodi Hill.** There is very little decoration, but walking around the hills to seek them out is peaceful and satisfying.

A trio of offbeat places, **Purandhar, Sasvad,** and **Jejuri,** are accessible on a day trip south from Pune. First, head for the great **fort of Purandhar,** perched 4,839 feet (1,475 m) above sea level. You have to walk the final 1,148 feet (350 m) up to the entrance—imagine taking this fort by force as Shivaji did in 1670 and Aurangzeb in 1705. Through the gate, pass the bold Bahmani walls (15th century) and continue up three levels to the ruined buildings; from here there

There are no cars in Matheran, so you either walk, take a rickshaw, or rent a horse to get about town and explore the narrow ridge and its viewpoints.

are good views of Wazirgad, the fortified hill to the east.

The pretty town of **Sasvad** has several of the Peshwas' fortified palaces, some with partly surviving carved wooden structures. **Sangameshvara** and **Changla Vateshvara Temples,** west of the town, are hybrids of Mogul and Hindu architecture with tortoises carved on the hall floors.

Jejuri is a popular pilgrimage center for Maharashtran merchants and farmers who follow the Khandoba cult, and it is especially lively during the April and December fairs. Find the temple through the town and up steps where peddlers sell brass masks of Khandoba. At the top of the steps, four lamp columns stand near a huge brass tortoise.

It's easy to visit the fort at **Sinhagad,** rising 2,296 feet (700 m) above the surrounding plain and once known as Kondhana: The road from Pune almost reaches it. The wonder is to see the walls of the three-pronged fort rising sheer from the steep cliffs, reinforced with ramparts and towers. Follow the steep path up through three gates. Although little remains inside, you can imagine Muhammad Tughlaq of Delhi trying to besiege it in 1340 and Malik Armad of Golconda taking it in 1486. Shivaji took it in 1647, when he changed its name to Sinhagad (Lion Fort), after which Marathas and Moguls vied for it.

It is worth the journey and the two-hour climb from Vajeghar, where the road ends, to see **Rajgad.** This spectacular fort rises sheer from its three-pronged hill and is so high that, once inside, you have views of Sinhagad, Torna, and Purandhar. Ruined stores, granaries, and halls fill the northern spur. Climb farther to reach Bala Kila (inner fort), 4,320 feet (1,317 m) above sea level, and find Shivaji's impressive palace remains. Having taken Torna Fort in 1646, Shivaji used its treasure to buy arms for Rajgad (King's Fort) and make it his seat of government until 1672, when he moved west to Raigad Fort. It was from there that he left to campaign on the Konkan coast in 1666. ■

Captured by Shivaji in 1656, Rajgad (Royal Fort) opened up the Konkan routes to him; it became his seat of government (1672) and place of coronation (1674).

Sinhagad
🅰 158 B3
✉ 20 miles from Pune

Rajgad
🅰 158 B3

Mumbai to Goa

THIS ISOLATED, BEAUTIFUL, AND SO FAR UNSPOILED AREA has become much more accessible due to new railroads and faster sea transportation. Hovercrafts and catamarans regularly leave the Gateway of India for Mandve; your ticket includes the bus ride on to Alibag, where there are taxi stands. If you are traveling by private car, the driver will meet you at Mandve. Alternatively, make use of the Konkan Railway (see pp. 204–205). Avoid driving out of Mumbai.

Alibag was the headquarters of Shivaji's Maratha fleet from 1662 on. Later, the Angres, who mixed trading with piracy, used it as a base from which to annoy European shipping until the British took it in 1840. You can visit the island **Kolaba Fort** (1820) at low tide or see it while you walk along the

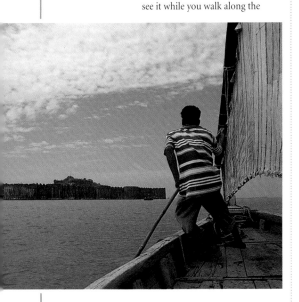

If you miss the low tide walk from Alibag to Kolaba Fort, you can sometimes take a ferry there to explore its 17 wall towers, teak doors, stables, and storerooms.

beach. The main road goes straight through dusty **Chaul,** reducing the pleasure of seeking out the remains of walls and churches that were once part of a major Konkan port governed by the Bahmanis of Gulbarga, then the Portuguese.

Quite simply India's most spectacular island fort, **Janjira** is reached by rowboat from Murud

town. As you roam the massive fortifications, guardrooms, cannon, and the four-story *durbar* (audience) hall, imagine its proud history. The Sidis, Abyssinian admirals in the service of the Adil Shahis of Bijapur, built it in 1511 but by 1618 had asserted their independence. Mixing piracy with providing armed escorts for pilgrims on *hajj* to Mecca, they never lost to Shivaji or the British. Today's former royals live in the hilltop palace; the creekside road south from Murud passes their tombs. Because Janjira is isolated, visit it after a night or so at **Chiplun,** a thriving town on the Vashishti River.

Almost as good as Janjira, the magnificent fort of **Vijayadurg** sits at the mouth of the Vaghotan Creek. The Adil Shahis of Bijapur built it but Shivaji took it, renamed it Vijayadurg (Victory Fort), and strengthened it. This, not Alibag, was his base for attacking Janjira, and the Angres later used it as a piracy base. You can explore the three concentric sets of fortifications, the residences, the barracks, and the granary. Continue to **Malvan.** It's well worth the somewhat simple accommodations to enjoy this charming town, its cafés, and cashew nut production. Take a boat ride out to the island **Sindhudurg Fort** to walk along some of the 2 miles (3 km) of fortifications built by Shivaji when he made this his coastal headquarters in about 1665. ∎

Buying fruit from local markets can be a form of entertainment.

More places to visit in Maharashtra

AHMEDNAGAR

Founded in 1494 by Ahmad Nizam Shah, who broke away from the Bahmanis of Bidar (see p. 241), this was the capital of the powerful Nizam Shahi rulers. Wars with Bijapur and Golconda ended when all three states, plus Bidar, formed a Muslim alliance to overthrow the Hindu kingdom of Vijayanagar in 1565 (see pp. 236–39). Later, despite an accord with Goa, Ahmednagar finally lost out to the Moguls in 1636, after which it belonged to Hyderabad, the Marathas, and, from 1808, the British. It was in the splendid **Circular Fort** (1563), with its moat and 22 bastions, that Jawaharlal Nehru wrote most of his book *The Discovery of India* while an imprisoned freedom fighter. See also the exquisitely decorated **Damris Mosque** (1568), the **Jami Masjid,** and **Mecca Mosque** in the heart of the city, the **Kotla** (1537), which was a Shia college of education, and **Ahmad's Tomb** (1509) in Bagh Rauza gardens. Out of town, the **Dargah of Alamgir** (1707) marks the spot where the Mogul emperor Aurangzeb collapsed and died (see Khuldabad, p. 175). Nearby stand two garden palaces: **Farh Bagh** and **Hayat Behisht Bagh.**

158 B3 ✉ 72 miles (116 km) northeast of Pune, 68 miles (110 km) southwest of Aurangabad, 90 miles (145 km) south of Nasik

KOLHAPUR

This busy commercial city in southern Maharashtra traces its history back to the Satavahana period, when it traded with the Mediterranean. More recently, it was the capital of the breakaway Maratha maharajas of Kolhapur, who commissioned fine Indo-Saracenic buildings by Maj. Charles Mant, better known for his Chennai buildings (see pp. 256–57). In the Old City, find **Rajwada** (Old Palace) and the popular **Mahalakshmi Temple.** Then visit Mant's splendid and influential buildings. There is **Kolhapur Museum** (1872–76, *closed Mon.*), built as the Town Hall, and Chhatrapati Pramila Raja Hospital (1881–84). His masterpiece, though, is **New Palace** (1884, *closed Mon.*), where former royals still live. The basalt and sandstone building has neo-Mogul cusped arches and a *durbar* hall with stained glass illustrating the life of Shivaji. The royal paraphernalia ranges from a silver elephant saddle to a veritable zoo of stuffed animals; one maharaja was an expert taxidermist. Take a look inside the **Shalini Palace** (1931–34), now a hotel overlooking Rankala Lake and furnished with fine Belgian glass. Do not miss the chance to buy Kolhapur leather shoes, to see *kusti* (wrestling) training near the Rajwada, to visit the spectacularly sited **Panhala Fort,** which guarded trade routes to the coast. This is a good base for visits to Vijayadurg and Sindhudurg (see p. 186), and is on the road to Bijapur (see p. 240) and Belgaum.

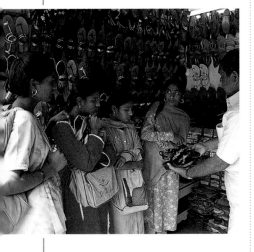 158 B2 **Visitor information** ✉ Kedar Complex, Station Road ☎ 0231-652935

MAHABALESHWAR

This is where the sacred Krishna River springs, making it a pilgrimage site for the faithful. The British, after making a treaty with the local ruler in 1829, exploited this lush, wooded site in the Sahyadri Hills as a hill station. Still popular for its views, streams, and fresh air, this is a good base for visiting Shivaji's **Pratapgarh**

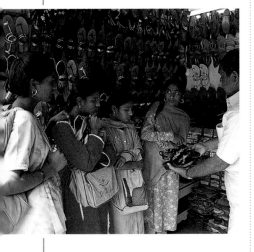

Kolhapur's visitors make time to shop for its famous *chappals* (sandals).

(1656), where he murdered the Bijapur commander, and **Raigad,** which he captured in 1636 and made his capital in 1672. He and his son were crowned here. Trips can be made to the island forts of Janjira (see p. 180) and Suvarnadurg, by Harnai, from here. There are more Shivaji sites at Pune.

158 B3 ✉ 74 miles (120 km) SW of Pune

NASIK

The sacred Godavari River, flowing through this ancient holy city, attracts a continuous stream of pilgrims, swelling to vast numbers every 12 years for the Kumbh Mela festival (last held in 2001, next in 2013, see p. 304). Hindus believe Rama spent part of his exile here, with Sita and Lakshmana. Join pilgrims to visit the riverside temples, including **Rameshvara** (18th century), leaving time to visit three sites out of town. **Pandu Lena** has rock-cut Buddhist caves (second century B.C. to third century A.D.); Nos. 3, 10, and 18 are especially interesting. Within the dramatic cliffs of Trimbak lies the source of the Godavari River, much visited during two annual fairs (*Oct.–Nov. & Feb.–March*). At Sinnar, on the road to Pune, **Gondeshvara Temple** (11th century) was built by the Yadava rulers and is one of Maharashtra's largest and best preserved temples.

158 B4 ✉ 81 miles (130 km) northeast of Mumbai; 130 miles (209 km) north of Pune **Visitor information** ✉ Golf Club, Old Agra Road ☎ 0253-570059

PAITHAN

This is a treat for archaeology and weaving enthusiasts. The thriving settlement founded by the Satavahana ruler Shalivahana as his capital in A.D. 78 is being unearthed at Nag Ghat: Local weavers create the distinctive Paithan designs in fine silk and cotton.

159 C3 ✉ 32 miles (51 km) south of Aurangabad

SOLAPUR

Down in southeast Maharashtra, on the road to Bijapur and Gulbarga, Solapur's strategic importance has made it the subject of many battles. Thus, in town there is an impressive **fort** with sloping walls, built by the 14th-century Bahmanis, with inner additions by the Adil Shahis of Bijapur. **Naldurg,** 28 miles (45 km) to the west, has a magnificent fort (16th century) built by the Adil Shahis on a bluff above the Bori River. If your route is to or from Ahmednagar, it is worth detouring to **Parenda** to see one of Maharashtra's most perfect early military forts, built around 1500 for the Bidar sultans.

159 C2 ■

With mountains to the east and ancient marine trade routes to the west, this strip of palm-fringed beaches, fishing villages, forts, and ports has a history and culture distinct from the rest of peninsular India.

West Coast: Goa & Kerala

A colorful umbrella shades a bargain-hunter at Mapusa market in Goa.

The lush Goan landscape is complemented by the rich colors of the traditional clothing worn by its inhabitants.

West Coast: Goa & Kerala

A NARROW BAND OF LUSH, VERDANT LAND RUNS DOWN THE WEST COAST of India's peninsula, sandwiched between the Western Ghat mountains and the Arabian Sea. From northern Goa to southern Kerala the visitor can relax on the beaches or take advantage of a variety of water sports. There is here something for everyone, in this mixture of east and west with its easygoing ambience.

The map shows how mountains and sea have played their part in the West Coast story. The mountains have been a barrier crossed more often by traders than by empire-builders, the seas a tool to bring trading wealth and introduce new cultures, peoples, and religions. Arabs, Romans, and, later, Europeans arrived, bringing Judaism, Islam, and various forms of Christianity. Coastal people have tended to look outward across the water, rather than inward to the great empires of the Deccan and Tamil Nadu, and their coast is littered with ancient forts and modern ports—Panaji, Mangalore, Cannanore, Kozhikode (Calicut), Kochi (Cochin), and others—all centers for shipbuilding.

None of India's great rivers empties here, but India's great southwest monsoon hits Kerala in July and soaks the Western Ghats in July and August, so hundreds of little rivers flow down to the coast. They run from the steep Sahyadri Hills to the Konkan coast of Goa and the Kanara coast of Karnataka. They flow from the even higher Cardamom Hills to the Malabar Coast of Kerala, slowed down by such quantities of inland lagoons and rivers that land and water become inseparable.

Today these busy rivers continue to carry the local merchants' traditional sources of wealth (pepper, cardamom, other spices, and quantities of rice) to the ports. They also carry tea from the Nilgiri Hills, coffee from

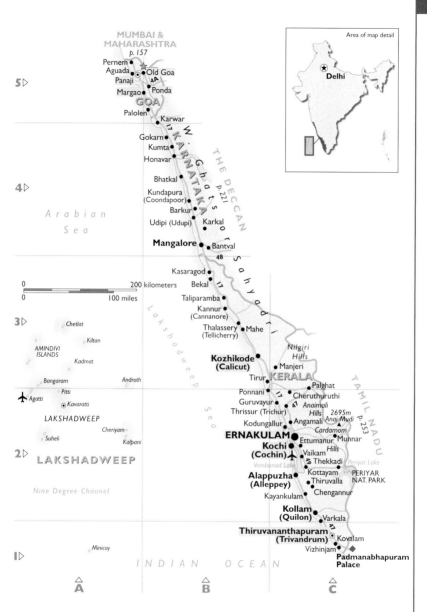

Karnataka's plantations, and lucrative rubber and turmeric (see pp. 214–15).

This coast that depended so much upon the sea has a new land connection: the Konkan Railway (see pp. 204–205). Opened in 1998, it stretches from Mumbai to Kochi and is already hauling the more isolated, undeveloped parts of the coast into the modern world. Goa and Kerala have been quick to respond with some charming upscale hotels. Visitors can comfortably explore a beautiful area of mostly unspoiled India, while enjoying palm-fringed beaches and outstanding local cuisines. A week or so spent in this region makes a relaxing and striking contrast to touring India's great monuments. ■

Goa is dotted with dazzling, white-washed colonial baroque churches that serve its substantial Roman Catholic population.

Old Goa
🄰 191 B5
State Tourist Office
✉ Trionara Apartments, Dr Alvares Costa Rd.
☎ 0832-225583

India Tourist Office
✉ Communidade Building, Church Sq.
☎ 0832-243412

Basilica of Bom Jesus
🄢 $

Cathedral of St. Catherine
🄢 $

Convent & Church of St. Francis of Assisi
🄢 $

St. Cajetan's Church
🄢 $

Old Goa & Panaji

PANAJI IS THE SLOW-PACED, FRIENDLY CAPITAL OF GOA, A tiny state of 1,429 square miles (3,702 sq km) created only in 1987, its language of Konkani given official status in 1988. Explore Panaji after your visit to Old Goa, the region's former capital, reached by road or by passenger boat up the Mandovi River.

OLD GOA

The few surviving churches and monasteries, with baroque high altars and encroaching palm trees, evoke Goa's most recent great city, for this ancient river port was used by the Ashoka, Satavahanah, and Chalukya empires. The Kadambas (11th–12th centuries) made it their capital on two nearby sites, attracting Khilji, then Tughlaq forces from far away Delhi. Later, Goa was wrested from the Bahmanis by the all-powerful Vijayanagas, won back (when the port capital was moved to this site), but in 1489 lost for good to the Adil Shahis of Bijapur.

Meanwhile, Portuguese explorer Bartolomeu Dias rounded the Cape of Good Hope in 1488. A decade later Vasco da Gama rounded the Cape and sailed across the Indian

Ocean to Calicut, and in 1503 Alfonso de Albuquerque built Fort Cochin. In 1510, Albuquerque sailed up the Mandovi and took Goa on November 25, establishing it as the capital of a fast-growing Portuguese maritime empire.

Goa was an entrepôt for trade up and down the coast, in and out of India, and from the Arabian Gulf across to Malacca. The Portuguese levied taxes on everything—cargoes of indigo, cotton, cinnamon, mace, nutmeg, Chinese silk, porcelain, and the very valuable pepper. For a century Goa was known as *Goa dourada* (golden Goa). It was an international city of churches, convents, palaces, mansions, docks, and markets, swarming with activity. It was a center for Roman Catholicism, for the Portuguese trading zeal was matched with a missionary zeal. Missionaries arrived early in Goa, closely followed by the Jesuits and their Counter-Reformation (1540) and Inquisition (1560).

But the Portuguese Empire faded. The reasons were many: loss of trade after the fall of Vijayanagar, the proselytizing zeal against Hindus, the taxation of Muslims on *hajj* (pilgrimage) to Mecca, plagues of cholera, deceitful Portuguese business practices, and the arrival of Dutch and English traders in 1595 and 1600. Goa sank into isolation that the removal of its capital from unhealthy Old Goa to Panaji

in 1843 did little to alleviate. Portugal clung to her colony until December 19, 1961, when Nehru's Indian forces liberated the city.

To enjoy Old Goa town, wander through the baroque colonial churches with their ebullient decoration, twisted columns, flying angels, and lashings of gilt. The three major churches (see p. 194) are the **Basilica of Bom Jesus** (1594–1605), the **Cathedral of St. Catherine** (1562–1619), and the **Convent and Church of St. Francis of Assisi** (1521 and 1661), which also includes the town's museum.

PANAJI

Still with a definite Portuguese air, Panaji sits at the mouth of the Mandovi River. It only became the capital of Goa when the port at Old Goa town silted up. It is worth paying a visit to the hilltop parish church, **Our Lady of the Immaculate Conception** (1619), built in Portuguese Baroque style with twin towers; then walk through the old area of Fontainhas to see old public buildings, such as the **Case Modea** (Mint) and **Idalcaon Palace** (Secretariat). The riverside area west of here is home to the colorful municipal market and Charles Correa's splendid **Kala Academy** (1973–1983), decorated with Mario Miranda's monochrome murals. ∎

Church & Monastery of St. Augustine
🅢 $

Festivals
Carnival, week preceding Lent: festivities throughout Goa
Holy Week, Easter, & Christmas, dates vary: grand processions, various churches; contact local tourist offices for specific information

Church of Our Lady of the Rosary
🅢 $

Panaji
🅐 191 A5

Our Lady of the Immaculate Conception
🅢 $

Kala Academy
🅢 $

St. Francis Xavier

Goencha Saiba (Lord of Goa) is the affectionate Konkani title Goan Christians, Hindus, and Muslims give to their local saint. Born in Spain in 1506, Francisco Xavier y Jassu met Ignatius Loyola in Paris, took a vow to convert infidels, and joined the Society of Jesus. The Portuguese king, Dom

Joao III, sent Xavier to Portugal's new colony, Goa. He arrived in May 1542, aged 36, and made Goa his base for five voyages to the Far East. After his death on Sancian Island in 1552, his body was returned to Goa in 1553 and carried in triumph from the riverside. St. Francis was canonized in 1662. ∎

A drive through Old Goa, Ponda, & Margao

This gentle day excursion takes in Portuguese monuments and mansions, and some of Ponda's most distinctive temples.

The Basilica of Bom Jesus is a focal point for Goa's Catholic population.

The road to **Old Goa ①** rises over a hill to give you a first glimpse of the overgrown city with St. Augustine's soaring tower. Head for the center, where the group of big churches stands. In the **Basilica of Bom Jesus** (1594–1605), built by the Jesuits next to their home, the Professed House (1589 and 1633), is St. Francis Xavier's elaborate mausoleum, given by the Duke of Tuscany, Cosimo III. Inside the casket, a light shines on St. Francis's body. Across the square stand the

grand **Cathedral of St. Catherine** (1562–1619), built for the Dominicans, and the beautiful painted **Convent and Church of St. Francis of Assisi** (1521), housing Goa's best museum with a collection of sculptures and portraits of Portuguese governors.

Take a walk west of the Cathedral to see the **Church of St. Cajetan** (1655–1700), whose dome was modeled on that of St. Peter's in Rome. Continue through the **Viceroy's Arch,** built by Francisco da Gama (viceroy 1597–1600), to the silent docks, where more than a thousand ships were loaded each year. From here either walk or drive up Holy Hill to the **Church and Monastery of St. Augustine** (1602), its pink laterite stone lit by morning sun. The 152-foot-high (46 m) church tower, eight chapels, 100 or so carved granite tombstones, and monastic buildings testify to a substantial community. A path across the road leads to the **Church of Our Lady of the Rosary** (1544–49), which overlooks the Mandovi River; here St. Francis preached at evening mass.

Leaving Old Goa, the temples of Ponda are a total contrast (see p. 198). Instead of riverside colonial style, you now have secret temple building in secluded valleys. Driving southward, the road twists and climbs into hills where spreading cashew trees and jackfruit trees grow. Here are three contrasting temples to visit. **Sri Mangesh Temple ②,** at Priol, has all the distinctive Goan elements and is Goa's richest temple. Up the steps, find the large courtyard with a *tulsi* (basil) pot, a lamp tower, and an elephant on wheels in front of the lemon-yellow and white-domed temple; inside, look for the tiles and Belgian glass. **Sri Lakshmi Narashimha Devashtan Temple ③,** dedicated to Vishnu and Lakshmi in the gods' abode, stands in an appropriately idyllic woodland setting at Velinga and is probably Goa's most beautiful temple. Finally, **Sri Shantadurga Temple ④,** near Queula, is Goa's most popular temple, especially crowded with people buying flowers before the main *puja* at 1 p.m., held in a *mandapa* (hall) of baroque splendor.

From here, the road goes through Borim before crossing the Zuari River. A detour left after Camurlim village leads through lanes to **Rachol Seminary** (see p. 202) **5**, with its great entrance hall, chapel, and museum.

Margao 6 (see p. 196) is southern Goa's main town. Bustling yet rural, it has two good areas to visit. As you drive in along the one-way street, you can already see some of the

A well-maintained Indo-Portuguese house with its *balcao* (veranda)

town's grand old houses. You can stop at **Largo de Igreja** (Church Square), the old central square, to see a cluster of old houses that overlook the gleaming white **Church of the Holy Spirit** (1564, rebuilt 1675), with its baroque and rococo interior. Then visit the **covered market,** where locals buy spices, vegetables, household goods, and, outside, fresh fish. In the Margao outskirts of Borda, reached by taking Agostinho Lourenco Street from Largo de Igreja, find the huge palace of **Sat Burnzam Gor.** ■

- ◩ See area map page 191
- ▶ Old Goa
- ⟷ 20 miles
- ⏱ 5–6 hours
- ▶ Margao

NOT TO BE MISSED

- Basilica of Bom Jesus, Old Goa
- St. Augustine's Church, Old Goa
- Sri Mangesh Temple, Priol, near Ponda
- Largo de Igreja (church square), Margao
- Covered market, Margao

Margao & around

Margao's well-kept, traditional colonial streets make the town a pleasure to visit.

GOA'S SECOND LARGEST TOWN IS A GOOD PLACE TO FEEL the influence of 450 years of Portuguese rule, partly because there are few tourists, partly because it forms part of the heartland of the Old Conquests (the rest of Goa was conquered in the 18th century).

Margao
191 A5
Margao Tourist Office
Tourist Hotel
0834-722513

As you approach Margao from the surrounding countryside, you notice the whitewashed baroque facades of colonial Catholic churches standing beside the paddy fields and rivers. Women often wear pretty dresses with puffed sleeves, rather than saris. Widows dress in European black, not Hindu white, and sit crocheting on the deep *balcaos* (porches) of their houses. These are painted blue, red-umber, and yellow, with the large windows outlined in white. The cuisine is a mixture of Portuguese and Indian traditions, and wine is readily available. Soccer, not cricket, is the favorite sport. Even the Portuguese siesta is maintained: Everything closes from 2 p.m. to 4 p.m.

When the city of Old Goa declined, the Old Conquests were barely affected. Here, the Portuguese-speaking Christian Goans ran the government and trade, and in due course they formed the local aristocracy in Margao and the villages. Prosperity here peaked in the 18th and 19th centuries, when the great houses were built.

For a breathtaking view over Margao and the Arabian Sea, go up to **Mount Church.** Down in the town, the markets are the hub for trading the fish and farming produce of southern Goa. Behind the big red-and-white Municipal Building you can find the fisherwomen, their saris tucked up, crouching beside baskets of shrimp, pearl spot, Indian salmon, and other catches of the morning. Nearby, you can buy fruit from the great piles of bananas, pineapples, chikoos, jackfruits, and, starting in

March, mangoes. Inside the old **covered market** you'll find dried mangoes, flowers, fresh Goan bread, tobacco leaves, and sacks full of turmeric, garlic, Goan red chilies, and the dried tamarind that gives a bitter richness to local dishes. The box-shaped stores stocking wines, jewelry, and hardware form the walls of the market.

To see a good cluster of old houses, go to **Aquerim** district and brave the thundering traffic to walk along the two one-way streets that lead in and out of town and run along both sides of Largo de Igreja (Church Square). These grand town houses with their painted walls, iron balconies, and carved balustrades surround the tall, dazzlingly white **Church of the Holy Spirit** (1564, rebuilt 1675), one of Goa's finest late baroque churches. If it is open, go inside to enjoy the coffered ceiling, grand gilt pulpit, rococo altar, and baroque transept altarpieces.

To see more fine houses, go along Agostinho Lourenco Street behind the church and toward Curtorim. About half a mile along stands the huge palace of **Sat Burnzam Gor,** built around 1790 by Inacio Silva and now lived in by his descendants. As well as a string of grand salons, it has one of Goa's earliest private chapels.

If this has whetted your appetite, you can follow a delightful circular route around the villages of this area, **Salcete,** to see more. Begin at the old Portuguese administrative center, **Loutolim,** found by turning north from Carmurlim on the Margao–Ponda road. The clutch of fine old buildings includes **Case dos Mirandos** (*Contact tourist office to arrange a visit*), still lived in by the Miranda family. Built early in the 18th century, it has a chapel, bedrooms, salon, and deep internal verandah on the first

floor and a great banqueting room, library, and main bedroom upstairs. Two other fine Loutolim houses are **Roque Caetan Miranda House** (1815), a typical Goan country house and **Salvador Costa House,** with its spectacular chapel. Visits to both houses should be arranged through the tourist office.

Continue to Chandor, through undulating land with old houses scattered around and flashy new ones built with money newly earned in the Middle East. You may wish to pause at **Rachol** (see p. 202) or to see Curtorim's splendid church facade. Chandor is dominated by the vast, ornate **Menezes-Braganza Mansion** whose second-floor rooms are furnished with gilt mirrors, four-poster beds, and quantities of elegantly carved chairs. Do not miss the ballroom, with its blue- and white-painted zinc ceiling, Italian chandeliers, Belgian mirrors, and portrait of the mansion's builder, Anton Francesco Santana Pereira. For more villages to visit, see Chinchinim (see p. 202). ■

The Menezes-Braganza Mansion, part of which dates from the 16th century, boasts historic furnishings.

Sat Burnzam Gor
- ✉ Borda
- ☎ 0834-235728
- ◷ Visits by written or telephone appointment

Menenzes Braganza Mansion
- ✉ Chandor
- ◷ Contact tourist office to arrange a visit
- 💲 $

Ponda's temples

WHEN PORTUGUESE MISSIONARY ZEAL SPARKED THE PUB-
lication of an edict to destroy Hindu temples in 1540, some Hindu
priests fled with the temple deity to the forested hills around Ponda,
outside the Portuguese territories. Thus, while more than 550 temples
were destroyed, many Hindus continued to worship in secret. Today,
about 50 of Goa's temples have deities who are, in effect, long-term
refugees, still situated close to, but outside, Ponda.

**Sri Mangesh
Temple, with
its soaring
deepastambha
(lamp tower),
encapsulates
the idiosyncratic
Goa temple.**

Ponda
🗺 191 B5

Hinduism flourished freely again
under more benign Portuguese rule
at the end of the 18th century.
Despite the number of churches
you see sprinkled across the state,
Goa is today 60 percent Hindu.
Furthermore, Christians sometimes
join Hindus to pay their respects to
an ancient deity worshiped by their
Hindu ancestors.

Goa's temples have a style all
their own. The laterite walls are
usually plastered and painted, and
there are often domed central roofs,
red-tiled side roofs, and tall *deepas-
tambhas* (lamp towers). Inside, you
may find Greek-inspired columns
and grand chandeliers.

The pick of Ponda's temples is
probably **Sri Mangesh Temple**
at Priol, whose Shiva *lingum* was
brought here for safety from

Cortalim and hidden until the 18th
century, when the temple was built.
The seven-story deepastambha,
elaborate doorway, and Belgian
glass testify to the temple's wealth
and status. **Sri Mahalsa Temple**
lies between here and Ponda, in
Mardol village. Do not miss the tall,
brass pillar topped by Garuda and
set on a turtle's back, signs that the
temple is dedicated to Vishnu. At
Velinga, **Sri Narashimha
Devashtan Temple** is especially
beautiful in its peaceful wooded
setting and is dedicated to Vishnu
and his consort Lakshmi. The
gleaming image of Narasimha,
Vishnu's fourth *avatar* (earthly
form), was brought here for safety
from Sancoale in the 1560s. The key
features are the original entrance
and the tank around the back. ■

Goa's beaches

EARLY MORNING SUN, BARE FEET ON FIRM SAND, FISHER-
men going out to sea, porpoises playing in the frothy waves, and infinite stretches of sand beneath a canopy of blue sky await you. Have
breakfast in a beachside café, go for a swim, and then retreat to the
shade to read until lunch—grilled giant shrimp are popular. After a
siesta, enjoy swimming and strolling along part of the 66 miles
(106 km) of beach until the spectacular sunset over the sea.

Goa

🗺 191 A5 & B5

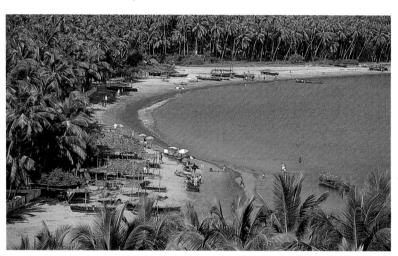

Goa's dark sand is clean and fine.
Some beaches are very long: The
uba dando ("straight rod") is the
great 12-mile (21 km) stretch in
southern Goa from Velsao to
Mobor. Each beach is named after
the fishing village nestling in the
coconut palms behind it, so the uba
dando has several names. Each
beach has its own character, from
isolated Agonda to sociable and
popular Calangute, or the almost
private coves like Vainguinim.
Different beaches attract different
crowds: Sinquerim Beach is next to
two upscale hotels, Anjuna is a hippie hangout, and Indians arrive in
busloads at Calangute and Colva.

It is easy to beach hop: Simply
walk to the next beach, rent a
bicycle or motorcycle, or take a taxi.
Where you need to cross a river,
your only problem is waiting for
the ferry to arrive; in Goa, there is
always time to wait.

Goa takes an active interest in
ecology. Heated local debates have
resulted in strict laws. New buildings must be 660 feet (200 m) back
from the high-tide line. Sand dunes
and their salt-tolerant vegetation
are encouraged and litter cleared
regularly. These laws particularly
affect the owners of beach cafés,
temporary structures where you
can have a drink. Try local *feni* (see
p. 201) or its lighter equivalent,
urrack; do nothing much and watch
the waves to a soundtrack of old
Motown and Beatles hits. Licenses
are given and taken away seemingly
arbitrarily, but there should always
be some friendly cafés waiting to
serve you.

**Goa's beaches
range from sandy
crescent shapes,
like this, to the
12-mile-long
(21 km) sweep of
uba dando south
of Panaji.**

After a night at sea, fishermen unload their catch on the beach at Colva.

Goa's beach etiquette is simple: Nudity is unacceptable, drugs are illegal, the sea should be checked locally for undertow, and peddlers need fierce bargaining or a polite "no, thank you." To help you find the right beach, here are the best of them, from north to south.

QUIET NORTHERN GOA BEACHES

To reach these peaceful spots, take the ferry from Siolim across the Chapora River into Pernem district, little influenced by the Portuguese. Isolated **Querim Beach** is best reached by a pleasant walk from Arambol (Harmal) Beach past a mixture of palms, fishing boats, Hindu-owned cafés, a handful of hippies, and a good local bakery. Turn left from the Chapora Ferry and follow the riverbank. **Morgim**

Beach (Morji) tends to be very quiet unless a busload of Indians arrives, and there is good bird-watching.

BUSIER NORTHERN GOA BEACHES

Six miles (10 km) of beach stretch from Baga down to Sinquerim along the coast of Bardez district. This is where the action is, with beach parties, a choice of restaurants, bars, and nightlife. Behind the beaches, old Portuguese houses and churches stand among paddy fields. **Anjuna Beach** is a social center for hippies and beach parties, with safe swimming, cafés, and the Wednesday afternoon market with vendors from Rajasthan, Gujarat, and Karnataka; nearby Mapusa's Friday market (see p. 202) is inland. Pretty, crescent-shaped

Baga Beach, in front of some very good accommodations, has tempting restaurants and a lively social life, which is also true of neighboring **Calangute Beach. Candolim Beach** is next, with its charming inns and cafés. Finally, **Sinquerim Beach,** lined with palm trees, runs right down to Fort Aguada, where you will find upscale hotels, cafés, water sports, and the inevitable peddlers.

BEACHES NEAR PANAJI
These are small beaches, where the sand has a silver tint because of the iron content. Some of the beaches are private, and thus free of peddlers. **Dona Paula Beach** is reserved for guests of the hotels overlooking it; **Vainguinim Beach** is reached through Cidade de Goa Hotel, whose garden encircles it.

LONG SOUTHERN GOA BEACHES
Uba dando's 12-mile (19 km) stretch is, so far, quieter than the main northern Goa beaches. Its sand is cleaner, and its sea is usually calm. Margao, Ponda, Panaji, and Old Goa (see pp. 192–98) are fairly accessible, but avoid Bogmalo, right on the airport flight path. Beaches

run from Velsao to lively **Colva,** with its fishermen, beach cafés, village market, and restaurants. Peaceful **Sernabatim, Benaulim,** and **Varca** beaches are surprisingly little-used by patrons of the nearby upscale hotels. **Cavelossim** fronts the pretty village of Carmona, and **Mobor** is home to a super-chic hotel. You then come to Betul village and the Sal River.

QUIET SOUTHERN GOA BEACHES
To enjoy nearly empty beaches with their wilder scenery, go for the day and take a picnic. **Agonda Beach** is usually particularly quiet, whereas **Palolem's** beauty is threatened by development. South of here are **Rajbag** and **Galgibaga**. ■

Anjuna's busy flea market (right) has a heady mix of goods from all over India, plus little restaurants and, of course, the beach.

Coconut palm

This versatile tree plays an essential role in Goan life. Seaside clumps help protect villagers from the sun, wind, and monsoon storms. Inland, more than half of Goa's agricultural land is devoted to coconut and cashew production, something the Jesuits encouraged: Tended, watered and fertilized, an acre (0.4 ha) of coconut palms will produce 7,000 nuts a year against 1,000 in the wild. The juice of green (unripe) coconuts is a refreshing drink. Ripe

nuts have their fibers twisted into ropes, fishing nets, and rigging, or woven into coir matting. Shells become fuel or eating-bowls. Coconut milk and the kernel are used in cooking; dried and pressed, they produce valuable coconut oil. The timber is used for building, its fronds for thatched roofs, fish traps, mats, and baskets. Sap is tapped to make jaggery (raw sugar) or to distill into the alcoholic drink *feni,* which can also be made from the bitter cashew fruits. ■

More places to visit in Goa

AGUADA FORT

Goa's strongest fort, built in 1612, defends Aguada Bay and the mouth of the Mandovi River. Built using the latest Italian engineering theories of low, broad walls, wide moats, and cylindrical turrets, it surrounded Sinquerim

Southern India's fresh, fragrant spices are on sale at village markets, the range tailored to local cuisine.

and Candolim villages and had 79 cannons. Reach it through Betin, Verim, or Nerul fishing villages. The fort archway leads to the church, lighthouse, and citadel which has views across the Mandovi to Cabo promontory and the governor of Goa's mansion.
✉ North of Panaji

CHAPORA FORT

The fort was a refuge for locals when Shivaji's son Shambhaji swept down here in 1739. The Portuguese treaty won them back this district, Bardez, in exchange for the Marathas having

Bassein (see p. 171). Hike up the hill to see the laterite battlements and bastions (1617) and to enjoy views down over Chapora estuary, past mango and cashew orchards.
✉ North of Panaji

COLVA, BENAULIM, & CHINCHINIM VILLAGES

These three Salcete district villages, are all situated west of Margao. Colva has a high baroque church, **Our Lady of Mercy** (1630, rebuilt 18th century), and nice old houses. Nearby Benaulim has the baroque **Church of St. John the Baptist** and more charming houses such as **Vincent Correia Fonsecos** (now apartments). Finally, twisting lanes lead through paddy fields and cashew orchards to Chinchinim. In the pretty square, Dr. Alvaro Loyola Furtado's **mansion** stands next to the peppermint green church.
✉ West of Margao

DIVA ISLAND

This is part of the northern Tiswadi district, but it is easily reached by ferry from near Old Goa. From 1510 on, this was Albuquerque's base, so many of Diva's 8,000 inhabitants are descended from Goa's first Christians. There are beautiful houses near the crossroads, such as that of leading Goan writer Mario Cabral e Sas. You can visit the hilltop church of **Nossa Senhora da Piedade** (1700–1724).
✉ South of Panaji

MAPUSA MARKET

Every Friday the main square of Mapusa is a hive of activity. Locals buy their fruit, fish, and household goods such as tiffin cans (lunch boxes); visitors look for Goan terra-cotta pottery, and crafts from other states. Stores sell cashews and Mumbai-made accessories.
✉ North of Panaji

RACHOL SEMINARY

All of Goa's 500 churches need priests, and Rachol Seminary is one of four seminaries devoted to training them. Founded in 1574, the fortlike building has a chapel with an ornately gilded altar and impressive relics, pulpit, and murals. The small **Museum of**

Christian Art, which opened in 1994, has exquisite pieces, including a gilded St. Ursula figure, processional flags, and the Loutolim priest's palanquin.

✉ 4 miles (7 km) east of Margao

SEA & RIVER CRUISES

Locals often run informal sunset boat rides up Goa's many rivers, where you can spot birds such as sandplovers, terns, ospreys, and sea eagles. Trips also go out on the sea to look for schools of humpbacked dolphins.

✉ South of Panaji

SPICE PLANTATIONS

Goa is less famous for its spices than Kerala. However, there are two fascinating spice gardens at Khandepar near Ponda, both well run for visitors: **Savoi Verem Spice Garden** and **Garden of Eden.** See tiny chilis; nutmeg fruits that must be pried open for the lacelike mace surrounding the nut; fragrant cinnamon bark; cloves drying in the sun; vines of black pepper (once known as black gold); and much more.

✉ East of Panaji

TAMBDI SURLA TEMPLE

A one-day trip inland from Panaji takes you to Goa's best building: a beautiful and evocative temple hidden in a clearing in the thick forested hills. Built of basalt stone, the decoration is crisp and deep, the roofs powerfully primitive. This is a rare survivor from the Kadamba empire, which ruled Goa in the 11th and 12th centuries, ran the west coast's major port, and was India's finest maritime power. Turn left at Molem crossroads, then right to Surla. Then take the next right turn; follow this road right to the end, and walk a short distance through the trees.

✉ East of Ponda

MORE NORTHERN GOA TEMPLES

Some of the best temples in northern Goa include **Mauli Temple** at Sarmalem, near Pernem, with graffito decoration and **Sri Bhagavati Temple** at Parcem. Eastward into Bicholim district, **Sri Saptakoteshwar Temple** at Naroa had a refugee deity brought here from Diva Island by Shivaji in 1668.

✉ North of Panaji

MORE SOUTHERN GOA TEMPLES

In southern Goa, near Ponda, you can find two temples in lush valleys near Bandora. **Sri Nagesh Temple** was founded here and has friezes of scenes from the great Hindu epics. At nearby Queula, **Sri Shantadurga Temple** (1738) was partly funded by Shivaji's grandson Shambhaji (see Chapora Fort,

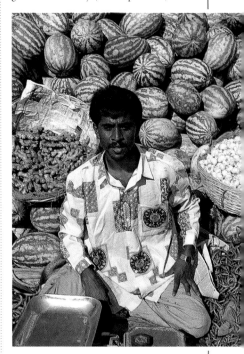

Fruit sellers provide on-the-spot drinks, often either coconut milk or, as here, watermelon juice.

p. 202). At 1 p.m., you can witness the main *puja* of the day, with men standing on the right and women on the left beneath a gilded ceiling. Mirrors outside spotlight the deity for the benefit of the overflow. Down in the south of Salcete district, there are two hilltop temples, founded in the fifth century or earlier, with splendid views. **Sri Chandranath** has its *lingum* carved out of the hill, while **Sri Chandreshwar Bhutnath Temple,** dedicated to Shiva as Lord of the Moon, has a similarly carved Nandi bull.

✉ South of Panaji ■

The Konkan Railway

While other countries abandon their trains, India wisely promotes this low-pollution form of transportation and even builds entirely new lines. The Konkan Railway is the country's most recent triumph, an engineering feat that runs 523 miles (999 km) through three states—Maharashtra, Goa, and Karnataka—from Mumbai (Bombay) down the coast to Mangalore. There it links up to an older railroad line to Kochi (Cochin).

चान्दर गोवा
CHANDOR GOA

Initiated in 1984, begun in 1990, and opened in 1997, Konkan was the largest railroad project of the 20th century. Billed as "A Dream Come True," it provides a north–south transportation infrastructure that will boost the economy and increase employment of a poor area where the monsoon regularly destroys roads and makes port connections by inland waterways and sea unnavigable.

Along the route, trains cross 143 major bridges, of which the longest is a mile (1.6 km), and 1,670 minor ones. They pass through 75 tunnels, the longest one more than 4 miles (6 km). They cross India's highest viaduct, 211 feet (64 m) high, roll over 85,630 tons (87,000 tonnes) of rails and 1.2 million railroad ties, and stop at up to 53 stations.

The railway has changed the lives of coastal people. They are less isolated; traveling distances and times have been reduced—a train journey from Goa to Mumbai is cut from 20 to 10 hours—and the fare is cheaper.

But ecologists and environmentalists, albeit pleased at the prospect of less pollution from trucks, are anxious. They fear the area's rich mineral resources—iron ore, bauxite, chromite, manganese, and silica sand—and its dense forests will be ravaged. Iron ore is already a major Goa industry. Maharashtra has the last tract of India's untouched coastal

forest. They also worry about increased population, urbanization, and industrialization, and the consequent pollution of the coast's fragile ecosystem.

Thermal plants, an oil refinery, and copper-smelting complexes are already planned, and train passengers are expected to reach 21 million each year by 2014.

For the visitor, the Konkan Railway opens up travel along the coast south of Mumbai. The grueling drive out of Mumbai can be avoided by taking a train from Victoria Terminus. Roha makes a good stop for visiting Janjira, and Chiplun for staying in a quaint hotel while exploring the Vashishti River and valley. Farther south, Sawantwadi is the station for seeing the forts at Malvan and Vijayadurg. In Goa, there are stations at Pernem, Old Goa, Margao, and Canacona. The scenic route continues down coastal Karnataka with stops that include Karwar, Coondapur, and Mangalore (see p. 206). Here the Konkan Railway links into the older Southern Railway, built to serve British trading needs, and continues down to Kochi, stopping at such towns as Kozhikode (Calicut) and Thrissur (Trichur).

The current schedule enables you to hop on a train in Mumbai at 4:40 p.m., enjoy a good night's sleep, meals on board, a day's window sightseeing, and arrive at Kochi at 9 p.m the next day. This is a fast train: You do not stop at every station. ∎

Trains chug slowly through Goa along the new Konkan Railway line (right), stopping at stations with smart and useful bilingual signs, as at Chandor (above). The new line crosses many rivers, including the wide Zuari near Cortalim, where fishing families continue to mend their nets (opposite above).

Coastal Karnataka

Coastal Karnataka
⬥ Map p. 191

Coastal villages celebrate their temple deities with gusto.

THE COASTAL STRIP OF GOA'S NEIGHBORING STATE Karnataka is called Kanara. Its landscapes are among the most scenic in India. Laterite cliffs alternate with almost empty beaches and mangrove-lined river estuaries. Tourists are rare; facilities are simple.

Gokarn visitor information
☎ 08386-58236

Jog Falls
☎ 08186-44732
🕐 Avoid monsoon season (Nov.–Jan.)

Mekkekattu visitor information
☎ 0811-29303

Mangalore visitor information
✉ Hotel Indraprestha, Lighthouse Hill Rd.
☎ 0824-442926

If you are traveling from Goa down the coast to Mangalore, you pass through **Gokarn** first—an ancient pilgrimage center focused on its **Sri Mahabaleshwar** and **Sri Mahaganpati** temples. Pilgrims shave their heads, take a holy dip in the sea, and then visit both temples to perform their *puja* (worship) and *darshan* (ritual viewing of the deity); the splendid *rath* (temple chariot) is still used for Shivratri, Shiva's festival *(Feb.).*

A string of perfect beaches follows, some the home of Goa's long-stay beachbums. On down the coast, a detour inland from Bhatkal leads to **Jog Falls,** although the drive there from Kumta is more spectacular. The falls are India's highest and set amid breathtaking hill scenery; hikers can follow the track down to the water, but should take a guide to avoid getting lost.

At Barkur, turn inland to **Mekkekattu** for a fantastic sight: about 170 new, bright red *bhuta* (spirit) images in the Nandikeshvara Temple complex (see also Mysore's Folklore Museum, p. 231).

Farther down the coast you come to **Udupi** (Udipi), famous through India as the birthplace of delicious *masala dosas,* the thin rice pancakes stuffed with vegetables and first made in the town's *brahman* hotels. Having sampled one or two in a café at the Hotel Sharada International or Kediyoor, go to the square to join pilgrims visiting the amazing wooden Krishna temple, with its copper-clad sloping roofs, founded by the Hindu saint Madhva (1238–1317). Look for the colorful temple chariot processions in winter.

Finally, you reach cosmopolitan **Mangalore,** a great port since the sixth century, later owned by the Vijayanagas, Portuguese, Tipu Sultan, and the British. From here, pepper, ginger, and other spices were traded with the Middle East. Today, its exports are coffee, cocoa, cashew nuts, and granite. Sadly, there are scant remains of its past— the **Manjunatha Temple** (tenth century) with its fine bronzes, and **St. Aloysius College Chapel** (1885), with its Italian frescoes and murals, are probably the best. ■

Kochi (Cochin) & Ernakulum

Kochi & Ernakulum

191 C2

Kochi (Cochin) Tourist Office

Willingdon Island, near the Taj Malabar Hotel

0484-668352

Kerala Tourist Office

Shanmugham Rd., Ernakulum (outpost at main boat jetty)

0484-353234

Kathakali shows
See p. 376 for information on shows.

SPREAD OUT OVER SEVERAL ISLANDS WHERE VEMBANAD Lake meets the Arabian Sea, Kochi's main center is peaceful, historic Fort Cochin and Mattancherry; its twin city, dynamic, expanding Ernakulum, lies across the water to the east.

St. Thomas the Apostle is believed to have come to the isthmus of Kochi in about A.D. 50 and created a Christian community called the Moplars. Jewish people came, too, then Syrian Christians, Chinese, and Persian travelers, and, in 1502, Vasco da Gama. He established a Portuguese factory to process spices for export. The following year, Albuquerque arrived with friars to begin the fort and church.

The English set up their spice factory in 1635 only to lose it in 1663 to the Dutch, who converted the Catholic church to a Protestant chapel and the cathedral into a warehouse. When the Netherlands fell to the French in 1795, the British were quick to grab Kochi and its lucrative and strategic port.

Gentle trading continues. You can still see spice go-downs (warehouses) in the Mattancherry area of Kochi, but its character is preserved thanks to the growth of Ernakulum on the mainland. Little fishing boats still bring their catch to the harbor at sunset, though Kochi's real wealth is its commercial port, which handles much of the state's phenomenal production of rubber, coconuts, tapioca, bananas, ginger, coir (coconut fiber), and cashews.

Ernakulum is a fast-growing, affluent city where flashy jewelry, silk, and other luxury boutiques thrive thanks to the wealth generated by spice-growers, rubber barons, and the many Keralites who work hard stints for high wages in the Middle East. ■

For the Kathakali dancer, applying make-up is part of the religious performance.

Kathakali dance

Kerala's distinctive culture has many traditions in dance, drama, sports, and religious ritual. One of the few that is easy to see is Kathakali, a highly sophisticated and dramatic dance-drama whose name means "story-play." Derived from a form of yoga, the ritual of the performance begins with the application of elaborate make-up and costumes, whose colors are symbolic. The dance itself is a stylized religious pantomime recounting stories from the great epics and can last a whole night. For once in India, the shortened tourist shows are of a high quality, are clearly explained, and give a good idea of the full-length performance. ■

Pulleys and weights lower and raise the teak frames of these huge Chinese fishing nets.

A walk around Kochi (Cochin)

The best days for this walk are Sunday through Thursday, as the Pardesi Synagogue closes on Saturday and the Dutch Palace on Friday. Reach Kochi by ferry from Ernakulum and Willingdon Island, rather than by car; or negotiate for a private boat. At Kochi, if walking is too tiring, hire a rickshaw or rent a bicycle.

The walk begins at **Mattancherry Jetty ❶,** where the shoreline has beautiful old tiled buildings with pastel-colored walls, many still used as go-downs (warehouses). Go to the main road and into the Mattancherry for **Dutch Palace ❷** (1557), in fact built by the Portuguese for the Kochi Raja, Veera Keralavaram (R.1537–1561), to help win a better trading deal; the Dutch merely renovated it in 1663. Inside, there are court dresses, paintings, and palanquins in the Coronation Room and India's most spectacular 16th- to 18th-century frescoes in the other rooms. Upstairs, a rich palette coats the walls with illustrations from the *Ramayana;* downstairs, the later paintings show Shiva and Mohini, and Krishna holding Mount Govardan and playing with the *gopies* (milkmaids).

Turn right on leaving the palace for a little walk through an area that is called Jew Town, past stores selling packaged spices and traders working in their go-downs. Turn right at the end, by the **Indian Pepper & Spice Trade Building,** and peek inside. You will find Synagogue Lane, and at the end is the **Pardesi Synagogue ❸** (*Sun.–Fri. 10 a.m.–noon & 2–5 p.m.*); enjoy the beauty and calm of its interior. Founded in 1568, then destroyed by the Portuguese, the synagogue was rebuilt in 1664 under Dutch approval and given its prized floor of Cantonese willow-pattern tiles in the mid-18th century by Ezekial Rahabi, who also gave the clock tower. As a result of emigration to Israel, the local Jewish community is so reduced that services are not always possible. The rabbi depends

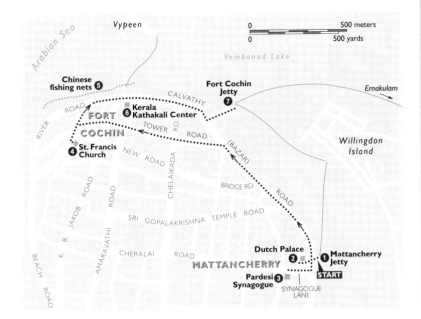

upon Jewish visitors to make up the required numbers, but he is often there to show them special copper plates. These record the grant of privileges to White Jews (see p. 60), made by King Ravi Varman (962–1020) to the Jewish merchant Joseph Rabban.

To walk to Fort Cochin, go back through Jew Town and along Calvathy (Bazaar) Road; then turn left on Tower Road to pass some old houses and lush walled gardens. You emerge in a parody of an English village: a lawn for Sunday cricket, surrounded by British coir merchants' houses and **St. Francis Church** ❹ (1546). The Portuguese Franciscan friars built the plain, massive structure to replace the earlier wooden one that was probably India's first European church. Inside, the memorial on the far right is to Vasco da Gama (viceroy 1524), who died here on Christmas Day 1524; his body was later moved to Lisbon. There are also fine tombstones of Portuguese, Dutch, and British traders. On Sundays, the congregation overflows and the church is cooled by *punkas,* the manual air-conditioning system.

Turn right out of the church and go down the road past some very handsome colonial traders' houses to the tip of Fort Cochin, finding a handful more on the right, shaded by

> 🗺 See area map page 191
> ▶ Dutch Palace, Mattancherry
> 🔄 2 miles (3 km)
> 🕐 2–3 hours
> ▶ Fort Cochin Jetty
>
> **NOT TO BE MISSED**
> - Dutch Palace, Mattancherry
> - Synagogue, Mattancherry
> - St. Francis Church, Fort Cochin
> - Chinese fishing nets, Fort Cochin

giant rain trees. At the water's edge, the cantilevered **Chinese fishing nets** ❺ were introduced to Kerala by traders from the court of Kublai Khan. Kerala's distinct temple architecture, conical fishermen's hats, paper, and porcelain also evolved thanks to Chinese trading. A complicated system of pulleys and weights lowers and raises each of these huge teak frames.

You are now near the **Kerala Kathakali Center** ❻ for Kathakali performances (see p. 207). Farther on, off Calvathy Road, is **Fort Cochin Jetty** ❼, where you can find boats back to Willingdon Island and Ernakulum, or sunset boat rides in the harbor. ■

The backwaters

Moving by boat through the Kerala backwaters, known locally as Kuttanadu, allows you to glimpse an enclosed world where bountiful nature and simple village life are in harmony.

THE GREATEST PLEASURE IN KERALA IS TO TAKE A BOAT slowly through the shimmering backwaters. You can watch kingfishers dive, boats deliver their goods, children catch water buses to school, boys splash in the water, and women prepare spicy Kerala fish dishes in the shade of towering coconut palms.

Kerala's coastal region is more water than land in places. There are 44 rivers that, with innumerable tributaries, meander their way to the Arabian Sea. Rivers, estuaries, deltas, and man-made canals interlink to create a vast, ancient, and labyrinthine water transportation system still used to carry spices, rubber and rice. The longest canal stretches 228 miles (367 km) from the capital, Thiruvananthapuram (see pp. 212–13), up to Tirur.

BACKWATER CULTURE

The bigger backwaters lie between Kochi (Cochin) and Kollam (Quillon), where **Vembanad Lake** spreads over 77 square miles (200 sq km). Known as Kuttanadu, this area is where life is spent beside, on, and often in the water, on narrow slivers of land. Here, in the dense tropical vegetation, families live in brightly painted houses that appear to float on the water. Tiny grocery stores and tailors somehow squeeze on, too, as do tightly planted orchards of jackfruit trees, coconut palms, and mango trees, and each homestead's chickens, ducks, and, of course, cows. Everything from the morning newspaper to the sari chest is transported by boat.

Locals may be skimming through the canals using a thick paddle at a furious speed. Or they may punt their narrow dugout boats along with a tall pole, which they plunge into the water, push hard, and then slip out just before it disappears. On bigger boats, carrying coir, *copra* (dried coconut flesh), and piles of coconuts or cashew nuts, locals have small palmyra palm leaf huts as their onboard homes. Lazy boatmen tag on to motor ferries; others put up sails; still others carve the prow.

Coir and fishing are the main industries here; you may see fishermen diving for freshwater mussels or simply dangling a rod and line. Farmers must harvest any paddy growing in the boggy fields before the monsoon, when the whole area is flooded—not surprisingly, since the water level of the canals is often higher than the fields on either side. But when the monsoon ends in August, Keralites celebrate the Onam festival, believing it to mark the return of the benign, mythical King Mahabali from his exile in the underworld. Great boat pageants and races are held, which used to be between rival princes. Today, the best are the snake boat races held near Alappuzha (Alleppey). Having slicked down their great *chandan vallam* (racing boats) with special oil to make them glide faster, a hundred oarsmen each hurtle through the water to great roars from the crowds. For the benefit of visitors, this and the Thrissur Puram (see p. 220) are now repeated in mid-January each year.

ENVIRONMENTAL ISSUES

The big threat to Kuttanadu life—apart from population growth and land reclamation—is African moss. This waterweed grows rampantly and threatens to throttle the waterways entirely. The velvety leaf with its thick cushion of intertwining fibrous roots was introduced about 30 years ago, but it has already had a drastic effect on the ecosystem. The water, cannot now be used for drinking or washing. Fish and aquatic life have reduced in numbers because no sunlight reaches them. Boats cannot pass through the blocked rivulets and canals.

HOW TO VISIT THE BACKWATERS

There are various ways of seeing the backwaters. One is to rent a converted country rice boat called a *kettuvallam*, the type that used to transport goods down to Kochi. It comes complete with crew, so you can opt out of "real life" to spend a few days being pampered in this watery paradise.

If this is too exotic, rent a private boat and driver for the day from Alappuzha or Kottayam (the waterscape from Kotch is dull for the first two hours); you can be dropped off at one of two upscale waterside hotels at Kumarakom, overlooking Vembanad Lake. Or simply join locals on a public ferry from one town to another. ■

Right:
For the boat races, crews of up to a hundred power each narrow snake boat with its lavishly decorated high prow.

Thiruvananthapuram (Trivandrum)

KERALA'S SEASIDE CAPITAL RAMBLES OVER SEVEN HILLS. IN contrast to other state capitals, it is laid back and easy, with little metropolitan buzz. Leafy parks and traditional red-tiled houses line the wide, quiet streets.

A corner of Shri Padmanabha-swamy Temple exemplifies Kerala's superb woodcarving.

Thiruvanantha-puram
🅰 191 C1

Thiruvanantha-puram Tourist Office
✉ Airport Counter
☎ 0471-451498

Kerala Tourist Information
✉ Thampanoor bus stand
☎ 0471-330031

Puttan Malika Palace
✉ Chalai Bazaar Rd.

Kuthiramalika Palace Museum
🕐 Closed Mon.
💲 $

When India won freedom in 1947, the princely states of Travancore and Cochin and British-administered Malabar were amalgamated to form Kerala, whose official language is Malayalam. Since then, the state has enjoyed a radical reputation. In 1957 it was the first in the world to democratically elect a Communist government. Reforms led to a fairer distribution of wealth, much improved education and health care, but little industrial development. Today, its birthrate is India's lowest, its health is among the best, and its literacy rate is an impressive 93 percent, the highest in India.

Thiruvananthapuram, called Trivandrum when it was the capital of Travancore state, took its new name to honor the god Vishnu. It means "holy city of Anantha," and Anantha is the coiled snake on which Vishnu rests in the cosmic ocean. It is in this form, called Padmanabha, that the royal family of Travancore worshiped their principal deity. When Raja Matanda Varma (*R.*1729–1758) moved the capital here in 1750, he dedicated the whole state of Travancore to her and built the temple his descendants still control, the **Shri Padmanabhaswamy Temple,** which stands in the historic heart of the city. Although non-Hindus cannot go inside, you'll find the surrounding area of interest. Walk around the temple, and at the front see the faithful bathing in the tank or buying souvenirs and *puja* offerings. Here, too, you may see students practicing the special Kerala martial arts exercise, Kalarippayat, in the early morning.

The Travancore rajas moved into nearby **Puttan Malika Palace** when they left Padmanabhapuram (see below). They still live here, visiting their great temple early each morning, but have opened some rooms to the public. The polished floors, delicately carved wooden screens, and royal crystal are superb treasures; see especially the fine murals and columns carved as rampant horses.

Beyond the old quarter, at the far end of M. G. Road, lie the **Public Gardens,** 64 acres (26 ha) of lawns and trees and the home to the **Arts & Crafts (Napier) Museum** (1874–1880). Inside R. F. Chisholm's brightly colored brick building with stained-glass windows, there are fine Chola bronzes and Kerala woodcarvings, masks and puppets, gold jewelry, musical instruments, and various royal memorabilia. The **Shri Chitra Art Gallery** is also in the gardens, as well as the **Natural History Museum** (*Closed Wed. a.m. & Fri.–Mon.*), whose models of the Kerala *taravad* (manor house) and traditional *nalekettu* (four-sided courtyard) house show you what to look for while driving through the countryside.

PADMANABHAPURAM PALACE

Although Padmanabhapuram

Visitors to Kerala can watch a demonstration of Kalariphayat, rigorous martial arts training.

Palace is in Tamil Nadu state, it makes sense to visit the Travancore rulers' former capital from Thiruvananthapuram. The splendid palace, one of southern India's finest royal buildings, dates from 1550, although Raja Matanda Varma (1729–1758) remodeled much of it. The teak rooms with their deep, overhanging roofs are arranged around four courtyards and enriched with elaborate carving, rosewood furniture displaying a strong Chinese trading influence, and spectacular murals, superior even to those in Mattancherry's Dutch Palace (see p. 208). It may still be closed to the public, for preservation purposes.

During your tour with the obligatory and informative guide, note the delicate perforated screens, foliated brackets, and *dhatura*-flower pendants. The many rooms include a carved open hall, where the king addressed his people. The upstairs council chamber has an ingenious air-conditioning system using herbs soaked in water, broad-seated chairs for ministers to sit on cross-legged, and a floor gleaming with polish achieved by mixing burned coconut, sticky sugarcane extract, egg white, lime, and sand. The tower's top room is reserved for the god, complete with bed and murals. There is also the **Ekandamandapam** (Lonely Place), the oldest section reserved for rituals for the goddess Durga. It has a stone-columned dance hall and includes the bedroom of the raja, whose bed was made from medicinal woods. The whole ensemble brings to life the very special Travancore royal house, where succession was matriarchal through the eldest sister's eldest son; the ruler did not marry, to prevent his love being diverted from his state to his children. ■

Arts & Crafts (formerly Napier) Museum
🕑 Closed Mon.
💲 $

Shri Chitra Art Gallery
🕑 Closed Mon.
💲 $

Natural History Museum
☎ 0471-62275
🕑 Closed Mon.
💲 $

Festivals
Arat festivals, March–April, Oct.–Nov.: activities and street processions during two ten-day festivals

Visitor tips
Entry to most of Kerala's temples is barred to non-Hindus.

Padmanabha-puram Palace
🄰 191 C1
✉ 34 miles (55 km) SE of Thiruvananth-apuram
🕑 Closed Mon. Best to avoid weekends
💲 $

India's spice box

Spices are essential to every Indian meal, even if the *masala* (blend) varies from region to region. Spices give each dish its distinctive flavor and character. The meat, fish, or vegetables are added after the spices have cooked a little.

From early times, Greeks, Romans, Arabs, and Chinese have paid highly for powerful spices to perfume themselves, improve room odors, help preserve food, act as medicines, and disguise the pungent smells of rancid meat. Southern India was the chief source, and prices could compare with gold.

In the 15th century the urge to break the Arab and Venetian stranglehold on the spice trade led to Christopher Columbus's arrival in America, while looking for a westerly route to India, and Vasco da Gama's discovery of the sea route around Africa. From then on, the Portuguese, Dutch, French, and British began to trade directly with India.

Pepper, once known as black gold, is the king of spices, and Kerala produces 95 percent of India's pepper crop. All over Kerala you can see the pepper vines growing up trees shading other crops, and peppercorns drying in the sun. Most pepper is grown alongside cashew, coffee, coconut, areca nut, tapioca, banana, and rice crops on homesteads lying between the high mountains and the coast.

In fact, most of India's spices are grown in the south of the country on small plantations. More than 60 percent of India's cardamom is grown on the high Kerala hills, alongside tea, coffee, and rubber, and in mountain forests.

Fresh red chilis are sorted for quality and size. They will be sold whole or ground in markets and factories.

The seeds sprout from the base of a big, broad-leafed bush and are picked by women who dry them and keep a few for use as aphrodisiacs. Ginger is part of the same plant family, and about 70 percent of the world's requirement is grown here; it is used in food and as a digestive medicine. *Haldi* (turmeric) is another rhizome, mostly grown in neighboring Andhra Pradesh. As well as being used in cooking, it is used in medicine as an antiseptic and rubbed onto babies' and women's skin to soften and lighten it. Thanks to such attractive properties, the domestic market consumes 98 percent of the 350,000 tons (371,350 tonnes) that are produced in India every year.

Buying these and other spices in the local markets is a lot of fun. Did you know that nutmeg is a fruit, from which we get mace? The kernel of the fruit is the nutmeg that we use in cooking; the strands of mace are wrapped around it. Cinnamon is the inner bark of the lateral shoots of pruned cinnamon trees, and it is sold in tightly curled quills. Chilis come in all sizes: The big ones are eaten as vegetables or are crushed to make mild paprika; the small ones have the "fire" in them.

Cashew nuts, most often ground and used in the gentle sauces of Mogul dishes, grow in a most interesting way. Just one pair of nuts grows outside each large, yellow, bitter fruit. When harvested, they must then be laboriously shelled and skinned by hand, then sorted according to size. This is the reason for their high cost. ■

Above: Peppercorns, here kept in a special wooden box, were once so valuable that they were used by traders as currency.

It is fascinating to visit the wholesale spice market in Jew Town, Kochi (above), where brisk business continues as it has for hundreds of years. Sackfuls of precious and fragrant seeds, pods, and bark are carted off to be sold again before they reach the marketplace (right), where grateful cooks buy them.

India's coastline is dotted with traditional fishing villages; here, Keralites haul their boat up onto the beach.

Kerala's beaches & Lakshadweep Islands

IF IT IS TIME TO CHILL OUT, YOU HAVE SEVERAL CHOICES. Very little of the long, sandy shoreline of the Malabar coast, stretching 342 miles (550 km) from Goa down to Kanya Kumari, is developed by Western standards. Unlike Goa (see pp. 190–203), Kerala has few beachside hotels or cafés, and locals may well be upset by scanty swimsuits. For a complete escape, head for Bangaram Island.

Kovalam
 191 C1

Varkala
 191 C2
✉ 33 miles (53 km) N of Thiruvananthapuram, 12 miles (19 km) S of Kollam

Danardhana Swamy Temple
✉ Varkala

Lakshadweep Islands
191 A2 & A3

The empty beaches punctuated with cliffs or fishing villages make wonderful places for refreshing and peaceful walks and a quiet swim. The two areas where beach life has developed are Kovalam and, to a lesser degree, Varkala; both are reached from Thiruvananthapuram.

To seek out the best of Kovalam, go to quiet **Samudra Beach,** watch the fishing boats on **Hawah Beach,** discover restaurants on **Lighthouse Beach** (with a nice afternoon walk down to Vizhinjam village), and find peace on **Pozhikkara Beach.**

Varkala is quite different from Kovalam, though it may well change. This pilgrimage center draws

Hindus to the **Danardhana Swamy Temple** overlooking the sea, where they pay respect to their ancestors; after 5 p.m. non-Hindus may enter. A lane next to it leads down to the beach, which so far retains its charm. You can enjoy its white sands and promontory walks. There are also natural springs, the local town's market, and, if you like, you can take an elephant ride into the nearby forest.

LAKSHADWEEP ISLANDS
Coming here is still a total escape because foreign tourism is tightly controlled. To conserve the islands' culture, only Bangaram Island is open to non-Indians. Visitor num-

Ayurvedic medicine

The ancient medicinal philosophy called *ayurved* has been practiced in India for at least 5,000 years, especially in Kerala. Unlike Western medicine, which seeks to discover and then eliminate what is making you sick, Ayurved considers that disease reveals a body that is totally out of balance. Thus the imbalance, rather than the disease, is treated. First, you must accept that the body is controlled by three forces: *pitta* (the sun's force over digestion and metabolism); *kapha* (the moon's cooling force over the body's organs); and *vata* (the wind's effect on movement and the nervous system). Diagnosis is by considering physical complaints, emotions, family background, and daily habits. Treatment may involve herbal preparations and yoga exercises. Ayurvedic doctors and pharmacies throughout India often have training in both Western and Ayurvedic systems, and can help tackle long-term problems such as migraines and asthma. To find out more, visit one of the many Ayurvedic centers, such as C.V.N. Kalari Sangam by Shri Padmanabhaswamy Temple in Thiruvananthapuram. ■

Getting to the Lakshadweeps
If you want to visit the Lakshadweep Islands, you will have to fly from Kochi, or alternatively book a cruise through a travel agent.

bers are limited, prices are high, and there is nothing much to do except relax. A snorkel and mask are essentials.

As you fly in, look down on the 36 coral islands lying in the azure Arabian Sea between 137 miles (220 km) and 273 miles (439 km) off the Kerala coast. They are India's smallest Union Territory: Just 52,000 people live here on the ten habitable islands, with Kavaratti the capital and Agatti the airport. Most inhabitants are Sunni Muslims, speak Malayalam, and live by fishing and coconut cultivation. Other crops here include jackfruit, banana, and wild almond.

Bangaram Island, with a resident population of 61, is reached by a two-hour boat ride from Agatti, 5 miles (8 km) away: Watch the boatman carefully avoiding the coral in the shallow sea. This beautiful teardrop-shaped island is surrounded by white sands and guaranteed warm calm water—about 79° F (26° C), perfect for spending hours watching the exotic underwater world. ■

The idyllic Lakshadweep Islands may take some effort and expense to reach, but peace and natural beauty are guaranteed after arrival there.

More places to visit in Kerala

As Kerala is so long and thin, the suggestions below are arranged in two sections, each with a good central base.

KOZHIKODE & NORTHERN KERALA

Bekal
Here you will find northern Kerala's best pre-served coastal **fort:** Grand ramparts, walls, and bastions (17th century), were built by Shivappa Nayaka of Nagar and later taken by Haider Ali in 1763.
191 B3   49 miles (79 km) north of Kannur, 37 miles (60 km) south of Mangalore

Kannur (Cannanore)
This was the capital of the powerful Ali Rajas, Kerala's only Muslim royal dynasty. They used the massive triangular Fort St. Angelo, built by the Portuguese (1505) in their 1770s alliance with Tipu Sultan against the British.
191 B3   14 miles (23 km) north of Thalassery, 57 miles (92 km) north of Kozhikode

Kozhikode (Calicut)
Make this the base for exploring northern Kerala. Kozhikode is a thriving, modern town trading in spices, timber, coffee, and tea. It is the former capital of the Samutiri rulers, bet-ter known as the Zamorins. They had close ties with Arab Muslim traders, who equipped their army and were threatened by the Portuguese, then the English, French, and Danes. See the **Tali Temple** and mosques with distinctive multi-tiered tiled roofs: **Mithqalpalli** (16th century), **Jama Masjid,** and **Mucchandipalli** (both 15th century).
191 B3

Taliparamba
Two of Kerala's finest temples are here, both founded in the ninth century but mostly rebuilt in the 16th and 17th centuries: **Rajarajeshvara Temple,** in town, and **Krushan Temple,** which stands in a pretty grove one mile (1.6 km) to the south and has beautiful friezes recounting the Krishna story.
191 B3   14 miles (23 km) north of Kannur

Thalassery (Tellicherry)
This attractive coastal town is where the British set up a factory in 1683. See their impressive **fort** (1708) and overgrown **cemetery,** the Mappila traders' traditional **warehouses** and **homes,** and the Kerala-style **Odothilpalli Mosque** (17th–18th century).
191 B3   34 miles (55 km) north of Kozhikode

AROUND KOCHI & ERNAKULUM

Alappuzha (Alleppey)
This pretty, affluent town, with enough bridges to make it an Indian Venice, owes its character to vigorous development by the Travancore rulers after they took it over in 1762. Merchants flocked here to use the new warehouses, and a shipbuilding industry blossomed, boosting trade with Bombay and Calcutta. Produce was, and still is, delivered here from the hills along the inland waterways, including quantities of coir for matting.
191 C2   35 miles (56 km) south of Kochi, 52 miles (84 km) north of Kollam

Angamali
Angamali has unusual 17th- and 18th-century Christian monuments: baroque **St. George's, St. Mary's,** with its nave murals showing the Last Judgment and Christ telling St. Thomas to go to India, and, at nearby Kanjoor village, another **St. Mary's,** whose murals curiously include the defeat of Tipu Sultan (see p. 226).
191 C2   20 miles (32 km) north of Ernakulum

Cheruthuruthi
This town is home to the **Kerala Kalamandalam,** the state's finest academy for classic Keralas Kathakali and other per-forming arts, such as Kutiyattam (an archaic kind of Kathakali). The academy was founded in 1927 by the Malayali poet Vallathol, and vis-itors are permitted to watch the fascinating training sessions and performances in the beautiful theater.
191 C2   18 miles (29 km) north of Thrissur   0492-622418

Guruvayur
At Kerala's most popular pilgrimage town, you can join pilgrims to enter the **Krishan Temple** (but not the sanctuary), then drive 2 miles (3 km) east to see the temple's elephants in the compound of the fine mansion at **Punnathoor Kotta.**
🔼 191 C2 ✉ 18 miles (29 km) north of Thrissur

Kayankulam
Kayankulam's **Krishnapuram Palace** is less ornate than Padmanabhapuram (see p. 212) but just as interesting. It was probably built by Ramayya Dalawa, who was governor of northern Travancore under Rama Varma (1758–1798); one room off the small interior courts has a beautiful mural of Vishnu riding on Garuda.
🔼 191 C2 ✉ 30 miles (48 km) south of Alappuzha 🕐 Closed Mon.

Kodungallur (Cranganore)
There's little to see, but the town is historically very important. It was from here that Arabs and Romans imported spices to Alexandria and Oman, and that early Jewish people, Christians, and Muslims arrived to make their first settlements in India. Christians claim St. Thomas arrived at Pallipuram, near here; Muslims claim that Malik bin Dinar, an Arab missionary, founded the Cheraman Mosque here in 630.
🔼 191 C2 ✉ 32 miles (51 km) north of Ernakulum

Kollam (Quilon)
A lively town between the sea and Ashtamudi Lake, the southern point of the backwaters, Kollam was already a port of call for seventh-century Chinese merchants. Traces of its Portuguese, Dutch, Travancore, and British administrators can be found around the town, attesting to Kerala's cosmopolitan history. **Ganapati Temple** stands opposite **Old Tobacco Godown,** while the baroque **cathedral** is a reminder that Kollam is probably the oldest Catholic diocese in Southern India, established in 1328. Also of interest is a **Syrian Church** (1519) with unusual 18th-century murals, the **Valiakada Arikade mosque,** and the **Travelers**

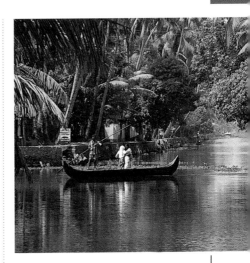

Kerala's ancient canals, their maintenance funded by local rulers, include one that stretches 228 miles (367 km) from the capital, Thiruvananthapuram, up to Tirur.

Bungalow, built as the British Residency.
🔼 191 C2 ✉ 53 miles (85 km) south of Alappuzha, 44 miles (71 km) north of Thiruvananthapuram

Kottayam
This affluent, charming town lies on the Minachil River, which connects with Vembanad Lake. Most of Kerala's hill produce arrives here before continuing to Kochi and Alappuzha, often by boat. You can happily stroll around for a few hours, catch water buses, watch life, and maybe visit the **Syrian Church** in Puthenangadi area. Kottayam is the headquarters of Kerala's Orthodox Syrian and Roman Catholic communities.
🔼 191 C2 ✉ 45 miles (72 km) south of Ernakulum

Munnar
A spectacular drive along a country road follows the ridge of the hills, with panoramic views of rolling tea gardens on either side. British tea, coffee, and cardamom planters created this mini-hill station at 5,000 feet (1,524 m), centered on the **High Range Club** and **Protestant Church** (1910), which appear unchanged since their foundation. While here,

go to **Lockhart Gap** for breathtaking views over the Annamalai Hills; serious hikers can tackle **Anai Mudi,** southern India's highest peak at 8,838 feet (2,694 m). From here you can visit Periyar, or continue through the hills to Kodaikanal (see p. 281).

191 C2 139 miles (224 km) east of Ernakulum

Palai

As this is the seat of a bishop of the Syrian Catholic church, the old **Cathedral of St. Thomas** (1002) is one of Kerala's grandest churches, with magnificent gilded altars.

10 miles (16 km) east of Ettumanur

Periyar National Park

After a beautiful drive up through the Cardamom Hills, you have 270 square miles (700 sq km) of hilltop deciduous woodland and a huge artificial lake to explore. Established in 1934, this is one of the best sanctuaries for watching wild elephants,

At the climax of the Puram and Elephants festivals, mahouts and their helpers dance on top of their caparisoned charges.

especially at either sunrise and sunset. The sanctuary also provides visitors with excellent forest walks and bird-watching for traveling nature lovers.

191 C2 74 miles (119 km) east of Kottayam, 99 miles (159 km) west of Madurai in Tamil Nadu

Thiruvalla, Kaviyur, & Chengannur

Thiruvalla's **Vallabha Temple** is one of Kerala's largest temple complexes, with elaborate tiered gables, porches, and carvings. Also here is the contemporary British architect Laurie Baker's **St. John's Cathedral,** inspired by Kerala traditions. Kaviyur's **Mahadeva Temple** has some of Kerala's finest carved woodwork and, nearby, a Chera period **cave temple** (eighth to ninth century), with fully rounded figures including a proud chieftain. Chengannur's **Narashimha Temple** also has exceptionally beautiful woodwork.

191 C2 **Thiruvalla** 17 miles (27 km) south of Kottayam

Thrissur (Trichur)

Thrissur is famous for its magnificent Puram festival *(April–May)*, when richly decorated elephants parade through the crowded streets, accompanied by music and fireworks. Their final destination is the huge **Vadakkunnatha Temple** (16th to 17th century) with its walled courtyards, tiered roofs, dancing hall, and several shrines. Thrissur was the Kochi rulers' second city, and the museum complex reflects its rich history. There are superb bronzes in the **Art Museum** and other interesting artifacts in the **Archaeological Museum** *(Closed Mon.)* and **State museums.**

191 C2 43 miles (69 km) north of Ernakulum

Vaikam, Kaduthuruthi, & Ettumanur

These are three places worth visiting on the Ernakulum–Kottayam road. Vaikam is where Mahatma Gandhi's 1925 *satyagraha* movement (see p. 150) resulted in temple roads being opened to all in the then highly caste-ridden Kerala. At Kaduthuruthi you can visit two fine Syrian Christian churches: the baroque **St. Mary's** (rebuilt 1599), with its very elaborate gilded altar (18th century), and the **Forane Church of the Holy Ghost,** one mile (1.6 km) away. At Ettumanur (6 miles/10 km north of Kottayam), the roadside **Mahadava Temple** (1542) has vivid murals painted inside its traditional gateway.

191 C2 **Vaikam** 24 miles (39 km) south of Ernakulum ■

Beneath the huge skies of the Deccan Plateau great Hindu and Muslim kingdoms rose and fell, battled for power, and left their magnificent monuments strewn across the dramatic, still rural landscape.

The Deccan

Piles of brightly colored, finely ground spices in Mysore's Devaraja Market

The Deccan

TRAVELING THROUGH THE DECCAN, WHICH COMPRISES MOST OF KARNATAKA and Andhra Pradesh states, can be demanding, but the region's magnificent monuments and stunning landscapes make it one of the most rewarding areas of India to visit. You encounter a succession of utterly different, wondrous sights.

There are two focal points: Bangalore and Hyderabad, the capitals of Kannada-speaking Karnataka and Telegu-speaking Andhra Pradesh states. Bangalore, once an elegant British town now a dynamic state capital, is India's Silicon Valley. Hyderabad, thick with the remnants of its royal Muslim Qutb Shahi and Nizam rulers, is following Bangalore's lead and exploding into the global economy.

Outside these great cities lies a challenging, rural landscape. The great Godavari, Krishna, and Kaveri Rivers and their tributaries, which all empty into the Bay of Bengal, feed the rich soil of the Deccan Plateau, where agriculture accounts for 70 percent of both states' employment. On your travels you will see fields of rice, ground nuts, chilis, cotton, and sugarcane, plus Andhra Pradesh's tobacco and Karnataka's mulberry bushes for its silk industry. One village will be sleepy, the next in the midst of a festival; a single goatherd and his flock will block a road; an empty field will transform into a livestock fair where cattle have been daubed with pink polka dots.

In the west, you can visit British hill stations nestling in the lush Nilgiri Hills and view the protected forests and wildlife of three adjoining national parks. If you feel a lack of romance, you have the palaces of Mysore. To the north, forgotten empires have left some of India's finest temples, from the earliest efforts at Aihole, which imitated wooden structures, to the final glories of Vijayanagar.

North and eastward again, the rulers of the great Bahmani kingdom, Vijayanagar's rivals, built citadels at Gulbarga and Bidar. Then they broke up into rival sultanates, decking their cities with romantic, bulbous-domed mosques and tombs, while facing the inevitable onslaught of Mogul expansion from the north. Finally, there are rarely visited sites along Andhra Pradesh's beautiful 621 miles (999 km) of coast at Tirupati and around Vishakhapatnam port and the Godavari and Krishna Deltas.

Amid all this, heroes abound. You can follow the stories of Vikramaditya, the eighth-century ruler of the Chalukyas, and Krishnadeveraya, who later ruled the Vijayanaga kingdom. You can also see evidence of the enlightened 18th-century expansionism of Haider Ali and his son, Tipu Sultan, which resulted in their clashes with the British. ■

After the searing heat of the Deccan Plateau, the Nilgiri Hills offer respite with their fresh air, luxuriant foliage, and rolling hills.

Adilabad

Satmala Range

Sirpur

Nirmal

Tandur

Jagtial

16

Chinnur

Nizamabad

odhan

Kamareddi

Karimnagar

Medak

Dudada

Warangal

Jangaon

Yellandu

Secunderabad

Bhongir

Musi

conda

HYDERABAD

9

Khammam

Nalgonda

Suriapet

A N D H R A

Vijayapura

Krishna

Amaravati

Mahbubnagar

Nagarjuna
Sagar

Nagarjunakonda

P R A D E S H

Guntur

adwal

Srisailam

Narasaraopet

Chilakalurupet

Alampur

Markapur

Kurnool

Chirala

False Divi Point

Nandyal

Giddalur

Kondukur

Tadpatri

Udayagiri

Kavali

antapur

Proddatur

Penner

armavaram

Cuddapah

Nellore

Seshachalam Hills

Puttaparthi

Gudur

Kadiri

Rayachoti

Pulicat Lake

Sri Kalahasti

akshi

Tirupati

Chik
Ballapur

Punganuru

Chittoor

Kolar

Eastern Ghats

4

T A M I L   N A D U

p. 253

△ C

E A S T E R N   I N D I A
p. 285

Ichchapuram

Ghats

Parvatipuram

Bobbili

Mukhalingam

Salur

Srikakulam

Paderu

43

Vizianagaram

Eastern

Sankaram

Bheemunipatnam

Konta

Narsipatnam

Vishakhapatnam

Anakapalle

Godavari
Gorge

Tuni

Kottagudem

5

△ F

Samalkot

Kakinada

Tadepallegudem

Drakasharama

Bay of Bengal

Eluru

Vijayawada

Bhimavaram

Gudivada

△ E

Tenali

Machilipatnam

Bapatla

Ongole

Bay of

△ D

Godavari

garreddi

Kamareddi

0   200 kilometers
0   100 miles

Area of map detail

★ Delhi

Visitors to Amba Vilas, the massive city palace at Mysore, enter through this suitably ornate gateway.

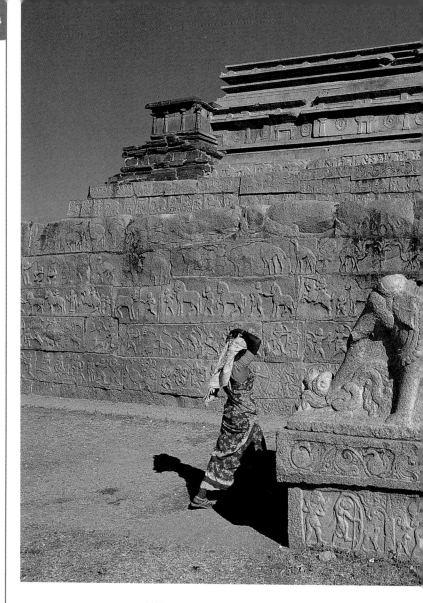

Karnataka

Karnataka's dramatic landscape ranges from giant boulders, seemingly dropped by the gods onto barren hills, to the bountiful paddy fields and leafy coffee plantations of the undulating Kodagu area. This is the backdrop for stunning monuments that have been the silent witnesses to the heady adventures of great Hindu and Muslim dynasties whose struggles for power survive in local tales. Dynasties rose and fell from the 7th to the 18th centuries, landmark events were the defeat, in 1565, of the last great Hindu empire, Vijayanagar, and the death of the enlightened hero Tipu Sultan in 1799.

Karnataka's capital is the dynamic city of Bangalore, where you may hear just as much English spoken as the official state language, Kannada. As India's foremost center for IT, office buildings, luxurious hotels, and quality shops make a stark contrast with Mysore, just three hours' drive away. This slow-paced historical city is dominated by grand and fanciful palaces. Either city makes an ideal stop between visiting the national parks of Nagarhole, Bandipur and Mudumalai.

The walls of the great Mahanavami Platform at Vijayanagar are coated in vivacious friezes showing dancing girls, horse traders, and hunting scenes.

But less than 30 percent of the state's population lives in the cities. As you travel through countryside irrigated by the great river systems of the Cauvery and the Krishna, you cross the high Deccan Plateau that gives Karnataka its name: it is Kannada for "lofty land." ■

Bangalore

ONCE KNOWN FOR ITS FRESH AIR, TREES, AND PARKS, which brought relief to visitors from the hot upper plains, Bangalore is now a thundering, commercial city whose climate is no longer so benign. It is still one of the cleanest cities in India, however.

Bangalore
222 B2
India Tourist Office
K.F.C. Building, 48 Church St.
080-5585417

State Tourist Office
Mitra Towers, 10/4 Kasturba Rd., Queen's Circle
080-2212901

Cubbon Park
M.G. Rd.

The city was founded by Kempe Gowda, a lord of the Vijayanaga kingdom (see p. 236), who built a mud fort here in 1537. The Wodeyars of Mysore (see p. 230) took the city in 1687. Haider Ali (R.1761–1782) took Bangalore in 1758 and three years later usurped the Wodeyar throne. Keeping Mysore and nearby Srirangapatnam as his base, he made Bangalore a crossroads for east–west southern trading and for exporting cotton and other crops from this rich agricultural area. He and his son, Tipu Sultan (R.1782–1799), whose palace remains are well worth visiting, could thus raise huge taxes. These funded the famous Mysore army of 60,000 men, with its superb light cavalry, Telugu marksmen, and herds of huge, white Deccan cattle. This army was used

to win ports on the Kerala coast, aiming to crush the Peshwas of Pune (see p. 182) and the Nizams of Hyderabad (see pp. 248–49), and to establish trade with Arabia and Persia. Far from being the despot painted by the British, Tipu was imitating their mercantile and expansionist ideology, which is why Arthur Wellesley (later Duke of Wellington) needed to defeat him.

After Tipu's death (see p. 246) in 1799, Bangalore became a flourishing British garrison town and continued to be important up to independence. The British cantonment had everything a homesick servant of the empire could wish for: horse-racing, tennis courts, a pretty park, Victorian Gothic bungalows with herbaceous bordered gardens, the obligatory statue of the Queen-Empress

Victoria, and grand clubs for cards, croquet, snooker (a game similar to billiards), and lavish parties.

These British buildings and the city's two green spaces—**Cubbon Park** and the **Race Course**—give Bangalore its spaciousness and lingering elegance today. It may have highrises, new affluence, a population of almost eight million, and top-quality stores, but you can easily imagine colonial times, not long ago, when servants in white livery and gloves served cucumber sandwiches and chili-cheese toast to *memsahibs* wearing flower-printed dresses. Try driving through Cubbon Park, walking around the High Courts or one of the many churches, or visiting **Lalbagh Botanical Gardens.** Founded by Haider Ali in 1760 and further planted by Tipu, their 240 acres (97 ha) contain rare trees and other plants, British pavilions, and greenhouses. In February and August, the quintessentially British flower shows staged here have dazzling arrays of dahlias, chrysanthemums, and roses.

It is significant that the Karnataka government chose to site its huge neo-Dravadian-style

granite **Vidhana Soudha** (Secretariat and State Legislative) right in the British area, opposite the Law Courts. Winston Churchill, who always opposed India's desired independence, would doubtless have taken this as flattery. He came to live here in 1937 as a young soldier and wrote happy letters home describing his huge bungalow with its two acres (1 ha) of gardens, rose beds, and deep verandas wreathed in purple bougainvillea. He and two of his friends kept about 30 horses and devoted themselves to the serious purpose of life: polo. ∎

This splendid Victorian pavilion in Lalbagh Botanical Gardens is the setting for Bangalore's set-piece flower shows.

Information technology

Bangalore is India's information technology (IT) capital and the world's third most important IT city. It is also India's software capital, with exports growing at 100 percent a year and accounting for 57 percent of national exports. IT, together with science, has made Bangalore a more international city even than Mumbai (Bombay). Glass skyscrapers rising above the parks and brick buildings indicate a sensational new affluence. Formerly, Indian IT brains went to work for U.S. companies in California. Today,

the tables have turned: They have now returned home, set up their own companies, and are busy buying out weaker U.S. firms. Many multinationals find they now need to finance sleek new office buildings in Bangalore. Meanwhile, their Indian counterparts stock their offices with Indian-made, not American, equipment, rigorously tested and proven to be comparable to the products of the best U.S. brands. Hyderabad, with an enlightened state government, is following Bangalore's lead. ∎

Race Course
 Race Course Rd.
☎ 080-560001

A drive around old colonial Bangalore

Hire a driver for a morning or afternoon to explore British life in Bangalore and to glimpse the town's past as southern India's elegant, relaxed garden city. It is best to go on Saturday or Sunday, when there is less traffic.

Start by going to the **High Courts** ❶ (Attara Kacheri), a classical, arcaded stone building, painted Pompeian red and originally built in 1868 as the public offices. A statue of Bangalore's commissioner from 1834 to 1861, Sir Mark Cubbon, stands in front. The jacaranda trees to the left add a cloud of contrasting mauve when they blossom in springtime.

Across a ceremonial road that is often the scene of farmers' union protests, the imposing polished granite **Vidhana Soudha** (1956) (see p. 227) stands as the symbol of the fulfillment of the Kannada-speaking peoples' long ambition—to unite in one state. K. Hanumanthaiah, chief minister when the building was completed, said this "people's palace" would "reflect the power and dignity of the people." Certainly, it is India's largest civic structure. Its design takes inspiration from Karnataka's temple architecture: See the projecting balconies, the curving eaves, and the temple-like, curving towers that are added to the huge wings.

Now ask your driver to take you through **Cubbon Park,** almost 300 acres (121 ha) laid out by Cubbon in 1864. You may wish to

Busy streets in colonial Bangalore

get out for a stroll near the **Seshadri Iyer Memorial Hall** ❷ (1913), built to house the Public Library and named to honor a prime minister of Mysore state. Leave the park at the southern corner and go up R. R. M. Roy Road to glimpse the timeless, stucco **Bangalore Club** ❸ *(members only)*, with some nice old houses nearby. Return along Kasturba Gandhi Road to find three public buildings on the left. The middle one is the

---

🅼 See area map pages 222–23
▶ High Courts
🔄 5 miles (8 km)
🕐 2–3 hours
▶ Kempe Gowda Road

NOT TO BE MISSED
- Vidhana Soudha
- Cubbon Park
- Russell Market

Government Museum **④** (1876), whose sculpture gallery, hero stones, and Mysore school miniature paintings are worth a look.

At the far end of Kasturba Gandhi Road, an incongruous trio of **statues ⑤** stands at the main gate of Cubbon Park: a memorial statue of Queen Victoria (1906) and statues of Edward VII, and Mahatma Gandhi.

Turn right along Mahatma Gandhi Road to see the neoclassic, domed **St. Mark's Cathedral** (1812) on the right. Then turn left to find the Victorian Gothic **St. Andrew's**

Church **⑥** on Cubbon Road (1867). Drive past the church facade and down to **Russell Market ⑦**, built so that British *memsahibs* could shop in safety after a scandal concerning a moneylender and an abortion.

From here, drive up across Infantry Road and turn right back on Cubbon Road again to pass the palatial, whitewashed **Raj Bhavan ⑧** (1831), built as the British Residency, and go down Race Course Road to the end. Turn left, and you will find **Kempe Gowda Road,** an excellent place for fixed-price silk stores such as **Karnataka Silk Industries Corporation (K.S.I.C.) ⑨**. Helpful assistants advise on the lengths needed for your requirements and the suitability of the various silk weaves—crêpe de chine, georgette, chiffon, soft and spun silk, stone-washed and raw silk.

If you are feeling inspired by this drive, and are energetic enough, you can continue on to see Tipu's Palace and Lalbagh Botanical Gardens (see p. 227). ■

Facade of the High Courts

The granite Vidhana Soudha

Mysore

THE WODEYARS, ORIGINALLY GOVERNORS OF SOUTHERN Karnataka under the Vijayanaga emperors (see p. 236), rose to be rulers of Mysore and to determine its delightful character, preserved today, partly because the city does not have an airport. The former royal family still lives in a corner of the vast, city-center Amba Vilas Palace, the place to begin exploring the city.

Mysore
🅰 222 B1
Karnataka & Mysore Tourist Offices
✉ Yatri Niwas, J.L.B. Rd.
☎ 0821-423652

Amba Vilas Palace
✉ Entry on south side only; shoes and cameras must be deposited before entering; socks permitted
🕐 Open daily

Extravagant, fantastical **Amba Vilas Palace** (1897–1912), also known as the Maharaja's palace, was designed by Henry Irwin and outstrips most Rajasthan palaces. It takes most of a morning just to follow the route around it and to see the outbuildings. The Wodeyars built a fort here in 1524 while governors, but they moved away when they became rulers. Tipu later razed Mysore, intending to rebuild it; when the British reinstated the young Krishnaraja III as a puppet Wodeyar ruler in 1801, Mysore still needed rebuilding.

After a fire in 1897, Irwin was awarded the commission to rebuild. He created an Indo-Saracenic palace that manages to be simultaneously imperial, traditional, and progressive. On your way through, details to look for include the maharajas' *howdah* (seat used to ride elephants), encrusted with 24-carat gold, and the eight enormous bronze tigers by Robert William Colton. In the octagonal wedding hall, see the long friezes recording the 1930 Dussehra procession, the cast-iron pillars shipped out from Glasgow, and the Belgian stained-glass peacocks. In the Durbar Hall are whole avenues of carved pillars, huge inlaid doors, walls coated in arabesques, and a Mogul-style floor. Before leaving the compound, explore the surviving rooms of the older palace, now housing a museum, and some of the old temples. The palace is illuminated by tiny lights on Sundays and festivals.

Nearby, part of **Jaganmohan Palace** (1900) was transformed into a museum of musical instruments and miniature paintings in 1915 by Krishnaraja IV, who followed tradition in his enlightened and progressive policies, in his energetic building program for his model state, and in his loyalty to the British. You will find the **Sri Chamarajendra Art Gallery** at the back of the building, where Lord Curzon attended Krishnaraja IV's coronation; do not miss the murals of royal pastimes.

Near Amba Vilas are the City Corporation Offices and the Public Offices. Up Siyaji Rao Road are hospitals, schools, and the grand **Government House.** On Kalidasa Road, the **Manasa Gangotri Folklore Museum** has wonderful wooden *bhuta* figures from Mekkekattu (see p. 206). **Dvaraja Market** has sacks of flowers, pyramids of spices, neat arrangements of polished fruits and vegetables, and piles of fresh herbs.

Chamundi Hill makes a pleasant afternoon trip. Drive to the top to see the **temple** (12th century) dedicated to Mysore's titular deity,

Chamuneswari (Durga), which is made of solid gold; then walk down steps past the huge **Nandi bull** (1659) carved out of black granite. End the day with a visit to **Lalitha Mahal Palace Hotel,** built in 1931 for the foreign meat-eating guests of the strictly vegetarian maharaja. It has a wonderful double staircase, a period bar, and dining in the former ballroom. ■

Shwetavara-
haswamy Temple,
inside the Amba
Vilas compound

Dussehra (Dassera)

Mysore celebrates with gusto this week-long festival of the triumph of good over evil that arrives in September–October and harks back to the annual extravaganza at Vijayanagar. It is symbolized in the goddess Chamundeswari's (Durga's) triumph over the demon buffalo Mahishasura, rather than the northern India version, of Rama's triumph over Ravana. Vijayadashami marks the finale to ten days of pageantry: Caparisoned elephants, horses, and cavalry, plus some movie-starlike deities parade to the Banni Mantap, and everything ends

in dramatic fireworks. A cultural festival runs in parallel to honor Saraswati, goddess of the arts. This is a good opportunity to experience the special Carnatic music and dance of Karnataka in the palace's Durbar Hall and grounds—and some *yakshagana* dance-drama. The Mysore royals, famous for their hospitality, would hold their Mysore Week at this time. Events included races at the city's pretty racetrack and an extravagant outing to witness the *khedda* (elephant roundup) in the forest at Nagarhole (see pp. 232–33). ■

Sri Chamarajendra Art Gallery
✉ Back of Jaganmohan Palace
☎ 0821-423693
🕐 Closed Wed.
❓ No photography

Manasa Gangotri Folklore Museum
✉ Jayalakshmi Vilas Mansion
☎ 0821-515525
🕐 Closed Sat. p.m. & all Sun.

Lalitha Mahal Palace Hotel
✉ Siddharth Nagar
☎ 0821-571265

Nagarhole, Bandipur, & Mudumalai National Parks

Nagarhole National Park

⚠ 222 B1

✉ 60 miles (96.5 km) SW of Mysore

☎ 0821-480901

💲 $. Game viewing extra

Bandipur National Park

⚠ 222 B1

✉ 50 miles (80 km) S of Mysore

☎ 080-3341993

💲 $. Game viewing extra

Mudumalai National Park

⚠ 222 B1

💲 $. Game viewing extra

EVEN THOUGH MUDUMALAI IS IN TAMIL NADU, THESE three parks are treated together, since they border each other. Their wildlife, notably the herds of Karnataka elephants, roams freely among them. Furthermore, they are now collectively referred to as the Nilgiri Biosphere Reserve and constitute India's most extensive tract of continuous protected forest. To protect the wildlife, access is limited and visits are usually only permitted at certain hours each day.

All three parks are relatively easy to reach from Bangalore (see pp. 226–29), Mysore (see pp. 230–31), or Ooty (see pp. 280–81). Roads are good, and the scenery around Ooty is spectacular. The parks also fit well into a southern India itinerary, so be sure to reserve accommodations in advance. As usual, prices tend to include all meals, guides, jeep rides, and elephant and boat rides where

Coracle boats ferry people, their bicycles, and livestock across the Tungabhadra River at Vijayanagar.

available. The best time to visit is from October to May, staying at least three nights to get the full benefit. It takes time to learn how to spot the animals and identify the birds. (In June the heat is punishing; in post-monsoon September the ground cover is too thick to see game.)

In addition to elephants, you may come across *gaur* (Indian

bison), sambhar, several other species of deer, crocodiles, and a rich selection of birds; lucky and patient visitors may see a tiger or leopard. The great variety of bird life is another bonus.

NAGARHOLE NATIONAL PARK

Centered on the Kabini River and the lake created by damming it, this is one of the best parks in India for seeing and learning about animals and birds in a variety of settings. Accommodations in the maharaja of Mysore's hunting lodge and viceroy's buildings add further charm, as does the team of expert naturalists and the almost certain chance of seeing wild elephants.

The 110 square miles (284 sq km) of mixed deciduous trees, swamps, streams, and soaring bamboo clumps are home to hundreds of elephants. This is where the maharaja's annual *khedda* (elephant roundup) was held, and where the movie *Sabhu the Elephant Boy* was made—movies of both events are shown in the evenings. To watch a group of elephants for an hour or so at sunset simply moving through the riverside grasses, the baby elephants frolicking under the watchful eye of their nanny carers, is a truly memorable experience.

The drier it is, the better your

animal sightings along the river banks will be. On an evening boat ride you may see fat crocodiles lounging on the banks, while many elephants, bison, and deer arrive to populate this Garden of Eden.

On arrival, plan your itinerary with your naturalist. This might include jeep drives, a sunrise expedition on the lake in coracles (small boats made of buffalo hide), observing a waterhole from a *machan* (blind), and cruising up the Kabini at sunset. At the elephant camp you can see the elephants being bathed and you can feed them their breakfast of lentils and rice hay. Each day includes a siesta period and ends with a simple dinner around a campfire beside the lake.

BANDIPUR NATIONAL PARK

Created in the 1930s by the maharaja of Mysore, then expanded in the 1940s to join the Nagarhole and Mudumalai land, this park covers 340 square miles (880 sq km) of dry, deciduous forest south of the Kabini River.

You may sight elephants anywhere in the forest. Bird-watching is good here, too, and you can enjoy fine views from Rolling Rocks, over the deep and craggy Mysore Ditch, or from Gopalswamy Betta, a high ridge overlooking Mysore Plateau.

MUDUMALAI NATIONAL PARK, TAMIL NADU

This tract of 150 square miles (400 sq km) of forest nestles under and into the Nilgiri Hills and attracts a variety of wildlife. You may see giant squirrels, and bonnet and common langur monkeys, as well as the usual gaur, sambhar, and deer. The bird life includes species of the plains and hills attracted by springtime fruit trees. There are also delightful accommodations and the Kargudi elephant camp to visit. ■

Within an elephant herd, the young are looked after not only by their mothers but also by special "nanny" elephants.

Badami

🅰 222 B3

🆂 $

Badami Medieval Sculpture Gallery

🕒 Closed Fri.

Pattadakal

🅰 222 B3

🆂 $

Badami, Pattadakal, & Aihole

THREE CLUSTERS OF EXQUISITE CAVES AND TEMPLES, isolated in the dry but beautiful Malprabha River Valley of rural Karnataka, rival those at Mahabalipuram in Tamil Nadu (see pp. 260–61). Together they form the foundation of the glorious achievements that followed in medieval cities throughout the subcontinent. They are worth every effort to reach them across the open Deccan plains from Vijayangar, Bijapur, or Hubli.

A succession of Early Chalukya rulers were responsible for these masterpieces. From their first base at Aihole, the Chalukyas rose from the fourth century to control most of Karnataka, as well as parts of Andhra Pradesh and Maharashtra, until the Rashtrakutas overthrew them in 757. Pattadakal was their religious center and coronation city.

BADAMI
Pulakeshin I (*R.* 543–566) moved the capital to Badami, doubtless attracted by the soaring, protective bluffs surrounding a beautiful lake. Later, Pulakeshin II (*R.* 610–642) left from here to defeat Harsha of Kanauj, the most powerful king of northern India, and to push the Chalukya boundaries south when he came into conflict with the Pallavas of Kanchipuram. After repeated Chalukya raids on Kanchipuram in 612 and after, the Pallavas retaliated and took Badami in 654. Pulakeshin lost his life, but his successor Vikramaditya I expelled the Pallavas, and his son Vinayaditya (*R.* 696–733) enjoyed a long and peaceful reign. Pallava troubles returned under Vikramaditya II (*R.* 733–744), whose son lost out to the Rashtrakutas.

To enjoy Badami's treasures in their best light, you need to see some in the morning and the rest in the evening. In the morning, see the cave temples cut into the southern cliffs. The morning sun illuminates

both the sculptures and the pinks and purples of the sandstone. Created in the sixth century, their bold and rounded sculptures have a stunning robustness, while the column, capital, and ceiling decoration is a delicate mix of figures, foliage, jewels, and garlands. Find images of Harihare (left) and Shiva with Nandi (right) in **Cave no. 1,** with a magnificent 18-armed dancing Shiva nearby. **Cave no. 2** has images of Vishnu as Varaha (left) and Trivikrama (right), while **Cave no. 3,** inscribed with the date 578, is even richer and has traces of painting; see especially Vishnu on the coiled serpent and the Narasimha composition. **Cave no. 4** is Jain, adorned with restrained images of Tirthankaras.

In the evening, you can take a pony and trap through the narrow lanes of Badami village and then walk along the lakeside to enjoy the sunset from **Bhutanatha Temple** (7th and 11th centuries). To explore further, see the two lakeside temples in town and, up the path behind it, three clifftop temples and gorgeous views. **Mahakuta,** a village not far from here, has a group of four temples built in the years between Badami's and Pattadakal's.

PATTADAKAL
Outside the village, set in manicured lawns beside the Malprabha River, these now isolated eighth-century temples

A sensuous carving adorns Sanameshvara Temple at Pattadakal, the eighth-century royal commemorative and coronation site for early Chalukyan rulers.

mix various styles to achieve the climax of Early Chalukyan building.

Unless you are a true temple addict, be selective here. Go across the lawns, past earlier and simpler temples, to see the two largest and most developed, dedicated to Virupaksha and Mallikarjuna, two forms of Shiva. Built by the queen in about 745 to commemorate Vikramaditya II's victory over the Pallavas, they are decorated with large sculptures full of a vitality that is almost contagious. See especially the panels flanking the east porch of Virupaksha; inside, there are the sensuous courting couples and delicate narrative friezes on the columns.

AIHOLE

The many Hindu and Jain monuments here, both rock-cut caves and temples, span the periods of the Early Chalukyas, the Rashtrakutas, and the Late Chalukyas (10th–13th centuries), who ruled northern Karnataka from Basavakalyan and built splendid temples at Ittagi (see p. 244) and Dambal. Their patrons were kings and merchants, since the town was then an important trading center. Together they display the bold experiments of this period. The best way to enjoy them is to make your base the little government rest house, whose staff can prepare food if asked on your arrival. ■

Aihole

222 B3

Aihole Archaeological Museum

Closed Fri.

Badami's soaring cliffs and lake make a dramatic yet peaceful setting for Bhutanatha Temple.

Vijayanagar

Vijayanagar
🅰 222 B3

Hampi
🅰 7 miles (11 km)
NE from Hospet
💲 $

CONSIDERED BY MANY TO EQUAL PETRA IN JORDAN WITH its impressive buildings amid large rocks beside the mighty Tungabhadra River, Vijayanagar's ruins were forgotten until a team of archaeologists started work here in the 1960s. Yet the powerful Hindu rulers of this once huge metropolis controlled all of southern India and provided the unifying power to keep the Muslim threat at bay until 1565. Today, royal, religious, and civic buildings dot the former city, sharing space with banana groves, paddy fields, and villages.

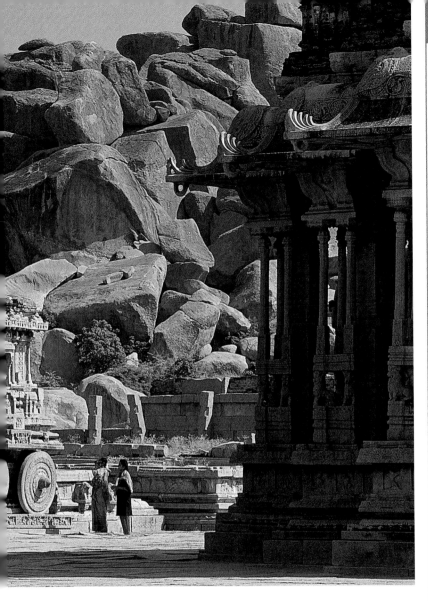

Vijayanagar's rulers rose in parallel, and in rivalry, with the Muslim Bahmanis based at Gulbarga and Bidar (see pp. 240–41). They established their base at Vijayanagar (City of Victory) in 1336, after seizing the waning Hoysala territories in southern Karnataka, then swiftly regained most lands lost to the Delhi sultans. Thus they achieved the allegiance of the newly liberated rulers of the whole region, down to the tip of Tamil Nadu, apart from most of the Malabar coast.

The consequent vast amounts of tribute money and taxes were used by Bukka I (*R*.1354–1377) and Devaraya II (*R*.1423–1446), then by Krishnadevaraya (*R*.1510–1529) and his brother-in-law, Achyutadevaraya (*R*.1529–1542) to create their imperial capital. Its size, trading

The fine carving of royal Vitthala Temple's granite stone chariot and magnificent *mandapa* (hall) contrast with the rough, boulder-strewn landscape.

These grand buildings probably housed the royal elephants.

Visitor tips
The five-hour drive, 209 miles (337 km) north of Bangalore, is relentless and best tackled by leaving very early. Or, you can take the overnight train to Hospet. Otherwise, approach from Badami (93 miles/150 km) or Bijapur (129 miles/207 km). It's best to stay at Hospet and explore Vijayanagar's various sights with a combination of driving and walking. Take a picnic if you are going to be out all day.

wealth, grand buildings, and grandiose rulers were compared to Rome by its visitors.

But on Achyutadevaraya's death the commander of the imperial forces, Ramaraya, took control and kept the rightful successor in prison. It was Ramaraya's high-handedness with the sultans who had emerged from the Bahmani breakup that led to war. In January 1565, at Talikota near Aihole (see p. 235), the combined forces of Bijapur, Bidar, Golconda, and Ahmednagar crushed the Vijayanaga army and then spent a reputed four years sacking the city of its vast wealth, burning the wooden buildings to melt off the gold decoration.

Many buildings survived because they were built of stone and a visit to see the remains of Vijayanagar is still highly recommended. There are two main areas to visit: The sacred and the royal, with extras for those with time.

A very good place to start is Hampi village. Here you can visit **Virupaksha Temple** (13th to 17th century, *$*), the only temple in the area still in use; its resident elephant helps with the *pujas*. Hemakuta Hill rises above it, a huge slope of granite that provides fine views up the river and has small temples and shrines. Through the great rocks there are two monolithic Ganeshas and Krishnadevaraya's 1513 **Krishna Temple** *(Hemakuta Hill)*, built to celebrate a military campaign in Orissa. Just beyond, a lane on the right leads through a banana grove to a huge monolithic Narasimha.

A second walk from Hampi goes up the main street of stores and cafés, then left along a path that passes the riverside Kodandarama Temple, where busloads of pilgrims come to worship Rama. Indeed, this is epic country:

Farther along the path, after a detour down a wide bazaar to see the 16th-century **Achyutaraya Temple** *(foot of Matanga Hill)*, you pass what is believed to be the cave where Sugriva hid Sita's jewel. The riverside path continues from here to Krishnadevaraya's 16th-century **Vitthala Temple** *($)* and surrounding city bazaars. Roaming the complex, you will find the piers carved into rearing animals and riders, the great stone chariot, and a basement frieze of Portuguese horse traders, who made rich profits from the Vijayanagas.

A third walk starts at the Royal Enclosure. First, see the private **Lotus Mahal** *(Zenana Enclosure, $)* and the amazing elephant stables. Return around the palace walls and go along the road to the **Ramachandra Temple** (15th century). Its outer wall is covered with an incredible relief showing the Mahanavami festival procession; there are more reliefs of Rama stories inside. Beyond the temple lies the area for royal public performance. You can find the platform for the hall of justice, the step-well, and the magnificent **Mahanavami Platform,** entirely covered with friezes of royal hunting, partying, and marching; the platform is thought to be the place where the king sat to watch the Mahanyvami festivities.

Finally, for a special atmospheric outing, choose either sunrise or sunset to climb Matanga Hill: There are a lot of big steps, but the trip is worth the effort. ■

A view from Hemakuta Hill over Hampi village and the tall *gopura* **(gateway) of its Virupaksha Temple, with the Tungabhadra River beyond**

Southern sultanates

ALTHOUGH SMALL TODAY, EACH OF THE OLD SULTANATE cities of Bijapur, Gulbarga, Bidar, and Golconda were at one time a great medieval fort city, powerful enough to hold back the invading Mogul armies. Each has left monuments, whose romantic designs and silhouettes are a rich amalgam reflecting the peoples who migrated there, initially to Gulbarga. Their rulers, lacking the traditional Islamic passion for recording events, have left a certain mystery: We know little about them. However, we have a number of their artifacts, especially some stunning miniature paintings, whose vivid colors and lyrical lines confirm strong cultural links with Safavid Iran, with the addition of the sensuality found in local southern Indian sculpture.

Bijapur
📍 222 B4
Bijapur Tourist Office
✉ Hotel Mayura Adil Shahi
☎ 08352-20359

Visitor tip
Bijapur Tourist Office is the only information post in this area, so it is best to collect information there, before moving on.

BIJAPUR
As you wander the streets of this laid-back provincial town, where a pony and trap is still a regular form of transportation, it is only the evidence of the immensely grand buildings and monuments at every turn that convinces you Bijapur was once great. This was the prosperous capital of the Adil Shahi dynasty (1490–1686), established by Yusuf Adil Khan (*R*.1490–1510). Its rulers tempered their extravagant patronage with an acute aesthetic sense. But protracted and expensive wars and then decline under Mogul rule finally extinguished Bijapur's power.

GULBARGA
Although little remains to testify to it, the sultanate story begins here, 103 miles (165 km) northeast of Bijapur (see map pp. 222–23). It is a story worth telling, because the history of this part of India, where north meets south, can be confusing.

A succession of incursions into southern India by the Delhi sultans began in 1296 and finally brought the Yadava, Kakatiya, Hoysala, and Pandya dynasties to a close. Muhammad Tughlaq even moved his capital down to Daulatabad (see p. 175) in 1327 to consolidate his triumphs. But when he returned to Delhi in 1334, the Muslim governors of Madurai and Daulatabad proclaimed their independence, and the Hindu Vijayanaga rulers began to liberate their fellow chieftains.

The governors of Daulatabad rose to become the powerful Bahmanis, moving to Gulbarga in 1347, then departing for Bidar in 1424. Their vast territories included Maharashtra, northern Karnataka, and Andhra Pradesh. Gulbarga became a metropolis attracting other Muslims—Persians, Arabs, Turks, and Abyssinians—and its buildings reflect this in their Persian forms and decoration.

Mosques and palaces filled the great circular **citadel,** whose 52-foot-thick (16 m) crenellated walls and 15 watchtowers now surround just one beautiful mosque (1367). Outside the walls the Bahmanis built their tombs and those of saints who boosted their image; see the lively **Dargah of Hazrat Gesu Nawaz** (died 1422), which, with its Persian painted neighbor, attracts many pilgrims but is open only to men. Early royal tombs lie in the fields west of the fort: massive cubic chambers with domes. Find later tombs at Haft Gunbad, near the Dargah.

Gulbarga's fate was to achieve independence and lose out to, first, the Adil Shahis of Bijapur, then the Moguls.

BIDAR

After moving its capital here in 1424, the Bahmani kingdom reached its zenith under Ahmad I (*R*.1422–1436), Muhammed Bahmani III (*R*.1463–1482), and Bahmani's able prime minister,

Mahmud Gawan. At its height, the Bahmani kingdom stretched from the Arabian Sea to the Bay of Bengal. Internal rivalries, however, soon broke up the kingdom and five sultanate states emerged. Qasim Barid (*R*.1488–1504) took control of a much reduced Bidar, and his successors mixed patronage with decline. Three other sultanates— Golconda, Bijapur, and Ahmednagar in Maharashtra—had Shia Muslim rulers, which contributed to their antagonism to the Sunni Moguls.

Today, a visit to Bidar transports you to those distant times, much more so than a visit to Gulbarga. The **fort,** whose massive walls and seven gateways are Baridi work, overlooks the plains. Inside are

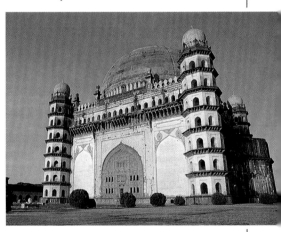

substantial remains of the royal palaces, including tiled and inlaid walls, the Solah Khamb Mosque (1327), the Diwan-i-Am (public audience hall), and the throne room. In the walled city, see the **Shihabuddin Ahmad Is Takht-I Kirmani gateway** and the huge **Madrasa** ("place of learning") founded by Mahmud Gawan in 1472 for Shia studies. Its minaret and front arcade have bold calligraphic motifs and, in places, still retain their richly colored tiles. ■

Gulbarga
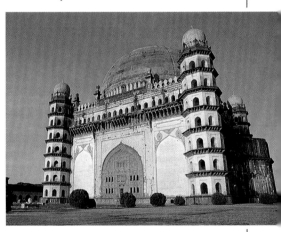 222 B4

Bidar
222 B4

Muhammad Adil Shah II built his own mausoleum in Bijapur, the Gol Gumbaz, whose huge dome, at 145 feet (44 m) in diameter, is one of the world's largest.

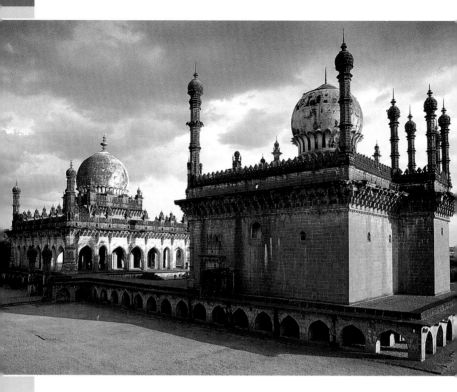

Outside Bijapur's city walls, the early morning sun illuminates the tomb of Ibrahim Rauza.

Bijapur by pony & trap

Bijapur's great black mosques, walls, and tombs look their most impressive in the early morning or late afternoon, and what better way to travel to them than by pony and trap? Women should cover their arms and legs and take a head shawl. Agree on a price with your pony and trap master before you start. Ask him to wait when you want to get down, and pay him at the end with a suitable addition for waiting time.

During your ride, imagine an exotic court of energetic patronage, funded by Vijayanaga booty. It found expression in buildings, miniature-painting, music, and religious Sufi learning and science. Only after the final Mogul onslaught and victory by Aurangzeb in 1686 did the decline set in.

Start at the landmark **Gol Gumbaz** ❶ (1655), the majestically simple tomb of Muhammad II, with a huge, hemispherical dome on a cube-shaped base; the interior is almost austere in its simplicity. Hop back on your trap and go straight ahead from the Gol

Gumbaz gateway; then turn right on Jama Masjid Road. Here, you will find a **trio of monuments** ❷: the incomplete but nevertheless monumental **Jama Masjid** (1576), **Yusuf's Old Jama Masjid** (1513), and, down a side street, the tiny **Ali Sahib Pir Masjid**, with fine plaster decoration.

Now go toward the citadel and past its entrance to find **Asar Mahal** ❸, built as a hall of justice but later converted into a reliquary to hold two hairs of the Prophet. Its civic origins give us a good idea of the character of Bijapur's palace buildings. Perhaps, like

Solapur

AZAD ROAD

TEMPLE ROAD

NEHRU ROAD

STATION   BACK   ROAD

8
■ **Sharza Bastion**

Gol
Gumbaz 1
START

Atke Gate

MAHATMA   GANDHI   ROAD

Malika Jahan
Masjid

Gagan
Mahal **Citadel**
4

JAMA   MASJID   ROAD

3 Asar
Mahal

Mecca
Gate

9
■
Ibrahim
Rauza

6 **5**

2 ■ **Jama Masjid**

7
Taj
Bauri

Jod
Gumbaz

Karimuddiin's
Mosque

■ **Yusuf's Old Jama Masjid**

Ali Sahib
Pir Masjid

JUMNAL ROAD

Hospet

| 0 | 600 meters |
| 0 | 600 yards |

[icon] See area map pages 222–23
[icon] Gol Gumbaz
[icon] About 2 miles (3 km)
[icon] 2 hours
[icon] Ibrahim Rauza

NOT TO BE MISSED
- Gol Gumbaz
- Asar Mahal
- Walking the walls
- Ibrahim Rauza

this building, they had slender timber columns, inlaid wooden panels, and murals of courtly scenes or floral patterns, and they overlooked formal gardens—images seen in some miniature paintings.

Go into the **citadel 4**, protected by thick inner walls, to find **Karimuddin's Mosque** (1310), begun when the Delhi sultans were in residence and built with stones from destroyed temples. Gangan Mahal, Ali I's audience hall, is easy to identify: Its great triple arch faces the open area where the people sat.

Outside the west wall of the citadel is the small and finely decorated **Malika Jahan Masjid 5**, possibly specially built for women. Nearby, **Jod Gumbaz 6** is a pair of tombs with elegant facades and slightly bulbous domes containing the remains of Khan Muhammad, commander of the Adil Shahi troops, and Abdul Razzaq, his spiritual advisor. The large, square tank with stepped sides and arcades is **Taj Bauri 7**, where the entrance steps descend to a big arched gateway.

Now go out of the city by the Mecca Gate, turn right, and go in at the next one, Atke Gate. Here, you can climb the wall to see the Malik-i-Maidan, Bijapur's famous gun, which sits on the **Sharza Bastion 8**. This is a good moment to look at Bijapur's magnificent **walls** (1565), built by Yusuf Adil Khan. They are 32 feet (10 m) high, reinforced by 96 round

bastions, and equipped with guardrooms and a parapet. You can walk along the broad path on top of them right around the city.

Your ride ends with a visit to the best of all, the Adil Shahi buildings: **Ibrahim Rauza 9** (1628). This is a tomb and mosque built by Ibrahim II for his queen, Taj Sultana, but later converted into a mausoleum for himself and his family. You enter through a single gateway and go through a formal garden to reach both buildings, which stand on a plinth. Take time to look carefully at the exterior of the tomb: It rises up in layers, crowned by a bulbous dome that sits on a ring of petals. Now go into the verandah to look closely at its outer walls, doorways, and windows, and enjoy the precision-cut geometric and calligraphic designs. Some are cut through as screens, others are cut in shallow relief. ■

More places to visit in Karnataka

ARSIKERE & ARALAGUPPE
For more 13th-century Hoysala temple elegance and richness, visit the towns of Arsikere and Aralaguppe. A second Aralaguppe temple, **Kalleshvara** (ninth century), has a beautiful ceiling panel.
🅰 222 B2 **Arsikere** ✉ 27 miles (44 km) northeast of Hassan

BAGALI, KURUVATTI, & HARIHAR
Bagali and Kuruvatti are villages with Chalukya temples. Bagali's **Kalleshvara** (tenth century) has surprisingly provocative sculptures. Kuruvatti's **Chalukya** (11th century) has masterpiece bracket figures on the east doorway. Harihar town has a splendid Hoysala temple, **Harihareshvara** (1224).
🅰 222 B3 **Bagali** ✉ 34 miles (55 km) southwest of Hospet

BELUR & HALEBID
The great Hoysala ruler Vishnuvardhana (*R*.1108–1142) built the Channekashava Temple at his capital, **Belur,** to celebrate his defeat of the Cholas in 1116. The dense, fluent carving riots over the squat yet refined building; note the high plinth, star-shaped plan, lathe-turned pillars, and polished surfaces.

At nearby **Halebid,** visit the incomplete double Hoysalesvara Temple, designed and begun by Kedaroja for the Hoysala ruler Narasimha I (*R*.1141–1182). Up on the platform you can follow the bands of decoration with their lively carving and precision, showing rows of elephants, stories from the epics, baroque scrollwork, and scenes from courtly life. Above them, the great sculptures include Shiva dancing with the flayed skin of the elephant demon and Brahma seated on a goose. The sumptuously bejeweled temple-guardian figures are especially fine, as is the fat Ganesh figure. To visit longer at the Hoysala temples, you can stay in Hassan.
🅰 222 B3 **Belur** ✉ 23 miles (38 km) northwest of Hassan; **Halebid** ✉ 20 miles (32 km) north of Hassan

CHITRADURGA FORT
At the halfway point of the Bangalore–Hospet road, this is a good place to stretch your legs. Go through several great gates to find two Hoysala temples and various tanks, palace buildings, and lamp columns.
🅰 222 B2 ✉ 124 miles (200 km) northwest of Bangalore

ITTAGI & OTHER TEMPLES
There are some very rural villages on the Hospet–Hubli road; Ittagi makes a wonderful picnic spot. Before this, you can visit the ninth- and tenth-century temples at **Kukkunur,** on the way to Ittagi, where you can enjoy the highly decorated **Mahadeva Temple** (1112). On toward Hubli, the

A Jain pilgrim worships at the foot of the 58-foot-high (8 m) statue of Gomateshvara at Shravanabelagola.

Silk, the state industry

Karnataka produces 85 percent of India's raw silk, and the industry is closely controlled by the government at every stage. Japanese male moths are mated with local Mysore females, who are carefully checked for disease. Once hatched, the pupa are sold at a fixed price to the mulberry-bush owner or to farmers, who rear them to cocoon stage.

This is when you can see woven mats propped up in the morning sun outside small farms. The worms on them eat mulberry leaves continuously for 26–28 days, during which they molt four times and grow to be 4–6 inches (10–15 cm) long. They then turn from white to yellow and for about four days furiously spin their cocoons with a viscous solution; each one of these will be unraveled to about 4,000 feet (1,200 m) of silk yarn. The cocoons are then sold for boiling, reeling, dyeing, and weaving. You will be made very welcome at most roadside silk-production units, where the managers are usually happy to explain the precise workings of each of the processes to you. ∎

temples at **Lakkundi** are Late Chalukya buildings of gray-green schist, all richly carved; this village is especially nice to wander in. Finally, the **Dodda Basappa Temple** (12th century) at **Dambal** is one of the most beautifully carved Late Chalukya temples. **Ittagi** ✉ 33 miles (53 km) west of Hospet

KODAGU (COORG)

This beautiful area mixes rugged mountains with cardamom jungle, paddy fields, and orderly coffee plantations established by the British. The tall and graceful people, known as Kodavas or Coorgis, have maintained their distinct culture, including heavy jewelry, very rich saris, ancestor worship, and cuisine. Driving through the area, pause at **Madikeri** (Mercara) with its fort-palace, and **Talakaveri,** where the Kaveri River springs from the wooded slopes of Brahmagiri Hill. ⛰ 222 B1 **Madikeri** ✉ 60 miles (96 km) west of Mysore

MALNAD

This wild, forested region offers a combination of waterfalls (for Jog Falls see p. 206), craggy peaks, and monuments created by the Nayaka rulers of the 16th and 17th centuries. Having done well under the Vijayanagas, they became independent, with capitals at Keladi, then Ikkeri. Your base can be **Shimoga,** whose restored **Shivappa Nayaka Palace** overlooking the Tunga River is worth visiting. One outing is to **Keladi** and **Ikkeri's temples,** another to **Nagar, Devaganga's** tanks and pavilions, and **Kavaledurga's** citadel. Take a trip north to **Balligave** and **Banavasi's** Hoysala and Late Chalukya temples, or south to **Amritpur's** outstanding Hoysala temple (1196). ⛰ 222 A2 **Shimoga** ✉ 97 miles (156 km) north of Hassan, 120 miles (193 km) southwest of Hospet

RANGANATHITTU BIRD SANCTUARY

An early morning or evening visit to this bird sanctuary near Srirangapatnam is magical. Take a boat out on the lake with an ornithologist for some peaceful bird-watching, looking out for electric blue kingfishers to great gan-gling herons, spoonbills, and openbill storks; there are also crocodiles in the water. ⛰ 222 B1 ✉ 12 miles (19 km) north of Mysore

SOMNATHPUR

Even if you think you have seen enough temples, you will delight in this little gem found down country lanes, a 90-minute drive out of Mysore. Built in 1268, the **Keshava Vishnu Temple** is the last and most complete of the three great Hoysala temples (see Belur & Halebid). Ask the guardian if you may go up onto the walls to enjoy fabulous views of the star-shaped plan and the densely carved roofs that top each of the shrines. ⛰ 222 B1 ✉ 21 miles (75 km) east of Mysore

SRIRANGAPATNAM (SERINGAPATAM)

The island fortress on the Kaveri River is synonymous with Tipu Sultan (see p. 226), killed here in 1799 when General Harris stormed the citadel, confirming British supremacy in southern India. Get a flavor of the fort's great ramparts and visit the possible site of the breach and the place where Tipu fell. Then find the pretty, Mogul-influenced **Daria Daulat Bagh** (1784), Tipu's pleasure resort, where there are delicate murals and drawings of his sons. A small formal garden surrounds the cenotaphs of Tipu and his father, Haider Ali, who are buried together underneath them. ⛰ 222 B1 ✉ 9 miles (14 km) north of Mysore

SHRAVANABELAGOLA

Southern India's most sacred Jain site is believed to have been where the Mauryan emperor Chandragupta died in about 300 B.C. If you are physically fit, the reward of walking up Indragiri Hill is to see the colossal, calm, monolithic figure of Gomateshvara (981) that has been carved out of the rock; or, visit the priest's house with its painted walls.

It is worth arranging a visit to **Nritgram dance village** (Tel 080-8466312), founded by dancer Protima Bedi, to learn about different forms of Indian dance and see dancing. ⛰ 222 B2 ✉ 56 miles (90 km) north of Mysore ∎

Andhra Pradesh

Andhra Pradesh has much to offer, though few visitors come here. Hyderabad is littered with dilapidated palaces, the backdrop to a dynamic city that today looks to Bangalore's IT success as its inspiration. Its infrastructure is being entirely rebuilt at a furious speed, adding overpasses, new airport terminals, a hi-tech city, and entertainment parks; a film city is already up and running.

In contrast, if you are feeling adventurous, leave the capital and venture into the rugged countryside, where you will be well rewarded with evocative, offbeat sites but expect simple accommodations. Not far from Hyderabad lie the remains of Nagarjunakonda and Warangal, whose ramparts and fort you might have to yourself.

At Tirupati, in southeastern Andhra Pradesh, you can join the seething masses of Hindu pilgrims in their daily *pujas* to Lord Venkateswara in what is believed to be the world's richest temple. Around Vishakapatnam is a rich landscape made up of the Kailasha Hills, Orissan temples, and Buddhist and Dutch ruins. ■

It is always worth climbing up India's forts for an overview of the surrounding city and countryside, as here at Golconda Fort.

Golconda & Hyderabad

GOLCONDA FORT IS NOT INDIA'S BIGGEST, BUT IT IS ONE of its most spectacular. Great crenellated walls with round bastions run 3 miles (5 km) around the bottom of a rocky bluff in a forbidding, boulder-strewn landscape. Inside, substantial remains cover the hill, with the royal Durbar Hall at the top. The adjacent city of Hyderabad developed as a result of Golconda's expansion.

Golconda Fort's many surviving buildings give a vivid idea of medieval fort life.

Golconda Royal Tombs
- ✉ Golconda
- 🕐 Closed Fri.
- 💲 $

Golconda
- 🗺 223 C4
Andhra Pradesh Tourist Information
- ✉ Yatrinivas, S.P. Rd., Secunderabad
- ☎ 040-843931

Already in the 12th century, Golconda was a wealthy fort city. Later, it was an important outpost of the Bahmani kingdom, whose Turkish governor, Quli Qutb al-Mulk (R.1494–1543), broke free to establish his own kingdom and Qutb Shahi line of sultans. An outstanding military leader, he consolidated his gains over rival rulers, including those of Vijayanagar and Orissa, putting Golconda on a level footing with Bijapur.

The royal necropolis, near the fort, reflects the magnificence of these rulers. Seven **tombs** stand in a formal garden. Each has an onion dome perched on a cube-shaped mausoleum, surrounded by a richly ornamented arcade, with additional corner minarets. In early morning or sunset light, the whole ensemble is hauntingly romantic.

The reign of Ibrahim Qutb Shah (R.1550–1580) marked Golconda's peak. Under his successor, Muhammad Quli Qutb Shah (R. 1580–1612), plans were made for expansion despite external threats, and in 1591 the city of Hyderabad was laid out beside the Musi River.

HYDERABAD
Comparative peace followed. Moguls and Marathas watched for opportunities to pounce on Hyderabad's wealth and its stocks of diamonds; in 1687 the Moguls conquered the city. Later, Mogul emperor Muhammad Shah's representative in Aurangabad, Nizam ul Mulk, declared independence and

took the title Asaf Jah I (R.1724–1748). Hyderabad, India's largest state (82,000 sq miles), recovered to withstand British, French, and Maratha threats. It finally gave in to the idea of independent India only in 1956.

Today Hyderabad is India's sixth largest city—a chaotic, ever-expanding urban sprawl that takes little care of its heritage. Encompassing Old and New Hyderabad plus Secunderabad, a station for British troops founded in 1853 after the British alliance, it is not an easy city to grasp. Here are a few things to look for.

Set the mood with a visit to the **Salar Jung Museum,** a vast and random collection made by the Nizam's prime minister, Salar Jung (1899–1949). Then find the land-mark pink **High Court** (1916), designed by Vincent Esch, whose carved Agra sandstone has lapis lazuli–glazed domes and gilded finials. Esch's boys' school is next door. Along Mahboob Shahi Road

there is a rare survivor of Quli Qutb Shah's original buildings, the **Badshahi Ashurkhana** (1592–96), the royal house of mourning, with beautiful enamel tile mosaics (1611). The Nizam's prime ministers lived in the **Diwan Deorhi** across the road and worth exploring to find the Chini Khana's mosaic walls. Farther up the same road you find the **Charkaman** (four arches, 1594) and Old Hyderabad's focus, the **Char Minar** (four towers, 1591), once the ceremonial gateway to the palace, now constantly threatened by developers.

In this area you can find *bidri* workers and pearl stores (see box). **Mecca Masjid** (1598) is one of India's largest mosques; the central arch has red stones made from earth brought from Mecca. Some of Hyderabad's many dilapidated palaces are found south of here: **Paigarh** and **Chaumhalla** near-by, **Jahannuma** and **Falaknuma** a mile (1.6 km) or so farther out. ∎

Hyderabad
🅰 223 C4

Hyderabad Tourist Office
✉ 2nd floor, Sandozi Building, 26 Himayat Nagar
☎ 040-7630037

Salar Jung Museum
✉ Sardar Patel Rd.
🕐 Closed Fri.
💲 $

Badshahi Ashurkhana
✉ Mahboob Shahi Rd.
🕐 May be closed to visitors

Diwan Deorhi
✉ Sardar Patel Rd.
🕐 May be closed to visitors

Mecca Masjid
✉ Sardar Patel Rd.

Pearls & *bidri* work

The fabulously rich Nizams of Hyderabad were famous for their love of pearls, which they wore, rubbed on their bodies, and even ate ground up. Hyderabad is still India's pearl market, where every wealthy bride-to-be wants to shop. In little workshops around Char Minar, pearls grown in Japan

are sorted, pierced, sorted again, and either sold or re-exported. Many go straight to the shops in nearby Pertheghatty Road, where they are sorted by color, size, and quality. Clients select their pearl type and the required number is counted out, priced by weight, and strung on silk; the family jeweler will add the gemstones and a fancy clasp. In the same area, the special Muslim craft of bidri ware can be seen in the little alleys. This is the technique of decorating metalwork with a very fine silver or brass inlay of arabesque, floral, geometric, or calligraphic patterns. ∎

A Hyderabad craftsman uses tiny pearls to decorate a bangle.

Eastern & southern Andhra Pradesh

TRAVELING FROM HYDERABAD THROUGH THE BARREN landscape to the northeast is quite a tough trip, but on the way you can explore the glories of the Kakatiya rulers of the 13th and 14th centuries, whose territories nudged the Gangas of Orissa to the north and the Cholas of Tamil Nadu to the south. Use a car and driver.

EASTERN ANDHRA PRADESH

First stop is the Kakatiyas' second capital, **Warangal,** laid out by Ganapatideva *(R.*1199–1262) and his daughter, Queen Rudramadeva *(R.*1262–1289); see the two rings of outer earthen walls, the monumental gateways, the massive granite inner fort walls, and the temple portals. Two miles (3 km) away, the fine gray-green basalt **Thousand-Pillared Temple** (1163) stands at Hanamkonda, the first Kakatiya capital. The enthusiastic can continue 42 miles (68 km) to **Palampet** for the superb Ramappa Temple (1213) and nearby Ghanapur's shrines; clever Kakatiya engineers created both lakes.

Travel southwest from Hyderabad to reach Vijayapuri in time to catch the morning boat (usually 9:30 a.m.) to an island in the Krishna River, to see tantalizing limestone sculptures that testify to **Nagarjunakonda's** former glory. In the third and fourth centuries the Ikshvakus, Andhra's most powerful rulers, made this their capital and patronized fine Buddhist and secular buildings that extended over more than eight square miles (20 sq km). Their monuments were rediscovered by archaeologists in the 1950s, but in 1960 the Nagarjuna Sagar Dam opened and almost the whole area was flooded; the island you visit was once the summit of Nagarjuna Hill. It is well worth visiting, however, to see the fort remains, the reconstructed stadium and monastery, *maha chaitya* (great *stupa,* third century) and other stupas, and the amazing sculptures on display in the museum.

If you follow the Krishna River to its lush delta, you will come to **Vijayawada,** an isolated and fascinating spot best reached by train or air, because it is a long road journey. It has been an important commercial center since at least the fifth century. In town, the **Victoria Jubilee Museum** has impressive local Buddhist finds. Set off to see **Kondapalle's** fort and **Undavalli's** rock-cut sanctuaries. Farther away, southward through tobacco, cotton, and paddy fields, **Guntur's Boudhasree Archaeological Museum** has more local Buddhist finds. Continue to **Amaravati,** once known as Maha Chaitya (Great Stupa), the site of India's largest and most elaborate stupa (third century B.C. to fourth century A.D.). The majority of its sculptures are now shared between Chennai Government Museum (see p. 259) and London's British Museum, but it is still worth going to this haunting site beside the Krishna River; its museum displays the many recent finds.

The verdant Godavari River Delta is a historically prosperous area dotted with fields of rice and sugar, with immensely beautiful scenery and fascinating places to visit. Stay in **Rajahmundry** and make an outing to see the temples of **Bikkavolu, Drakasharama,** and, best of all, **Samalkot,** an 11th-century temple and the area's largest East Chalukya monument. Alternatively, cross the Godavari to visit **Guntupalle's** Buddhist relics in a wooded ravine. And do not leave without taking the boat trip up the Godavari to visit **Godavari Gorge** in the wooded hills of the Eastern Ghats.

Vishakhapatnam, a huge port founded by the English in 1689, faces onto a fine broad bay that opens into the Bay of Bengal. As India's principal port, naval base, and industrial center on the east coast, it is equipped with good hotels from which to explore the beautiful surrounding rural area. In the nearby forested Kailasha Hills, you can find **Simhachalam's** hilltop Varaha Narasimha Temple (1268) at the end of a winding road; the patron of this pure Orissa temple was commander of the armies of the Eastern Ganga kings

of Orissa (see p. 294). Inside the granite temple enclosure find carved lions, friezes and garlands, royal princes, gods, and life-size prancing horses.

Meanwhile, hilly **Sankaram** is known for its Buddhist remains while coastal **Bheemunipatnam,** a major Dutch settlement, has sandy beaches, a Dutch fort, houses, and grand tombs. Farther up the coast, **Ramatirtham** and **Salihundram** have more Buddhist remains, and remote **Mukhalingam,** the early capital of the Eastern Gangas, has good temples, including the early **Madhukeshvara** (ninth century), with its curved tower and beautiful sculptures.

SOUTHWESTERN ANDHRA PRADESH

Many fine but isolated monuments lie in this rarely visited region. If you are traveling through it on National Highway 7, which runs from Hyderabad to Bangalore, you may wish to stop and see one

This vast monolith, found a mile east of Lepakshi town, shows Shiva's mount regally decked in garlands and bells.

Anantapur

⚐ 223 C3

Penukonda

⚐ 222 B2

Lepakshi

⚐ 223 C2

Alampur

⚐ 223 C3

Puttaparthi

⚐ 223 C2

Prasanthi Nilaya Ashram

☎ 08555-8758; no advance reservations

Tirupati

⚐ 223 C2

or two. For a closer look, stay overnight at **Anantapur.** You can take a walk up to **Gooty's Fort,** dramatically sited on a granite out-crop right beside the highway; east of here, Tadpatri's two major **Vijayanaga temples,** one in town and the other overlooking the Penner River, have very ornate sculpture and even some surviving ceiling paintings.

Back on the highway and beyond Anantapur, **Penukonda** is a convenient stop. After 1565, this fort is where the defeated Vijayanaga rulers fled before they moved on to Chandragiri. Among the ruins you can find the Hoysala-period **Parshvanatha Temple** and the **Rama and Sita Temples,** whose facades are carved with the *Ramayana* and Krishna legends.

Farther south, **Lepakshi** lies 7 miles (11 km) west of the highway. Here, past the huge Nandi monolith, you find the **Virabhadra Temple** (16th century), built by two brothers who were Vijayanaga governors of Penukonda. Its sculpture is glorious, and its ceiling frescoes the best surviving from the period: Note the costumes, faces, rich colors, and the donor brothers worshiping Shiva and Parvati (east side).

At **Alampur,** Andhra Pradesh's earliest large group of Hindu temples has been saved from the Srisailam Dam, a huge hydroelectric project on the Krishna River, which stretches east from here to Srisailam, 53 miles (85 km) away. Built by the Early Chalukyas of Badami in the seventh and eighth centuries, the temples overlooked the Tungabhadra River; now they are protected from the water by a barrage, and other threatened temples have been dismantled and re-erected here.

Restrained and simple, each has enriching sculpture, especially **Svarga Brahma Temple** (689). If you are driving from Hyderabad,

you could pause at Srisailam, where **Mallikarjuna Temple** (14th century), with its wonderful and unusual wall reliefs, overlooks a deep gorge in the Krishna River.

Puttaparthi is a remote, quiet village in the arid rocky hills of southwest Andhra Pradesh. It has leaped to fame because it is the birthplace, and the home from July to March, of one of India's best-known living saints, Sri Sathya Sai Baba. Thousands of disciples visit him each year, staying in the new **Prasanthi Nilaya Ashram,** which is like a model village. Born in 1926, the saint is credited with possessing supernatural abilities. He claims that his miracles are to shock materialists, while his message is really universal love: his image is seen all over India. At the ashram he gives *darshan* twice daily, which anyone may attend.

SOUTHEASTERN ANDHRA PRADESH

With the pilgrimage temple-city of Tirupati as its main attraction, this area is best visited from Chennai (see pp. 256–59). Traveling here from Hyderabad is best done over several days, with stops at some of the sites mentioned on these pages.

If you arrive at **Tirupati** from the rural peace of Andhra Pradesh, it may come as a shock. Every day, overcrowded busloads of pilgrims arrive from Chennai for a one-day visit. From the town they continue through the trees and up the switchback roads to worship at the **Venkateshvara Temple** (tenth century and later), on Tirumala Hill in the Seshachalam Hills. As the temple is open to non-Hindus, this is an opportunity to observe closely many aspects of Hinduism, from the preparatory cleansing head-shave on arrival to the almost intoxicating spiritual ecstasy of the chanting faithful at the sanctum. ■

This lush land fed by two monsoon seasons is peppered with some of India's prettiest villages, each with ancient stone temples whose soaring and tapered gateways are landmarks across the viridian fields of paddy.

Tamil Nadu

A sacred cow with gaily painted horns

An elaborate *kolam,* a ritual pattern created using colored *muggu* (rice flour)

Tamil Nadu

THE STATE OF TAMIL NADU PULSATES WITH ENERGY AND VITALITY. MOST OF
its monuments are busy places, so you can experience the vigor and purity of the great
Dravidian culture in huge temple complexes thronged with people (see pp. 262–63). You
can visit the British-built High Court of Chennai (Madras), busy with lawyers. Tamil
Nadu also presents strong contrasts. Madurai's sprawling temple feels like a medieval temple town; hilltop Ooty is still reminiscent of its British hill station origins; Thanjavur
retains some of its regal Chola majesty.

Furthermore, Tamil Nadu is comparatively
compact. The relatively short drive from place
to place through the clean, quaint villages is
pure pleasure. You can easily drive from the
British Victorian elegance of Chennai to a
simple bronze-casting atelier, from the formal
excitement of the Bharata Natyam dance to
the bells and smells of Hindu worship aided
by the temple's resident elephant.
Undoubtedly, Tamil Nadu makes the gentlest
introduction to India.

Look at the map, and it is clear why this is
so. Tamil Nadu almost fills the southern tip of
India. On the east, the Bay of Bengal's surf laps
the sandy beaches of the Coromandel coast,
which has for centuries brought international

trade and cultural exchange with west and
east. On the west, the steep and rugged
Western Ghats are the barrier between Tamil
Nadu and Kerala and Karnataka. British hill
stations nestle in the northern Nilgiri Hills.
South of here, the Anamalai (Elephant) Hills
are a mixture of dense forest and velvet-
smooth tea gardens. South again, more tea
gardens and the hill station of Kodaikanal sit
in the Palani Hills. Thus, as you can see, all the
rivers flow eastward, including the great Kaveri
(Cauvery), southern India's most sacred river
(see p. 265).

Pallava, Chola, and then Pandya empires
fueled the distinct and very sophisticated Tamil
culture beginning in the seventh century. With

Area of map detail

Delhi

THE DECCAN p.221

5▷

Pulicat

Ambattur
Tiruttani   Avadi   CHENNAI
                      (MADRAS)
Arcot
Vrinchipuram   Sriperumbudur   Coast
Vellore   Kanchipuram
Ambur   Chengalpattu
Krishnagiri   Vaniyambadi   VEDANTANGAL   Mahabalipuram
                              BIRD   Tirukkalukkundram
                              SANCTUARY
Tiruppattur
4▷   Tiruvannamalai   Gingee   Tindivanam
THE DECCAN p.221   Vettavalam
Dharmapuri   Panamalai   Auroville
              Villupuram   PONDICHERRY
Yercaud   Pondicherry
                          (Puduchcheri)
Salem   Cuddalore
Attur   Neyveli   Bay of
2636m   Bengal
Doda-Betta
amandalam   Coonoor   Bhavani   Tiruchengodu   Chidambaram
(Ooty)   Nilgiri   Mettuppalaiyam   Jayamkondacholapuram   Gangakondacholapuram
         Hills   Erode   Namakkal   Kilaiyur
              Tiruppur   Punjai   Perambalur   Kumbakonam   Tarangambadi
                        Karur   Kaveri (Cauvery)   Karaikal
Coimbatore   Srirangam   Tiruvaiyaru   Darasuram   PONDICHERRY
                                                        Thiruvarur   Nagappattinam
Pollachi   Tiruchchirappalli   Thanjavur   Velanganni
3▷   (Trichy)   Kiranur
              Palani   Kodumbalur   POINT CALIMERE   Vedaranniyam
Anaimalai   Palani   Nartamalai   Pudukkottai   WILDLIFE
Hills   Hills   Dindigul   SANCTUARY   Point
                                                        Calimere
         Kodaikanal   TAMIL NADU
Teni   Alagarkoil   Chettinad
Thirupparankundram   Madurai   Karaikkudi
                     Sivaganga   Devakottai
Srivilliputtur   Virudunagar
2▷   49
Sivakasi   Ramanathapuram
Rajapalaiyam   Kilakkarai   Rameswaram   SRI
              Dhanushkodi   LANKA
                                        (CEYLON)
Kalugumalai
Tenkasi
Tirunelveli   Tuticorin
Palayankottai   Gulf of
Papanasam   Krishnapuram   Mannar
         Alvar   Kayalpattinam
Tirunagari   Tiruchchendur
Padmanabhapuram   Manapadu
47   Nagercoil
Suchindram   Kanniyakumari
         Cape
         Comorin
A   B   C   D
1▷

0   100 kilometers
0   75 miles

little interference from the Moguls or the British, their monuments and culture survive today in this affluent, culturally rich, traditional, yet dynamic and modern state.

Tamil Nadu's capital, Madras, was renamed Chennai in 1996. Its economy mixes the historically important rice (see p. 266), sugar-cane, and cotton with export business and industrial activity so rampant that Tamil Nadu currently has India's top industrial investment growth rate—even higher than Maharashtra's. As you might expect, literacy is high, and the state language of Tamil is often supplemented with skills in English rather than Hindi. ■

Chennai (Madras)

A view of bustling Chennai, with its wide streets, exotic skyline, and, in the distance, port cranes and the Indian Ocean

Chennai

🗺 255 D5

India Tourist Office

✉ 154 Anna Salai

☎ 044-8524295 or 044-8519459

🕐 Closed Sat. p.m. & Sun.

Visitor tip

Strong currents make it unwise to swim at Chennai.

TAMIL NADU'S SPRAWLING COASTAL CAPITAL IS TUCKED UP in the northern corner of the state, just south of its huge port. With a population of around six million, this is India's fourth largest city, but its seaside position and relative spaciousness make its center pleasant to explore.

There is certainly plenty to see while strolling around the very fine streets or taking advantage of the busy beach. Chennai is also the place to prepare for your inland temple tours by watching a performance of Bharata Natyam (see p. 257) and visiting the small but exceptional museum collections. So even if you opt to bypass the city in favor of relaxing at a beach hotel to the south, Chennai deserves at least a long day's visit, possibly two.

Founded on the Cooum and Adyar Rivers in 1639 by the British merchant Francis Day, the city's site was chosen for its cheap local cotton. Despite having no port and ferocious surf, which meant much cargo was lost as it was landed in small boats, Madras grew fast. By 1644 the East India Company was building its fort and had a workforce of around 400 weavers working in the surrounding villages. This textile trade continues to be vital to Chennai today, as important as its leather and auto industries. In 1688 James II (R.1685–88) granted a municipal charter, India's first, to a city that by then had about 300,000 inhabitants. (The population of London, Europe's largest city by far, was 575,000.) Soon there were twin towns on the site: the Europeans' Fort St. George and the Indians' Chennaipatnam, or Black Town, which was renamed Georgetown in honor of the King-Emperor George V's visit in 1911.

By 1740, British trade in India was so substantial that it represented 10 percent of all

Britain's revenue and made a major contribution to London's Georgian wealth and affluence. Much of this trade passed through Madras, which remained the nerve center of British influence in India until the move to Calcutta in 1772 (see p. 289). The city's established merchants built their famous stuccoed houses outside the walls of the fort and ensured that their departed loved ones were remembered in style in the fort's St. Mary's Church.

Madras was a relaxed, elegant, gleaming garden city cooled by sea breezes. The French occupied it in 1746–49, but the young general, Robert Clive, crushed them at the Battle of Arcot in 1751, consolidating Britain's supremacy in southern India; Britain's position in Bengal was confirmed at Plassey in 1757 (see p. 315). Even when the British focus moved to Calcutta, Madras remained an important city. To give the capital of the Madras presidency a promenade worthy of its status, Governor Grant Duff (1881–86) laid out the splendid 3-mile-long (5 km) **Marina,** which runs right along the waterfront. Soon this classical city was adorned

with a string of spectacular waterfront Indo-Saracenic buildings, several designed by Robert Fellowes Chisholm and Henry Irwin. Today the Marina is one of the most beautiful promenades to be found in any city, and is much loved by Chennai's residents, who come down here in the cool of the evening for a stroll, small talk, a snack of freshly barbecued fish, or a cooling frolic in the waves. ∎

Water is a public commodity for many Chennai citizens. A man washes at a street pump, while women wait to fill buckets or traditional water pots.

Bharata Natyam

This is probably India's oldest classical dance, created in the Tamil Nadu temples as a form of worship and now enjoying a vigorous revival. A woman performs the solo dance that begins with *alarippu,* symbolizing the body unfolding to offer itself to the gods. *Nritta* (pure dance) follows, when the dancer uses a combination of formalized face, hand, body, and dance expressions to expound on a poem sung by the *natuvangari* (conductor), accompanied by musicians. Rhythm is all-important,

emphasized when the dancer replies to the music by stamping her feet to sound the bells of her ankle bracelets. A dancer's initiation performance should be for the gods in one of the great temples such as Chidambaram (see p. 265). You can find regular performances at Chennai's many *sabbas,* arts societies, and venues, and there are more than 500 dance and classical music performances during the December–January Chennai Festival; the tourist offices carry full details. ∎

State Tourist Office

✉ 143 Anna Salai
☎ 044-830752
🕐 Closed Sat. p.m. & Sun.

A drive around Chennai (Madras)

This drive works around Chennai's current system of one-way streets to give you a good introduction to the city. Enjoy a walk on the splendid beach before you start—and maybe another after you finish.

Start with a visit to **San Thome Cathedral ❶** (1547, 1896), where St. Thomas the Apostle's relics are kept. It is believed that he came to India from Palestine in A.D. 52 and was killed in A.D. 78. Around 1100 the saint's remains were moved inland and a new church was built, possibly by the Persian Christian community. It stands in Mylapore, once the Tamil port, where the Portuguese made a settlement in 1522. Nearby **Kapalishvara Temple** is lively with plenty of festivals, singing, and busy bazaars.

Enthusiasts can detour to the southwest to see **St. Thomas's Mount,** believed to be where the saint was stoned to death. **The Old Cantonment** is nearby, with lots of old flat-topped Madras villas; return via the racetrack and **Raj Bhawan** (1817), the former Government House built for Sir Thomas Munro.

The drive follows the Marina, renamed **Kamaraj Road,** for a group of Victorian buildings that are collectively as impressive as Mumbai's (Bombay). Moving up it, pause to see the circular former **Vivekananda House ❷** (1842), once the Ice House, where the Tudor Ice Company used to store blocks of ice imported from America; the Lutyens-style **University Examination Hall;** and **Presidency College.** Its older part was designed by Chisholm (1882) in a style mixing French and Italian Renaissance and various local details.

Next come the **Public Water Works** (1870), **Chepauk Palace** (1768) built for the anglophile Nawab of the Carnatic, with Chisholm's later tower (1870), and Chisholm's university **Senate House** (1873). This time he went for the Gothic-Saracenic style, with polychrome stones and arcades. A Golden Jubilee statue of Queen-Empress Victoria (1887) stands outside. Both she and Chantry's bronze equestrian statue of popular Sir Thomas Munro (1839), seen on the right after crossing the Cooum River, have survived postindependence cleansing of Raj memories.

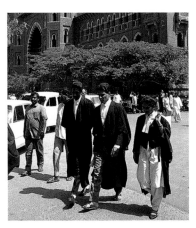

A group of aspiring advocates in front of Chennai's magnificent High Courts

Continue north to **Fort St. George ❸,** begun in 1644. Drive or walk through it to find **St. Mary's Church ❹** (1678–1680), the spiritual heart of old Chennai and the East's oldest surviving Anglican church. Inside, look for the original, intricately carved teak gallery balustrade and the black Pallavaram granite font where Job Charnock, who would later found Calcutta, had his daughters baptized. A stunning collection of funerary monuments includes several by John Flaxman and John Bacon. Elihu Yale (governor 1687–1692) married here and was later a benefactor to Yale University.

Now for a contrast: the spectacular Indo-Saracenic warren of the **High Courts ❺** (1888–1892), whose design by J. W. Brassington was revised by Irwin and J. H. Stephens. Up the stairs by the statue of Sri T. Muthasamy Iyer, the first Indian judge, the public courts have beautiful stained glass and tiles. Finally, drive past the Gothic arcades of **Chennai Central Station ❻** (1868–1872) to find, on the right, **St. Andrew's Kirk ❼** (1818–1821), considered India's most accomplished neoclassic church; the circular interior has its original louvered doors and cane pews.

The **Connemara Hotel** **8** has an excellent lunch buffet of local dishes. You can get dance performance information from the tourist office on nearby Anna Salai.

The **Government Museum Complex** **9** (*closed Fri.*), also grandly called The Pantheon, is exceptionally good and deserves a whole afternoon. Founded in 1851, it has three main sections: stone carvings, including the Amaravati sculptures upstairs; bronzes, many from Chola temples; and musical instruments, photographs, and Chettinad carvings. ∎

See area map page 255
San Thome Cathedral
About 4 miles (6 km)
Allow a full day, with lunch as indicated
Government Museum Complex

NOT TO BE MISSED
- Strolling up the Marina
- St. Mary's Church
- Government Museum Complex

Mahabalipuram
(Mamallapuram)

GREAT CAVES, ROCKS AND BOULDERS, CARVED STONES and frie and monolithic temples testify to the former importance Mahabalipuram, port city of the Pallavas, the first great dynasty of south India. Their royal capital was at Kanchipuram (see pp. 264–65).

Mahabalipuram

◪ 255 D4

Tourist Office

✉ North end of the village

🕐 Closed Sat. & Sun.

Visitor tip

If you find the stone-carving interesting, visit the Government Collection of Sculpture on the road north of Mahabalipuram toward Chennai (tel 04133-42261).

Rising from local rulers to wealthy emperors, the Pallava dynasts believed in divine right and, in Hindu tradition, traced their ancestry back to Brahma. They called their empire Dravidia and extended it over present-day Tamil Nadu and into the Deccan, coming into repeated conflict with the Early Chalukyas of Badami (see p. 234). The Pallavas created much of the blueprint by which Tamil Nadu would live for centuries and promoted the village and temple culture known as Dravidian. They encouraged agriculture to increase both produce and taxes. Rice was the main crop and bartering unit,

but coconuts, mangoes, plantains, cotton, and gingelly (sesame) were also grown. Each village built its own brick-lined tank as its essential water reservoir; many are still in use today. Taxes were levied on everyone and everything, from marriage parties to letter carriers; only weavers to the royal court were exempt.

Mahabalipuram's survivors are Tamil Nadu's earliest monuments. Mostly dating from the seventh and early eighth centuries, they seem to show a relentless thirst for experimentation, and much of the temple carving is sublime. It is best to go early, stopping for drinks in a café.

It was under the politically powerful Mahendravarman I (*R. 600–630*), a dramatist and poet who converted from Jainism to Shaivism, that some of the earliest rock-cut temples were chiseled. He was succeeded by Mamalla (*R. 630–668*) and later by Rajasimha (*R. 700–728*).

Here there is a selection of especially wonderful monuments to look for. Start by visiting the so-called **Tiger Cave,** found in the trees about a mile (1.6 km) north of the village. A huge boulder has been carved to create a small portico surrounded by fierce masklike *yali* heads and two elephants. Along a path, find another early temple, a tiny living shrine roofed in coconut leaf. Beside it, a row of upright stones placed in the sand to face the sunrise has its origins in pre-Hindu nature worship.

In the village, clamber up the hill behind the center to find **Varaha Cave Temple.** Colossal, bold, and vigorous sculptures fill the interior: Varaha lifting up Dhudevi (left), Trivikrama (right), and Lakshmi and Durga on the rear wall.

Back in the village center, there are two treats: first, **Arjuna's Penance,** a remarkable piece of top-quality relief carving, whose composition, of great complexity and intellect, coats some 50 feet (15 m) of a rock face. Using delicate modeling and carefully observed detail, mixing naturalism with stylization, and taking advantage of a cleft in the rock, the craftsmen have enriched their story. Today, we interpret it as either the penance of Arjuna (standing on one leg) or the sage Bhagiratha persuading Shiva to receive the Ganga River in his matted locks. Next to this, find the **Krishna Mandapa,** whose back wall has a gentle and bucolic scene of Krishna protecting the *gopies* by lifting Mount Goverdhana as an umbrella; see the farmer milking his cow.

Now drive past the stone-carvers' workshops and climb the steps up to **Mahishamardini Temple,** whose veranda sculptures are yet more masterpieces: Vishnu sleeping on the serpent (left) and Durga killing the buffalo-headed demon (right).

Beyond the village, standing alone in a sandy enclosure, the **Pancha Rathas** are five monolith temples; that is, they are huge boulders carved to become temples. Their names mean little, but their variety of shapes and their carvings reveal an intensely creative period. See especially the tallest and most elaborate *rath* (chariot), whose

sculptures already have a recognizable iconography; the south side shows Shiva with the royal patron, Mamalla.

Early in the eighth century, later than all these different caves and monoliths, Mahabalipuram's **Shore Temple** was built. Together with Kailasanatha Temple at Kanchipuram, this is the first significant structural temple in Tamil Nadu and provides the blueprint for the Dravidian temple (see pp. 262–63). ∎

Part of the Krishna Mandapa relief at Mahabalipuram, a farmer milks his cow.

Dravidian temples

Tamil Nadu's temples were built by the villagers to be their religious, social, cultural, and political focus—a position many still hold today. Funded by the king or a local man of means, they kept thousands of people employed for life, and still do. Temples remain the bedrock of Tamil Nadu communities.

The temple itself follows a basic format. One principal *gopura* (gateway) through the wall leads into a courtyard and so to the porch, *mandapa* (hall), and main shrine; the mandapas and shrine have increasingly lofty *vimanhas* (roofs). The elements are in line, so the worshiper progresses from the open spaces and their ebullient, symbolic sculpture to the increasingly dark, mysterious, simple, and womblike sanctum.

This pilgrim has rubbed his forehead and arms with ashes as a sign of penitence.

Many temples were founded by the Pallavas and Cholas, then enlarged by the Vijayanagas and Pandyas. They sometimes added subsidiary shrines for the consort or family of the principal deity; thus a temple to Shiva could be given shrines for his consort, Parvati, and his sons, Ganesh and Kartikeya. They might add extra mandapas for dance or special festivals, and around the central core they might build rooms for administration, facilities for cooking, sleeping rooms for the ever growing numbers of temple inmates, and libraries for study. Storage rooms were also needed for the festival chariots and for the coconuts, sugar, flowers, and spices sold in the temple to the faithful as offerings during their *puja* (worship). You can see this arrangement in many temples.

As the temples got bigger, extra and taller walls were built to increase the space for these buildings and to protect the increasingly large treasuries from attack by greedy Muslim armies. Temples at Tiruchirappalli and Madurai have several concentric walls and still function as complete cities. These later walls, whose tops were frequently decorated with Nandi bulls (Shiva's vehicle), have gopuras with higher and higher pyramid-shaped roofs covered with carvings of all the deities of the Hindu pantheon. This was because the untouchables, the lowest caste, were not permitted to enter the temples, and they therefore worshiped by looking up at the gopuras. It was for their benefit, as well as for that of the old and infirm that, at the many festivals, the temple deity was hauled around the village on an elaborately carved wooden *rath* (chariot).

Locals used their temples for much more than just simple worship. Their devotions became increasingly passionate, stimulating the great devotional poetry and music, the Bharata Natyam dance (see p. 257), and the legendary silk-weaving to clothe the deities. Locals went to Sanskrit school in the temple; later they traded, held meetings, and celebrated there, too. Today, a Hindu may well do a special puja before making a journey or opening a store, or after landing a good job. In the past the income of whole villages was given to a temple—the inscriptions running around temple platforms are often a record such donations. Nowadays, wealthy Hindus may pay for special pujas, maintenance work, or meals for the poor. The wealthy industrial Birla family has even completely funded several entirely new temples. ∎

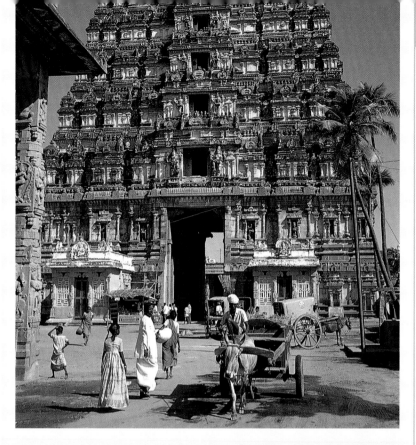

The temple is often still the focus of daily life, which goes on all around a Kanchipuram temple (above), while vendors take up positions outside Madurai's Minakshi Temple (below).

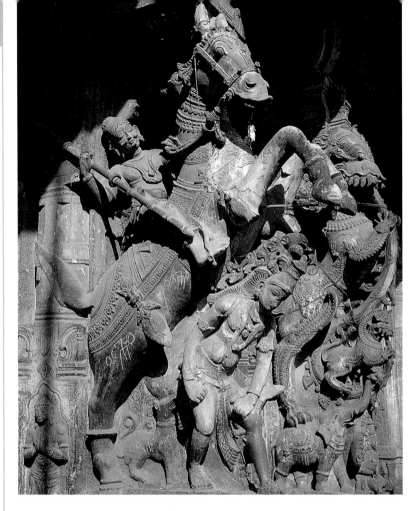

This Vijayanagar-
period temple
sculpture of a
rearing horse
crushing his
enemy symbolizes
good triumphing
over evil, Hindus
over Muslims.

Kanchipuram
▲ 255 C5

A temple odyssey

THIS TOUR FROM CHENNAI (MADRAS) TO THANJAVUR
visits a handful of the many glorious temples, some now empty,
others functioning just as they have done for centuries.

KANCHIPURAM
The only one of the Seven Sacred
Cities dedicated to both Shiva and
Vishnu, Kanchipuram was enriched
by the Pallava rulers (see p. 260),
who made it their capital. Chola,
Vijayanaga, and Nayaka rulers further embellished it. Today this busy
town, 35 miles (72 km) southeast of
Chennai, has 50 or so functioning
temples whose rituals gave birth to

one of southern India's most
important silk-weaving centers.
(Buy here, or, for more choice and
better prices, in the big cities.)

The buildings span a thousand
years of creative and devotional
output. Begin with the simple
sandstone, eighth-century
Kailasanatha Temple (0.5
mile/1 km west of the city center),
the finest of the Pallava ruler

Rajasimha's buildings, dedicated to Shiva as lord of Kailasha, his mountain home; you can see a variety of Shiva images. Late eighth-century **Vaikuntha Perumal Temple** stands to the east, near the train station. Built by Nandivarma II, the temple has one *mandapa* that leads to three shrines dedicated to Vishnu as the boar and lion; the rear wall sculptures illustrate Pallava historic events.

The later **Ekambareshvar Temple** (mostly 16th and 17th century), dedicated to Shiva as lord of the mango tree, is the city's largest temple (north of the center). Built in 1509 by the Vijayanaga emperor Krishnadeveraya, it has a soaring *gopora* (192 feet/58 m high), which leads toward an equally huge mandapa and corridor. The 12th-century **Varadaraja Temple** (1.5 miles/3 km southeast of the city) has a Vijayanaga addition, whose columns are elaborately carved with Vaishnava iconography and rearing horses.

KANCHIPURAM TO CHIDAMBARAM

As soon as you leave Kanchipuram, you're on country roads. On the way to Mahabalipuram,

Uttarmrur has two fine late Pallava temples built by Dantivarman *(R. 796–817).* If you want to see more Pallava monuments, spend a very quiet but long rural day inland; otherwise drive right down to Pondicherry (see p. 267).

The rarely visited early cave temple at **Mandagappattu,** near Gingee has an inscription that refers to Mahendravarman I *(R. 580–630).* Continue to the huge but clearly laid out **Arunachaleshvara Temple** (16th to 17th century) at **Tiruvannamalai** (major festival, *Nov.–Dec.),* where Shiva is worshiped as Lord of the Eastern Mountain. Finish with the hilltop temple (early eighth century) at **Panamalai,** 19 miles (30 km) east.

CHIDAMBARAM TO THANJAVUR

Chidambaram's **Nataraja Temple** (12th to 13th century) is like a fair every day. Nataraja is Shiva as the cosmic dancer, the Cholas' favorite form of Shiva. Try to arrive in time to witness the busy and elaborate main morning puja, usually around 9:30 a.m.; temple management and pilgrims' gifts make this one of India's richest

Chidambaram

🅰 255 C3

Chidambaram Tourist Office

✉ Next to T.T.D.C. Hotel Tamil Nadu, Railway Feeder Road

Visitor tips
Neither Kumbakonam nor Kanchipuram has a tourist office. You can obtain a detailed map of Kanchipuram from the T.T.D.C. Tamil Nadu Hotel. A pleasant way to explore the temples more thoroughly is to rent a bicycle.

Kaveri (Cauvery) River

Southern India's most sacred river rises in Karnataka and carries its life-giving waters into Tamil Nadu. Here its delta is used for intensive rice cultivation before emptying into the Bay of Bengal. For southern Indians the Kaveri is as important as the Ganga, and its banks have many temples and special *ghats* (steps) for death ceremonies—Trichy's Ranganathaswamy Temple occupies a whole island.

Blessed by two monsoons, in July and November, the river usually flows generously—although the governments of Karnataka and Tamil Nadu argue over how much water each may draw off. This is nothing new. Historically, Tamil Nadu harnessed the Kaveri to its advantage. To fund arts patronage, agrarian administrative units called *nadus* (hence Tamil Nadu's name) promoted better irrigation for more efficient farming. Paddy crops increased from two to three a year, creating a surplus of rice that was their most lucrative export. ∎

His power and transport combined, a farmer's precious bullocks have their horns brightly painted for Pongal festival.

temples. Then explore the warren of halls and corridors, mostly built in the late Chola period; do not miss the carvings of Bharata Natyam dance positions on the inside walls of the main gates.

The ride to evocatively named **Gangakondacholapuram** goes inland through villages where rope-making is a thriving cottage industry; you can pause to see how it is done. Then, seemingly in the middle of nowhere, you arrive at the windowless wall surrounding **Brihadishvara Temple.** Built by Rajendra I (*R.*1012–1044) in his new capital, it celebrated his victory in eastern India up by the Ganga

River and was intended to surpass his predecessor, Rajajraja I's Thanjavur temple. Only a few village names (meaning "watchman's area," "firework makers," etc.) and some brick debris give clues to the extent of Rajendra's city. But the temple is testament enough. It is superb, neither big nor complex: Its glory is the monumental simplicity and its sculpture. Large panels on the out-side of the shrine, mostly of Shiva, include one magnificent composition of Shiva garlanding Chandesha.

It is a short drive to **Kumbakonam,** a busy and ancient religious center between the banks of the Kaveri and its tributary, Arasala. Here are bronze-workers, traditional gold and jewelry dealers, and, of course, temples. The ritual core of the city is **Mahamakam Tank,** the focus of the festival held here every 12 years (next one 2004). The finest temple, however, is found just outside the city, across the Arasala at **Darasuram,** where the Airavateshvara Temple (mid-12th century) built by Rajaraja II (*R.*1146–1172) is probably the finest late Chola building; the compact structure is coated in fine sculpture. From here the lanes twist through paddy fields and villages to Thanjavur (see pp. 268-69). ∎

Importance of rice

If you are in southern India in early January, you may witness Pongal, the rice harvest festival. Farmers scrub their bullocks and paint their horns. On Pongal morning, each village home boils newly harvested rice amid a complicated ritual. When it boils over it is *pongal*, a sign indicating a rich harvest to follow.

Here, rice is more than a staple part of the diet and economy. It is a fundamental part of life. Before a child goes to school, there is a rice ceremony to Saraswati, goddess of learning. A bride tips a bowl of rice into her new home to symbolize fertility and prosperity; a mourning family offers rice balls at the *sradh* ceremony to help the spirit find peace. Throughout the state you can see *kolams*, intricate patterns of rice powder made by women to encourage prosperity and happiness and to ward off black ants from their houses. ∎

Pondicherry

Pondicherry

▲ 255 C4

**Pondicherry
Tourist Office**

✉ Goubert Salai

☎ (0413) 339497

**Pondicherry
Museum**

◷ Closed Mon.

ABOUT A CENTURY AFTER THE PORTUGUESE ARRIVED TO trade on the east coast, the English, Dutch, and French followed. The French bought land from the sultan of Bijapur in 1672, and two years later, François Martin set up a trading post. Although Pondicherry was lost to the Dutch once and to the English several times, the Marquis de Dupleix, who dreamed of a French empire in India, restored its prestige, and Jean Law laid out the grid-plan town (1756–1777) that still survives. After independence the French hung on to their territories, only relinquishing them in 1954. Today, about 14,000 French nationals live here.

You can spend a pleasant day wandering the deserted streets of the old core, catching a hint of French colonial times as you pass by old colonial houses with louvered windows. Start in the main square. **Dupleix's statue** (1870) stands near the gleaming white **Raj Niwas,** a fine French colonial house (1752) built as his palace. (There is a brief but splendidly formal ceremony here each sunset.) Across the square, **Pondicherry Museum** occupies the French former Government Library and displays all sorts of bits and pieces, including Dupleix's bed.

Down on the waterfront, eight pillars from Gingee and a statue of Mahatma Gandhi stand at the entrance to the pier. South of here is a statue of Joan of Arc, the **Église de Notre Dame des Anges** (1855), and, in the cemetery opposite, the tomb of Dupleix's enterprising follower, Charles, Marquis de Bussy (1785).

North of the pier, **Sri Aurobindo Headquarters** is on Rue de la Marine. Sri Aurobindo Ghosh (1872–1950), a Bengali educated at Cambridge, retired here to practice yoga. He and his disciple, a Parisian known as the Mother (1878–1973), established the *ashram* here. In 1968, she founded the nearby futuristic city of Auroville, designed by French architect Roger Anger. There is a fascinating handmade **paper factory** around the corner *(Closes 3 p.m.),* and daily tours go to **Auroville** (see p. 282).

Finally, see whether the home of the 18th-century diarist Ananda Rangapillai, one of Dupleix's protégés, is open to the public. His house, at 69 rue Rangapillai, mixes Indian and French colonial styles. ■

The pretty Church of the Sacred Heart of Jesus on South Boulevard

Two bullock carts trundle through the unusually quiet courtyard of the great Brihadishvara Temple.

Thanjavur

LIFE IN THIS MODERATE-SIZED, MODERATELY PACED town still centers on the monumental royal Brihadishvara Temple (circa 1010) built by Rajaraja I *(R. 985–1014)*, who donated the gilded pot finial on top of the 217-foot-high (66 m) tower. In the morning, locals hurry in through the sun-drenched gates to pray before work. In the evenings they come in their hundreds as the last rays of sun are glowing on the tower and enliven the whole compound with their prayer, chattering, music, and religious readings.

Thanjavur

▲ 255 C3

Thanjavur Tourist Office

✉ Gandhi Rd., opposite the Post Office

☎ 04362 33017

Thanjavur was Rajaraja I's capital, built up under previous Chola rulers, chieftains in the area for centuries. One leader conquered Thanjavur in the ninth century and quickly claimed descent from the sun. Expansion of land and power followed under Rajaraja I and his son Rajendra I *(R. 1012–1044)*. Campaigns in Kerala, the Maldives, Sri Lanka (Ceylon), and right up to Orissa brought most of the Indian peninsula under Chola control until the Hoysalas of Halebid and the Pandyas of Madurai expanded in the 12th century.

Chola trading in cottons, silks, spices, drugs, jewels, ivory, sandal-wood, and camphor was lucrative, while at home agriculture was made more efficient. Caste differences became stronger. The poor were encouraged to win spiritual and social respect by giving their skills and time to the temple, the wealthy to acquire prestige by donating whole villages to the temples. Church and state became intertwined: The god-king cult was promoted through image worship of past rulers and temple buildings, and the *raja-guru* (king's priest) became the king's chief spiritual and temporal adviser.

The thoroughly royal **Brihadishvara Temple** epitomizes this increasingly controlled and centralized state. The biggest and richest Chola temple was conceived as a temple-fort and dedicated to Shiva as the Great Lord. The gateway leads into a large, rectangular court, where a Nandi bull lies in a high pavilion in front of the steep steps up to the temple. Rich sculpture decorates the porch and exterior; see especially the Shiva images on the outside of the sanctum. Inscriptions run all around the platform, like a public notebook documenting the construction of the temple and the donations, together with the names of the donors. Inside, join the faithful to see the colossal *lingum*. There are Chola period paintings here, too, including one of a royal visit to Chidambaram (west wall) and another of Shiva riding in a chariot drawn by Brahma (north wall); many others were overpainted by the Nayakas. The compound has a

delicate 17th-century subsidiary temple dedicated to Subramanya, one of Shiva's sons, and a treasury, museum, and library.

In the royal palace compound is the **Nayak Durbar Hall Art Museum,** a collection of Chola bronzes found in the area, exhibited with beautiful simplicity in open rooms around the palace courtyard, together with fine stone carving. Several show Shiva as Nataraja (see box below); the best were found at Tiruvelvikudi and Jambavanodai. Others show him as the archer, with his consort Parvati, or with their son Skanda. The masterpiece is Shiva with Parvati, one arm outstretched. ■

Cholas & Shiva Nataraja

Hindu temple sculpture is the most sublime achievement of Indian art, reaching one of several peaks under Chola patronage. Shiva is a favorite deity. He represents dynamic energy, both creative—hence his symbol of the *lingum*—and destructive, which suited the powerful warring temple patrons. His developed personality was at once outrageous, amoral, and wild, yet ascetic and that of the perfect family man.

The Chola rulers worshiped Shiva Nataraja—Lord of the Dance. Shiva dances in a wild, ecstatic frenzy or in a withdrawn yogic state, eyes downcast or closed, within a ring of flames. With his hands he carries the fire of destruction and the double drum, whose beat summons up creation, and calms and protects the worshiper. Shiva's matted hair contains the Ganga River-goddess; below him, the demon Apasmara, personifying ignorance, looks up in hope. In all, Shiva symbolizes both endings and beginnings. ■

Chola bronze of Shiva as Nataraja

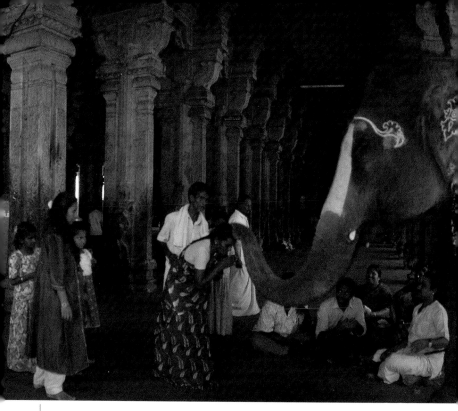

Tiruchchirappalli

THE SMALL TOWN OF TIRUCHCHIRAPPALLI, BETTER KNOWN
as Trichy, lies beside the sacred Kaveri River. Just north of the town
the waters split to flow on each side of a long island, thus considered
especially holy. Here, at Srirangam, one of southern India's largest
and most complete sacred complexes, Sri Rangarathaswamy, was
built. Founded by the Cholas, it received patronage from both the
Pandya and Hoysala rulers, was sacked twice by 14th-century Muslim
armies from Delhi, then expanded unabated during the 16th and
17th centuries.

Tiruchchirappalli
🅜 255 C3
Tiruchchirappalli
Tourist Office
✉ Williams Rd.
☎ 0431-460136

Today, Tiruchchirappalli is a
vibrant temple city dedicated to
Ranganatha—Vishnu when he is
reclining on the serpent Anata.
Pilgrims swell the resident population daily, especially at festival time.
It is a timeless yet thriving world.
The first, huge gateway, with
writhing sculptures painted bright
yellows, greens, and pinks, was
completed only in 1968. As you

move forward, past stores selling
everything from temple offerings
and souvenirs to chilis and light
bulbs, the sacred mystery of the
temple increases.

The temple itself begins at the
fourth wall, where you leave
your shoes. Here you see the
Ranganayaki Temple and the
richly carved thousand-pillared
Kalyan Mandapa. Even more

spectacular carving has transformed the pillars of the **Sheshagiriraya Mandapa** into rearing horses carrying hunters armed with spears, a typical Vijayanaga double symbol of good triumphing over evil—that is, of brave Hinduism protecting the temple against Muslim invaders. In contrast, the Nayaka-period **Venugopala shrine** on the south side is delicately carved with maidens leaning against trees.

At the fourth wall, ask to climb onto the roof to enjoy the splendid view right across all the walls to the gold-encrusted sanctum; the *gopuras* diminish toward the center. Inside the third courtyard, continue to the **Garuda Manadapa,** a hall carved with maidens and donors that surrounds the shrine to Vishnu's man-eagle vehicle. Only Hindus can continue to the inner sanctum to see the image of reclining Vishnu.

As well as its stupendous temple, the town has a Chola-period earthen dam, the **Grand Anicut;** the great rock with temples including the **Lower Cave Temple** (Pandya, eighth century) and **Upper Cave Temple** (Pallava, 580–630); and the **Church of St. John** (1816) in the cantonment. ■

Rooftop level view of the gopuras protecting the gold-roofed inner sanctum and treasury of Sri Ranganatha-swamy Temple

Rural routes from Trichy

THE DRIVES FROM TRICHY TO THANJAVUR AND TO
Madurai are not long. If you have time and a good driver, a detour
from either one takes you right into peaceful, sometimes dramatic
country with magical sites. Take water and snacks.

TRICHY TO THANJAVUR

From Trichy, take the road southeast to Kiranur. Along this 34-mile
(55 km) route you can stop to look
at a group of hundreds of dilapidated, abandoned *ayyanars* on the
right. These are heraldic terra-cotta
figures of equestrian deities, sometimes with horses and elephants,
often brightly colored, found on
village outskirts throughout Tamil
Nadu. Their functions are to protect the village from calamities such
as plague, make barren land fertile,
bring good harvests, and protect
night watchmen. A priest regularly
performs *pujas* at each group. On
special occasions, such as the time
of sowing seeds, new ayyanars are
added and special pujas performed.

At Kiranur, turn right for the village of **Nartamalai.** Once there,
leave your car at the far end of the
village and walk for about 15 minutes up the granite hill to find a cluster of early Chola temples. One is
cut into the granite and has 12 iden-
tical high-relief Vishnu figures
carved into the back wall. The freestanding temple has guardian figures
flanking the door, and fading murals.

It is about an hour's drive from
Nartamalai to **Mallaiyadipatti.**
Here you find superb late Pallava
caves (ninth century), one carved
with a huge Vishnu reclining on the
Cosmic Ocean, another carved with
the nine gods. From here continue
to the main Trichy–Thanjavur road,
and turn right. Soon you will see on
the left a memorial—two standing
stones and a crossbar—to a death
in childbirth, which travelers use to
rest their load. A little farther along,

on the right, a group of ayyanars
stands beneath a banyan tree
across a small field. The road continues to Thanjavur.

TRICHY TO MADURAI

Leave Trichy on the country road
to Madurai (88 miles/140 km), not
the main one, toward Kodumbalur.
You will pass brightly colored
ayyanars, whose creators have kept
them up to date by giving them
wristwatches. At Kodumbalur, the
isolated double **Muvakoil
Temple** (ninth century) built by
the Cholas is all that remains of
the original nine shrines. Their
sculptures are glorious; it's worth
coming here just to see the Shiva
Nataraja on the east side of the
south shrine.

Continue to **Sittannavasal** to find a Jain cave temple (ninth century) cut into a long granite outcrop. Inside the hall, find images of Parshvanatha (right), Mahavira (left) on the sides, and more Jinas in the rear walls. Delicate paintings survive, too: dancing maidens and royal figures on the columns, a lotus pond in full blossom on the hall ceiling, a design with knotted patterns on the shrine ceiling. A rocky overhang on top of the hill has a natural cavern with polished beds for Jain monks and an inscription that dates from the second to first century B.C.

Pudukkottai is the next stop: Its Tondaiman rajas supported the British against Tipu Sultan and the French; thus they received titles and security and left a well-built city. In the old area, Tirugorakarna, find the **Gokarneshvara Temple** (begun in the seventh century), with its 18th-century *Ramayana* paintings and rock-cut Pallava inner chamber, whose carvings include a set of Matrikas (mother goddesses).

Near the temple entrance, **Government Museum** (*Closed Mon.*) displays quality local finds.

You can now go direct to Madurai or make four final stops. First is at the village of **Avudaiyarkoil,** where the broad temple passageway has supports carved with Tondaiman royals, their ministers, and, at the end, Shiva in his fierce aspects. Farther into the temple, find a shrine dedicated to the local saint, Manikkavachakar.

A road leads cross-country to **Karaikkudi** in the heart of the Chettinad communities, where merchants made their money in the 19th and 20th centuries in trade and finance with Madras, Burma, and Malaya. Their mansions have some of the finest wood carving in Tamil Nadu but display a masonry facade to orderly streets in small settlements. See them here and in **Devakottai** to the south and **Chettinad** village to the north from where it is about 59 miles (95 km) to Madurai (see pp. 274–75). ■

As you drive through rural areas watch for ayyanars, protective terra-cotta figures grouped outside villages.

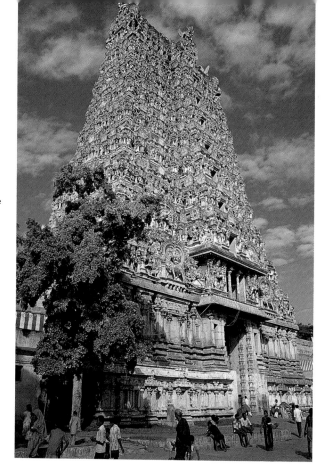

The riot of gaily painted, dancing and cavorting gods and goddesses decorating this *gopura* at Madurai's Minakshi temple heralds the richness of color and carving to be found inside.

Madurai

PILGRIMS FLOCK TO MADURAI'S BUSY, COLORFUL, AND HUGE complex of the Minakshi Sundareshvara Temple, dedicated to Shiva's consort, Parvati (Minakshi), giving it a lively yet medieval atmosphere.

Madurai
255 B2
Madurai Tourist Office
W. Veli St.
0452-734757

Built on the banks of the Vaigai River, Madurai was founded by the Pandyas, who made it their capital while they ruled south Tamil Nadu (7th to 13th centuries). However, in 1323 Malik Kafur's Tughlaq forces from Delhi took Madurai and stayed until 1378, when the Vijayanagas liberated it. Their governors, known as Nayakas, slowly asserted their independence; Tirumala (R.1623–1660) was an especially active builder throughout

his kingdom. Resisting Moguls and Marathas, the Nayakas held on to their throne until the British established control in 1763.

Madurai's temple is thus a testament to Nayaka royal and aristocratic patronage through the 17th and 18th centuries. Remodeling and redecoration continue to keep the ceilings, murals, and *gopura* as colorful as when built. If you can, make both a morning and an evening visit to find *pujas,* elephant processions, music, and singing in the various halls. The 12-day festival in April–May, to celebrate the coronation of Minakshi and her marriage to Shiva, is spectacular.

While simply wandering through the corridors and halls will be rewarding, there are some special things worth seeing. Entering the **Ashta Shakti Mandapa**, notice how elegant and tall the gopuras are. Then find the lively dancing men flanking the corridor to the **Potramarai Kulam** (Golden Lily Tank), behind which you find superb carvings of the *Mahabharata* heroes in the **Panch Pandava Mandapa.** Just near here, in the gloom, find a beautiful and sensuous freestanding group of Shiva and Parvati. See also the **Kambattadi Mandapa** with its seated Nandi, the huge, corridor-like **Viravasantaraya Mandapa,** the **Temple Art Museum'**s carvings, and the **Pudu Mandapa,** whose columns are sculptured into portraits of all the Nayaka kings up to Tirumala, each with his family and ministers. ■

MADURAI'S TEMPLE

Madurai's temple is best appreciated by wandering the corridors and halls; only the inner sanctuaries of the shrines are off-limits to non-Hindus. All day, processions, worshipers, and visitors throng the temple. Climb the south gopura for a wonderful overview and don't miss the Temple Art Museum's carvings.

1. **Entrance through the Ashta Shakti Mandapa (Porch of the Eight Goddesses)**
2. **Potramarai Kulam (Golden Lily Tank)**
3. **Minakshi shrine**
4. **Kambattadi Mandapa**
5. **Sundareshvara (Shiva) shrine**
6. **Viravasantaraya Mandapa**
7. **Pudu Mandapa**
8. **South gopura**

N

Southern Tamil Nadu

WHAT THE SOUTH OF TAMIL NADU LACKS IN ARCHITEC-
turally stunning temples, it makes up for in coastal beauty, some
fascinating offbeat sites, and the chance to visit Kanniyakumari,
where the waters of three seas mingle.

Rameswaram
◭ 255 C2
**Rameswaram
Tourist
Information**
✉ 14 East Car St.
☎ 04573-21371

Tirunelveli
◭ 255 B1
**Tirunelveli Tourist
Information**
✉ Train station
☎ 0462-26235

The far south of India has attracted
devotion rather than war, inspiring
temple-building rather than forts.
Rameswaram, the 35-mile-long
(56 km) peninsula jutting out from
mainland India toward Sri Lanka,
plays a vital role in the climax and
finale of the great Hindu epic, the
Ramayana. The huge **Ramanatha
Temple** (mostly 17th to 18th century) marks the spot where Rama,
having killed the demon Ravana,
worshiped Shiva to purify himself.
Today's pilgrims imitate this by
bathing in the sea and then being
doused with water from the 22 wells
in the temple complex. Many also
visit **Gandhamandana Hill** to see
Rama's footprint, and **Dhanushkodi,**
where Rama received submission
from Ravana's brother.

On the way to the peninsula,
you can stop at the village of
Ramanathapuram to see the
local Setupati rulers' palace, where
the Ramalinga Vilasa rooms are
lavishly decorated with 18th-
century paintings recounting the
Hindu epics and Setupati royal life.
Farther south on the Gulf of
Mannar, huge maritime fossils
have been found on the shores
near Kilakkarai.

Set in the lush valley of the
Tambraparni River, **Tirunelveli**
makes a good base for visiting the
tip of India. If you are driving here
from Madurai, pause at Kalugumalai
to see the monolithic **Pallava
Temple** (eighth century) chiseled
out of a granite outcrop and exten-
sively decorated. In Tirunelveli
itself, a major Nayaka city, the
Nellaiyappa Temple (mostly

16th to 17th century), dedicated to
Shiva and Devi, has a riot of fine
stone and wood carving; in the first
enclosure find donor sculptures of
the Tirunelveli chiefs.

The first stop on a tour southeast from Tirunelveli is the village
of **Krishnapuram,** whose
Venkatachala Temple, dedicated to
Vishnu as Lord of the Venkata Hills,
has glorious 17th- to 18th-century
carvings and fine figural piers in its
Virappa Nayaka Mandapa. The Iron
Age site of **Adichanallur,** beside
the Tambrapani River, has fascinating ancient sepulchral urns. At the
town of Alvar Tirunagari, the high-
ranking Vishnu saint Nammalvar,
born here in the ninth century, was
the inspiration for the **Adinatha
Temple** (mostly 16th to 17th
century) and its lively carvings.
When you reach the coast, there are
three places to visit overlooking the
Gulf of Mannar: **Kayalpattinam,**
with its mosques for locals
descended from Arab traders;
Tiruchchendur's pilgrimage
temple; and **Manapadu,** whose
Catholic associations go back to St.
Francis Xavier's visit in 1542.

The tip of India is a rocky
promontory overlooking the
mingling waters of the Bay of
Bengal, the Arabian Sea, and the
Indian Ocean. The town of
Kanniyakumari is named after
Kumari, the Hindu goddess who
protects the shores, and pilgrims
come here to bathe near the temple. Two great Indians have memorials here: Mahatma Gandhi,
whose ashes were thrown into
the ocean here; and Vivekananda,

the Bengali philosopher who came here as a monk in 1892 and founded the Ramakrishna Vivekananda Missions. Headquartered in Kolkata, the missions still thrive today.

West of Kanniyakumari, you can stop at Suchindram to see the **Sthanumalaya Temple** (13th to 18th century) beside the large tank. Dedicated to Vishnu and Shiva, grand and gaily painted *gopuras* and colonnades lead to the earlier shrines. Before Shiva's, see the splendidly carved corner columns of the small pavilion. Similarly, the pavilion housing the image of Vishnu's vehicle, Garuda, has columns carved with portraits of Nayaka donors and their queens. In the corridor inside the perimeter walls, **Alankara Mandapa** has carvings of royals, including Martanda Varma of Tiruvananthapuram (see pp.

212–13). It is an easy drive northwest from Suchindrom to the astonishing palace of the Travancore kings at **Padmanabhapuram.**

Another good route from Tiruneludi goes to Kollam (Quillon). Stop at **Tenkasi** to visit the capital of the Pandya in the 15th to 16th centuries. Their **Vishvanatha Temple** has very fine carvings; see Shiva with the wives of the sages on the gopura walls, and the huge carved piers of the hall in the first enclosure.

A different, more rural route west to Kollam goes through the village of **Tiruppudaimarudur.** Its **Narumbunatha Temple,** on the banks of the Tambraparni River, has unusually well-preserved sculptures and paintings. At **Papanasam,** up in the hills, you simply enjoy the beauty of the spot. ∎

Indians travel from all over their huge country, often in village or school groups on subsidized train or bus tickets, to visit Gandhi's memorial at Kanniyakumari.

As Ooty's popularity has grown since independence, its eclectic mix of colonial buildings has been joined by modern Indian housing, stores, and billboards.

Tamil Nadu's hill stations

ALTHOUGH THE EARLY BRITISH ADVENTURERS ADOPTED Indian ways and dress, and had Indian wives, by the 19th century an altogether more powerful and bureaucratic British presence seemed determined to remain as British as possible. Rather than adapting to the hot and humid climate and self-preserving ways of Indians, they wore too many clothes, ate and drank in quantities suited to northern Europe, and dreamed of green hills, gentle rain, and rose gardens.

As a result, they fell ill and many died of typhoid, cholera, and malaria. Soldiers stationed in the hill forts, however, did not. So sanitariums were built in the hills for ailing servants of the empire. Once it had been proved that the hills were healthier, enterprising officers set off to discover suitable sites. British hill stations were born.

Shimla, then called Simla, was the first, dating from 1819 (see p. 124). During the next 30 years more than 80 hill stations were established at elevations of between 4,035 feet (1,230 m) and 8,071 feet (2,460 m), and vast resources were spent on constructing mountain roads and railroads to reach them. Built on open hilltops with no

Scotch trout streams and Lusitanian views." She and her compatriots loved the colder climate, tolerated the leaking houses and discomforts, and built British-style houses with names like Rose Bank and Glenthorn.

But India was never far away. For all the attempts to create a drop of pure "home," every British hill station had a certain Indianness about it. Today, it is the reverse: Every Indian hill station has a certain Englishness about it.

UP TO COONOOR

Leaving the hot, lush, and sparkling paddy fields of the Tamil Nadu plains, roads twist and turn up gentle slopes into the fresh air and forests of the Western Ghats. These are truly spectacular drives, so it is worth allowing time to stop and enjoy panoramic views, do some bird-watching, and visit tea or coffee gardens. From north to south, the Ghats run more than 1,000 miles (1,609 km), reaching their height in the Nilgiris (Blue Mountains) at Ooty, which stands at the foot of the 8,615-foot-high (2,626 m) Doda Betta Peak.

Affluent **Coimbatore** is strategically placed near Palghat, the broadest pass through the hills. Coimbatore serves as a gateway to the Nilgiris. Its industrial wealth soared after hydroelectric power was harnessed from the Pykara Falls in the 1930s, boosting cotton manufacture. Most people drive through because it has no tourist attractions, but if you stay overnight here, you could take a morning stroll in the **Botanical Gardens,** established around 1900.

From Coimbatore drive north to Mettuppalaiyam, where the steep ascent begins, bringing hairpin bends, wonderful views, and a canopy of dark foliage. Northwest of Mattuppailayam is **Coonoor,**

fortifications, they represented a British confidence in themselves, their power, and their home culture.

The hill stations were cocktails of ideal British countryside, town activities, and beach town resorts. Highly social, elitist, and yet trapped in an isolated dream far from home, the British in the hill stations lived life to the full. The theater, clubs, churches, sports, flower shows, and promenades along the Mall ensured a continuous whirl of activity and a fair number of romantic flings.

But underneath there was homesickness, too. Lady Betty Balfour wrote from Ooty in 1877 of "such beautiful English rain, such delicious English mud. Imagine Hertfordshire lanes, Devonshire downs, Westmoreland lakes,

The Collector's Office in Ooty is a typical example of colonial British architecture.

Udagamandalam (Ooty)

⛰ 255 A3

Udagamandalam (Ooty) Tourist Office

✉ Commercial Rd.

☎ 0423-443977

Botanical Gardens

✉ Garden Rd.

Sim's Park

✉ Upper Coonoor

Raj Bhawan

✉ Garden Rd.

🕐 Closed to visitors

Savoy Hotel

✉ 77 Sylks Rd.

☎ 0423-444142

💲 $

which stands at 6,096 feet (1,858 m). It is at the head of the Hulikal Ravine in the Doda Betta Range and is less wet and cool than "The Queen" (see below). Huge tree-ferns, rhododendrons, and roses flourish in **Sim's Park,** where the prestigious Coonoor Fruit and Vegetable Show is held annually, after Ooty's flower show.

This is a marvelous area for hiking: Visit **Lady Canning's Seat** (2 miles/3 km); **Lamb's Rock** (3½ miles/6 km), with dramatic views; **Dolphin's Nose** (7½ miles/ 12 km), with views of Katherine Falls and the Coonoor Stream; and **Law's Falls** (3 miles/5 km), named after the man who constructed the Coonoor Ghat Road. You can also hike the 2 miles (3 km) up to **The Droog** (Pakkasuram Kottai) for exhilarating views of the plains.

OOTY

At an elevation of 7,349 feet (2,240 m), Udagamandalam (Ootacamund, or Ooty) is the highest Nilgiri hill station and is surrounded by rolling, grassy slopes, natural woodland, and imported eucalyptus and conifers.

The original inhabitants here were four tribes, including the Todas, a tribe who tended herds of sacred buffalo. Today, their few surviving members have, sadly, been turned into something of a tourist curiosity. Following the death of Tipu Sultan in 1799, the East India Company annexed the Nilgiris and their tribes. In 1818 two assistants of John Sullivan, Collector of Coimbature, saw the possibilities of the area; in 1823, Sullivan built his Stone House. Word spread, the British arrived, and Sullivan planted English vegetables and trees. He enlarged the lake and introduced fast-growing eucalyptus trees from Australia.

By 1861 Ooty, as it was known, was the summer capital of the Madras Presidency and "The Queen of Hill Stations." The governor and his staff, servants, and all their families arrived, soon followed by other Europeans and anglophile Indian princes. According to their means and position, they came on foot or on horseback, were carried in palanquins, or, later, took the train; the first passengers arrived in Ooty in 1908. Nowadays the train can be taken from Mettuppalayam or, for a longer journey, from Coonoor.

French botanist M. Perottet introduced tea here; coffee had already been grown near Mysore since the 1820s. Visitors in the early years included the first governor-general of India, Lord William Cavendish Bentinck (1774–1839), and historian Thomas Babington Macaulay (1800–1859). Snooty Ooty, as the hill station was known, has changed radically and now feels more like a midscale Indian town transplanted to the hills; but its popularity is unabated.

To visit some of British Ooty, start with a walk through the orchids, trees, ferns, and medical plants of the glorious hillside **Botanical Gardens,** founded in 1848 by the Marquess of Tweeddale with the help of Mr. MacIvor from Kew Gardens in London. Above the gardens lies **Raj Bhawan** (1877, *closed to the public*), built for the Duke of Buckingham when he was governor of Chennai. Ooty's biggest events, the annual flower and dog shows, are held here.

Among the verdant lanes, you can get a feel of British Ooty by surveying the Ootacamund Club (founded 1843, *closed to non-members*), and the Ooty Gymkhana Gold Club on Wenlock Downs. Then go to **St. Stephen's Church** (1831), full of memorials to those who could not be saved by Ooty's fresh air, and to the **Savoy Hotel,** whose wood fires burn each night. Go down past the lake to see the racetrack, station, and beyond them, **St. Thomas's Church** (1870). Farther on down is the **Fernhill Palace** (1842), which once belonged to the ruler of Mysore and is now a hotel (*closed for renovation*). In town, find Sullivan's **Stone House** near Charing Cross, the **Nilgiri Library** (1885), and the **District and Sessions Court** (1873).

There are good excursions and hikes, or you can make arrangements through your hotel for an accompanied horseback ride. Try going to Doda Betta Peak for fine views, or to Marlimund Lake, Tiger Hill, Kalhatti Falls, and Pykara Lake or Pykara Falls, 20 miles (32 km) west of Ooty. A scenic road leads to Avalanche, and from Mukerti Lake you can hike up Mukerti Peak.

KODAIKANAL
Set in a natural bowl in the Palani Hills and surrounded by terraced hills, Kodaikanal has only recently lost its peaceful charm in favor of lucrative tourism. Known as "The Princess of Hill Stations," it was founded in 1844 by the American Madurai Mission, whose members moved up here from Madurai in a desperate search for renewed health.

If you can, avoid the two monsoons Kodaikanal receives and arrive here along picturesque Laws Ghat Road between January and March, when there are few visitors. You can rent rowboats from the Boat Club and find good views over the plains along Coaker's Walk.

YERCAUD
Across in the Eastern Ghats, the thickly forested Shevaroy Hills rise sharply. Here, at Yercaud, 4,920 feet (1,499 m) up, the first real hotel opened in 1971, offering a convenient respite from the heat for people living in Madurai and Bangalore. Until then it had been a place for coffee estates since the 1820s and, more recently, for Catholic schools. Leaving the whitewashed, red-tiled houses of the town and its planters' club, there are pleasant walks through the wooded lanes around the coffee estates. ■

You may see tea-pickers plucking new shoots, which are processed on site to preserve their flavor.

Kodaikanal
⚠ 255 B3
Kodaikanal Tourist Office
✉ Rest House Complex
☎ 04542-41675

Yercaud
⚠ 255 B4
Yercaud Tourist Information
✉ Rjaram Nagar
☎ 04281-66449

More places to visit in Tamil Nadu

ALAGARKOIL
The **Algar Perumal Temple,** beside a forested hill, is dedicated to Vishnu as Kallalagar, Minakshi's brother; so the temple is part of Madurai's great festival (see p. 275). Note the elegant donor figures with Nayaka queen, and the rare Pandya central shrine.
🏔 255 B2 ✉ 7 miles (12 km) north of Madurai

AUROVILLE
Inspired by The Mother (see p. 267), about 800 families live in this ideal coastal city founded in 1968. Houses with names such as Grace form an outward spiral, symbolizing continuous motion and the universality of faith; Matrimandir (meditation house) is central. Stores in the city stock quality homemade goods.
🏔 255 C4 ✉ 6 miles (10 km) north of Pondicherry

CHENGALPATTU (CHILGLEPUT)
Chengalpattu is famous for its fort, which was disputed by the French and English. Roam the remains and, at nearby **Vallam,** see three very early, fascinating Pallava cave temples from the reign of Mahendravarman I (*R.*580–630).
🏔 255 C5 ✉ 36 miles (58 km) west of Chennai

CHENNAI–MAHABILIPURAM DRIVE
There are two places to stop: **Cholamandel** coastal artists' community, with its permanent arts exhibition, and Muttukadu's **Dakshinachitra** (*Tel 04114-45303, closed Tues.*), to see old vernacular buildings rescued from destruction. A building from each of four southern states is preserved, together with information on their respective ways of life.
✉ 13 miles (21 km) south of Chennai

GINGEE
Tamil Nadu's most spectacular fortified site, Gingee was built by the Vijayanagas and contested by most subsequent armies in the south; see the three impressive citadels.
🏔 255 C4 ✉ 42 miles (68 km) northwest of Pondicherry

KILAIYUR & TIRUVAIYARU
Kilaiyur's finely finished twin temples, built in the ninth-century by local chieftains, make an interesting combination to visit in conjunction with nearby Tiruvaiyaru's temple, famous more for its music festival than for its architecture.
🏔 255 C3 **Kilaiyur** ✉ 20 miles (33 km) north of Thanjavur

PANAMALAI
On the Villupuram–Vettavalam road, the important hilltop **Talagirishvara Temple** (eighth century), dedicated to Shiva, is built of reddish granite and has a hemispherical roof, some nice sculpture, and traces of paintings.
🏔 255 C4 ✉ 46 miles (75 km) west of Pondicherry

POINT CALIMERE WILDLIFE SANCTUARY
Saltwater tidal swamps are home to flamingoes and other waterbirds. On a trip from Thanjavur, you can return via **Velanganni,** a Catholic pilgrimage center, and **Nagappattinam,** an ancient port and Buddhist center whose Karikop Cemetery has early Dutch tombs.
🏔 255 C3 ✉ 56 miles (90 km) southeast of Thanjavur

PULICAT
Right on the border with Andhra Pradesh, Pulicat Lake attracts resident and migratory waterbirds such as pelicans and flamingoes. The town's Dutch cemetery is especially rich in old tombstones.
🏔 255 D5 ✉ 25 miles (40 km) north of Chennai

PULLAMANGAI
The splendid **Brahmapurishvara Temple** (tenth century), dedicated to Shiva, sits quietly at the end of this rural village where in almost every house there lives a master silk-weaver. Walk around the back to see the fine sculptures on the outside of the sanctuary.
✉ 6 miles (10 km) from Thanjavur

SRINIVASANALLUR

There is fine sculpture on this early Chola temple (927) overlooking the Kaveri River and dedicated to Koranganatha, a form of Shiva. Westward, **Punaji** has a similarly good temple, while **Namakkal's** eighth-century Pandyan shrine, with vigorous and large sculptures, is hidden behind later additions.
✉ 28 miles (45 km) northwest of Tiruchirappalli

SRIPERUMBUDUR

Believed to be the birthplace of the Vaishnava saint Ramanuja, the temple (16th to 17th century) has splendid *Ramayana* friezes.
255 C5 ✉ 25 miles (40 km) southwest of Chennai

SRIVILLIPUTTUR

This temple town is focused on two temples. One of them, **Vatapatrashayi,** dedicated to Vishnu, has a 17th-century Nayaka period *gopura* 207 feet high (63 m) with an 11-stage tower. Said to be the tallest of all gopuras, it is Tamil Nadu's official emblem.
255 B2 ✉ 46 miles (74 km) southwest of Madurai

SWAMIMALAI (TIRUVALANJULI)

Find the **Kapardishvara Temple,** dedicated to Shiva, in the hamlet of Tiruvalanjuli; the Srivilliputtur's Adal Temple, a twin to Vatapatrashayi Temple, has brass-encased portraits of its patrons, the Madurai ruler Tirumala Nayaka and his brother, by the temple swing.

Chola-period hall has unusual bulbous pilasters. In the village, you can watch craftsmen make religious bronzes by the traditional lost wax method; you can buy direct from them.
✉ 5 miles (8 km) west of Kumbakonam
(255 C3)

TARANGAMBADI (TRANQUEBAR)

From 1620 to 1807 this town was the headquarters of the Dutch East India Company, and the European character survives intact today in the houses, churches, and fort with museum *(Closed Fri.)*.
255 C3 ✉ 39 miles (63 km) east of Kumbakonam

TIRUCHENGODU

There are two Chola foundations to see here, much enlarged by the Nayakas and Wodeyars. Midtown **Kailasanatha** is crowded with stores and temple chariots; walk up the hill to **Ardhanarishvara** for the best entrance, fine woodcarving, and good views.
255 B3 ✉ 31 miles (50 km) southwest of Salem

TIRUKKALUKKUNDRAM

One of the most ambitious temples to be built by the Nayakas of Gingee, and dedicated to Shiva as Bhaktavatsaleshvara, Tirukkalukkundram's grand *gopura* has fine sculptures and paintings of royal visitors (west gopura).
🅜 255 D4 ✉ 9 miles (14 km) west of Mahabalipuram

TIRUMANGALAKKUDI

The 18th-century paintings on the corridor ceiling in **Pramanatheshvara Temple,** dedicated to Shiva, make a trip across the Kaveri worthwhile. They depict local legends and, interestingly, the shrines along the river.
✉ 9 miles (15 km) northwest of Kumbakonam (🅜 255 C3)

THIRUPPARANKUNDRAM

The sacred granite hill of this town is where its **Murugan Temple,** dedicated to Shiva's son Subramanya, began as a fine Pandya-period cave temple (773). To reach it, go through the later additions of painted and sculptured halls. See Travelwise for details of the major 14-day festival *(March–April).*
🅜 255 B2 ✉ 4 miles (6 km) southwest of Madurai

TIRUTTANI

Follow the path to this hilltop Subramanya temple. Then go through ascending terraces to find a Pallava period shrine with fine images of Subramanya and, in the outer enclosure, a row of stone soldiers as his army.
🅜 255 C5 ✉ 53 miles (86 km) NW of Chennai

TIRUVADAIMARNDUR

There are two Chola shrines to Shiva here. First, see the grand and large corridors and halls of the **Mahalinga Perumal** temple complex (17th to 18th century), with its Chola shrine, then Tribhuvanam's royal **Kampahareshvara Temple,** built by Kulottunga III *(R.*1178–1218).
✉ 6 miles (10 km) northeast of Kumbakonam (🅜 255 C5)

TIRUVANNAMALAI

The **Arunachaleshvara Temple** in this town is one of Tamil Nadu's grandest, dedicated to Shiva's fiery *lingum* (phallus). The temple is the focus of a crowded 14-day festival *(Nov.–Dec.),* which coincides with the cattle fair. If you are going north from here, pause at **Tirumalai** to see the 16th-century Jain complex.
🅜 255 C4 ✉ 23 miles (37 km) west of Gingee

TIRUVARUR

This is one of the area's most important Chola temples, dedicated to Shiva as Tyagaraja, whom Tamil saints such as Appar and Sambandar glorified in their devotional hymns. Massive gopuras lead through halls to the shrine, whose Somaskanda form of Shiva (Shiva, his consort Parvati, and their son Skanda or Subramanya) was a favorite Chola image.
🅜 255 C3 ✉ 33 miles (53 km) east of Thanjavur

VEDANTANGAL BIRD SANCTUARY

A lake and marshy, low-lying ground attract a variety of waterfowl, including ibises, purple moorhens, gray pelicans, and night-herons.
🅜 255 C4 ✉ 25 miles (40 km) southwest of Mahabalipuram

VELLORE & ARCOT

Vellore's **fort,** a fine piece of military architecture, has haunting associations with the Vijayanagas (their temple here is superb), Marathas, Moguls, British (courthouse, church), and Tipu Sultan, whose family was kept here after the fall of Srirangapatnam (see p. 246). A mile (1.6 km) northeast, find the **dargah** (tomb) of Tipu's mother and wife. At Arcot to the east, the famous battles fought with the Nawabs of Arcot have left few remains.
🅜 255 C5

VRINCHIPURAM

Rising grandly above its modest village of lanes and thatched houses, the **Marghabandhu Temple,** dedicated to Shiva, was substantially funded by the Nayakas of Gingee. It has a huge gopura, a columned hall, twin marriage halls possibly inspired by Vellore's superb temple (see above), and with donor portraits of the Nayaka patron and his wife (in the northwest hall).
🅜 255 C5 ✉ 9 miles (14 km) west of Vellore ∎

The Ganga's great delta brought prosperity to empires from the early Mauryas to the British. Trace the legacy of these cultures and visit their distinctive monuments in a verdant land that is home to the Hindus' sacred Varanasi city.

Eastern India

**An intricately carved wheel
at Konark's Surya Temple**

Eastern India

STEEPED IN HISTORY, EASTERN India is surprisingly little visited by foreigners. East of Delhi, India is for the most part quiet and very accessible; there is little of the aggressive tourism found west of Delhi, in Rajasthan.

You can trace the path of the Ganga (see pp. 304–305) through three very different states: Uttar Pradesh, Bihar, and West Bengal. Uttar Pradesh has the highest population of any Indian state—more than 140 million; yet its literacy is just 41 percent, a telling yardstick. Its cities vary from the Moguls' Muslim Agra (see pp. 96–99), the Hindus' sacred Varanasi, and Buddhist Sarnath, to Lucknow, now the state capital. Out in the fields, farmers produce more cereals than any other state and half of all India's sugarcane.

Neighboring Bihar is even more densely populated but less fortunate: Literacy is just 38 percent. However, it is India's richest state in minerals and is responsible for 42 percent of the country's production. Around the capital, Patna, you can follow the story of Buddhism at Bodh Gaya and Nalanda.

Kolkata (Calcutta) is West Bengal's capital and eastern India's commercial and cultural center. The state's recent history is one of reduction: It once stretched to Agra and included Bihar and Orissa, but it was divided in two in 1905, a move that fed the area's awakening patriotism. It was further divided at independence to form East Pakistan (now Bangladesh) and West Bengal. Kolkata has a state literacy rate touching 60 percent, and still maintains Bengal's cultural tradition, while the farmers produce much of India's rice, jute, and, up in the hills, tea.

Between these three states and the Deccan Plateau to the south lie Madhya Pradesh, Tharkand, Chhatisgarh, and Orissa. A vast landscape of dry plains and forested hills, Madhya Pradesh is India's largest state; yet apart from the area around Delhi it is rarely visited by tourists. Orissa, bordered by the Eastern Ghats on one side and the Bay of Bengal to the

other, is home to some of India's most interesting tribal communities. As in Bihar, you can visit vestiges of remarkable early empires in and around the capital, Bhubaneshwar.

The tropical Andaman and Nicobar Islands form India's most remote state, more than 600

Bananas are traded briskly in Kolkata.

Area of map detail

Delhi

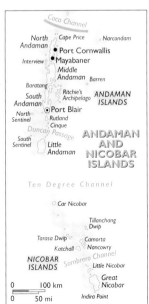

miles (1,000 km) east of the mainland. Only a few of the islands are open to foreign visitors, but they offer fabulous beaches and pristine coral reefs off the coast.

Kolkata, Varanasi, and Lucknow may not be picturesque or easy to visit, but they are rich in history and are well worth the effort needed to explore them. ■

Kolkata (Calcutta)

THERE IS A STRENGTH AND SPIRIT IN KOLKATA THAT, DESPITE all it has suffered, makes it one of the world's great cities. If you are looking for prettiness, this is not a city for you. But Kolkata allows you to touch the pulse of Bengal's great culture, past and present, and see, through the decay, the grandeur of a great colonial city.

Former colonial grandeur is the backdrop to contemporary Kolkata life on Bentinck Street, named for Lord William Bentinck, governor-general between 1834 and 1835.

Kolkata
🗺 287 D3
Kolkata Tourist Information
✉ 4 Shakespeare Sarani
☎ 033-2421402 or 2421475

In fact, Bengalis consider themselves, with some justification, the intelligentsia of India. The Bengali Renaissance of the 19th century witnessed a flowering of talent, led by Raja Ram Mohan Roy (1774–1833), which created a new intellectual elite whose legacy continues today; do try to visit one of the city's art centers.

Kolkata is relatively new. In 1690 Job Charnock, a maverick agent for the British East India Company,

leased three swampy villages from Mogul Emperor Aurangzeb. Trading began, and six years later the company built Fort William, but times were uncertain. When Suraj-ud-Daula of Murshidabad took the city and incarcerated British soldiers in a dark room later dubbed the "Black Hole of Calcutta," Robert Clive arrived from Madras and crushed him at the Battle of Plassey in 1757. Seven years later, Sir Hector Munro led the

British triumph at the Battle of Buxar, wresting most of Bihar from the Nawabs of Bengal, who had recently won it from the weakening Moguls.

The fortunes of the British— and the city—took off. In 1772 Kolkata (Calcutta) usurped Chennai (Madras) as the British head-quarters in India and appointed its first governor of British India, Warren Hastings. Kolkata's rich hinterland became the main source of the company's vast wealth (which, after 1858, went directly to the British govern-ment). Dazzling white stuccoed mansions with a lifestyle to go with them made Kolkata the great-est colonial city of the Orient.

Kolkata's position held until 1931, when New Delhi was inaugurated as the new capital, and kept its commercial prowess until independence, when colonial com-panies were obliged to become Indian. Since independence, the city's population has swelled first with Hindu immigrants from newly created Muslim East Pakistan, then with refugees from the Indo-Pakistan war of 1965 and the Pakistan-Bangladesh war of 1972, prompting the start of high-profile charity work (see box). Today, Kolkata covers 40 square miles (104 sq km) and has a population of more than 11 million.

To begin your exploration of the city, try driving around downtown (see pp. 292–93). Then explore one of the areas described on pp. 290–291. Early mornings are best, when you can imagine the past elegance of this City of Palaces.

High Court
🕐 Closed Sat. & Sun.

Town Hall
🕐 Closed Sat. & Sun.

Raj Bhavan
✉ Red Rd.
🕐 Closed to visitors

Writers' Buildings
☎ 033-2215858
🕐 Closed to visitors

Marble Palace
✉ Muktaram Babu St., off Chittaranjan Ave.
🕐 Closed Thurs. & Mon.

Rabindra Bharati Museum
✉ Dwarkanath Tagore Lane, off Chittaranjan Ave.
☎ 033-345241
🕐 Closed Sat. p.m. & Sun.
💲 $

Charity in Kolkata

Despite Kolkata's tremendous spirit, the outward image is one of poverty. In fact, much is being done to help Kolkata's poor. Mother Teresa (1910–1997) was the beacon bringing support for the many charities working in the city. Born in Albania, Mother Teresa joined the Sisters of Loreto. She was sent to Darjiling, where she took her vows in May 1931. Seeing the poverty in Kolkata, she founded the Missionaries of Charity, which focuses on helping the dying. Never shy in criticizing the powerful, she was an outspoken campaigner, who was awarded the Nobel Prize for Peace in 1979.

Some charities help street chil-dren and children's homes or women's education; others give inoculations or eye treatments. ■

B.B.D. BAGH & AROUND

Start early in the morning west of Assembly House, by the statue of Khudiram Bose, the first martyr for independent India, who was hanged in 1908 at the age of 19 for killing two British women with a bomb. In front of Walter Granville's very fine Gothic **High Court** (1872), well worth exploring, stands a statue of the revolutionary Surya Sen (died 1930).

John Garstin's **Town Hall** (1813) is a handsome Tuscan-Doric building, remodeled in the 1990s. Beyond it, on your way around the back of Raj Bhavan's huge garden, find the statue of the political leader Subhas Chandra Bose's equally revolutionary brother.

Raj Bhavan (Government House) is the West Bengal governor's residence. Beyond this take Old Court House Street past the Great Eastern Hotel to **B.B.D. Bagh** (Dalhousie Square), renamed for Benoy, Badal, and Dinesh, three freedom-fighters hanged by the British. B.B.D. Bagh was the hub of company power. **Writers' Buildings** (1780, refurbished 1880) spanning the north side of the square, was built for company clerical staff and is still a bureaucratic hive.

On the west side of B.B.D. Bagh is Walter Granville's **G.P.O.** (General Post Office, 1864–68), with its Corinthian columns standing over the site of the Black Hole of Calcutta (see p. 288). Try to imagine the lives of Robert Clive, Warren Hastings, and Clive Francis, who all lived nearby. Francis wrote: "Here I live, with a hundred servants, a country house, and spacious gardens, horses and carriages…."

Finally, down Government Place West, visit **St. John's Church** (1787), designed by Lt. James Agg and based on London's St. Martin-in-the-Fields. In the cool interior, memorials to Kolkata's British heroes include John Bacon's to Maj. James Achilles Kirkpatrick; the altarpiece (now in the south aisle) depicts famous Kolkata residents as Christ's apostles; the churchyard has memorials to the Rohilla War (1794) and Job Charnock (circa 1695), who founded the city.

HAORA (HOWRAH) STATION & BRIDGE

A good way to see this area is to visit the early morning **flower market** under Howrah Bridge (1943), where gymnasts and wrestlers train at Armenian Ghat. Then drive over

Durga Puja

This is the most spectacular of Kolkata's many festivals, which fill the city's calendar. It falls in September–October, generates a near collapse of the city's offices, and brings families together for constant celebrations. The focus is Durga, Shiva's wife in her destructive form. Idol-makers living in the Kumartuli area work all year to create hundreds of Durga images, painting their straw and unbaked clay models gaudy colors to look like the latest film stars. Offices, local groups, or whole streets then create unashamedly glitzy settings for their goddess, who, fierce and furious with her ten arms, is shown either on or with her lion, slaying the demon Mahisasura, who has deviously taken the form of a buffalo to threaten the gods. For the ten days before Mahadashami, when the images are paraded down to the Hooghly and immersed in the water, Kolkatans take evening strolls to visit as many as possible of these spectacular creations. ∎

the bridge to explore Halsey Ricardo's magnificent **Howrah railroad station** (1854–1928), which is always busy. From here you can take a ferry across the Hooghly to land at **Babu's Ghat** on the Maidan, or one upriver to **Kumatuli Ghat** to see craftsmen making inlaid woodwork and the Durga Puja clay deities.

NORTH KOLKATA

North of B.B.D. Bagh was where rich Kolkatans once lived, and some old families still do. Here you can explore narrow alleys and find facades of crumbling mansions. Try **Barabazaar** and its Armenian church (1724). North of M.G. Road, find the vast and decaying **Marble Palace,** begun in 1835 by Rajendra Mullick when he was 16 years old. It abounds with Belgian chandeliers, Venetian mirrors, and paintings by Rubens and others. Northeast of here, visit the restored house of Rabindranath Tagore, which is now the **Rabindra Bharati Museum,** and trace the story of the Tagores and the Bengal Renaissance. Finally, visit College

Street in the university area, where the **Ashutosh Museum of Indian History** has Bengali crafts and *kantha* embroidery.

SOUTH KOLKATA

Alipore and Ballygunge, Kolkata's wealthy residential areas, developed around the Deputy Governor's House, now the **National Library.** Alipore's **Horticultural Gardens** are half a mile (1 km) south of here. At the **Kolkata Zoo,** the snake, bird, and big cat collections are especially interesting.

Still farther south **Kalighat,** the temple to Kali, patron goddess of Kolkata, is best reached on India's only underground transit system. Opened in 1984, it is Russian-designed, clean, and efficient. Zip down to Kalighat station, then walk five minutes to the city's most important temple. Indeed, such is its importance that the East India Company servants used to give high-profile but controversial devotional offerings here. Excellent brass is sold in the market outside the entrance. ∎

A stallholder finds his wares make a handy pillow.

Horticultural Gardens
✉ Alipore
🕐 Closed Mon., flower shows in Feb.
$ $

Ashutosh Museum of Indian History
✉ Centenary Building, College St.
🕐 Closed Sun. & university holidays
$ $

Rabindra Bharati Museum
✉ 6 Dwarakanath Tagore Lane

Kolkata Zoo
✉ Jawahar Rd.
$ $

A drive around colonial Kolkata

After Clive's victory (see p. 288), the East India Company rebuilt the fort (1757–1770) and cleared thick jungle in front of it to create the defensive Maidan (open space) that is Kolkata's great lung today. This drive takes you past some of the colonial public buildings, churches, monuments, and houses built in Kolkata's heyday.

Ranks of yellow taxis wait among the crowds outside Howrah Station.

Start at **Babu's Ghat ❶**, from where ferries go to Howrah Station (see pp. 290–91). Near the Ghat, **Eden Gardens ❷** contain Kolkata Stadium, where test cricket matches are held. Look across the Maidan to Jawaharlal Nehru and Chowringhee Roads: Enough buildings survive to help your imagination furnish them with 18th- and 19th-century grandeur.

Drive along Esplanade past Col. John Garstin's handsome, refurbished **Town Hall** (1813) and grandiose **Raj Bhavan ❸** (Government House, 1797–1803), begun by Viceroy Lord Curzon and designed by Capt. Charles Wyatt in imitation of Robert Adam's Kedleston Hall in Derbyshire, England.

At the corner with Jawaharlal Road, the **Ochterlony Monument ❹** (1828) is a tall column in remembrance of Sir David Ochterlony, the eccentric British hero of the Nepal War (1814–1816). Your drive down Chowringhee Road begins with the **Oberoi Grand Hotel** (1911, much changed), which stoically holds on to its Raj character through every restoration. Down Lindsay Street bustling lanes are centered around **New Market ❺**; if you want to shop, a coolie will follow you around and carry your purchases on his head.

Proceed to the **Indian Museum ❻** (opened 1814), India's first national museum. Despite its shabbiness, it holds exceptional stone and metal sculptures rescued from eastern Indian sites. See the second-century B.C. sculptures from Vidisha, Sravasti, and Bharhut; the second-century A.D. panels from Mathura; India's finest collection of first- to third-century schist sculptures from Gandhara; and other treats from Khajuraho, Halebid, Konark, Nalanda, and Nagappattinam. Farther down Chowringhee Road, you pass the **Asiatic Society of Bengal,** founded by Sir William Jones in 1784, and the forerunner of such British learned societies.

Turn left on Park Street, then right into Middleton Row to find more buildings from Kolkata's past. The **Convent of Our Lady of Loreto** was once home to the great collector Sir Elijah Impey. On Shakespeare Sarai, the **Royal Calcutta Turf Club** (1820), built as the home of a shipping magnate, is now one of many traditional British clubs that have changed little apart from the nationality of their membership. Stop to take a stroll around **South Park Street Cemetery ❼**, where pyramids, catafalques, pavilions, and obelisks, all saved from destruction, tell the amazing story of the city's growth and heyday. The cemetery guide, sold on site, is worth buying.

⓫ See area map pages 286–87
▶ Babu's Ghat, Maidan
⟳ 6 miles (10 km)
⏱ 4–5 hours: Leave early enough to reach the Indian Museum at 10 a.m., when it opens.
▶ Victoria Monument

NOT TO BE MISSED
- South Park Street Cemetery
- St. Paul's Cathedral
- Victoria Memorial

Back along Shakespeare Sarai **St. Paul's Cathedral** ⑧ (1839), overlooking Chowringhee, is the British Empire's first Church of England cathedral. Treasures inside include Sir Edward Burne-Jones's west window (1880), Clayton and Bell's east window (1860s), Sir Arthur Blomfield's reredos, the pre-Raphaelite monument to Lord Mayo, and much more.

Finally, you reach the symbol of British imperialism in the east, the **Victoria Memorial** ⑨ (1921). Designed by Sir William Emerson and faced in Makrana marble from Jaipur state, it is topped off with a bronze figure of Victory. A statue of Lord Curzon, who conceived it, stands at the unused south entrance. In front, there is Sir George Frampton's striking art nouveau statue of the Queen-Empress Victoria. Inside, find quantities of huge oil portraits of self-regarding servants of the empire, plus an excellent new gallery in the back, which explains Kolkata's history. ∎

Bhubaneshwar

📍 287 C2

India Tourist
Information

✉ B/21 B.J.B. Nagar

☎ 0674-412203

Orissa Tourist
Information

✉ 5 Jayadev Nagar,
near Panthaniwas
Hotel

☎ 0674-431299

Orissa State
Museum

✉ Lewis Rd.

🕐 Closed Mon.

💲 $

Orissa's capital,
Bhubaneshwar,
offers relative
tranquility and
delightful
temples.

Bhubaneshwar, Puri, & Konark

BHUBANESHWAR, THE STATE CAPITAL OF ORISSA, HAS A long and glorious history. In the fourth century B.C. it was the capital of ancient Kalinga. Ashoka fought here in 260 B.C. before turning to Buddhism (see p. 31); he later placed one of his rock edicts there. During the city's golden age of prosperity and religious fervor, the 7th to 12th centuries, more than 7,000 temples were built around Bindu Sagar (Ocean Drop Tank) by the Bhauma-Kara, Somavansi, and Ganga rulers, as offerings to the gods and symbols of authority.

Visitor tip
Both tourist information
offices in Bhubaneshwar
have information on
Orissa's many festivals.

Many temples survive, including three groups of stunning ones on the town's southern outskirts, best reached by rickshaw. By visiting just five temples in chronological order, you can trace the development of distinctive Orissan style. These are the temples to see: **Parasumaresvara Mandir** (late seventh century), **Vaital Deul** (late eighth century), **Mukteshvara** (late tenth century), **Lingaraja** (late 11th century), and **Yameshvara** (late 13th century). The curved tower grows higher and more complex; the *mandapa* (hall) becomes larger with a pyramid roof; sculpture is increasingly fully modeled, more elaborate, and focused on the niches.

In town, the **Orissa State Museum** has an excellent collection of Orissa's archaeological finds, as well as ethnographic items and illustrated manuscripts. India's largest zoo is in **Nandankanam Botanical Gardens.**

Farther afield, a one-day trip south to **Puri** winds through quaint villages with decorated houses, including **Pipli,** center of Orissa's colorful cotton appliquéwork. Puri is best known for its soaring Jagannath Temple *(closed to non-Hindus),* and this is a true pilgrim town, especially during the annual Rath Yatra festival *(June–July).* You can also take a promenade along the waterfront (the sea is not especially clean here).

Then drive up the coast to **Konark,** whose splendid **Surya Temple** (13th century), built by the Ganga king Narasimha *(R.* 1238–1264) marks the climax of all you saw at Bhubaneshwar: The temple is built as the sun god's chariot drawn by a team of horses. ■

Orissa's early monuments

ORISSA'S ELABORATE, ROCK-CUT CAVES AND SUBSTANTIAL Buddhist remains testify to the prosperity of the Kalinga empire of the fourth century and its mercantile strength, military power, and opulent lifestyle.

In two sandstone outcrops overlooking Bhubaneshwar are some remarkable Jain caves left by a large Jain community that thrived here in the first century B.C. under the benevolent Chedi rulers. About 35 massive and austere caves, some natural and some dug out, provide our earliest evidence of the art found here in Orissa.

The dozen caves on the Khandagiri Hill are fairly simple. Those on the **Udayagiri Hill** include **Cave no. 1,** the largest and most elaborate. Two levels of cells surround a large courtyard. See the guardian figures, some in foreign dress (upper story, right wing), and the relief carvings over the doorways that show pious couples, musicians, dancers, and nature scenes. **Caves no. 3–5, 9,** and **10** are also interesting.

If these have whetted your appetite, take a long but rewarding one-day trip north to find more caves at Lalitagiri, Udaiayiri, and Ratnagiri, and to enjoy stunning countryside. On your way, you pass through Orissa's former capital, **Cuttack,** crammed onto a narrow island on the Mahanadi River. In the old quarter's bazaars, find Orissa's distinctive filigree jewelry (in Balu and Nayasarak bazaars).

The caves are hidden amid lush farmland sprinkled with tiny villages. It is easy to imagine how each of these hill sites was an ideal place to found a Buddhist university with the great expansion of Buddhist teaching from the 5th to the 12th centuries. At that time the sea reached farther inland and

would have been, in the monks' view, thoroughly appropriate because their patrons were often affluent merchants trading by sea. Some of these monasteries

were training centers for Buddhist missionaries who were to spread the word eastward.

At **Lalitagiri,** remains of platforms, shrines, mounds, and monastic buildings are still being excavated on Parabhadi and Landa Hills. At **Udaiayiri,** archaeologists are finding more of these plus a colossal image of Buddha seated and panels of Bodhisattvas. Last and best of all, **Ratnagiri,** once the center of Buddhism in Orissa, has a great hilltop *stupa* and two monasteries; one still has its courtyard, cells, and a Buddha figure. ■

Udayagiri Hill caves

- ✉ 4 miles (6 km) W of Bhubaneshwar
- 💲 $

Cuttack

- 🔺 287 C2
- ✉ 30 miles (48 km) N of Bhubaneshwar

Two wonderfully realistic elephants stand in the compound of Konark's isolated Surya Temple, matched by two rearing horses on the other side.

Ratnagiri

- 🔺 287 D2
- ✉ 85 miles (135 km) NE of Bhubaneshwar
- 💲 $

India's tribal communities

About 70 million of India's billion inhabitants still live their traditional tribal lives. Known collectively as Adivasis (original inhabitants) or by their official government grouping of Scheduled Tribes, they trace their origins right back to pre-Aryan times. For many, their lifestyle has changed little over the centuries. Until recently, they had remained separate from all the great empires and their developments, and had rarely encountered Hindu, Muslim, Western, or other cultures—even though the British encouraged them to settle so they could be taxed.

Naga tribeswomen living in Nagaland, wearing their distinctive shawls and jewelry

their buffaloes, which has been eroded by close encounters with the British and with Hindu Indians. The Bhils of southern Rajasthan, on the other hand, have for centuries been close allies with the rulers of Mewar, and this symbiotic relationship of mutual respect continues today. The Abors and Apatamis of Arunachal Pradesh in northeast India, however, continue to manage their own affairs.

But the pulls of tradition against modernity are increasingly causing friction. The more than three million Santhals of West Bengal and Bihar, who form the largest tribe of southern Asia, capture best these contrary pulls. Back in the 19th century, rapacious Hindu moneylenders dispossessed them of their land to the extent that they rebelled in 1855–57; yet they wanted high-caste Hindu privileges. In the 20th century they were drawn into the emerging industrialization that arrived on their doorstep, and its attendant education and modernization opportunities: Tata Iron and Steel Company opened at Jamshedpur in Bihar in 1908.

Today India has more than 500 named tribes speaking more than 40 different languages and following ancient customs and religious rituals. Each one has its own lineage or clan. Tribes still live on the periphery of society, with their distinctive lifestyles, although environmental pressure has forced the traditional hunters among them to change to cultivation. Most live in the thickly forested regions of India—where the terrain is unattractive for urban development or just plain inaccessible—such as southern Bihar, western Orissa, parts of Madhya Pradesh, the Andaman Islands, and the northeastern states.

Some tribes, such as the Jarawas of the Andamans, live at subsistence level, hunting and gathering in tiny communities of fewer than 500; others account for almost an entire population, such as the Mizos of Mizoram or the Nagas of Nagaland, who have adopted Christianity and Western lifestyles. India's tribal life has been under threat since the British period. The Todas of the Nilgiri Hills in Tamil Nadu had a rich culture, centered on

Today, with improved communications and a ballooning population, ideas and people reach most of India's tribes. So does outside competition for land where the tribes have lived for centuries; that these people are exposed to secular life and political awareness, and must make choices about them, is unavoidable but acceptable to them. That they are ruthlessly exploited, dispossessed, used as cheap labor, and left hungry is not. However, the Scheduled Castes and Tribes do have a voice in parliament: In each state, the number of constituencies reserved for them is in proportion to the state's total population. ∎

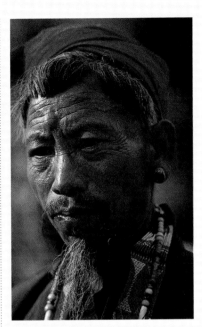

India's Scheduled Tribes, known as Adivasis, are scattered throughout the country. In the Lower Himalayas, a Kulu woman (above) living in Himachal Pradesh shops for a water pot.

In Gujarat, Maghwal *harijans* living in the town of Bhuj (below) lost their beautifully decorated homes in the devastating earthquake of 2001 (see p. 147).

Above: A Naga tribesman from Khonsa district in Arunachal Pradesh state

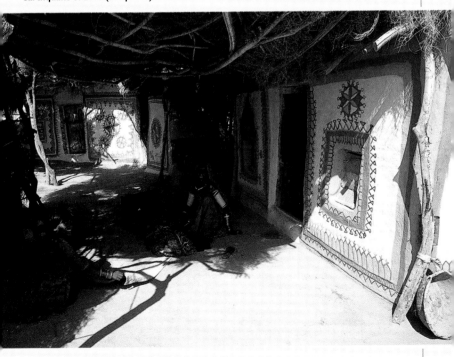

**The Andaman &
Nicobar Islands**

🅰 287 box inset

**Andaman &
Nicobar Tourist
Office**

✉ Opposite Indian
Airlines, Port Blair

☎ 03192-32694

**Port Blair
Tourist Office**

✉ VIP Rd., 189, 2nd
Floor, Jungli Chat

☎ 03192-33006

**Cellular Jail
National
Memorial**

💲 $

**Samudrika
Marine Museum**

🕐 Closed Mon.

💲 $

**Fisheries
Museum &
Aquarium**

🕐 Closed Mon.

💲 $

**Anthropological
Museum**

✉ Gandi Rd.

🕐 Closed Mon.

💲 $

**Mini Zoo &
Forest Museum**

✉ MG Rd.

🕐 Mini Zoo closed
Mon.

💲 $

Visitor tip
You can visit some of the
islands but not all. Consult
the Tourist Office.

The Andaman &
Nicobar Islands

IN THE BAY OF BENGAL, IN THE ANDAMAN SEA, MORE THAN
300 tiny islands make up a far-flung Indian possession that is important predominantly for its strategic position. Difficult to reach, these
islands offer a complete escape to superb beaches and wonderful
underwater sight-seeing on the coral reefs.

These forested islands, some 808
miles (1,300 km) from Kolkata and
746 miles (1,200 km) from
Chennai, form two groups: the
Andamans in the north, where Port
Blair is the capital on Middle
Andaman Island, and the Nicobars
(which you cannot visit) in the
south. Geologically, they were once
part of the landmass of southeast
Asia. The total population of about
300,000 people live on fewer than
40 of the islands.

In the past, the Portuguese,
Dutch, British, and Japanese have
controlled the islands; in 1857 the
British sent some 4,000 convicted
rebels to prison here. In 1956 the
Indian government passed the
Aboriginal Tribes Protection Act
to help protect the island tribes'
culture. However, this has not been
wholly successful: Many Sri Lankan
Tamils have migrated to the islands,
swelling the population sixfold in
just 20 years, and much forest has
been felled in favor of rubber
plantations. Even the islands' most
valuable possessions—their tribal
people and unique ecology—are
threatened by mismanagement.
Tribal people now account for less
than 10 percent of the population,
and numbers continue to fall.

Tourism, on the other hand, is
doing little damage. So far, just a
few of the 260 islands, most with
superb beaches and coral reefs, have
been developed. This policy works
well in the Maldive Islands, lying off
the west coast of southern India.

In Port Blair, where all the hotels
currently are, there are several
places to visit. The **Cellular Jail
National Memorial,** once a
British jail, is now a shrine to India's
freedom fighters. The **Samudrika
Marine Museum** provides a
good introduction to the islands'
geography, archaeology, and marine
life. For more specialized information, visit the **Fisheries Museum
& Aquarium** to discover more
about the Andaman Sea, the little
Anthropological Museum to
learn about the indigenous but
threatened tribes, and the **Mini
Zoo** and **Forest Museum** to

find out about the 200 or so animals exclusive to these islands. Out of town, you can visit **Mount Harriet National Park** and climb its mountain; sometimes you can stay in the Forest Guest House. A trip to **Ross Island** is worthwhile to see the British administrative buildings that are now very overgrown.

But the real joy of the islands lies in the water surrounding them. Beautiful coral reefs and very clear water combine to offer some of the world's best snorkeling. (Diving here is still in its infancy.)

BEACHES NEAR PORT BLAIR

Corbyn's Cove is the nearest beach, 4 miles (7 km) south of Port Blair. **Snake Island** is surrounded by a coral reef; take a boat there rather than swim, since the current can be strong. At Wandoor, the **Mahatma Gandhi National Marine Park** is 15 islands with mangrove creeks, tropical rain forest, and reefs supporting more than 50 types of coral. From Wandoor village, you can take a boat (*except Mon.*) 18 miles (29 km) southeast to **Jolly Buoy** and **Red Skin** islands to explore coral reefs for a couple of hours. **Chiriya Tapu,** 19 miles (30 km) south of Port Blair, is a tiny fishing village with mangroves and beaches; just over a mile (2 km) south lies an especially attractive beach. From here you can sometimes arrange a boat to the Cinque Islands (see below).

OTHER ISLANDS

Havelock Island, 33 miles (54 km) northeast of Port Blair, has perfect, white sandy beaches, clear turquoise water, and good snorkeling, plus dolphins, turtles, and large fish. **Long Island,** off Middle Andaman, is tiny, with one village and several perfect beaches. **North** and **South Cinque Islands,** some of the most beautiful of all, are part of Wandoor's national park; day visits only. ■

Mount Harriet National Park
🕐 Closed sunset to sunrise
💲 $

Mahatma Gandhi National Marine Park
✉ 19 miles (30 km) SW of Wandoor
💲 $

Port Blair Library
✉ Near the Post Office; reference section 1st floor

Pristine tropical beaches await visitors to these isolated islands.

Tibetan monks chant and pray in the shade of the bodhi tree at Bodh Gaya, in Bihar.

The Buddha trail

NON-BUDDHISTS RARELY VISIT INDIA'S EIGHT SITES associated with Buddha—Sravasti, Sankasya, Lumbini, Kushinagar, Sarnath, Bodh Gaya, Rajgir, and Vaishali—yet these places are as fascinating as Hindu, Muslim, and Jain sites. So consider joining the groups of Buddhists that flock to these fascinating places.

Lucknow
286 A4 & A5

Sravasti
286 B5

Kushinagar
286 B5

If you have time, and a strong interest, begin your trip from Lucknow by first visiting **Sravasti,** where the Buddha spent 24 rainy seasons: See where he stayed, plus monastic ruins and Jetavana Park. **Sankasya,** west of Lucknow, is where Buddha reputedly descended from heaven. **Lumbini,** just across the border in Nepal, is Buddha's birthplace, and at nearby **Kapilavastu** there is the palace of Buddha's father and a stupa. **Kushinagar** (30 miles/50 km

east of Gorakhpur) is where Buddha died and attained Mahaparinirvana; see the stupa built after his cremation, monastic remains, and a large reclining Buddha made of stone.

Or you could start at the next site, **Sarnath,** near Varanasi in Uttar Pradesh, the leading Buddhist pilgrimage center. Here Buddha preached his first sermon, usually called Dharmachakra ("Setting in Motion the Wheel of Righteousness"), on the July full moon

Leaving G.T. Road, you enter a quiet, rural area. **Bodh Gaya** is where Buddha meditated, was tempted by the demon Mara, and finally received *bodhi* (enlightenment), making the place an important pilgrimage site. The bodhi tree that is believed to spring from the one he sat under stands at the back of a Hindu temple; Buddhists sit here to meditate, chant, and read. There is also an excellent **Archaeological Museum** displaying fine sculptures and some modern temples built by Japanese, Vietnamese, and other Buddhist communities.

Country lanes twist past medieval Gaya to **Rajgir.** Buddha and Mahavira, who spread Jainism, often visited the ancient Magadha kingdom, whose capital was here. Its rulers Bimbisara and Ajatashatru (circa 543–459 B.C.) converted to Buddhism, and the First Council was held here. You may need a guide to help find the many localities associated with Buddha: **Venuvana bamboo grove**, which became the first Buddhist monastery; **Saptaparni Caves**, where the First Council was held; Pippala stone house, where the senior monk Mahakashyapa stayed, and others. Take the walk up **Gridhrakuta Hill** (Vulture Peak) past two caves to the high terrace to experience a peaceful, restorative sunset. Rajgir has a quality hotel.

Nearby, **Nalanda** was a huge monastery and university from the 5th to 12th centuries, and it was the seventh-century Pala rulers' principal seat of learning and place of art patronage. Beneath the farmers' fields, nine brick Buddhist monasteries facing four temples have been unearthed; even some floor tiles survive. Treasures in the **Archaeological Museum** range from a *Naga* deity to ancient rice grains.

Complete the trail at **Vaishali,** 20 miles (32 km) north of Patna, where Buddha preached his last sermon. ∎

night (see p. 58); this was the basis of all future development of the religion. Buddha also founded his *sangha* (monastic order) here. As you wander around the monasteries, the Dharmarajika Stupa (third century B.C.), and Main Shrine (mostly fifth century), you will soak up the strong historical-religious atmosphere. Visit the excellent **Sarnath Museum;** its Ashoka pillar capital is now the official symbol of India.

Now turn eastward into Bihar along the Grand Trunk Road, or G.T. Road, described by Kipling as "the backbone of all Hind…" with "such a river of life as nowhere else exists in the world." After 60 miles (97 km), detour to **Sasaram** to see Sher Shah Sur's five-story, midlake tomb (1540–45), considered by some to be one of India's best buildings.

Sarnath
🗺 286 B4

Sarnath Museum
✉ Ashoka Mara
☎ 0612-225411
🕐 Closed Fri.
💲 $

Sasaram
🗺 286 B4

Bodh Gaya
🗺 287 C4

Bodh Gaya Archaeological Museum
🕐 Closed Fri.

Rajgir
🗺 287 C4

Nalanda
🗺 287 C4

Nalanda Archaeological Museum
💲 $

Vaishali
🗺 287 C4

Visitor tip
Most facilities in this area are very simple; always carry water and snacks.

Patna

THIS ANCIENT CITY OF GREAT HISTORICAL IMPORTANCE, founded in the fourth century B.C. as Pataliputra, was the center of the legendary Magadhan and Mauryan empires. From Patna, Chandragupta Maurya extended his rule to the Indus, and his grandson Ashoka pushed it even farther (see p. 31). Under the Guptas (fourth century) and Sher Shah Sur (16th century), the city enjoyed revivals. However, this narrow city beside the Ganga has little to offer visitors today.

Patna

🗺 287 C4

Patna Tourist Office

✉ Sudma Palace, Kankur Bagh Rd.

☎ 0612-345776

Patna Museum

✉ Budh Rd.

🕐 Closed Mon.

💲 $

There are few remains to testify to its glory, except in the **Patna Museum.** So, start here. The superb collection includes a wooden Maurya wheel (third century B.C.) and pillar in the entrance hall, which come from Pataliputra's palace. Don't miss beautiful sculptures, such as the woman holding a *chauri* or flywhisk (third century B.C.), recently retrieved from Delhi's National Museum. Another is the woman with a parrot (third to seventh century), which was once part of a door. There are rooms full of gentle Buddhas and Bodhisattvas, Hindu carvings, and, upstairs, prints by the uncle–nephew team of

Sonpur Fair

India's largest livestock fair, held outside Patna at the confluence of the Gandak and Ganga Rivers, lasts a full month and is a parade of nonstop color and amazing sights. It is so big that the local train station has India's longest platform, specially built to accommodate freight trains bringing farmers and their sheep, cows, goats, horses, and other wares for sale. The fair begins on Kartik Purnima, the night of the November full moon, which is the climax of the Chath Festival. After pre-dawn *puja* at the tiny Hari Hari temple, the faithful go down to the river. There you can rent a boat and be punted past saffron-saried women performing their pujas, to see mahouts scrubbing their elephants. Back on land, see the elephants, all painted up to look their best for sale, the animal-trading, and the latest agricultural tools. ■

Elephants for sale are taken for their morning bath in the river during the fair.

Thomas and William Daniels, superb bronzes, and a hall full of lively proto-Mauryan terra-cottas (2000 B.C.).

To see old Patna, you can avoid the worst of the city's constant traffic congestion by setting off very early and using the Old Bypass Road to reach **Har Mandir Sahib,** one of the four holy temples for Sikhs (see p. 59). It honors the tenth Guru, Guru Gobind Singh, who was born here. As in the temple at Amritsar (see pp. 122–23), there is an aura of peacefulness.

When the British lopped Bihar and Orissa off Bengal to make an independent administrative unit, Patna once again became a capital. New Patna, contemporary with

New Delhi, was laid out as a modern imperial town, with wide avenues ending in vistas of grand buildings and a central axis called King George's Avenue. To see it, you need to drive or take a rickshaw and pass by **Raj Bhavan** (Government House), the **Secretariat** (1929) and **Council Chambers** (1920), and the **High Court** (1916).

West of Patna, 17 miles (29 km) along the road to Ara, lies **Munar** (Maner). Here, in a clearing in the woods stands **Choti Dargah** (1616), the tomb of Shah Daulat, built by Ibrahim Khan. Its fine proportions, delicate *jali* (stone lattice) work, and surface ornament make it eastern India's finest Mogul monument. ■

Ganga River

The dominant force of eastern India is the Ganga. Its hundreds of tributaries trickle down the Himalayan slopes, link up into rivers, and create the life-giving Gangetic Plain and Delta. On the map on pp. 286–87 you can see how the Ganga flows past Kanpur, near Lucknow in Uttar Pradesh, then continues to Allahabad, where it takes in the Yamuna River, which has already watered Delhi and Agra. On it flows through Varanasi and into Bihar state. Here, at the city of Patna, major tributaries swell its waters: the Ghaghara, the Son, and the Gandak. Soon the great river begins to split into hundreds of threads to become the vast delta whose blessings of nourishment and punishments of flooding are shared by West Bengal and Bangladesh.

The Ganga is sacred to Hindus. A Hindu's Ganga *yatra* (journey, pilgrimage) begins at the river's source, Gangotri, near Rishikesh, then descends to Haridwar, Allahabad, and Varanasi. At each stop the river's water is revered; just a few droplets, not a hard scrub, can purify. The Ganga's water is especially purifying since Hindus believe it to be the goddess Ganga flowing eternally from the summit of Mount Meru, the abode of the gods, down through Shiva's matted locks. To bathe in the waters is to cleanse oneself of the *karma* of previous and current lives and so be prepared for death and rebirth into a better life. Hindus from all over India attend the mass ritual bathings that take place during the Kumbh Mela festival held every three years at one of Haridwar, Allahabad, Nasik, and Ujjain in turn. Of these, Allahabad, also known as Prayag (confluence) because the Yamuna and Ganga meet there, is especially sacred so the Kumbh Mela held here is known as Maha

(Great) Kumbh Mela; the city also has an annual Magh Mela *(Jan.–Feb.)*.

At Chunar, upstream from Varanasi, the Ganga turns sharply north and then makes a great arc through the holy city. This, combined with the high west banks and the flat land on the east banks, creates an extraordinary, almost tangible bowl of light, especially at sunrise. Hindus have for centuries thought of Varanasi as Kashi (City of Divine Light), or as Kashika (The Shining One), referring to the light of Shiva.

Historically, the Gangetic Plain was the hearth of Indian culture, and settlements spread eastward from this core region more than three millennia ago. The Ganga was a highway for east–west trade across the subcontinent, and it irrigated and fed the soil to produce rich farmland. Thus, early cities such as Pataliputra (Patna) grew to be capitals of great empires. Later, the Moguls made Allahabad one of their capitals. The British pushed their influence up the Ganga from Calcutta to protect their vital trading route.

Today the rich alluvial plains formed by deposits from the Himalayan Mountains form one of the world's most densely populated regions. Deforestation of the Himalayan Mountains means additional silt is carried down river and helps cause flooding; more than a third of Bangladesh is flooded annually. Ironically, this rich silt is essential to the nourishment of the rice crops being intensively farmed throughout the Ganga basin. ■

Devotees wash away their sins by bathing in the Ganga at Haridwar (above and far right), while others (right) bathe at the confluence of the Ganga, Yamuna, and Saraswati Rivers.

During the Maha Kumbh Mela festival of 2001 (above), more than two million Hindus gathered at Allahabad to witness the moon's eclipse.

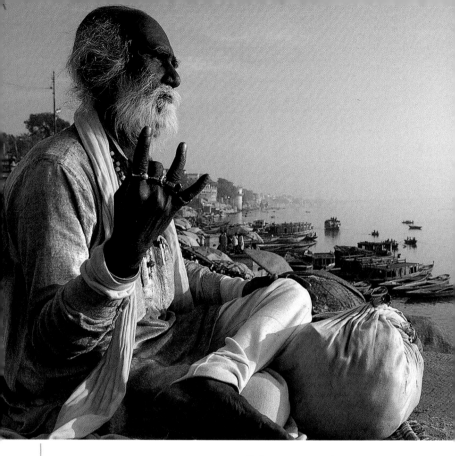

Varanasi

THE HINDUS' HOLIEST CITY, VARANASI IS PERPETUALLY overflowing with pilgrims. To visit it once in a lifetime is every Hindu's goal; to die here is to have the greatest chance of *moksha* (salvation, release). It is, therefore, not an easy city for a Western person to visit. But once you do, it may well become one of the most fascinating places of all your travels.

Varanasi
🅜 286 B4
**India Tourist
Office**
✉ 15-B The Mall
☎ (0542) 343744

**Uttar Pradesh
Tourist Office**
✉ Tourist Bungalow,
Parade Kothi
☎ (0542) 343413

Walk down to the river for a boat ride (see pp. 308–309), either early in the morning or in the late afternoon when the sun's rays are enjoyable rather than punishing. Give this city some time; zipping in for a dawn boat ride and then out again is rarely satisfying. Varanasi is about watching a nonstop pilgrim city going about its business.

A city as old as Babylon, Varanasi is, for Hindus, quite simply Kashi (City of Divine Light). Of the Hindus' Seven Sacred Cities, it is the most sacred. The others are Haridwar, Ujjain, Mathura, Ayodhya, Dwarka, and Kanchipuram. Each is dedicated to Shiva or Vishnu, except Kanchipuram, which is dedicated to both.

Thus, although it is a center for Hindu culture and has fine music and art, Varanasi's daily trade is pilgrims, India's most numerous and free-spending visitors. From the most humble upward, pilgrims often make their *yatras* (pilgrimages) by bus on an excursion, singing *bhajans* (religious songs) along the way. At their destination, the aim is to receive *darshan* (the meritorious glimpse of the god) and to bathe in the sacred waters. Emotional outpourings of religious fervor are common. Meanwhile, priests, gurus, peddlers, and con-men of all kinds abound, often all too ready to relieve pilgrims, unused to the city and emotionally vulnerable, of their hard-earned money.

Varanasi was already thriving 2,500 years ago when Buddha came to Sarnath to deliver his first sermon (see p. 300), making it sacred to Buddhists, too. Later, Muslims periodically plundered the city; the widowed Shah Jahan forbade temple-rebuilding, and pious Aurangzeb converted one temple into a mosque. Early British arrivals wrote of being intoxicated by Varanasi's exoticism and mystery. Winding your way through the maze of narrow, filthy alleys swarming with cows and pilgrims, you feel something of this as you peek into temples of all sizes, some simple, some flashy, like **Tulsi Manasmunda,** funded by the Birla family. Pilgrims flood in and out of them ceaselessly.

Despite the city's squalor—for no other word will fit—the holiness of Varanasi has been the inspiration for some of the most sublime creations in Hindu culture. Classical music was nurtured in the temples, and today the city produces many of India's top musicians and stages important music festivals. Sanskrit and classical Hindu studies thrive in back rooms, on rooftops, and at the Banaras Hindu University, known as B.H.U.

Top right: Some Hindu rituals demand a child mendicant.

Here, too, is the **Bharat Kala Bhavan,** where you can see some exquisite miniature paintings, whose religious message is heightened by the use of a rigid and highly symbolic iconography and intense colors.

Then there is the silk, originally woven to clothe the temple deities. Varanasi's weavers developed Baranasi brocade, a lusciously extravagant weave that includes threads of gold and silver. Much loved by the Moguls, it is still woven today. To see it, go to the daily **silk market,** found through an arch off Thatheri Bazar. In the late afternoon the weavers hurry through the maze of tiny alleys, more like corridors, with their wooden boxes full of completed saris. They sell them to plump dealers sitting in cubicles on white cotton, their tools of trade a moneybox, a calculator, and a telephone. Outside the silk market, find the **brass market** and continuous bazaars down to the water, where you can rent a boat and boatman for an evening cruise on the river, your boat lit by tiny oil lamps. ■

Varanasi Tourist Information
✉ 15-B The Mall
☎ (0471) 451498

Bharat Kala Bhavan
🕑 Closed Sun.
💲 $

A boat ride on the Ganga at Varanasi

Take this boat ride in the early morning to see the sunrise and morning Hindu rituals, or go in the evening for pretty views of the ghats. Drive a hard bargain for your boat, and do not be persuaded into a short, hurried trip.

If you can do it, get up at 4 a.m., put on warm clothes, and go down to **Dasaswamedh Ghat ❶** in the dark. Be on your boat as dawn creeps in, when you may hear the notes of the *shehna* reed instrument played by the musicians of the Shiva Temple to welcome the day. The dawn light is thin, liquid, and like no other light. It is easier to accept the various oil lamps and flowers pressed on you by aggressive children, and pay them off, than to spoil the mood by entering into a bargaining session.

First, go upstream (to the right) to **Asi Ghat ❷,** or as far as you can persuade your boatman to go. As the boat slides through the water, the city begins to wake, and pilgrims sleeping beneath the high walls of the maharajas' old riverside palaces rouse themselves.

By the time you turn around to go downstream, a pale sun rises, the light changes, and a steady stream of people flows down to the holy water. From the city's 80 or so *ghats*, each with its Shiva *lingum*, the faithful begin to bathe and do their *puja* (worship) to the new day. Each ghat has its own importance; ideally, a Hindu should worship at each one. Asi Ghat marks the confluence of the Asi and Ganga waters. Right next to it, **Tulsi Ghat ❸** commemorates the 17th-century poet Gosain Tulsi Das, who translated the *Ramayana* from Sanskrit into Hindi and later died here.

A little farther along, **Shivala (or Kali) Ghat ❹** is owned by the former royal family of Varanasi, whose fort across the river at Ramnagar is where the great Ram Lila festival is held annually. The ghat has a large Shiva lingum. Nearby **Hanuman Ghat ❺** attracts pilgrims who worship the monkey god, whereas **Dandi Ghat** is used by ascetics called Dandi Paths. **Harishchandra Ghat** is one of the city's two burning ghats; the other is Jalasai Ghat, which you see later.

Kedara Ghat ❻ has fine linga and a temple. **Mansarowar Ghat** is named after a lake in Tibet near the Gangotri, the Ganga's source. **Man Mandir Ghat ❼** is in front of the Maharaja of Jaipur's palace; beside it Jai Singh built one of his observatories (see pp. 131–32).

As the sun rises over Varanasi, boatloads of pilgrims and visitors share the sacred Ganga water with bathing worshipers.

📐 See area map pages 286–87
▶ Dasaswamedh Ghat
↔ 2–4 miles (3–6 km)
🕐 1–2 hours
▶ Dasaswamedh Ghat

NOT TO BE MISSED
- Dasaswamedh Ghat
- Asi Ghat
- Man Mandir Ghat
- Jalasai Ghat

(Ask your boatman to point them out)

Moving downstream you pass by **Dasaswamedh Ghat,** your starting point, where *brahmans* are by now setting themselves up for the day's business, sitting cross-legged beneath their shabby umbrellas. Continue to **Jalasai Ghat 8**, the famous burning ghat with a heap of lopsided temples (absolutely no photographs may be taken of this); the ghat is named after Vishnu when he is sleeping on the Cosmic Ocean. It adjoins **Manikarnika Ghat 9**, the most sacred of all ghats, for here Mahadeo (Shiva) dug the tank to find Parvati's

earring. As if to emphasize the Hindus' inequality in death, only the most privileged families are burned on the Charanpaduka slab marked with the imprint of Vishnu's feet.

With the sun warming your back, the boatman will row you back upstream to Dasaswamedh Ghat. ∎

Lucknow & Kanpur (Cawnpore)

THE CAPITAL OF INDIA'S MOST POPULOUS STATE, UTTAR
Pradesh, Lucknow is spacious and calm. The relative lack of visitors
and distance from industry make this an easy city to explore. Its key
sites are in two groups: the faded, romantic Muslim buildings of the
old city and the practical brick British buildings of the Residency, a
silent and poignant reminder of a complete breakdown in the two
countries' long relationship, a breakdown that also engulfed Kanpur,
an important British garrison town.

Lucknow

🅰 286 A5

India Tourist Office

✉ 10 Station Rd.

☎ 0522-246205

State Tourist Office

✉ 3 Newal Kishore Rd.

☎ 228349

Great Imambara

🕐 Closed during prayers

The city's Shia Muslim rulers, called
the Nawabs of Avadh (Oudh, in
Bihar), rose to power in the
vacuum of 18th-century Mogul
decline and made their final capital
Lucknow. The ten lazy, plump,
pleasure-loving, and debauched
rulers set the tone for a distinctly
self-indulgent yet highly sophisticated Muslim culture, especially under
Asaf-ud-Daula (*R.* 1775–1797) and
Saadat Ali Khan (*R.* 1798–1814).
Today, the fruits of the Nawabs'
extravagant patronage of buildings,
artists, craftsmen, musicians, and
Urdu poetry retain the atmosphere
suitable for a decaying, decadent,

and introverted court that ended in
tragedy: The British deposed the
last incompetent ruler, one of several actions that triggered the
Rebellion of 1857.

The best of the Nawabs' buildings is the **Great Imambara,** or
House of the Imam (1780s), one of
the world's largest vaulted halls,
entered through the Rumi
Darwaza. Designed by Kifayat-ullah
for Asa'f-ud-Daula as a famine
relief project, its purpose is to be
the focus of the Muharram festival.
This is when Shia Muslims have a
procession in memory of the martyrdom of Hussain and his two

sons. Inside, see the *tazias,* ornate paper reproductions of the Shia Imam's shrine at Karbala in southern Iraq. Upstairs, there are good views of other buildings worth visiting: the **Jami Masjid,** the **Small Imambara,** the **Tower** for watching the moon at Id, the **Clock Tower,** and various royal tombs and Muslim shrines.

Chowk, the old market area, is a maze of alleys perfumed with the spices of *paan* ingredients, a Lucknow specialty. On Chowpatia Street, near Akbari Gate, you can find the essentials of any Lucknow sophistication: gold leaf being beaten, *bidri* work (see p. 249), gold thread-makers, *chikankara* (white-on-white cotton embroidery), silk brocade, Koran bookstands, heavy *attar* (perfume), and delicious fresh breads, kebabs, and confections. To see taziamakers, go to Hazaratganj area.

The **Residency** complex (see pp. 312–13) is the surreal, frozen reminder of the 1857 Rebellion, which staged some of its bloodiest scenes at Lucknow and Kanpur. This is the site of the epic siege and relief in 1857. The rebellion broke out in Meerut on May 10, when 47 battalions of the Bengal army mutinied. The next day it reached Delhi (see p. 75) and quickly spread to Kanpur, where there was a massacre on June 27, then to Lucknow.

Here the British endured a double siege, then reaped a vile revenge. Events began on June 30, 1857, when *sepoys* (Indian soldiers) poured over the Gomti River to join citizens already angry that their Nawab had been deposed. The British garrison of about 3,000, under the command of Sir Henry Lawrence, quickly took refuge in the Residency. Fighting was both above ground and underneath it in tunnels and mines. Meanwhile, gangrene, scurvy, cholera, and general lack of hygiene took their toll on the British garrison. Gen. Sir Henry Havelock arrived with reinforcements after three months, retaking the fort on September 25 only to lose it immediately. On November 17 Sir Colin Campbell led the final relief. Just 979 of the original 3,000 had survived.

KANPUR

Another significant site of this intriguing period of history, for India and Britain, is **Kanpur,** a two-hour drive away. This, one of the most important British garrisons on the Ganga, was also besieged during the "mutiny." In the cantonment, Walter Granville's Lombardic-Gothic **All Souls Memorial Church** (1862–1875) has poignant tablets around the apse wall, and the adjoining **Memorial Garden** has equally eloquent angels and a screen that remember the British women and children massacred and put in Bibighar well in revenge for British atrocities. In the nearby scrub find General Sir Hugh Wheeler's entrenchment, where the siege took place. You can also visit nearby **Sati Chaura Ghat,** where British fleeing Fatehgarh down the Ganga were massacred in their boats—a bleak, chilling spot. ■

Small Imambara
🕐 Closed during prayers

The magnificent Great Imambara at Lucknow is dedicated to three imams—Ali, Hassan, and Hussein.

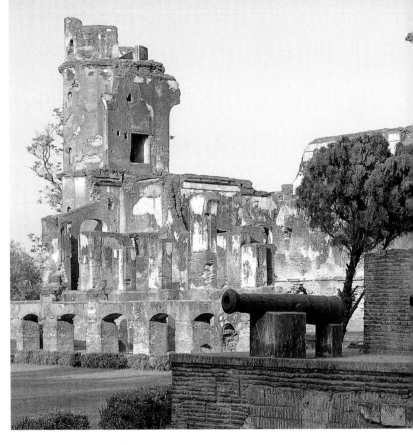

The Residency at Lucknow

THIS IMPORTANT SITE, WHICH MARKED A WATERSHED IN British and Indian history, has been cleaned up but left almost as it was at the end of the siege on November 17, 1857. Under the spreading banyan, neem, and bel fruit trees, you can visit the eerie remains of buildings where men, women, and children survived for five months, from the monsoon of July to the chilly days of November.

Lucknow Residency

💲 $. Free Fri.

Through the Baillie Guard gateway, you find the **Treasury** on the right, whose long central room was used as an arsenal in 1857. Next door, the grand and once sumptuous **Banqueting Hall** was the siege hospital. Dr. Fayrer's House, to the south, is a large, one-story building where women and children stayed; a tablet marks the spot where Sir Henry Lawrence died—there is a memorial cross to him on the lawn, and he is buried in the cemetery. **Begum Kothi** is where Mrs. Walters, a British woman who married the Nawab, once lived.

The elegant **Residency** building itself stands on the northeast side of the complex and was built by Nawab Saadat Ali Khan in 1800. The wives and children of high-ranking officers lived here in appalling and dank conditions in the basements. The second floor

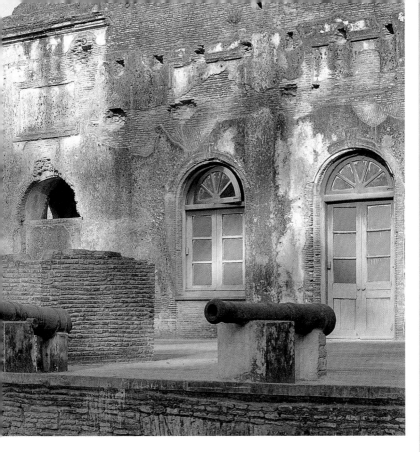

is now a little **museum** with a model of the whole residency complex in 1857, and some horrific prints. On the wall there is a poignant plaque to Susanna Palmer, killed by a cannonball on July 1, 1857. After this incident, the residents buried their snobbery and moved to Dr. Feyrer's House. In the **cemetery** find simple graves of Lawrence and of Brig.-Gen. J. S. Neill, whose frightful revenge on the Kanpur mutineers was not repeated at Lucknow; he was killed here on September 25, 1857. As for the hero Havelock, he died of dysentery a week after Campbell arrived. ■

The poignant remains of the Residency are well-maintained, perhaps to remind Indians of their hard-won freedom, whose beginnings here are called by some "The First War of Independence" rather than the "Mutiny" or the "Rebellion."

More places to visit in Eastern India

BARAKAR, GHURISA, & KABILASPUR

This pleasant rural trip northwest from Kolkata is for visiting more temples. Stop at Barakar for a ninth-century Orissan-style temple with miniature figures adorning its curved tower; at Ghurisa for a Bengali hut-style temple (1633) with terra-cotta panels, with some figures in European dress; and at Kabilaspur for a beautiful temple that lacks all decoration.

BARAKPUR

Once the summer residence of the British governors-general, this model cantonment on the east banks of the Hooghly, opposite Serampore (see p. 316), retains its layout and spaciousness, and it is well maintained by the army. Drive around to the many original houses and bungalows, several of them part of the Ramkrishna Vivekananda Mission. Access is restricted to some parts, but try to see **Government House** (1813), the **Temple of Fame, Lady Canning's Grave,** and **Semaphore Tower.**
 287 D3 ✉ 15 miles (24 km) north of Kolkata

BISHNUPUR

Come to the capital of the cultured Malla rulers of Bengal, now a rural backwater, to see their group of exquisite Bengali hut-style 17th- to 18th-century temples faced with beautiful terra-cotta story plaques, usually showing scenes from the *Ramayana*. See especially the **Shyam Rai Temple** (1643), **Keshta Raya Temple** (1655), and **Madana Mohana Temple** (1694).
▲ 287 D3 ✉ 93 miles (150 km) northwest of Kolkata

BUXAR

This Hindu pilgrimage site on the Ganga was the scene of Sir Hector Munro's decisive victory on October 23, 1764, when he used clever tactics to reverse near defeat against the forces of Shah Alam, Shuja-ud-Daula, and Mir Qasim, taking their entire camp and 160 guns. This built on Clive's victory at Plassey in 1757 (see below) and confirmed Britain's supremacy in Bengal. On the way here from Patna, pause at Ara, where 12 British and 50 Sikhs held the Little House of Ara from July 27 to August 3, 1857, against more than 2,000 *sepoys* and rebels.
▲ 286 B4 ✉ 73 miles (117 km) west of Patna

GAUR & AROUND

A wonderful trip from Kolkata takes you through rural Bengal to seek out the extensive, fine, and rarely visited Muslim capital of the Afghan rulers of Bengal during the 15th and 16th centuries. Later sacked by Sher Shah Sur (1537), Gaur became part of Akbar's Mogul empire in 1576. Find substantial ruins dotted among villages and farms covering some 20 square miles (52 sq km), there is a central group within huge embankments that includes a fort, mosques, tombs, a victory tower, and gateways. From here the intrepid can continue to **Malda** (Islamic buildings), **Pandua** (the Afghan capital before Gaur),

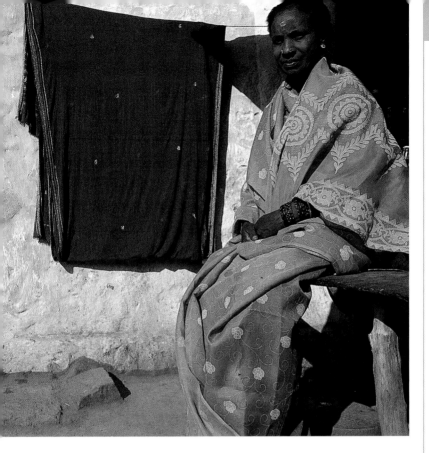

Bangarh (archaeological site of an ancient city), **Rajmahal** (good Mogul city remains 4 miles/6 km west of the modern city), and **Sultangunj** (eighth-century carvings on granite rocks at Jahangira), ending at Patna. ⚑ 287 D4 **Gaur** ✉ 200 miles (320 km) north of Kolkata

GOPALPUR-ON-SEA & AROUND
A delightful beach, small village, and a few cottages make this the best beachside escape from Kolkata. You can reach it by train to Brahmapur, where you may see silk-weavers around the temple. North of here, **Chilka Lake** is a large lagoon rich in migratory birds from December to February.
⚑ 287 C1

MURSHIDABAD & AROUND
The drive from Kolkata to Murshidabad passes Plassey and Brahmapur. At the former, little remains to mark Clive's victory beside the

Two women sit outside their simple coastal home at Gopalpur-on-sea.

Bhagirathi River on June 23, 1757, against the Nawab Suraj-ud-Daula of Murshidabad. At the latter, the early British cantonment is interesting, with its grid-pattern streets interspersed with ditches and water tanks for defense. Murshidabad became the capital of Bengal in 1704 when Murshid Quli Khan moved the capital here from Dacca and Rajmahal. After Plassey, the law (1772) and then the bureaucrats (1790) were forcibly moved to Kolkata. Reminders of past splendor to see in the town include: the **Palace of the Nawab, Imambara, Medina, mosques,** and **tombs.** North again, **Baranagar's** 18th-century hutlike temples contain fabulous terra-cotta story plaques. From here you can link in to the Gaur trip (see p. 314).
⚑ 287 D4 **Murshidabad** ✉ 122 miles (196 km) north of Kolkata

SERAMPORE & NORTH OF KOLKATA

Leave very early to avoid city traffic on this day trip from Kolkata, up the west bank of the Hooghly to visit sites evocative of intrepid European merchants and fine Bengali temples. First stop is Serampore, a Danish settlement (1755) where an English Baptist missionary set up Kolkata's first printing press (1799); see **Serampore College** (1821), **India Jute Mill,** and **St. Olave's Church** (1821). Continue to **Belur Math Temple** (1938), built by Swami Vivekananda, a disciple of Ramakrishna; a mile (1.6 km) or so beyond, Kolkata's popular **Dakshineshwar Temple** (1855) stands across the Bally Bridge. At **Chandannagar,** crumbling yet grand buildings testify to a successful French factory (1688). Beyond Hooghly and Bandel, both early European settlements, find first **Bansberia's** lovely terra-cotta-ornamented Bengali temples, then many more at **Kalna,** maintained by the former royal Burdwan family.

A gaily painted modern temple decoration

⬛ 287 D3   **Serampore**   ✉ 13 miles (21 km) north of Kolkata

SHANTI NIKETAN & AROUND

This is a peaceful escape from the steamy city. Founded by Bengal's great writer and poet Rabindranath Tagore in 1921, as a settlement and center of study to promote Bengali culture, Shanti Niketan was the Bengali Renais-sance's most ambitious and successful project. Tagore designed the **Uttaraya** complex of buildings, which includes a **museum** *(Closed Wed.),* **gallery** *(Closed Wed.),* and departments for art, music, and drama.

⬛ 287 D3   **Shanti Niketan**   ✉ 84 miles (135 km) north of Kolkata

SIMHANATHA & RANIPUR JHARIAL

This is an adventurous trip inland from Bhubaneshwar. Simhanatha's well-preserved temple (eighth century) stands on an island in the Mahanadi River. Continue into the hills to **Ranipur Jharial,** two villages whose rocky outcrop has more than 50 little temples.

⬛ 286 B2   **Ranipur Jharial**   ✉ 180 miles (290 km) west of Bhubaneshwar

SIMILIPAL NATIONAL PARK

The inhospitable, thickly wooded slopes of the Eastern Ghats have preserved this park, founded in 1957, from any form of taming—even today, the effort of reaching this very beautiful landscape, and the simplicity of accommodations, mean it has few visitors. However, the mixture of deciduous forest, streams, and open savannah provide the habitat for a varied wildlife, from leopards and tigers to porcupines, elephants, and mugger crocodiles, plus more than 230 species of birds. Permits and reservations with exact dates are essential; otherwise, join an organized tour.

⬛ 287 D2   ✉ Field Director Project Tiger, Baripada 757002, Mayurbhunj District, Orissa ☎ (06792) 52593

THE SUNDERBANS

Where the great Gangetic Delta meets the Bay of Bengal, water and land intermingle. The Hooghly River creates an estuarine delta of more than 965 square miles (2,500 sq km). Here is the Sunderbans Tiger Reserve, a group of mangrove-covered islands whose Royal Bengal tigers have adapted to the landscape and both swim and eat fish. To visit, stay at Sajnekhali Tourist Lodge 75 miles (120 km) south of Kolkata; explore the area by boat and with a Project Tiger guide. Permits available from the West Bengal Tourist Office in Kolkata; best visited November to March.

⬛ 287 D3 ∎

The great Himalayan range that forms India's dramatic northern border supplies hikers, painters, botanists, and those in search of relief from the plains' heat with lush, cool valleys; sparkling, clear rivers; forested hillsides; and spectacular mountain views.

The Himalaya

A woman from the western Himalaya Ladakh Valley

Kaylong Khardong village sits in the dramatic, bare landscape of the Lahaul district.

The Himalaya

THE HIMALAYA, THE WORLD'S HIGHEST MOUNTAINS, ARE LESS THAN 130 million years old and still growing. When the ancient Indian Plate of the peninsula, some 3,000 million years old, moved under the Asian Plate the dramatic crumpling and fissuring began, and the Himalaya began to rise.

Looking at the map on the inside front cover, you can see what a formidable barrier the Himalaya are, effectively isolating the subcontinent from the rest of Asia. Varying in width from 93 miles (150 km) to 210 miles (400 km), and with 95 peaks reaching an elevation of more than 24,000 feet (7,500 m), they stretch 1,553 miles (2,500 km) from Pakistan's Pamirs to Assam's Brahmaputra River. Two large chunks of these mountain ranges are in India.

The mountains are made up of several ranges, where some of India's great rivers rise. In the west, the young Indus flows between the Karakoram Range in Pakistan and the Zaskar Range. Moving east, you find many beautiful lakes in the frontier Vale of Kashmir, the region's most famous valley, which suffers from Indo-Pakistan political tensions. Eastward, Himachal Pradesh's hills belong to the Siwalik Range—massively folded and faulted mountains with longitudinal valleys known in the western part as "duns." Lowland

0   100 kilometers
0   50 miles

Area of map detail

Delhi

orchards and maize fields rise through sub-tropical forests to steep, pine mountains and inhospitable ice fields, from which the Sutlej River hurtles down deep, craggy gorges. Eastward again into Uttar Pradesh, the young Yamuna River takes one path down through mighty gorges, while the Ganga River takes another. From Gangotri Glacier it foams and crashes down to Haridwar, where it becomes more sedate for the long journey through the Sarawik Hills, here called the Garhwal.

East of Nepal the mountains of the central Himalayan range receive the full deluge of the annual monsoon rains, and the postmonsoon waters of the Brahmaputra River thunder through Assam. This isolated region has wild rhododendrons and orchids, Kaziranga and Manas wildlife sanctuaries, tea plantations, and individual cultures and peoples.

The Moguls loved Kashmir; later, the British discovered the vast, cool, and expansive beauty of all the Himalayan mountain scenery from lush lowlands to stunning high mountain passes. Today, the best way to experience it is to hike. This is nature in its most raw and awesome state, with the occasional Buddhist monastery, Hindu shrine, and British hill station. Choose an area that appeals; then make reservations for the right trek for you: anything from gentle day walks to a challenging ten-day journey sleeping in tents (see pp. 332–34 for trekking ideas). The more adventurous you are, and the less fussy about comfortable accommodations, the more rewarding your visit will be. ∎

The Suru Valley is a welcome ribbon of green in the high, parched region of Ladakh.

Western Himalaya

AS A CONTRAST TO THE HEADY COCKTAIL OF MONUMENTS, history, heat, and city crowds, a hike in the foothills of the Himalaya invigorates you. The cool air, mountain scenery, culture, and lifestyle offer relaxation after touring the plains, and the lower slopes in the Uttar Pradesh or Himachal Pradesh easily accessible from Delhi. The more ambitious can press on north to Ladakh.

Uttar Pradesh Garhwal area

Map p. 319
Regional Tourist Office

G.M.V.N., Hotel Drona, 45 Gandhi Rd. See also Mussoorie (p. 124), Haridwar (pp. 124– 25), Rishikesh (p. 125). For the Kumaun area: Nainital (p. 125) is the base.

UTTAR PRADESH

An easy drive or train ride from Delhi, the Garhwal and Kumaun Hills in the north of Uttar Pradesh state border Nepal and Tibet and are known as the Uttaranchal, or Uttarkhand. From the fertile plains, or *terai*, they rise through summer mountain meadows called *bugyals* to a series of snowpeaked mountains, including Nanda Devi (25,643 feet/7,816 m), the highest mountain completely in India. These hills have scenic variety as well as charming hotels (see p. 371); the sacred Hindu pilgrimage center of Haridwar, Rishikesh, made famous by the Beatles; the protected forests of Corbett National Park; and the gentle, still slightly Victorian British hill stations of Mussoorie and Nainital (see pp. 124–25 for all of these).

The history of the area is complex, since each of the deep

river valleys has its own distinct culture, and the Garhwal and Kumaun regions have their own languages. Furthermore, although Hinduism dominates, a shrine may reveal elements of animism and Buddhism; it was through the Himalayan mountains that Buddhism was carried to China. Indeed, so distinct is Uttarkhand that there is a strong local political movement fighting for autonomy from Uttar Pradesh.

The sources of the Yamuna and Ganga Rivers give the Garhwal special status and popularity. Here are the four *yatra* (pilgrimage) temples known as the Char Dham: **Badrinath, Kedarnath, Gangotri,** and **Yamnotri.** The hundreds of thousands of pilgrims who come here via Rishikesh from May to November each year have influenced the indigenous culture of this area. To experience purer Garhwal beauty, hike through the **Harki Dun valley** or the **Tehri Garhwal.** The less popular **Kumaun Hills,** however, retain much of their original charm. The temples receive fewer pilgrims, the landscape fewer trekkers, and hill towns such as Almora, with its cobbled alleys and wood and stone houses, fewer visitors.

For trekking ideas, see pp. 332–34. Rewarding trips to consider are the day-long walk to **Gangotri Glacier,** the source of the Ganga, or the varied five-day trek to **Pindari Glacier.**

HIMACHAL PRADESH

The gateway to this small state of hills and mountains, sandwiched to the east and west by Tibet and Pakistan, is **Shimla** (see p. 124), queen of all India's hill stations. North of here the mountains and gorges are the boundaries for remote and distinct districts, boundaries crossed by the Gaddi and Gujjar,

semi-nomadic shepherds. The area has seen Rajputs ruling Kangra, and Tibetans ruling Lahaul and Spiti; and since the 18th century control has passed from the Sikhs of the Punjab to the Gurkas of Nepal and finally to the British until independence.

After the lush valleys of the southern Sirmaur area, including delightful **Nalagar,** the landscape north of Shimla becomes more dramatic. Moving northeast past Narkanda you can follow the Sutlej River to find the wooden temple of **Sarahan** and, with a special Inner Line Permit, the Kinnaur district's isolated and austere beauty up on the Tibetan Plateau. Ambitious treks lead through to Spiti and the Kullu Valley; simpler walks are along the Sutlej Valley.

Just north of Shimla, passengers can enjoy spectacular mountain views.

Himachal Pradesh Kinnaur area

Map p. 319

Shimla Tourist Office

The Mall

0177-255 279

Dhauladhar Range

Map p. 319

Dharamsala Tourist Office

Main bazaar, lower town, near bus stand

North of Shimla, the road divides at Mandi. Keeping to the north, **Manali** is the increasingly developed base for exploring verdant Kullu Valley's terraces, forests, and diminishing apple orchards, and for white-water rafting at Vashisht. But farther north, across the treacherous Rohtang Pass (13,051 feet/3,978 m), fewer people visit the bare mountains and snowfields of the great Himalayan Range that encase Lahaul and Spiti Valleys. The 300-mile-long (500 km) **Manali–Leh Highway,** one of the world's great drives, is open June through October. The mountain and valley views are incredible as it switchbacks through Keylong, Sarchu Serai, and the passes of Langlacha La (16,597 feet/5,059 m) and Tanglang La (17,480 feet/5,328 m).

Northwest of Mandi, the well-trodden trail leads through the heavily populated Kangra Valley toward the Dhauladhar mountains, where the Dalai Lama and his Tibetan exiles live at **Dharamsala.** From here, gentle treks lead through the tea-growing area of Palampur; more adventurous ones cross the mountains into the Chamba Valley toward the Pir Panjal Range.

LADAKH

High in the Zaskar and Ladakh mountain ranges and stretching up to the Karakoram, **Ladakh** (appropriately meaning "land of

Ecology

Mountain farmers have to terrace their fields. Seen from a distance in the Garhwal area of Uttar Pradesh, the terraces look like rippling water.

India, so rich in resources, faces an ecology crisis. Rampant population growth is one reason, though the average Indian consumes a tiny fraction of resources compared to the average Westerner; local politics, modernization, and unplanned development are others. Ancient forests and their ecosystems are being destroyed by uncontrolled lumber industries, mining, cultivation, and dams. An estimated 5,800 square miles (15,000 sq km) are lost each year. As a result, tribal groups are losing their means of survival, as are species of flora and fauna. As industry increases, so land is overfarmed for its raw materials—cotton, paper, rubber, jute, tobacco, and sugar—at the expense of food. The huge dam projects, such as the Tungabhadra and Narmada, have displaced communities totaling more than 20 million people. They have also affected fish-breeding, wildlife, and animal migration; increased the dangers of waterborne diseases; and often silted up. Disadvantages, often not foreseen, have outstripped advantages.

Meanwhile, despite the green revolution making India self-sufficient in food, Western farming methods, fertilizers, and high-yield strains of crops have damaged the soil, demanded extra irrigation, and affected the environment and traditional by-products.

But there is hope: An increasingly energetic ecology movement is making its voice heard, and successful local projects may soon have state and national backing. ■

high mountain passes") is a high-elevation desert crossed by razor-sharp peaks. Here, where the land is frozen for eight months a year and scorched for four, rainfall is the same as in the Sahara. Yaks, goats, and sheep are essential for wool, milk, and butter, and for bartering in exchange for grain and fuel. Open to general visitors since 1974, the current unrest makes this the only area of Jammu and Kashmir state that it is advisable to visit.

Such an isolated and starkly beautiful spot is one of the large refuges of Mahayana Buddhism (see p. 58), Ladakh's principal religion, which historically has looked to Tibet for its inspiration; the Dalai Lama is head of its most popular sect, the Gelug-pa ("yellow hat"). As you travel through the area, the thin mountain light sparkles on brightly colored prayer wheels, rooftop flags, and whitewashed *chortens* (stupas). Furthermore, Ladakh's medieval monasteries, perched on craggy cliffs and known locally as *gompas,* are still centers of learning and worship. These house remarkable artifacts—brass Buddhas, walls painted with fierce divinities, *thangkas* (scroll paintings), and unusual musical instruments.

If you arrive by taking the Manali–Leh Highway (see p. 322), you go through the most concentrated area of these monasteries as you progress up the Indus Valley from Upshi to Leh, Ladakh's capital and once a staging post on the Silk Road. Having benefited from past trade and religious patronage, Leh is now buffeted by summer visitors. While acclimatizing to the elevation, you can visit the old palace, **Namgyal Tsemo gompa,** and the old quarter. One-day trips down the valley can take in pretty villages, **Shey**'s derelict palace, and the stunning **Tikse gompa,** returning via **Hemis gompa** and **Stok palace. Spitok** and **Phyang** gompas lie to the north, as do the 11th-century murals of **Alchi,** best seen during the breathtaking drive to **Kargil,** beyond which lies the beautiful Suru Valley and stunning but remote **Zaskar,** the goal for serious trekkers. The intrepid can visit the stark Nubra Valley, opened to visitors in 1994. ■

The view from Ladakh's best-known *gompa*, at Tikse near Leh, has changed little since the gompa was built in the 15th century.

VISITOR TIPS

Some of the hill areas are politically volatile, so it is wise to follow your own government's advice; currently, visits to Kashmir are discouraged, except to Ladakh. The Indian government requires foreign visitors to obtain special permits for some northeastern states. It is best to do your research, make your reservations, and obtain your permits before you arrive in India.

Fabrics of India

Until you first visit India, your experience of Indian fabrics may well be limited to seeing pictures of old woolen Kashmir shawls with richly patterned borders. They are glorious. The best were woven in Kashmir from the 15th to the mid-19th centuries, using fleece imported from Central Asia. Sophisticated Moguls and other rulers prized them for their intricate flower designs and precision craftsmanship: Each shawl required a dozen specialists, from pattern-drawers to dyers, and took many months to make. Introduced into European high fashion in the 1770s, the Kashmir shawl became an essential chic fashion accessory, especially in France. A century later, however, the Jacquard looms of Lyons and Paisley made the shawls so inexpensively that they lost their appeal.

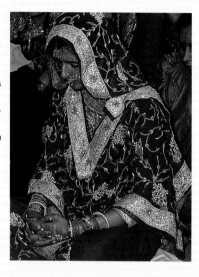

Most Hindu women, however modern, choose to marry in traditional clothes.

Today's Western fashion for so-called pashmina shawls (from the Persian word *pashm*, meaning wool) is a pale imitation of past glories and India's present weaving skills. That the variety and quality of India's weaving is unequaled, is quickly evident if you simply keep your eyes open as you travel around India.

The incredible colors, patterns, and weaves both in the markets and being worn by the people are infinite. These remarkable fabrics may be woven in many kinds of cotton, silk, and wool. For instance, cotton may be fine muslin, handspun and handwoven *khadi* made famous by Mahatma Gandhi, or mill-spun but handwoven "handloom" cotton. Indians tend to drape rather than cut and tailor their fabrics, wearing them as shawls, saris, or *lunghis* (or *dhotis*, a cloth worn by a man). Depending where you travel, you may also see local people in finely woven or intricately embroidered jackets, skirts, tight shirts, hats, and even shoes.

Weaving has been serious business in India since at least the period of the Indus Valley Civilization, from which spindles and pieces of cotton cloth wrapped around a silver vase survive. In the 1630s, the British established their first major foothold in India at Madras expressly to buy cotton from the nearby weavers. Today, textiles are a major part of the economy. India has about three million cotton handloom weavers. Sericulture (silk farming) and silk-weaving, first introduced by Buddhist monks from China, is a government-controlled industry in Karnataka state. Master weavers are revered and receive national awards, and fine silks dress temple deities. A bride-to-be is the focus of a serious family outing to choose her wedding saris; it may be a shopping trip to Varanasi to buy a luxurious Barnasi brocade encrusted with silver and gold threads, or a more modest outing to Jaipur's cotton market.

The best way to buy local weaves is to visit the village and town markets. If you are in a weaving area, maybe traveling through the villages of Tamil Nadu, weavers will welcome you into their homes, where the great wooden looms dominate the living space.

To see the range and quality of Indian fabrics, visit the National Crafts Museum in Delhi (see p. 72), the Calico Museum in Ahmedabad (see p. 148), and the Delhi street lined with fixed-price, high quality stores representing each Indian state, Baba Kharak Singh Marg at Connaught Place. ∎

Above: Traditional dress continues to be popular among Indian women, including those working in offices in the modern financial center of Mumbai.

Traditionally hot-toned, hand-dyed silk saris are put out to dry in Jodhpur, Rajasthan (above). These colors stand out against the ancient stones of Chittaugarh Fort (right).

Eastern Himalaya

THIS WHOLE HIMALAYA REGION SHARES MOUNTAINS, wildlife, and flora, but the presence of Bangladesh divides it in two—only Indian citizens may take the train from West Bengal to Assam. Getting to the Eastern Himalaya is easiest by plane from Kolkata (see pp. 288–93) or Delhi (see pp. 62–93). The necessary acquiring of permits and the long journey are richly rewarded.

**West Bengal
& Sikkim
Siliguri Tourist
Information**
✉ Hill Cart Rd., Siliguri

Darjiling
🅰 326 A3
**Darjiling Tourist
Information**
✉ Above Indian
Airlines office,
Chowrasta, Darjiling

Gangtok
🅰 326 A4

**Sikkim Tourist
Information**
✉ SNT Colony, Siliguri
✉ M.G. Rd., Gangtok

**Northeastern
states
India Tourist
Office**
✉ B.K. Kakati Rd.,
Ulubari, Guwahati
(provides information
on the whole
northeastern area)

**Assam Tourist
Information**
✉ Tourist Lodge,
Station Rd.,
Guwahati
✉ Tourist Lodge, M.G.
Road, Jorhat

WEST BENGAL & SIKKIM

The 56-mile (90 km) trip from Siliguri up to Darjiling is spectacular. You can drive or make the nine-hour journey by the Darjiling Himalayan Railway, known as the Toy Train because of its resemblance to a toy train set, built in 1879–1881 and still pulled by steam engines. Less patient people take a short run from Darjiling to Ghoom and back.

Up in the mountains, there are two hill stations to visit. **Darjiling** (7,218 feet/2,200 m) makes up for its faded British style with its spectacular mountain views toward Kanchenjunga, the world's third highest mountain. Tiger Hill, an unparalleled viewpoint from which to watch the sunrise, the Ghoom monasteries, and a tea garden are essential visits. In town, get a taste of Victorian Darjiling by walking along Chowrasta, then down the Mall to see The Planters' Club, founded in 1868. At the other end of town, the Botanical Gardens' paths lead down to dilapidated but atmospheric greenhouses filled with ferns and orchids. From here, treks leave to see Everest.

Smaller **Kalimpong** (4,101 feet/1,250 m) is ideal for investigating mountain flora, especially orchids; you can visit commercial orchid nurseries. Nearby Rachela Pass (10,341 feet/3,152 m) leads into **Sikkim,** India's smallest state,

which combines deep valleys and soaring mountains. From the capital, **Gangtok** (5,164 feet/1,574 m), trekkers through the Teesta and Rangit Valleys enjoy orchids, rhododendrons, magnolia blossoms, and other flora. Sikkim has almost 70 Buddhist monasteries, many with fine murals and images; try to see Phodang, Rumtek, Tashiding, and Pemayangtse.

NORTHEASTERN STATES

This region was all Assam until the 1960s, when separatist movements led to the creation of six new states Arunachal Pradesh, Nagaland, Manipur, Mixoram, Tripura, and Meghalaya. These states surround the now reduced but fertile valley of Assam and rely heavily on its road, rail, and air transportation routes.

Area of map detail

Delhi

CHINA

5▷

ARUNACHAL PRADESH

Anini

5108m

Along
Pasighat
Tezu

37

52

Lohit

NAMDAPHA
NATIONAL
PARK

Daporijo

Selek
Tinsukia

38

7089m
Kangto

Ziro

52

Dibrugarh

Tawang
Bomdila

Seppa
Lakhimpur

37

Khonsa

Itanagar

52A

Sibsagar

N

KAZIRANGA
NATIONAL
PARK

Jorhat
Mon

Tezpur

Golaghat

Mokokchung

MANAS
ATIONAL PARK
Mangaldai

52

37

Brahmaputra

Wokha
Tuensang

31

NAGAON

39

Zunheboto

Barpeta

ASSAM

NAGALAND

alpara

Dispur

Diphu

36

3826m

GUWAHATI

Dispur

Dimapur
Kohima

37

40

William
Nagar

Shillong

Jowai

Karong

39

MEGHALAYA

44

Ukhrul

Khasi   Hills

Haflong

Tamenglong

Cherrapunji

40

53

Imphal

Thoubal

Karimganj
Silchar

Bishnupur

△
E

△
F

MANIPUR

39

2▷

Dharmanagar

Churachandpur
Chandel

0   100 kilometers
0   50 miles

TRIPURA

Aizawl

44

Agartala

MIZORAM

Udaipur

Mizo
Hills

BANGLADESH

54

Lunglei

II▷

Lawngtlai

△
C

△
D

Children of the Apatani tribe from central
Arunachal Pradesh

MYANMAR
(BURMA)

Dihang

Dihang

Sprawling Gangtok, capital of Sikkim, straddles a hill that was a major India–Tibet trade route.

Assam Tourist Information
✉ Station Rd., Guwahati
☎ 0361-547102

Arunachal Pradesh Tourist Information
✉ Naharlagun, Itanagar

Nagaland Tourist Information
✉ Near Japfu Ashok Hotel, Kohima

Guwahati, Assam's capital until the new one is built at Dispur, sits on the great 1,800-mile-long (2,900 km) Brahmaputra River, which sweeps through the state. Assam is mostly peopled by Hindu Bengalis, mingled with the Ahoms and Bodos originally from Thailand and Tibet. Some 750 tea estates produce half of India's tea (see pp. 330–31), their clipped bushes giving way to rice fields and then the forested slopes of the mountains.

Guwahati's Kali temples and tea auctions are interesting. Out of town, the spectacular national parks of **Kaziranga** and less developed **Manas** both World Heritage sites, deserve every effort to reach them. Kaziranga, home to 1200 rhino, is 172 miles (215 km) from Guwahati; the park offices are in Kohara. Manas is a Project Tiger reserve, contact Assam Tourist Information for details.

The name Arunachal Pradesh means "land of the dawn-lit mountains," aptly romantic for this unspoiled wilderness of forested mountains, rushing rivers, and few roads. Out of reach of developers, this is a tantalizing glimpse of how the Himalaya was when Europeans first explored it, not so long ago. From **Itanagar,** the capital, you can take treks through magical scenery rich in flora and fauna.

Nagaland, only recently fully charted, is a state of densely forested mountains inhabited by the fiercely independent Nagas. The British built the capital, Kohima, but for something more ethnic, visit nearby **Bara Basti.**

The mainly Hindu Meitheis live in **Manipur** state. Their distinct culture includes classical dance, martial arts, and, in September, the colorful Heikru Hitongba Boat race—all found in the capital, **Imphal** (2,575 feet/785 m).

Mizoram state is home to the peaceful, egalitarian, and predominantly Christian Mizo people who live on forested and bamboo-covered hills sprinkled with churches and farms. Beautiful handicrafts can be found in and around **Aizawl,** the capital.

A diversity of people, including Bengalis, lives in **Tripura** state, whose Manikya rulers traced their ancestry to Rajput *kshatriyas* (see p. 29). See the capital **Agartala's** Ujjayanta Palace (1901), **Udaipur's** Tripura Sundari Temple, associated with female power, and **Neermahal** water palace.

In **Meghalaya,** orchid forests benefit from the monsoon that makes this one of the world's wettest places. The lakeside capital, **Shillong** (16,102 feet/4,908 m), retains some of the character of its Scots tea-planter founders. ■

Cricket is unavoidable in India: Here, young Buddhist students near Darjiling take a break from their monastic studies.

Manipur Tourist Information
✉ Hotel Imphal, Imphal

Mizoram Tourist Information
✉ Chandmari, Aizawl

Tripura Tourist Information
✉ Ujjayanta Palace, Agartala

Meghalaya Tourist Information
✉ Jail Rd., Shillong

Kargyudpa sect monks at Rumtek dress up to parade and dance during the Lohsar (New Year) celebrations.

Tea

When you drink a cup of tea, ponder for a moment on the precision skills required to produce the apparently simple dried tea leaf. It was the British who introduced tea production into northeastern India in the 19th century, using tea seed imported from China. In 1841 Dr. Campbell raised his first tea bushes at his home in Darjiling. Soon the government set up tea nurseries, whose bushes were planted in India's first commercial tea gardens in 1852. By the 1870s there were 113 tea gardens, and tea had joined other cash crops such as cotton, sugar, jute, and coffee, which the British were producing in India for international trading.

While Darjiling planters continued to grow Chinese tea, considered by tea connoisseurs to be the champagne of teas, British adventurers clearing plots of thickly forested land to lay out gardens in Assam discovered a more robust local bush. Land was parceled out on the almost uncharted maps in Kolkata, and many of the men with dreams died before their boats reached Guwahati.

Those who survived faced a tough and isolated life, whose highlight was the weekly gathering at the distant planters' clubs. It changed little until the 20th century when the telephone and television arrived. Still known as tea planters, the gardens' managers work a day that begins before sunrise and ends late. They must oversee their workforce, often composed of whole villages transplanted from Bihar in central India. They build temples and schools for them, and provide child care and medical care. To the workers, the manager is *ma-bapu* (mother-father), the person to whom they bring disputes; who sits in judgment, punishes, and even presides over marriages. Meanwhile, the manager also oversees the job of producing the tea, from trimming the bushes to deciding when to pluck the precious shoots, from keeping rogue elephants from trampling through the gardens to keeping standards high enough to satisfy the frequent visits of the company tea taster.

During the season, women pluck the leaves in the morning, delivering their full baskets to the on-site factory; they do a second picking in the afternoon. At the factory the fresh leaves immediately undergo a succession of carefully monitored processes: They are withered, rolled to bruise them and bring the juices to the surface, and then left to ferment to develop the flavor. They are then dried and sifted into ever more precise grades.

The bigger the leaf, the better the flavor—so the whole and unbroken leaves of Darjiling's Golden Flowery Orange Pekoe is the top grade, and Dust, literally the tea dust, is the cheapest. The tea is sent to auctions in great wooden chests, then on to the blenders. Almost every tea needs to be blended to produce the right balance of color, flavor, strength, and perfume, and each country has its own preferred blend.

Since independence, ownership of tea gardens has moved into Indian hands, although there is still a strong British interest. Assam's 750 tea gardens, many owned by big conglomerates such as Tata, produce more than 55 percent of India's tea needs and about 16 percent of the world's. Overall, tea production in India has doubled since 1950, despite political upheavals. ■

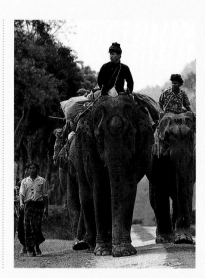

The manager of the tea garden (right) is up before dawn to inspect the bushes and decide which should be picked that day. For faster picking, some workers hang their baskets high up their backs and toss the tender leaves over their shoulders, into the baskets (below).

Trekking

A WIDE VARIETY OF TREKS IS POSSIBLE—HERE ARE JUST A few. They range from a few days to two weeks, from gentle walks and drives to challenging hikes that demand considerable physical fitness. See pp. 377–78 for more information.

WESTERN HIMALAYA

The Harki Dun Valley trek is an easy, four-day trek from **Mussoorie** through the beautiful and interesting **Harki Dun** (Valley of the Gods), a sparsely populated area of northwest Garhwal; the local people have their own customs and religious traditions, they live in alpine houses with carved wooden doors. You will stay in bungalows, except for the last night. On the first day, drive or take a bus via Netwar to Purola; the next day,

continue by road to Sankri and trek to Taluka (6,233 feet/1,900 m). On day three, trek beside the Tons River to Osla (7,411 feet/2,259 m). On day four, continue up to Harki Dun (11,679 feet/3,560 m), an excellent base for several days of trekking. From here, either return down or, if physically fit and prepared, continue across the challenging Yamnotri Pass.

The **Pindari Glacier** makes an easy and varied five-day trek from **Bageshwar** into the heart of the forested Kumaun region; there are simple bungalows along the way. From the pilgrimage town of Bageshwar, drive or take the bus to Bharari and hike through the Sarayu Valley to Song (or bus/drive all the way); from here, walk to Loharkhet. Day two is a hard trek over the Dhakuri Pass (9,301 feet/2,835 m), with its spectacular views, and down to Dhakuri. Days three and four are gentler hikes along the Pindar Valley to Khati, and then beside the Pindar River and its great waterfalls to Dwali and on to Phurkia—worth this last effort to be well-placed for the final day. The culmination of this trek takes you up to Zero Point (12,532 feet/ 3,820 m), marking the foot of the Pindari Glacier, and back down again unless you wish to camp.

The trek through **Kullu Valley,** from Nagar to Jari, with **Manali** as your base, is justly popular. It is the best way to enjoy the alpine scenery and the varied landscape and flora, especially from mid-September to late October. For this five-day route you need to camp, but there are many other simpler and shorter options. From Nagar, hike through a beautiful forest and grazing pastures, and camp above the tree-line or continue to the base of Chandrakani Pass. Day two is a hike over the Chandrakani Pass (12,008 feet/3,660 m) with fine mountain views, and on to Malana, whose people have distinctive houses and follow a strict cultural behavior (your guide will help you on this). You can stay two or three nights in a guest house and do day treks into the surrounding rugged country. Finally, take the steep descent into the Parvati Valley to Rashol, and go on to Jari.

The trek from **Shimla** to **Leh** is a 15-day combination of walking with driving or buses, to the remote mountain reaches of **Kinnaur** and

Spiti. These spectacular drives are not for the faint-hearted. It is essential to acclimatize to the high elevation; possibly you should allow extra days for this. In the first week, drive to Sarahan via Narkanda and Rampur; then trek to Sangla to see wooden Bhimkali Temple and the beautiful temples in the Baspa Valley. Continue to Kalpa via Chitkul, and hike through mountain terrain to the medieval villages of Kothi, Tehlangi, Pangi, Chini, and Peo; see Hubulankar Monastery at Chini. Drive on to Nako (12,008 feet/3,660 m) and visit Lotsabalhakhang Monastery. In the second week, drive on to Tabo, where the frescoes of Chos Khor Monastery (A.D. 996) compare with Ajanta's (see pp. 178–79). Continue through Pin, then on via Ki and Kibber to Rangrik and across the Kumzum La pass (14,931 feet/4,551 m) to Chatru. Keylong lies over the Rohtang Pass (13,057 feet/3,980 m), from where you drive over the Baralacha La pass (15,912 feet/4,850 m) to Sarchu, enjoying breathtaking mountain scenery. The Lachaalang La pass (16,617 feet/5,065 m) and Tanglang La pass lead to Leh.

The **Markha Valley** trek is the classic Ladakh trek. It lasts eight to ten days, goes from **Spiti** or **Stok,** near Leh, to **Hemis,** and there are plenty of camps along the way. Best done mid-June to mid-October (the valley can be crowded during July and August), the trek offers a good variety of landscape, some of it stunning, and mostly keeps within the **Hemis National Park.** Two gentle days start the trek, going through the Markha Valley. From Spiti (10,498 feet/3,200 m), you proceed via Jingchan and Yurutse to Rumbak (12,467 feet/3,800 m), then on to Yurutse and Shingo (13,615 feet/4,150 m). The next stage is through a spectacular gorge to Skiu (11,154 feet/3,400 m). From there you continue to Markha (12,139 feet/3,700 m) and enjoy glorious views of Mount Nimaling (20,9997 feet/6,400 m). Continue to Tahungste, the remote and charming camp at Nimaling (15,485 feet/4,720 m), and so through the Longaru La pass (16,732 feet/5,100 m) to the pretty camp at Shang Sumdo (12,008 feet/3,660 m). End with a visit to Hemis monastery.

EASTERN HIMALAYA

The trek from **Maneybhanjan** to **Rimbik** is a relatively easy six-day trek along the **Singalila Range** to enjoy spectacular views of four of the world's highest mountain peaks: Everest, Kanchenjunga, Makalu, and Lhotse. It is best done in October and November or from February to May. Stay in trekking huts, and take warm bedding.

On day one, drive or take the bus from Darjiling to Maneybhanjan; then hike to Meghma and on up to Tonglu (10,072 feet/3,070 m), or sleep at a lodge in Jaubari; reach Sandakphu (11,929 feet/3,636 m) the next day. On days three and four, enjoy spectacular views along the ridge, first hiking to stay overnight at Molley, then returning to Sandakphu on to Phalut (11,811 feet/3,600 m). On days five and six, trek to Gorkhey and on to Rammam (8,398 feet/2,560 m) for the night, before ending at Rimbik.

More of a tour than a trek, the journey from **Darjiling** to **Kalimpong** involves a gentle week of moving from West Bengal into Sikkim and staying in hotels, mixing drives with walks and visits to monasteries, nurseries, and a botanical garden; excellent for seeing Himalayan flora. It is best enjoyed in October and November or in February and March (orchids are best in March).

First, spend a day in Darjiling (see p. 326), and visit the Himalayan Mountaineering Institute on Birch Hill. On day two, drive through the Teesta River Valley to Gangtok (5,075 feet/1,547 m), where you can visit the Orchidarium, the Cottage Industries Institute, and the unique Research Institute of Tibetology the next day, or do a local trek. On day four, drive to Ramtek (5,085 feet/1,550 m), visit its monastery, and the next day enjoy a full day trek. On day six, drive along the Teesta River valley to **Kalimpong** (4,101 feet/1,250 m), the region's floriculture center, for two nights; you can mix local treks with visits to nurseries, Tarpacholing Monastery, and the School of Tibetan Medicine at Brang Monastery.

The **Dzongri Trail** is a nine-day, high-elevation trek through Sikkim's lush forests from **Yoksum** to **Dzongri** and back on a circular route, taking in wonderful mountain views and, in May, rhododendrons in bloom. Do this trek in an organized group, so that food, guides, and other things are arranged for you. On day one, walk from Pelling to the official start, Yoksum. On day two, hike up into the cloud forests to Tsokha (10,000 feet/3,000 m); then spend day three hiking in the area to acclimatize to the altitude. On day four, hike up through pines and rhododendrons to Dzongri (13,221 feet/4,030 m); then again spend a day acclimatizing. On days six and seven, trek on to Thangsing (12,467 feet/3,800 m), then on to Samiti Lake (13,320 feet/4,060 m); camp here or continue to Zemanthang. On day eight, ascend to Gocha La (16,207 feet/4,940m) and return. On day ten, descend directly to Tsokha. ■

Travelwise

Living a modern life: A sari-clad woman balances on the back of a scooter.

TRAVELWISE INFORMATION

PLANNING YOUR TRIP

India has such a wide range of climates and attractions that you can enjoy a visit at any time of the year. Its variety of history, crafts, monuments, wildlife, and activities can satisfy almost any interest. Spend some time planning your itinerary. Remember that if you spend a few days in one place, you usually experience much more than if you are bouncing from place to place, constantly on the move. India is vast, and no one can see it all in one visit. If you enjoy your first experience there, you will go again.

WHEN TO GO

India has three seasons: October to February is winter, with warm sunny days, but chilly nights in the north. April to June is summer, progressively hot and humid, except in the hills. July to September is the monsoon, which moves up across India from the south (see p. 20).

To visit the forts, temples, and palaces of India, as well as its beaches, the best time to go is from September to March. High season is from October to February, when you'll need to reserve hotel rooms in advance to be sure of a place to stay. To see India's wildlife, visit between February and August, when it gets drier and hotter and the undergrowth is less lush, as you are likely to spot more of the animals going to water holes. Bird-watchers can see an astounding variety of migrating birds in winter, especially from December to February.

The searing heat from April to July, which pushes most visitors up into the hills, breaks with the arrival of the monsoon, which can be a fantastic experience and has the advantage of being a time when India is almost tourist free. Up in the hills, trekkers will find the spring and summer months, from May to October, best. It is worth arranging your itinerary to coincide with one of India's many colorful festivals (see pp. 379–82), although you are likely to bump into delightful minor festivals and village fairs wherever and whenever you go.

TOURIST INFORMATION

For further information, maps, brochures, and help planning the trip that matches your interests, contact one of the Government of India Tourist Offices.

Website
www.tourindia.com

In the United States
3550 Wilshire Blvd., Room 204, Los Angeles, CA 90010, tel 213/380-8855, fax 213/380-6111, e-mail goitola@aol.com

1270 Avenue of the Americas, New York, NY 10020, tel 212/586-4901, fax 212/582-3274, e-mail andy@tourindia.com

In Canada
60 Bloor St. (West), Suite 1003, Toronto, Ontario, M4W 3B8, tel 416/962-3787, fax 416/962-6279, e-mail india@istar.ca

In the U.K.
7 Cork St., London, W1X 2AB, tel 020-7437 3677, fax 020-7494 1048, e-mail info@indiatourist office.org

TRAVEL AGENTS
To make your holiday in India go smoothly, use a travel agent who is experienced in advising on India and booking holidays there. If you wish to travel independently, an agent should be able to work within your budget, and to cater to your required levels of adventure, culture, and comfort. The agent should recommend sights and tours that suit your interests—while one person's dream is to visit temples galore, another's is to palace-hop in Rajasthan, walk in the hills, or explore the fort cities of Karnataka. An agent will handle the whole booking, using reliable agents in India, and should save you time-consuming long-distance booking and remove much of the worry. Once in India, local agents will ensure that your bookings for hotels, cars, guides, and other facilities are honored, and can amend itineraries and hotel choices if necessary.

PACKAGE DEALS
However much you may prefer to plan and make your own arrangements directly, when going to India it is definitely easier to take a tour. That way, you benefit from other people's experience and hard work, and when in India you can enjoy the sites while someone else organizes hotel reservations and transportation.

Nowadays, there is a tour to suit most interests, most budgets, and most preferred pace of travel. Many clubs and museums run tours to India, too. The price usually includes the airfare, transportation, hotels, some meals, and guide or lecturer; and many are very good value. Your local Indian tourist office (see above) can suggest reliable travel agents. Since the British have a particularly long and close relationship with India, it is well worth looking at tours departing from London, both for range and good prices.

Tours vary from the simple to the deluxe in content and in price. Look at a number of the brochures published by the travel agents listed below to get an idea of the range of trips— and prices. Even if your starting point is the U.S., do not discount using a British agent; the British are enthusiastic and experienced visitors to India. Finally, should you find yourself in India wanting to explore the country, these agents suggested here all have countrywide knowledge and can create itineraries quickly.

U.S. TRAVEL AGENTS
Esplanade Tours
581 Boylston St., Boston, MA 02116, tel 617/266-7465 or 800/426-5492, fax 617/262-9828, e-mail ej@esplanadetours.com

Geographic Expeditions
2627 Lombard St., San Francisco, CA 92008, tel 415/922-0448 or 800/777-8183, fax 415/346-5535, e-mail geox@geox.com

Great Adventure Travel Co., Inc.
645 North Michigan Ave., Suite 800, Chicago, IL 60611, tel 773/880-5764 or 800/874-2826, fax 773/880-5760, e-mail grtadvtrvl@aol.com

Himalayan Travel
110 Prospect St., Stamford, CT 06901, tel 203/359-3711 or 800/225-2380, fax 203/359-3669, e-mail worldadv@netaxis.com

International Ventures and Travel Inc. (IVAT)
225 West 35th St., Suite 1401, New York, NY 10001, tel 212/947-7075 or 800/338-2624, fax 212/563-7048, e-mail victor@ivat.com

Journeys International
107 April Dr., Suite 3, Ann Arbor, MI 48103, tel 734/665-4407 or 800/255-8735, fax 734/665-2945, e-mail info@journeys-int.com

Myths and Mountains
976 Tee Ct., Incline Village, NV 89451, tel 775/832-5454 or 800/670-MYTH, fax 775/832-4454

The following agents cover the world and include India:

Abercrombie & Kent Int. Inc.
1520 Kensington Rd., Suite 212, Oak Brook, IL 60523, tel

630/954-2944 or 800/323-7308, fax 630/954-3324, e-mail info@abercrombiekent.com

TRAVCOA
2350 S.E. Bristol, Newport Beach, CA 92660, tel 949/476-2800 or 800/992-2003, fax 949/476-2538, e-mail travcoa@aol.com

U.K. TRAVEL AGENTS
The following all have people on their team with extensive knowledge of India and of planning holidays there. You can usually join a tour in London or in India.

Bales Worldwide
Bales House, Junction Rd., Dorking, Surrey RH4 3HL, tel 0870-2413214 (brochure), 0870-2413208 (reservations), fax 01306-740048, e-mail enquiries@balesworldwide.com

Kuoni Travel Ltd.
Kuoni house, Dorking, Surrey RH5 4AZ, tel 0870-07458664 (brochure), 01306-740500 (reservations), fax 01306-744222, e-mail fareast.sales@kuoni.co.uk

Ultimate Travel Company
20 Pimlico Rd., London, SW1W 8LJ, tel 020-7259 0259, fax 020-7259 0256, e-mail diana@ultimate-travel.co.uk

World Wide Journeys
27 Vanston Place, London, SW6 1AZ, tel 020-7386 4646, fax 020-7381 0836, e-mail wwj@wjournex.demon.co.uk

INDIAN TRAVEL AGENTS
The following agents have a good reputation for reliability and fin-ancial integrity. They are accred-ited to the Ministry of Tourism and members of IATO (Indian Association of Tour Operators). All cover the whole of India except Cosmopol, which concentrates on southern India. All have a network of local agents.

Cosmopol Travel
A/301 Queens Corner, 3 Queens Rd., Bangalore 56001, tel 080-220 2410 or 080-220 2411, fax 080-220 0154, e-mail costours@vsnl.com

Equinox
Apartment 3, First Floor, 1 Rao Tula Ram Marg, New Delhi 110021, tel 011-616 3518 or 011-616 3522, fax 011-618 5130, e-mail equinox.india@vsnl.com

First Tours India
205 Park & Shop Complex, DLF City Phase II, Gurgaon 12202, Haryana, tel 0124-354400 or 0124-635 5515, fax 0124-635 0326, e-mail firstours@vsnl.com

International Ventures and Travel Inc. (IVAT)
C-233 Defence Colony, New Delhi 220024, tel 011-464 9194, 011-464 9195 or 011-464 9196, fax 011-465 5918, e-mail ivat@vsnl.com

Micato Tours
B-525 Sarita Vihar, New Delhi 110044, tel 011-6949107 or 011-6943781, fax 011-6940898, e-mail micato@vsnl.com

PL Worldways
B-5/47A Safdarjang Enclave, New Delhi 110029, tel 011-616 7340 or 011-616 7341, fax 011-616 7346, e-mail plholidays@vsnl.com

Travelscope
C-58 Malviya Nagar, New Delhi 110017, tel 011-668 0895 or 011-668 7593, fax 011-668 3979, e-mail travelscope@vsnl.com

WHAT TO TAKE

The old rule applies: The less the better. India has changed hugely in the past decade. Today, if you forget something and you are not far off the beaten track, you can usually buy it easily and far cheaper than back home. This includes quality camera film, face creams, batteries, books, maps, and other essentials. The major exceptions to this rule are high quality sunscreen, quality razor blades, and makeup. Adventurous travelers need to be better prepared, but even they can top up supplies with anything from film equipment to mountaineering gear in the main cities in India.

CLOTHES

Cottons, not man-made fibers, are the most comfortable clothes, but you will need extra layers for chilly mornings and nights in the north—hotel laundries are good and fast, so you do not need to take much. Shorts are acceptable, pants best for wildlife parks and trekking, a hat for sun protection, and swimsuits for pools and the sea—topless bathing is frowned upon. Shoes need to be comfortable for walking, yet easy to slip off when visiting religious buildings. On these occasions, some people like to slip on a pair of socks rather than go barefoot. Indian people are informal, so it is not necessary to dress up in the evenings.

MEDICINES

You may feel happier taking your own selection of pills, potions, and lotions. However, hotel doctors and local drugstores are very good. The best way to remain healthy is to drink plenty of bottled water and to eat freshly cooked vegetarian versions of local dishes. Stomach-calming, nutritious bananas can often provide an effective and simple remedy to minor upsets caused by unfamiliar foods.

There are, however, certain essential precautions. For the latest information on vaccinations or inoculations and malaria prophylaxis you should contact your doctor or travel clinic. Owing to the numbers of migrant workers, no area of India is now free of malaria. You should keep a note of the name of your tablets, so that if you lose them, more can be bought in India. The same applies to most medicines, so carry a copy of your prescription from home.

OTHER ITEMS

Other miscellaneous items that may be useful for your India trip are: sunscreen, rehydration tablets or powders (the local equivalent is Electrol), antiseptic cream, throat lozenges (the dust can irritate your throat), lip balm (the sun dries the skin), sterilized wet wipes, insect repellent, and soft toilet paper.

SPECIAL INTERESTS

Take a pair of binoculars for looking at birds, wildlife, and architectural detail. A notebook is useful to list the order in which you see buildings. This makes identifying your photographs later much easier. Bartholemew's Map of India (not available in India) helps you keep your location in perspective; state maps give more detail. Those interested in design and crafts should remember to take small swatches of fabrics or paints, so that you can match colors when you are buying bargain-priced silks and cottons.

GADGETS

Electricity is now much more reliable than it was. Voltage is 220, occasionally 230. American appliances will require both a voltage transformer and plug adapter. Gone are the days of packing candles and matches. It is worth taking a small, light antimosquito machine, a traveling iron, a CD player or personal stereo, and some favorite music for long journeys. A flashlight is useful for unlit palaces and sculpted temples and caves. Arrange for your cellular phone to operate in India (see p. 340) and remember to pack the battery charger as hotel telephone prices are high. You can also use public phones (see p. 340). If you need to keep in touch by e-mail, Internet cafés abound.

(see p. 340)

INSURANCE

Be sure to take out adequate insurance policies for health, possessions, and cancellation. If you have opted for a package deal, you may want to have more insurance than is included in the price—always check.

ENTRY FORMALITIES

PASSPORTS & VISAS

You will need a valid passport and a visa. The visa, of which there are many types, ranging from tourist to business, must be obtained before arrival. A tourist visa costs around $30. These and special permits for visiting certain areas (see p. 321, p. 323 and p. 324) are available from the Indian embassy or consulate in your home country.

(see p. 321, p. 323 and p. 324)

CUSTOMS ON ARRIVAL

Items brought into India for personal use are exempt from duty. So are gifts up to the value of Rs4,000, one liter of wine, one liter of spirits, and 200 cigarettes or 50 cigars or 250g of tobacco. Commercial goods must be declared, as must currency over $10,000 or its equivalent. Drugs and narcotics, apart from prescription drugs supplied by your doctor, are strictly prohibited.

CUSTOMS ON DEPARTURE

Several items are prohibited from export without an export license. These include gold jewelry valued above Rs6,000, animal skins and products made from them, art objects over 100 years old, and wild plants. To verify art objects, contact the Archeological Survey of India, Janpath, New Delhi, tel 011-301 9451.

INDIAN MISSIONS

For detailed information on any of the above, you should contact your nearest Indian mission. These include:

In the U.S.

Embassy of India, 2107 Massachusetts Ave., NW,

Washington, DC 20008, tel 202/939-7000, fax 202/265-4351

Consulate General of India, 3 E 6th St., New York, NY 10021, tel 212/861-3788, fax 212/861-3788

Canada

High Commission of India, 10 Springfield Rd., Ottawa, Ontario KIM IC9, tel 613/744-3751 or 613/744-3752, fax 613/744-0913

U.K.

High Commission of India, India House, Aldwych, London, WC2B 4NA, tel 020-7836 4331, fax 020-7836 4331

HOW TO GET TO INDIA

INTERNATIONAL FLIGHTS

Most national carriers fly to India. The main international airports are New Delhi, Mumbai (Bombay), Kolkata (Calcutta), and Chennai (Madras). Air India also flies into Bangalore, charter planes fly into Panaji (Goa) and Trivandrum (Thiruvanantha-puram, Kerala). It is worth considering flying into one city and home from another, an option offered by many large airlines at no extra cost. Consider, too, whether to fly across the Pacific into Kolkata (Calcutta) or Chennai (Madras), or across Europe into Delhi or Mumbai (Bombay). Shop around for a good deal as prices vary and may be particularly cheap if you travel via Hong Kong or London. Ensure that the price includes all airport taxes.

GETTING AROUND

ON ARRIVAL

Once you have passed through immigration, collected your luggage, and gone through customs (see above), if you are not being met, it is best to go

to the official taxi desk where rates and drivers are controlled, rather than accept an ad hoc driver.

TRAVELING WITHIN MAJOR CITIES

India has more transportation options than most countries. The trick is to select the one most suitable for your journey or sight-seeing. In Delhi, for instance, you might use a taxi for long journeys, a motorized rickshaw for shorter ones, and a bicycle rickshaw for exploring Old Delhi. In Mumbai (Bombay) you can use a combination of taxis and local trains; in Kolkata (Calcutta) you can choose between taxis, underground trains, river ferries, and, possibly, rickshaws. The adventurous might like to tackle the local buses, but this is challenging.

Taxis may or may not have meters that work. So for these and for all rickshaw journeys, agree on a price with the driver before starting your journey, make stops where you wish, then pay at the end adding extra money for "waiting time." Your hotel concierge should give you a clear idea of the local rates, which vary considerably.

TRAVELING AROUND THE COUNTRY

Traveling is part of your holiday in India. It is fun to collect your methods of transport. See if you can travel by air, car, coach, bus, and train; by camel, pony, and elephant; and by auto-rickshaw and tempo. Air travel is useful for big leaps across the country, but planes can be delayed and are best avoided for short trips such as Delhi–Agra, when the train is fastest and easiest.

India's roads are like no others. Your car, coach, or bus may share the tarmac with a herd of goats, some bicyclists, and overloaded bullock carts carrying farm produce. What

appears at first merely to be movement between one palace or temple city and another becomes a colorful and memorable experience.

Riding an animal, though, is quite different. Even the shortest journey on a camel may be too much, so ensure you have tested your endurance before you embark on a five-day camel ride through the desert. Ponies are easier, and often used on treks, and to sit atop an elephant to spot exotic birds and, perhaps, a tiger, is special indeed).

You can hire a car (which comes with a driver; it is madness to drive oneself in India, see p. 340).

BY AIR

Three large domestic airlines plus a handful of small ones service India's extensive network of 115 domestic airports: **Jet Airways, India Airlines,** and **Sahara Airlines.** Your travel agent will have the most up-to-date information, as schedules change in October and April. The three large carriers offer special discount fares for visitors, on the lines of a 15- or 21-day validity for unlimited travel at a flat rate, but with some restrictions. Check-in time for all domestic flights is one hour before departure.

BY TRAIN

For many visitors to India, a train journey is essential. India's vast railroad network (see p. 108) operates about 7,800 passenger services each day.

At the top end of the market, where tickets should always be reserved well in advance, you can choose between tourist trains such as The Palace on Wheels and regular passenger trains such as the Rajdhani and Shatabdi super-fast trains.

Indian Railways offers Indrail Passes valid from just half a day

GETTING AROUND/PRACTICAL ADVICE

up to 90 days, at very good prices.

Tourist trains

The Palace on Wheels circles around Rajasthan in eight days, departing from Delhi each Wednesday.

The Royal Orient Express operates from September to April taking passengers from Delhi through Rajasthan and Gujarat over eight days.

Superfast regular trains

The deluxe, air-conditioned Rajdhani Express trains connect large cities and have sleeping berths, while the Shatabdi Express trains connect cities less far apart, such as Delhi with Agra, Gwalior, and Bhopal.

The Konkan Railway

India's newest railroad runs down the west coast from Mumbai (Bombay), see p. 204.

Toy trains

With the demise of most steam trains, and India's commitment to making all of its train track broad gauge, the charming, British-built lines up to the hill stations are rare opportunities to evoke earlier times. Routes include the Kalka–Shimla journey, 43 miles (69 km); the **Shivalik Queen,** offering the same run but with private rooms aimed at honeymooners; the **Nilgiri Mountain Railway** to Ooty; the **Matheran Railway;** and the **Darjiling Hill Railway** with the narrowest gauge of all and uninterrupted views of the Himalayan Mountains. **The Fairy Queen,** the world's oldest running locomotive, is now used for weekend trips from Delhi to Alwar and back.

BY CAR & DRIVER

To "drive" in India means to rent a car with a driver. Budget permitting, this is the most luxurious way to travel around India. It is often the easiest way

to reach interesting sites. You are free to go where you wish, when you wish, and to stop whenever you see anything interesting.

A good driver knows your route, knows the best restroom stops and the best *dhabas* (roadside cafés), protects you from untrustworthy guides and tiresomely pestering peddlers, keeps the car stocked with bottled water and soft drinks, helps with minor practical shopping, and generally looks after your interests. Many travelers strike up strong friendships with their drivers, who should be well rewarded when you part (see tipping, p. 342).

When you first have your car and driver, it is important that you feel confident about both: If not, be sure to talk to your local agent immediately and request a change.

Your travel agent should arrange a car and driver, and include the cost as part of the price of the travel arrangements they make.

BY BUS

There are several classes of Indian public bus. At the top end of the market, deluxe buses are the most comfortable and have air-conditioning. Good lines include Jaipur's **Pink Line** and **Silver Line.**

BY WATER

Sometimes a boat journey is an integral part of the sight-seeing. Sunrise at Varanasi seen from a boat on the Ganga River is magical (see pp. 308–309), as is exploring the backwaters of Kerala by boat (see pp. 210–211); you can even stay on one. The best way to move from south to north Kolkata (Calcutta) is to take the public ferries on the Hooghly. On the west coast, ferries leave Mumbai (Bombay) for Elephanta Island

(see p. 169), while hydrofoils and hovercrafts cross the harbor to the Maharashtran coast.

PRACTICAL ADVICE

COMMUNICATIONS

To bypass the hotel markup on telephone bills, either bring your own cellular phone, or use the local pay phones that usually have yellow advertising boards marked "PCO-STD-ISN." Internet cafés abound.

Note that American cellular phones normally operate on the frequency 1900 mHz. The operating frequency in India is 900/1800 mHz; contact your network operator to check whether your phone will work on those frequencies.

CONVERSIONS

Temperature is measured in degrees Celsius, distance in kilometers, liquids in liters, fabric in meters, gold in grams. However, as some of the world's greatest traders, Indians will be able to adapt any measurement, from shoes to silk, to facilitate your understanding.

ETIQUETTE & LOCAL CUSTOMS

You will almost certainly encounter beggars in India. This can be distressing. The solution is not necessarily to give alms, which may not be kept by the person begging and in any case perpetuates the begging culture. Consider instead giving to one of the many charities based either in India or abroad that are focusing their efforts on a particular aspect that you feel strongly about—health, education, children, village water supplies, etc. If you feel you must give to a beggar, do so just before you leave the site to avoid being mobbed.

Indian people are so polite and so anxious to put visitors at ease that it is easy to be ignorant of causing offense, especially to people in the more traditional, rural areas. To help show your respect for different customs, here are some tips:

Remove your shoes when entering a temple, *gurudwara,* or mosque; dress conservatively in all places of worship.

The left hand and foot are considered unclean, so do not use your left hand to touch a holy object, point to anything, or eat food.

Respect any rules in holy places, such as "no cameras" or "no leather objects."

When shopping, you are expected to bargain hard, except when a store has fixed prices. Bargain when taking public transportation, too, unless the taxi has a working meter.

When things do not run on time, try not to mind too much. See it as an opportunity to write in your diary, read, or take a short walk to look at life around you.

Indian hospitality is unusually generous, and not to accept it may well cause offense. Furthermore, if you are invited to someone's house, try to arrive with some flowers or with a present brought from your own country. It is a good idea to purchase small, inexpensive items for this purpose before you leave home.

Skimpy T-shirts and short shorts are frowned upon, and on the beach you should wear appropriate swimwear—nudity and topless sunbathing are rarely tolerated.

Some people, especially women in rural places, do not wish to be photographed—respect their wishes.

HOLIDAYS

In addition to the many festivals (see pp. 379–82), most offices close for the following official public holidays:

Jan. 26, Republic Day
Aug.15, Independence Day
Oct. 2, Mahatma Ghandi's birthday
Dec. 25, Christmas Day

LIQUOR LAWS

Almost all hotels serve beer and spirits in their bars and restaurants. However, depending upon the political party in power, individual states may call for certain days of the month to be "dry." It is important to respect these rules and restrict liquor consumption to your hotel room on these occasions.

MEDIA

More than 40,000 newspapers and periodicals are published in 100 languages and dialects in India each year. Many are in English, including the *Times of India,* the *Hindu,* the *Hindustan Times,* and the *Indian Express,* each with several local editions. One or two will be delivered to your hotel room, and foreign newspapers are usually on sale in hotel shops. *India Today* is India's answer to *Newsweek.*

While India's own television networks may be worthy of only cursory investigation, most hotel rooms are supplied with satellite TV channels including BBC World Service and CNN.

MONEY MATTERS

Indian currency is the rupee. Bills come in denominations of Rs500, 100, 50, 20, 10, 5, and 2. The rupee is divided into 100 paise. Small bills and coins are useful for tips. However, visitors will find that large sums are often quoted in U.S. dollars, from hotel rooms to upscale shopping. Major credit cards are accepted in hotels, hotel shops and restaurants, and in larger stores. It is best to carry U.S. dollar traveler's checks and to change them at your hotel, where the rate is usually favorable, as the long lines at banks move slowly. When changing money, ask for an encashment certificate so that you can change back any money that you have left over at the end of your trip—it is not permitted to take rupees out of India.

OPENING TIMES & ENTRANCE FEES

Sites in the care of the ASI (Archaeological Survey of India) usually open sunrise to sunset. Admission fees are minimal but for a handful of notable exceptions such as the Taj Mahal, for which the fees are regularly revised. Museums often have quirky opening hours that vary from week to week; if you are somewhere where the museum is known to be good, then check out its opening times upon arrival.

Government offices are open Monday through Friday from 9:30 a.m. to 5 p.m., plus some Saturdays from 9:30 a.m. to 1 p.m. Stores are mostly open between 9:30 a.m. and 6 p.m., but those in hotels and at tourist sites are open whenever there is a chance of business. Bazaars keep longer hours.

PLACES OF WORSHIP

Most towns have active places of worship for Christians, Hindus, and Muslims; many have Gurudwaras for Sikhs. The cities historically linked with Jewish people, such as Mumbai (Bombay), Kolkata (Calcutta), Delhi, and Kochi (Cochin), have synagogues.

REST ROOMS

Rest rooms in hotels and upscale restaurants are modern

and clean, although water restrictions may mean that the flush is replaced by a bucket and tap. When traveling it may often be more comfortable (and more hygienic) to stop at the roadside near some bushes than to use a modest public lavatory; so carry a roll of toilet paper and packs of antiseptic wipes.

TIME DIFFERENCES

India has one time zone. It is 5.5 hours ahead of GMT; this means that it is 10.5 hours ahead of U.S. Eastern Standard Time, and 13.5 hours ahead of U.S. Pacific Standard Time.

TIPPING

As a general rule any service in India requires a tip. In a hotel, Rs10 is suitable for carrying luggage, delivering room service, returning laundry, etc. In a restaurant, tip 10 percent of the total bill. A good tourist guide deserves Rs100 tip per day, a good driver the same, more if he has driven a hard and long route. In both cases, give the tip at the end of the service, when you say goodbye; do not feel obliged to tip for bad service.

Be careful to note which tips are included in a package deal, checking with the local agent if necessary. The one place where double tipping is customary is on tour buses; here a small personal thanks to the driver and his helper is in order.

TRAVELERS WITH DISABILITIES

In India, where respect for the infirm and elderly is considerable, travelers with disabilities should have no problem, and there are always plenty of people to help. Being in a wheelchair does not mean you will not be able to ride on an elephant. You should be sure to inform your travel agent of any specific requirements that you might have, and reconfirm

these with your Indian agent upon arrival.

VISITOR INFORMATION

There are 21 Government of India Tourist Offices in India, and another 19 in other countries (see p. 337), mostly staffed by knowledgeable and helpful people. In addition, each state and union territory has its own web of tourist offices in its area, plus one in the capital, Delhi.

EMERGENCIES

EMBASSIES

U.S.A. Embassy
Shanti Path
Chanakyapuri
New Delhi 110021
Tel 011-688 9033
Fax 011-332 9499

U.K. Embassy
Chanakyapuri
New Delhi 110021
Tel 011-687 2161
Fax 011-687 288/20065

ACCIDENTS

If you witness a crime, are involved in an automobile accident, have something stolen, or experience anything that might require police assistance, make a clear note of the event at the time and include any necessary sketches. Then try to go to the local police station with your travel agent, your hotel manager, or, if serious, a representative of your embassy or consulate who will help with the bureaucracy and paperwork. It is important to report a crime if you are intending to claim on your insurance.

DIFFICULTIES

If something goes wrong in your hotel, contact the duty manager. If something goes wrong while

touring, your driver or guide will deal with it. For any other problems, contact your travel agent's local representative. However, should you suffer a significant robbery, you should go to the local police station with your travel company representative to report it.

HEALTH

If you need to use local medical facilities, these are usually of a high standard. In fact, India trains some of the world's finest doctors who are often know-ledgeable in both Western medicine and complementary remedies. If you have any health problems, your hotel will have a doctor on call 24 hours a day. Drugstores are well staffed and well stocked and hospitals in the big cities are of a high standard. Those anxious about hygiene should carry a set of disposable syringes and needles, and you can even travel with some of your own blood. Keep receipts for all medical help and drugs as they will be needed for insurance claims.

FOOD & DRINK

Eating and drinking are either perpetual worries or perpetual delights. If you worry, then make sure you always carry bottled water with you and, if you are unhappy about the food available away from your hotel, buy and eat a few bananas every day to keep up your strength.

If you find the aromas of cafés too tempting to pass by, then take basic precautions and you should come to no harm. Always eat freshly prepared local food in a popular café with a bustling trade (which means regular clients know it is reliable and food does not hang around). Stick to vegetables, dhal, rice, and bread unless absolutely sure of the storage systems and hygiene levels. Take bottled water, biscuits, and fruit you can peel on a journey or sight-seeing.

HOTELS & RESTAURANTS

India's accommodations and restaurants began to experience a total revolution in the 1990s. With the increase in international tourism and domestic travel, coupled with favorable tax breaks for heritage hotels, there has been a great growth of hotels of all sizes and qualities opening up across India.

Here is just a tiny selection of what is available. As elsewhere in the world, a change of hotel manager may quickly bring even a famous hotel up or down. That said, a well-run palace hotel with plenty of character, old charm service, and fine facilities is a very special experience, the stuff of dreams.

If you are planning your own trip, rather than opting for a preplanned package deal, beware: Upscale hotels and their in-house facilities from telephones to bar prices are not cheap, plus there are hefty taxes. Use websites to find the best deals. Consider staying in one or two memorable hotels, then economize with modest ones when you are sightseeing most of the day.

As for food and drink, the Indian tradition of eating at home where the wife or cook knows just how the family prefers its spice blends is becoming much more liberal. Large hotels often have several restaurants, some highly fashionable with locals so it is wise to reserve a table; they also have a "coffee shop" that offers informal eating and stays open long hours. The advantages of eating in such hotels is the range of cuisines (Chinese is especially good, Western food is known as Continental), fresh fruits from papaya to pineapple, and drinks—a favorite thirst-quencher is a fresh lime juice with soda, drunk either plain or with added salt or sugar syrup.

However, smaller hotels and independent cafés and restaurants often produce fresher and more authentic local food, especially if asked—Indians love to talk about food. A simple roadside café known as a *dhabba*

can be the best of all, especially for a "rice-dhal" meal or a *thali* (a whole meal arrives on one platter) in the south, or a kebab with a *naan* or *paratha* along the Grand Trunk Road in the north, washed down with hot, sweet, milky *chai* (tea) and some bottled carbonated drinks. Drivers and guides, once briefed, are very good at seeking out the best ones.

Suspicion and fear all too often lead foreign visitors to stick to disappointing, format food in upscale hotels. It's far better, and safer, to eat freshly cooked local food. Include plenty of rice or bread with your meal; stick to vegetable dishes unless you are sure of the freshness of fish or meat; have a daily bowl of yogurt; and drink lots and lots of bottled water. All hotels have their own restaurants but the author has flagged special ones below with a restaurant symbol. As quality varies between cities and towns, particular ones may be flagged because they are the best option in the area.

TYPES OF ACCOMMODATIONS

India's large deluxe hotel chains

Each of these has a central reservations system, where a full list of hotels is available—only a selection is listed below.

Ashok Group (government run, countrywide): tel 011-334 4422, fax 011-334 3162, e-mail reservation@theashokgroup .com; website www.theashokgroup.com

HRH Group: tel 011-294 528016, fax 011-294 528006, e-mail resv@udaipur.hrhindia.com; website www.hrhindia.com

Neemrana Hotels: tel 011-

461 6145, fax 011-462 1112, e-mail sales@neemranahotels.com

Oberoi Hotels and Resorts: tel 800/6-OBEROI (U.S.), 00 800 1234 0101 (Eur); fax 212/223 8500 (U.S.), 0207-222 9696 (U.K.); website www.oberoihotels.com

Taj Hotels, Resorts, and Palaces: tel 022-202 2626, fax 022-287 2719; website www.tajhotels.com

Welcomgroup: tel 011-685 0242, fax 011-686 3715; website www.welcomgroup.com. Some hotel reservations can be made through Sheraton Hotels.

International hotel chains

India's liberalization and a global increase in upscale travel mean that familiar hotel groups with hotels in India include Best Western, Country Hospitality (Regent, Radisson, Country Inns, TGIF), Four Seasons, Hilton, Holiday Inn, Hyatt, Inter-Continental, Kempinski, Mandarin Oriental, Marriott, Meridien, Park Plaza, Quality Inns, and Sheraton.

Heritage hotels

From sprawling palaces to modest hunting lodges, from

PRICES

HOTELS
An indication of the cost of a double room without breakfast is given by **$** signs.
$$$$$	Over $280
$$$$	$160–$280
$$$	$100–$160
$$	$40–$100
$	Under $40

RESTAURANTS
An indication of the cost of a three-course dinner without drinks is given by $ signs.
$$$$$	Over $80
$$$$	$50–$80
$$$	$35–$50
$$	$20–$35
$	Under $20

---

imposing forts to cozy family homes, the former royals and aristocrats of India have taken full advantage of tax benefits to transform their properties into hotels. A few are part of the big hotel chains or run by businesspeople; most are run by descendants of their creators. The majority are in Rajasthan, but there is a growing number in Gujarat, Madhya Pradesh, Himachal Pradesh, and other states. Although romantic and often very beautiful, their success in delivering a comfortable room, hot water, good food, and lively service to their guests varies. That said, the ones that are run well provide a remarkable and personal experience that no big hotel can match—and good local food, too. To find out more: Heritage Hotels Association, 9 Sardar Patel Marg, C Scheme, Jaipur 302001, Rajasthan, tel 0141-381906, fax 0141-382214.

Other lodging

Owner-managed hotels can be especially charming, and several are selected below. Individual states run some hotels, indicated in the lists below with their state initials in brackets after the title. Some modest, British-built Tourist Bungalows and Traveler Lodges in off-beat places are also run by the states. Kerala's country boats once used to transport rice are now pretty houseboats. Delhi, Goa, Mumbai, Kolkata, Chennai, and a dozen Rajasthan cities including Jaipur run paying-guest programs where you stay with an Indian family; all reserved through the local tourist offices. India's youth hostels are very cheap and often centrally located; contact Young Hostels Association of India, 5 Nyaya Marg, Chanakyapuri, New Delhi, 110021, tel 011-6116285, fax 011-6113469.

STANDARDS & PRICES

Local star ratings have little significance in India; and it would be misleading to imply the membership of upscale

international hotel groups means a hotel will be the equivalent of, say, a hotel in New York belonging to the same group; so such information is omitted. All hotels and most enclosed restaurants have air-conditioning, of varying types. Nonsmoking rooms are very few and far between, as are nonsmoking areas in restaurants. Most hotels will change foreign currency into rupees; most accept payment with the major credit cards. Hotel rooms above a certain prices are subject to extra luxury taxes. Very often the best restaurants in town are in the hotels.

CREDIT CARDS

Most of the bigger hotels accept the major credit cards. Smaller ones may only accept some, as shown in their entries, or none at all. Unless restaurants are in hotels, you should not expect them to accept credit cards. Abbreviations used in this guide are AE (American Express), DC (Diner's Club), MC (Mastercard), and V (Visa).

ORGANIZATION

The hotels and restaurants below have been grouped according to chapter, first alphabetically then by price category.

DELHI

The capital's many hotels are often full, so reserve in advance. For eating, northern Indian cuisines include the simple Northwest Frontier and the very rich, complex, and courtly Mogul food.

🏨 HYATT REGENCY
🍴 DELHI
$$$$$
BHIKAJI CAMA PLACE, RING RD.
TEL 011-679 1234 OR 011-679 1150
FAX 011-679 1122
E-MAIL hyatt@del2.vsnl.net.in
Large, gleaming south Delhi hotel, 5 miles (8 km) from the center and geared to the upscale business person. All

PRICES

HOTELS
An indication of the cost of a double room without breakfast is given by $ signs.
$$$$$	Over $280
$$$$	$160– $280
$$$	$100–$160
$$	$40–$100
$	Under $40

RESTAURANTS
An indication of the cost of a three-course dinner without drinks is given by $ signs.
$$$$$	Over $80
$$$$	$50–$80
$$$	$35–$50
$$	$20–$35
$	Under $20

modern conveniences are on hand and there are two executive club floors as well as two tennis courts. The hotel's restaurants include the good Delhi Ka Angan (northern Indian cuisine) and TK's (Oriental grill).
🛏 518 � 🔲 🚭 All major cards

🏨 MAURYA SHERATON
🍴 HOTEL & TOWERS
$$$$$
SARDAR PATEL MARG, CHANAKYAPURI
TEL 011-611 2233
FAX 011-611 3333
E-MAIL maurya@welcomgroup.com
A Welcomgroup hotel situated in the diplomatic enclave of southwest Delhi. The tower has a nonsmoking floor. This hotel is a pioneer in commissioning Indian art for its decor and reviving authentic cuisines in its restaurants—Northwest Frontier food is served in the *Bukhara*, sealed pot roasts from Lucknow in the Dum Pukht, while Bali Hi serves Polynesian dishes.
🛏 516 (including 44 suites) 🔲 � 🔲 🚭 All major cards

🏨 OBEROI
🍴 $$$$$

DR. ZAKIR HUSSAIND MARG
TEL 011-436 3030
FAX 011-436 0484
E-MAIL reservations@oberoidel
.com

Delhi's oldest deluxe business hotel, part of the Oberoi group, is constantly refurbished to maintain it at its best. Set right by the golf course in midtown Delhi, it is loved by high-flyers. Every service is available, from a butler to a nonsmoking floor. Restaurants include Kandahar (Mogul), Baan Thai (Thai), La Rochelle (Continental), and Taipan (Chinese).

🛏 290 📶 🏊 💪 🗝 All
major cards

🏨 TAJ MAHAL
🍴 $$$$$

1 MANSINGH RD.
TEL 011-302 6162
FAX 011-302 6070
E-MAIL tajmahal@giasdel01.vsnl
.net.in

Both Delhi's Taj group hotels (see p. 343, and Taj Palace p. 346) create a good atmosphere for visitors and businesspeople. This is the smaller of the two and is very central, with three restaurants: House of Ming (Cantonese and Szechuan), Captain's Cabin (bar with Continental seafood dishes), and Haveli (northern Indian).

🛏 300 🏊 💪 🗝 All
major cards

🏨 ASHOK
🍴 $$$$

50B CHANAKYAPURI
TEL 011-611 0101
FAX 011-687 3216
E-MAIL ashoknd@ndb.vsnl.net.in

Built in 1954 before space was at a premium, the Ashok has large guest rooms, spacious public rooms and lawns, and some charming and very good restaurants—try Samova (a coffee shop) overlooking the gardens, Durbar (Mogul food) for a buffet lunch, Frontier (Northwest Frontier), or Tokyo (Japanese).

🛏 550 🏊 💪 🗝 AE, DC,
MC, V

🏨 CLARIDGES
🍴 $$$$

12 AURANGZEB RD.
TEL 011-301 0211
FAX 011-301 0625
E-MAIL claridge.hotel@
gems.vsnl.net.in

Refurbished old hotel situated in the heart of New Delhi's elegant tree-lined avenues. Much patronized by locals for its choice of restaurants: Dhaba (northern Indian, especially Mogul), Corbett's (Northwest Frontier), and Jade Garden (Cantonese and Mandarin).

🛏 162 🏊 💪 🗝 All
major cards

🏨 GRAND HYATT DELHI
🍴 $$$$

VASANT KUNJ PHASE II,
NELSON MANDELA RD.
TEL 011-612 1234
FAX 011-689 5891
E-MAIL info@hyattdelhi.com
WEBSITE www.hyatt.com

There are extensive leisure facilities at this out-of-town hotel, which opened in April 2001. It is situated between the upscale residential area southwest of downtown Delhi and the airport and boasts seven restaurants, a serious health club, outdoor spa bath and tennis courts, and both body jet showers and Japanese showers.

🛏 390 🏊 💪 🗝 All
major cards

🏨 IMPERIAL
🍴 $$$$

1 JANPATH
TEL 011-334 1234 OR
011-334 5678
FAX 011-334 5678
E-MAIL hotel@imperialindia.com

Built to the latest designs between 1933 and 1936 and now laboriously restored and refurbished by the original owners, the Singh family, this is once again one of Delhi's best hotels with a rare dose of original character. Being downtown, the coffee shop and garden are a welcome haven for exhausted shoppers. The Spice Route (Southeast Asian) restaurant is worth trying.

🛏 263 🏊 💪 🗝 All
major cards

🏨 INTER-CONTINENTAL
🍴 NEW DELHI
$$$$

BARAKHAMBA AVENUE,
CONNAUGHT PLACE
TEL 011-341 1001
FAX 011-341 2233
E-MAIL newdelhi@interconti.com

Huge and very central, this hotel's lobby is usually buzzing with locals and visitors trying to find their way to a party or meeting in one of a dozen banqueting rooms. There are four executive floors and six restaurants—including Baluchi (North Indian), Blue Elephant (Thai), and the Grill Room (Continental).

🛏 444 🏊 💪 🗝 All
major cards

🏨 LE MERIDIEN
🍴 $$$$

WINDSOR PLACE, JANPATH
TEL 011-371 0101
FAX 011-371 4645
E-MAIL meridien@nda.vsnl.net.in

Superbly located for sight-seeing, this less than attractive landmark with its huge atrium and capsule elevators has rooms overlooking Lutyens' New Delhi. Its pool is on the fourth floor. Being French, its Pierre restaurant is good; so are Pakwan (northern Indian) and Golden Phoenix (Cantonese and Szechuan).

🛏 353 🏊 💪 🗝 All
major cards

🏨 METROPOLITAN
HOTEL NIKKO NEW
DELHI
$$$$

BANGLA SAHIB RD.
TEL 011-334 2000
FAX 011-334 3000

HOTELS & RESTAURANTS

E-MAIL nikko@hotelnikkodelhi
.com
Opened in April 2001, this
state-of-the-art hotel lends its
guests laptop computers and
cellular phones, supplies
interactive TV, and keeps
them in shape with a health
spa, and happy with a
photographer; every room
has a shower. There is a
nonsmoking floor.
🛈 178 🖾 🗗 🅂 All
major cards

🏨 THE PARK
$$$$
15 PARLIAMENT ST.
TEL 011-373 3737
FAX 011-373 2025
E-MAIL resv.del@park.sprintrpg
.ems.vsnl.net.in
Right in the heart of New
Delhi, The Park offers good
walks around Lutyens'
centerpiece direct from the
hotel. Special rooms are
available for visitors with
disabilities.
🛈 224 🖾 🗗 🅂 All
major cards

🏨 RADISSON HOTEL
🍽 DELHI
$$$$
NATIONAL HIGHWAY 8,
TOWARD GURGAON
TEL 011-677 9191
FAX 011-677 9090
E-MAIL raddel@del2.vsnl.net.in
Close to both the
international and domestic
airports, this hotel is ideal for
those who want to catch a
few hours' sleep pre-, post- or
between flights; nonsmoking
rooms are available
on request. Choose between
three restaurants and
three bars before catching
the plane.
🛈 256 🅂 🖾 🗗 🅂 All
major cards

🏨 SURYA
🍽 $$$$
NEW FRIENDS COLONY
TEL 011-683 5070
FAX 011-683 7758
E-MAIL suryahot@ndf.vsnl.net.in
Located in a pleasant

residential area of New Delhi,
the hotel's residents are
pampered with a butler service
while locals come here to
enjoy the Sikandra (Mogul)
and Sampan (Cantonese and
Szechuan) restaurants.
🛈 234 🖾 🗗 🅂 All
major cards

🏨 TAJ PALACE
🍽 $$$$
2 SARDAR PATEL MARG,
CHANAKYAPURI
TEL 011-611 0202
FAX 011-611 0808
E-MAIL bctdp@tajgroup.sprintrpg
.ems.vsnl.net.in
Newer and larger than its
sister Taj Mahal (see p. 345),
the Taj Palace is centrally
located for sight-seeing.
Restaurants include Orient
Express (French), Handi
(northern Indian) and Tea
House of August Moon
(Chinese).
🛈 422 🖾 🗗 🅂 All
major cards

🏨 VASANT
CONTINENTAL
$$$$
BASANT LOK, VASANT VIHAR
TEL 011-614 8800 OR
011-614 1177
FAX 011-614 5959
E-MAIL hvc@del3.vsnl.net.in
A conveniently placed hotel
set midway between the
airports and downtown Delhi
in a fairly new and upscale
residential area. Classy locals
use the Canacona coffee
shop.
🛈 123 🅿 🅂 🖾 🗗
🅂 All major cards

🏨 CONNAUGHT
🍽 $$$
37 SHAHEED BHAGAT SINGH
MARG
TEL 011-336 4225
FAX 011-334 0757
E-MAIL prominenthotels@gems
.vsnl.net.in
This high-class international
business hotel has immaculate
rooms and personal service.
Thoughtful touches include
fruit and biscuits supplied in

each room. The rooms on
the upper floors have great
views of the city, and there is
a choice of restaurants.
🛈 80 🅿 🅂 🗗 🅂 All
major cards

🏨 SAMRAT
🍽 $$$
KAUTILYA MARGI
TEL 011-611 0606
FAX 011-688 7047
In an excellent location, this
establishment offers
economical apartments if you
are planning a long stay. The
facilities are comprehensive
and include the Baradari
(Indian and Continental)
restaurant.
🛈 255 plus16 apartments
🖾 🗗 🅂 All major cards

🏨 AMBASSADOR
$$
SUJAN SINGH PARK
TEL 011-463 2600
FAX 011-463 8219 OR
011-463 2252
E-MAIL ambassador.delhi@
tajhotels.com.
Like the Imperial and
Claridges (see p. 345), this is
an early New Delhi hotel
built near Lodi Gardens in
1951 by the entrepreneurial
engineer Sir Shoba Singh.
Spacious lawns surround the
hotel. Part of the Taj chain.
🛈 88 🅂 All major cards

🏨 HANS PLAZA
🍽 $$
15 BARAKHAMBA RD.
TEL 011-3316861
FAX 011-331 4830
E-MAIL hansotel@nde.vsnl.net.in
This no-frills hotel on the
16th–20th floors of a building
on Connaught Circus has
superb views over the city; the
Clay and Coal (northern
Indian) restaurant is a plus.
🛈 67 🅂 All major cards

🏨 INDIA HABITAT
CENTRE
$
LODI RD.
TEL 011-468 2222
FAX 011-468 2052

E-MAIL enquiry@habitatworld.com.

The concept here is of a balanced ecological environment: Guests are accommodated within a major downtown arts complex, which, as well as hotel rooms and facilities, is equipped with theaters, auditoria, exhibit halls, and specialty restaurants.

🛈 58 ❄ 🏊 🏋 🅰 All major cards

🏨 JANPATH
$$
JANPATH
TEL 011-334 0070
FAX 011-334 7083
E-MAIL janpath@ndf.vsnl.net.in
In a good location as a base for sight-seeing, this hotel has simple facilities, but offers the Gulnar (Mogul) and Orbit (Continental) restaurants.

🛏 213 🅰 All major cards

🏨 NIRULA'S
🍽 **$$**
L BLOCK,
CONNAUGHT CIRCUS
TEL 011-332 2419
FAX 011-335 3957
E-MAIL delhihotel@nirula.com
Best known among Delhi's young people for its ice-cream parlor, pastry shop, and **Chinese Room** (Szechuan) restaurant. What you lose in peace, you gain in location and value for money.

🛈 29 🅰 DC, MC, V

🏨 OBEROI MAIDENS
$$
7 SHAM NATH MARG,
CIVIL LINES
TEL 011-397 5464
FAX 011-398 0771
E-MAIL bsparmar@tomdel.com
Situated north of Old Delhi, this hotel was built in 1900 by Mr. Maiden when this area was backwater Delhi. Sir Edwin Lutyens stayed here while his New Delhi was being built to the south. Charming period furniture, well-tended gardens, and tennis court.

🛈 54 🏊 🅰 All major cards

🏨 ASIAN INTERNATIONAL
$
JANPATH LANE
TEL 011-334 0101
FAX 011-334 0202
E-MAIL asian@hotels asian.com
On a quiet lane between Connaught Place and Lutyens centerpieces.

🛈 40 🅰 AE, MC, V

🏨 BROADWAY
🍽 **$**
4/15A ASAF ALI RD.
TEL 011-327 3821
FAX 011-326 9966
E-MAIL owhpl@nda.vsnl.net.in
Located between Connaught Place and Old Delhi, this is a simple hotel for those on a tight budget, and contrasts with its in-house upscale Chor Bizarre restaurant (which also has a branch in London's Mayfair). If you're on a tour of Old Delhi, this is a good option for lunch.

🛈 28 🅰 All major cards

🏨 CENTRAL COURT
🍽 **$**
N BLOCK, CONNAUGHT CIRCUS
TEL 011-331 5013
FAX 011-331 7582
One of the oldest hotels in Connaught Place, with a large terrace and three restaurants.

🛈 36 🅰 All major cards

🏨 RANJIT
$
MAHARAJA RANJIT SINGH RD.
TEL 011-323 1256
FAX 011-323 166
Well situated for Old Delhi sights, this hotel has a good restaurant serving northern and southern Indian dishes.

🛏 185 🏊 🅰 DC, MC, V

🏨 YORK
$
K-BLOCK,
CONNAUGHT CIRCUS
TEL 011-332 9169

PRICES	
HOTELS	

An indication of the cost of a double room without breakfast is given by **$** signs.

$$$$$	Over $280
$$$$	$160–$280
$$$	$100–$160
$$	$40–$100
$	Under $40

RESTAURANTS

An indication of the cost of a three-course dinner without drinks is given by $ signs.

$$$$$	Over $80
$$$$	$50–$80
$$$	$35–$50
$$	$20–$35
$	Under $20

FAX 011-335 2419
Conveniently set in the busy commercial hub of Delhi, the York is a no-frills but quiet establishment on the upper floors. Its two restaurants cover five cuisines.

🛏 27 🅰 AE, MC, V

🏨 MAHARANI GUEST HOUSE
$
3 SUNDAR NAGAR
TEL 011-469 3128
FAX 011-462 4562
E-MAIL maharani@newdelhi.net
Situated in a central, upscale residential area near Purana Qila. A simple, clean, comfortable, and friendly hotel with good bathrooms and 24-hour room service.

🛈 24 ❄ 🅰 All major cards

🏨 SHERWANI FORT VIEW
$$
11 SUNDAR NAGAR
TEL 011-463 5831
FAX 011-469 4226
Situated close to the Maharani Guest House (see above), the Sherwani offers a slightly higher standard of accommodation, with comfortable rooms.

🛈 16 🅰 All major cards

❄ Air-conditioning 🏊 Indoor/🏊 Outdoor swimming pool 🏋 Health club 🅰 Credit cards   **KEY**

🏨 YMCA TOURIST HOTEL

$

JAI SINGH RD.

TEL 011-336 1915

FAX011-374 6032

E-MAIL ymcath@ndf.vsnl.net.in

Open to both men and
women, despite the name. In
a superb location, with family
rooms available. Reservations
essential.

ⓘ 106   🚭 AE

🏨 YWCA INTERNATIONAL GUEST HOUSE

$

SANSAD MARG (PARLIAMENT
ST.)

TEL 011-336 1561

FAX 011-334 1763

E-MAIL ywcaind@del3.vsnl.net.in

As with the YMCA hotel, this
is open to both men and
women. Situated on Parliament
Street, it lies close to Lutyens'
Delhi. Accommodation is
fairly basic, but still a good
value. Reservations are
essential.

ⓘ 24   🚭 AE

🍴 COCONUT GROVE

$$

ASHOK YATRI NIWAR,
19 ASHOK RD.

TEL 011-336 8553

Discerning southern Indians
detour here for the home-
style food.

🍴 LA'ZEEZ AFFAIRE

$$

MALCHA MARG MARKET

Try the rich regional dishes
of the Punjab, Lucknow,
Hyderabad, and Kashmir from
the wide-ranging and varied
menu offered here.

🍴 COFFEE HOUSE CAFÉ

$

BABA KHARAK SINGH MARG

Enjoy a restorative coffee
and sambar snack here when
you are worn out from
shopping at the string of state
emporia. Conveniently
situated between blocks A
and B, it is an essential shop-
until-you-drop stop.

🍴 NATIONAL MUSEUM OF HANDICRAFTS

$

PRAGATI MAIDAN,
BHAIRON RD.

TEL 011-331 7641 OR
011-337 1887

One of the few museums in
India to have a café, and a
excellent one at that. A good
stop even if you're not visiting
the museum.

🍴 VILLAGE BISTRO COMPLEX

$

12 HAUS KHAS VILLAGE,
NEAR DEER PARK

TEL 011-685 3857

Several rustic restaurants in
one building, including a
rooftop one, overlooking Khilji
and Tuglaq remains and
surrounded by upscale
boutiques. A variety of
cuisines is offered, as well as
live entertainment. Popular for
brunch.

🚭 All major cards

🍴 VILLAGE RESTAURANT COMPLEX

$

SIRI FORT,
OFF SRI AUROBINDO RD.

As at the Village Bistro
Complex (see above),
picturesque ruins are the
setting for good food and a
fun atmosphere.

🚭 All major cards

SOMETHING SPECIAL

🍴 KARIM'S

For the adventurous
gourmand, a trip to Karim's,
one of Old Dehi's few surviving
traditional restaurants, is a must.
Find it down Gulli Kababian
(Alley of the Kebab), a tiny lane
on the south side of the Jami
Masjid. As you enter you pass
the kebab cooks and find five
dining rooms that serve a hearty
breakfast of *nahar* (morning
lamb curry) and *khameeri roti*
(bread) and then go nonstop
until midevening. You can watch
chefs brewing up their cauldrons

and bakers rolling and stuffing
their dough, then maybe try
some *shami kebabs*, a dish of
badam pasanda (aromatic lamb)
and, of course, hot fresh breads
such as *roomali roti, kulcha,* or
naan.

$$

GULLI KABABIAN

WEEKENDS AWAY

Here are five hotels ideal for a
weekend of peace in the
country.

🏨 THE MUD FORT, KUCHESAR

$

KUCHESAR,
UTTAR PRADESH

About two hours' drive east
of Delhi, Neemrana Hotels
has beautifully refurbished
part of a rambling fort.
Isolated amid farmland and
villages, it offers simplicity and
total peace. Make reservations
through Neemrana hotels
(see p. 343)

🚭 All major cards

🏨 NEEMRANA FORT

$

NEEMRANA,
RAJASTHAN

Midway between Delhi and
Jaipur, this beautifully
renovated, magnificent 15th-
century fort is a favorite for
Delhi escapes. Exquisite suites
are available. Excellent food.
Make reservations through
Neemrana Hotels (see p.
343).

ⓘ 41   🚭 All major cards

🏨 PATAUDI PALACE

$$

PATAUDI,
DIST. GURGAON

TEL 0124-74082

Lutyens-inspired country
house with original furnishings,
set amid rose gardens in a
quiet village off the Delhi–
Jaipur road. The house is still
used by descendants of the
Nawabs of Pataudi.

ⓘ 15   🚭 All major cards

🏨 RAMGARH LODGE
$$
JAMUVA RAMGARH
TEL 01426-552217 OR
01426-52079
Two 19th-century British-built bungalows, immaculately restored and furnished in period style, set in orchards and gardens northeast of Delhi. With fine views of the Kumauns, this is an ideal escape or pause en route to either Corbett National Park or the hills.
🛏 5　⊗ AE, DC, MC,

🏨 TIKLI BOTTOM
MANENDEER FARM,
GAIRATBUR BAS, TIKLI,
GURGAON, HARYANA
TEL 0124-636 1881
FAX 011-335 1272
E-MAIL honiwala@vsnl.com
Two long-standing residents of Delhi, Annie and Martin Howard have created a spacious and luxurious Lutyens-style mansion in the country, an hour's drive west of Delhi. Very tranquil.
🛏 4　⊗ None

AROUND DELHI

The Delhi–Agra and Delhi–Jaipur roads are home to several well-run restaurants with good rest rooms and, sometimes, gardens. Try the ones at Hodel and Kosi. For trekkers, the Kumaun Mandal Vikas Nigam (KMVN) runs almost 50 modest places to stay scattered through the Kumaun Hills region. Reserve through KMVN, Oak Park House, Mallital Nainital, tel 05942-36209.

AGRA

Most Agra hotels are fairly laid-back, but royal Mogul food can be very good.

🏨 AMARVILAS
$$$$$
TAJ EAST GATE RD.
TEL 0562-231515
FAX 0562-231516

E-MAIL reservations@amarvilas .com OR gm@amarvilas.com
Part of the Oberoi group, this is a super-deluxe, Mogul-style palace hotel that opened in 2001. It has the best hotel room views of the Taj Mahal in town. All rooms include butler service. (Oberoi also has a more modest Trident hotel here.)
🛏 16　❄　🛁　⊗ All major cards

🏨 JAYPEE PALACE
$$$
FATEHABAD RD.
TEL 0562-330800
FAX 0562-330850
E-MAIL jaypeeag@ned.vsnl.net.in
Huge hotel sprawling over 25 acres of gardens. Plenty of sports facilities are available to complement the vast indoor spaces and seven restaurants that include Mogul and Chinese cuisine, and a huge buffet.
🛏 350　❄　🛁　⊗ AE, V

🏨 MOGHAL SHERATON
$$$
TAJ GANJ,
FATEHABAD RD.
TEL 0562-331701
FAX 0562-331730
E-MAIL mughal@welcomgroup .com
This Welcomgroup hotel is housed in an elegant, low-lying, and award-winning Mogul-influenced building set in 27 acres of gardens. Higher rooms have views of the Taj Mahal. Good Mogul food is served in the restaurant.
🛏 300　❄　🛁　⊗ All major cards

🏨 TAJ VIEW
$$
FATEHABAD RD.
TEL 0562-331841
FAX 0562-331860
E-MAIL tajview.agra@tajhotels.com
Good for its view of the Taj Mahal from rooms on the upper floors, and for its swimming pool. Its restaurants are less impressive.
🛏 100　❄　🛁　⊗ All major cards

🏨 MANSINGH PALACE
$
FATEHABAD RD.
TEL 0562-331771
FAX 0562-330202
E-MAIL mansingh.agra@ mailcity.com
A well-run, unpretentious establishment in a good location.
🛏 97　❄　🛁　⊗ AE, MC, V

🍴 DASAPRAKASH
$
1 GWALIOR RD.
TEL 0562-260269
Locals come here for the good southern Indian food. The menus can be limited, but the eating is always good. Try the onion *rawa masala dosas*.

AMRITSAR

🏨 RITZ PLAZA
$$
45 THE MALL
TEL 0183-226606
FAX 0183-226657
E-MAIL ritz@del3.vsnl.net.in
Amritsar's oldest hotel, now comfortably refurbished, stands in gardens in a quiet northern suburb.
🛏 35　❄　⊗ All major cards

🏨 MRS. BHANDARI'S GUEST HOUSE
$
10 CANTONMENT
TEL 0183-222390
FAX 0183-222390
Family-run colonial home conveniently close to the railway station, unchanged since the 1950s. It boasts a devoted clientele of overland travelers who appreciate the home-style atmosphere.
🛏 12　❄　⊗ None

BANDHAVGARH NATIONAL PARK

🏨 BANDHAVGARH JUNGLE CAMP
$$$
TALA
TEL 011-685 4626

HOTELS & RESTAURANTS

FAX 011-686 4614
Riverside tents with hot
showers are pitched in the
gardens of a Maharaja's
hunting lodge. Make
reservations through B/21
Greater Kailash Enclave II,
New Delhi.
🛈 10 twin-bedded tents
🚭 None

BHARATPUR

🏨 LAXMI VILAS PALACE
$
KAKAJI-KI-KOTHI,
RAGHUNATH NIVAS,
AGRA RD.
TEL 05644-22722
FAX 05644-22864
WEBSITE www.laxmivilas.com
Pavilioned and painted *haveli*,
with original furnishings and a
homey atmosphere.
🛈 25 🏊 🚭 None

BHOPAL

🏨 NOOR-US-SABAH
$$
VIP RD.
LOHE-FIZA
TEL 0755-749101
FAX 0755-749110
E-MAIL reliable@bom4.vsnl.net.in
A renovated 1920s royal
palace with rooms
overlooking the city's lake.
Good food, nice pool. A
Welcomgroup hotel.
🛈 70 🏊 🚭 All major
cards

CHANDIGARH

🏨 MOUNTVIEW
$$
SECTOR 10
TEL 0172-740544
FAX 0172-742220
This hotel makes for a
practical base for visiting both
Chandigarh and Patiala.
🛈 59 🏊 🏋 🚭 All major
cards

🏨 NALAGAR FORT-
PALACE
NALAGAR
TEL 01795-23009
FAX 01795-23021

En route from Chandigarh to
Shimla. This family-run 15th-
century palace hotel has views
looking over the small town of
Nalagar, and across to the
Shivalik Hills.
🛈 35 🚭 All major cards

CORBETT NATIONAL
PARK

Some basic accommodations
(cabins, log huts, etc.) are
available within the park, but
these are disappointing (see
p. 126).

🏨 INFINITY RESORTS
$$
RAMNAGAR
TEL 05946-85279
FAX 05946-85280
EMAIL info@tigertopsindia.com
On a bluff overlooking the
Kosi River—great for a swim.
The resort offers spacious
rooms, good food, and
excellent naturalists who will
take guests into the forest for
one-day treks or overnight
stays.
🛈 24 🚭 All major cards

GWALIOR

🏨 USHA KIRAN PALACE
$$
JAYENDRAGANJ, LASHKAR,
BESIDE JAI VILAS (CITY
PALACE)
TEL 0751-323993
FAX 0751-321103
WEBSITE www.fhrai.com
High 1930s architecture and
furnishings in a royal guest
house. Once providing guest
accommodation for the local
maharaja, this is now a
comfortable hotel run by
Welcomgroup.
🛈 28 🚭 All major cards

KANHA
NATIONAL PARK

🏨 WILD CHALET
RESORT
$$
MOCHA
TEL 07649-77205
FAX 07649-77203

Well outside the park, but the
all-in-one price includes a
river view chalet, good food,
and resident naturalists.
🛈 16 🚭 AE for bookings

KHAJURAHO

All hotels and restaurants are
near the western group of
temples.

🏨 CHANDELA
$$
JHANSI RD.
TEL 07686-72355
FAX 07686-72365
E-MAIL chandela.khajurao@
tajhotels.com
Serviceable hotel with two
stories of rooms around the
pool and situated just a short
walk from the temples.
🛈 94 🏊 🏋 🚭 All major
cards

🏨 JASS OBEROI
$$
TEL 07686-42344
FAX 07686-42345
The low-rise, whitewashed
rooms at this hotel overlook
the gracious lawns and
swimming pool.
🛈 94 🏊 🚭 All major
cards

🍴 MEDITERRANEO
$$
JAIN TEMPLE RD.
Israeli and Korean dishes
served in addition to the
regular menu, an inspiration
on the part of the Italian
proprietor.

MANDU

🏨 JHIRA BAGH PALACE
$
MANDU RD,
DHAR
TEL 07292-322850
FAX 07292-35097
Accommodations in Mandu
are fairly basic, so this heritage
hotel, located a 40-minute
drive away, may be more
appropriate for those needing
greater comfort.
🏊 🏋 🚭 All major cards

MATHURA

🏨 MADHUBAN
$

KRISHNA NAGAR
TEL 0565-420058
FAX 0565-420064
Clean and practical, this hotel makes a good base for visiting both Mathura and the nearby Braj villages.

🏊 🏋️ All major cards

MUSSOORIE

🏨 CLARIDGES NABHA
$$

BARLOWGANJ RD.
TEL 0135-631426
FAX 0135-631425
This is a former palace of the maharaja of Nabha, which still retains its elegance and period furnishings. The extensive gardens are planted with both cedar and oak trees. No single or twin rooms available.

🛈 22 🏋️ All major cards

NAINITAL

🏨 BELVEDERE PALACE
$$$

AWAGARH ESTATE,
MALLITAL
TEL 05942-37434
FAX 05942-35082
E-MAIL belvederepalace@
vsnl.com
Built in 1897 as the summer palace of the rajas of Awagarh, this palace has been renovated as a hotel.

🛈 18 🏋️ MC V

ORCHHA

🏨 SHEESH MAHAL
$

TEL 07680-52624
This hotel is made up of simply furnished rooms situated inside part of Orchha's fort complex. The setting is glorious, and there is a rooftop suite complete with a terrace and panoramic view.

🛈 8 🏋️ All major cards

RISHIKESH

🏨 THE GLASSHOUSE
$

14 MILES (23 KM) NW OF
RISHIKESH
Peaceful bungalow set among an orchard and gardens overlooking the Ganga and the mountains 14 miles (23 km) above Rishikesh. Ideal for reading, painting, swimming, and walking. Vegetarian food and beer are served in the restaurant; no meat or spirits are available. Reservations should be made through Neemrana Hotels (see p. 343)

🛈 5 plus cottages 🏊 🍴
🏋️ All major cards

SANCHI

🏨 TRAVELLERS LODGE
$

ON BHOPAL RD.
TEL 0755-534340
FAX 0755-552384
Simple lodge, situated a brisk walk from Sanchi's *stupa*, making it ideal for sunrise and sunset visits to the site. Make reservations through Bhopal office of Madhya Pradesh Tourist Office (see p. 114).

🛈 8

SHIMLA

🏨 CECIL
$$$$

CHAURA MAIDAN,
THE MALL
TEL 0177-204848
FAX 0177-211024
E-MAIL reservations@thececil.com
The Oberoi group's first hotel, now restored to its Edwardian splendor, which makes the most of its prime location. Even if you don't stay here, sampling the full afternoon tea in the vast lobby is an essential experience of your trip to Shimla.

🛈 79 🏊 🍴 🏋️ All major cards

🏨 WILD FLOWER HALL
$$$$

MASHOBA,
CHHARABARA
TEL 07748-0808
FAX 07748-0909
Lord Kitchener's rebuilt country house set in the glorious and peaceful forested Dhauladhar and Garhwal Mountains, a 40-minute drive from Shimla. High standards and superb facilities include open-air Jacuzzi and spa.

🛈 86 🏊 🍴 🏋️ All major cards

🏨 WOODVILLE PALACE
$$$

RAJ BHAWAN RD.
TEL 0177-223919 OR
0177-224038
FAX 0177-223098
WEBSITE www.fhrai.com
Half a mile from The Mall, this is a 1930s mansion built by the Raja Rana of Jubbal. It retains its fine craftsmanship, decor, and furnishings, and is set in four acres (1.5 ha) of lush gardens. Indian, Chinese, and Continental cuisine served in the restaurant. Reservations essential. Part of the Oberoi group.

🛈 15 🏋️ AE, MC, V

RAJASTHAN & GUJARAT

This colorful area of India, so popular with first-time visitors to India, has numerous charming heritage hotels, with more opening each year. These hotels should be very much a part of your vacation.

Note: Much of western Gujarat is still recovering from the devastating earthquake of January 2001.

RAJASTHAN

ALWAR, DIG, & SARISKA NATIONAL PARK

🏨 KESROLI HILL FORT
$

KESROLI
Isolated, 14th-century turreted fort containing surprisingly delicate rooms. Come here for rural peace. Make reservations through Neemrana hotels (see p. 343).

🛏 21   🅰 All major cards

🏨 SARISKA PALACE
$$$

JAIPUR RD.,
SARISKA
TEL 0144-841322 OR
0144-841324
RESERVATIONS: 011-617 2346
FAX 0144-841323
E-MAIL sariska@del2.vsnl.net.in
A huge hunting lodge that once belonged to the colorful Alwar rulers of this region. With extensive gardens, it is situated right by the entrance to Sariska National Park.

🛏 112   🅿   🛗   🅰 All major cards

AMER & PUSHKAR

During the Pushkar Cattle Fair (see p. 382), Welcomgroup (see p. 343) pitches its mobile Royal Camp in Pushkar. For details e-mail udp@ndf.vsnl.net.in or see website www.marudharhotels.com.

🏨 DEOGARH MAHAL
$

DEOGARH
TEL 02904-52777
FAX 02904-52555
E-MAIL deogarh@datainfosys.net
An established, imaginatively restored, family-run heritage hotel, with attractive rooms scattered around the rambling hilltop palace. A favorite with discerning travelers, it provides facilities for disabled travelers.

🛏 36   🅿   🅰 MC, V

🏨 KUCHAMAN FORT
$$$

KUCHAMAN
TEL 01586-20476/20882 OR
01586-20882
FAX 01586-20884
E-MAIL sariska@del2.vsnl.net.in
Fairy-tale bastioned hilltop fort north of Amer, which was closed to the public for most of the 20th century. Pleasant rooms. You can ramble around the fort, swim in the old outdoor built-in pools, and explore the village.

🛏 51   🅿   🅰 All major cards

BIKANER

🏨 KARNI BHAWAN
🍴 PALACE
$$$

GANDHI NAGAR
TEL 0151-524701 OR 0151-524703
FAX 0151-522408
E-MAIL lphm.hrh@axcess.dot.in
This attractive hotel was built in art-deco style by a local maharaja and stands on landscaped grounds. A feature of the hotel is its restaurant, serving authentic Marwari cuisine.

🛏 10   🅰 AE, MC, V

🏨 LALLGARH PALACE
$$$

GANGA AVE.
TEL 0151-540201
FAX 0151-522253
E-MAIL gm.bikaner@itchotels.co.in
Built during the last half of the 19th century to Sir Samuel Swinton Jacobs' designs, this spectacular palace features delicate stone carving inspired by the local fort. As at Jodhpur, guests stay in one part of the palace, while former royals and museum exhibits fill the rest. Doctor and astrologer on call. A Welcomgroup hotel.

🛏 38   🅿   🅰 AE, MC, V

🏨 GAJNER PALACE
$$

GAJNER, TEH
TEL 01534-55063
FAX 0151-55060
E-MAIL resv@hrhindia.com
Built in the 1890s as an extravagant, lakeside royal hunting lodge with Waring and Gillows furniture that survives today. Good for bird-watching.

🅿   🍴   🅰 AE, MC, V

🏨 MAAN BILAS PALACE
$$

LALGARH PALACE COMPLEX
TEL 0151-524711 OR
0151-540220
FAX 0151-522408
This comfortable and attractive hotel is set on the grounds of historic Lalgarh Palace. The dining room offers a choice of Continental cuisine or traditional Rajasthani dishes.

🛏 9   🅰 AE, MC

🏨 BHANWAR NIWAS
$

RAMPURIA ST.
TEL 0151-529323
FAX 0151-200880
Right in the old town, this family-run *haveli* is beautifully decorated and furnished.

🛏 14   🅰 All major cards

BUNDI

🏨 HAWELI BRIJ BHUSHANJI
$

TEL 0747-412127
A charmingly run, beautifully restored house in the heart of medieval Bundi.

🛏 16   🅰 None

CHITTAURGARH

🏨 CASTLE BIJAPUR
$
TEL 01472-40094
FAX 01472-40769
This small, family-run, and friendly hotel has rooms overlooking the fort's inner garden. Good horseback riding offered.
🛏 16 🔲 All major cards

JAIPUR

The large and formerly wonderful Rambagh Palace and Jai Mahal Palace have a certain tired splendor, and equally uncommitted staff. The following suggested hotels retain their character and have a more charming and helpful staff. In addition, more than 150 Jaipur homes belong to the paying guest program: To reserve rooms contact the Rajasthan Tourist Reception Center, tel 0141-365256.

🏨 RAJVILAS
$$$$
GONER RD.,
OFF THE JAIPUR–AGRA HWY.
TEL 0141-640101
FAX 0141-640202
E-MAIL reservations@rajvilas.com
Once inside the classy Oberoi's specially built, luxurious resort, you could easily forget about driving 40 minutes to sight-see in Jaipur. Villas and tented rooms overlook the swimming pool of this delightful oasis in the dry lands of Rajasthan. Rajvilas was voted Hotel of the Year 2001 by the U.K.'s *Tatler* magazine.
🛏 71 🌊 🎽 🔲 All major cards

🏨 RAJ PALACE
$$$
CHOMU HAVELI,
JORAWAR SINGH GATE,
AMER RD.
TEL 0141-634077
FAX 0141-630489 OR
0141-373119
E-MAIL grvhotel@jpl.net.in

This lavishly renovated, beautifully decorated and furnished palace makes an excellent hotel. Very central.
🛏 25 🌊 🔲 All major cards

🏨 RAJPUTANA PALACE SHERATON
$$$
PALACE RD.
TEL 0141-360011
FAX 0141-367848
Jaipur-inspired, specially built downtown hotel. Strong on character, food, and local entertainment.
🛏 216 🌊 🎽 🔲 All major cards

🏨 TRIDENT
$$$
OPPOSITE JAL MAHAL,
AMER FORT RD.
TEL 0141-630101
FAX 041-630303
E-MAIL trident@jp1.vsnl.net.in
The Oberoi chain's more modest alternative to Rajvilas. Opened in 1997, this custom-built hotel has state-of-the-art facilities.
🛏 138 🌊 🔲 All major cards

🏨 RAJ MAHAL PALACE
$$
SARDAR PATEL MARG
TEL 0141-383260
FAX 0141-381887
E-MAIL rajmahalpalace@
sancharnet.in
Used as the British Residency from 1821, this hotel maintains an elegant and relaxed family feel, and is set among lush gardens. Formerly run by the Taj group, it has now been returned to its owners, the former Jaipur royal family.
🛏 21 🌊 🔲 All major cards

🏨 ALSISAR HAVELI
$$
SANSAR CHANDRA RD.
TEL 0141-368290 OR
0141-36485
FAX 0141-364652
WEBSITE www.haveli.com

Intimate and pretty 1890s hotel in the center of town, run by the owners.
🛏 30 🌊 🔲 All major cards

🏨 RAMGARH LODGE
$$
JAMUVA RAMGARH
TEL 01426-52217 OR
01426-52078
FAX 01426-52079
For a perfect escape from India's bustle, stay at the isolated hunting lodge of Ramgarh, about half an hour's drive from Jaipur. The hotel overlooks Ramgarh Lake.
🌊 🔲 All major cards

🏨 ARYA NIWAS
$
SANSAR CHANDRA RD.
TEL 0141-372456
FAX 0141-361871
E-MAIL aryahotl@jpl.net.in
Good inexpensive accommodations in a quiet side-street near the heart of Jaipur. No frills, but spotlessly clean, and with a high quality of service. Hostel-style restaurant serving good, simple cooking (including Western staples) to a high standard.
🌊 🔲 AE, MC, V

🏨 KARAULI HOUSE
$
NEW SANGANER RD.,
SODALA
TEL 0141-211532
FAX 0141-210512
E-MAIL karauli@jp1.dot.net.in
WEBSITE www.karauli.com
Spacious gardens surround the Jaipur residence of the maharaja of Karauli. Home stay in this attractive villa offers plain but elegant rooms, and an unhurried atmosphere.
🌊 🔲 All major cards

🏨 NARAIN NIWAS
$
NARAIN SINGH RD.
TEL 0141-561291
FAX 0141-561045
One of a number of *havelis* (courtyard houses) built by

Jaipur courtiers south of the walled city. Popular with discerning, experienced visitors to India.
🛏 31   🏊   💳 AE, MC, V

🏨 SAMODE HAVELI
$
GANGAPOL,
INSIDE AMER GATE
TEL 0141-632407
FAX 0141-631942
E-MAIL reservations@samode.com
The historic town house of the Samode family (see p. 133), with nicely decorated rooms and a relaxing courtyard. Reservations essential.
🛏 22   💳 All major cards

JAISALMER

During the Jaisalmer Desert Fair (see p. 380), Welcomgroup (see p. 343) pitches its mobile Royal Camp in Jaisalmer. For details e-mail udp@ndf.vsnl.net.in or visit website www.marudharhotels.com

🏨 GORBANDH PALACE
$$$
1 TOURIST COMPLEX,
SAM RD. (15.5 MILES/25 KM FROM JAISALMER)
TEL 02992-53801
FAX 02992-53811
E-MAIL jaisalmer@hrhindia.com
This HRH group hotel is a traditional stone building around a central courtyard with a great swimming pool.
🛏 67   🏊   💳   💳 All major cards

🏨 JAHAWAR NIWAS PALACE
$$
1 BADA BAGH RD.
TEL 02992-52208
FAX 02992-52288
E-MAIL jawarniwaspalace@yahoo.com
Once the palace of the former ruler of Jaisalmer, it has been redeveloped into a charming small hotel. Situated right near the fort.
🛏 22   🏊   💳 AE, MC, V

🏨 RAWAL-KOT
$$
JODHPUR–JAISALMER RD.
TEL 02992-51874
FAX 02992-50444
Overlooking Jaisalmer, this Welcomgroup Hotel features modern yet traditional style, and furnishings. Indian, Chinese, and Continental cuisine served.
🛏 31   🅿   💳   🏊   💳 AE, MC, V

JODHPUR

🏨 BAL SAMAND PALACE
$$$
MANDORE RD.
TEL 0291-572327 OR 0291-572321
FAX 0291-571240
E-MAIL ubp@ndf.vsnl.net.in
WEBSITE www.marudharhotels.com
Suites and garden rooms in a large, sandstone royal recreation palace 5 miles (8 km) outside town. The hotel overlooks a lake built in the 13th century as a reservoir to supply Jodhpur with drinking water. Lovely gardens. Ayoma and ayurvedic health spa.
🛏 35   🏊   💳 AE, MC, V

🏨 UMAID BHAWAN PALACE
$$$
CHITTAR HILL (3 MILES/5 KM FROM CITY CENTER)
TEL 0291-510101
FAX 0291-510100
E-MAIL ubp@ndf.vsnl.net.in
WEBSITE www.marudharhotels.com
This hotel is the ultimate royal extravagance. The hotel fills just a third of the vast palace, built as a famine relief project to designs by H. V. Lanchester and completed in 1945. There are huge rooms, fun suites, a circular indoor pool, brass beaux arts front doors, and more. Sensitively maintained by the Welcomgroup. Good food.
🛏 98   🏊   🍴   💳 AE, MC, V

🏨 ROHIT GARH
$$
ROHIT GARH
TEL 0926-68231
FAX 0926-649368
A small lakeside royal Rathore home, 25 miles (40 km) from the capital. Horseback riding or jeep rides can be arranged to visit local Bishnoi villages.
🛏 25   🏊   💳 All major cards

🏨 JHALAMANDGARH
$
POST JHALAMAND
TEL 0291-740481
FAX 0291-741125
An 18th-century castle in Marwar style situated 7 miles (12 km) south of Jodhpur. The arcaded courtyard makes an attractive lobby. Folk music and dances offered some evenings. Safaris arranged to the Guda Bishnoi Lake wildlife sanctuary.
🛏 18

KISHANGAR

🏨 ROOPANGARH FORT
$$
ROOPANGARH
TEL 01463-7217
The Kishangar rulers' old capital centered on this impressive, rambling 1653 fort. Rooms are in a later part of the building that features great views. There is a charming village below the fort.
🛏 20   💳 All major cards

KOTAH

🏨 BRIJ RAJ BHAWAN
$$
CIVIL LINES
TEL 0744-450529
FAX 0744-450057
WEBSITE www.heritagehotels.com/brijraj
This modest palace brims with charm and original furnishings. The colonial-style building, with attractive lawns and terrace gardens, is set on the banks of the Chambal River.
🛏 8   🍴   💳 MC, V

KEY   🏨 Hotel   🍴 Restaurant   🛏 No. of bedrooms   🍴 No. of places   🅿 Parking   🕐 Closed   🛗 Elevator

PALKYIA HAVELI
$$
MOKHA-PARA
TEL 0744-327375
Family-run, traditional
courtyard house in the center
of town. A peaceful hotel with
pretty rooms.
[] 8 None

UMED BHAWAN PALACE
$$
PALACE RD.
TEL 0744-325262
FAX 0744-451110
The maharao of Kota's richly
carved warren of a home has
huge rooms with original
furnishings. Good food. A
Welcomgroup hotel.
[] 32 [] All major
cards

KUMBHALGARH

AODHI HOTEL
$$
OUTSIDE KUMBHALGARH
FORT
TEL 02954-42341
FAX 02954-42349
In harmony with the rugged
and hilly landscape, this
beautiful, modern stone hotel
has good food and, remark-
ably, a pool. Ideal for visiting
the finest of 32 fortresses
built by Rana Kumbha. Run by
HRH group (see p. 343).
 AE, V

MOUNT ABU

CONNAUGHT HOUSE
$$
RAJENDRA MARG, OPPOSITE
BUS STAND
TEL 02974-38560
FAX 02974-38900
E-MAIL udp@ndf.vsnl.net.in
WEBSITE www.marudharhotels
.com
In the hills tradition, this
English-style country cottage
with a pretty garden was once
a summer retreat for Marwar
state's chief minister. A
Welcomgroup hotel.
Reservations essential.
[] 14 V

NAGAUR

ROYAL CAMP, NAGAUR
$$$
NAGAUR FORT
TEL 0291-572321
FAX 0291-571240
E-MAIL ubp@ndf.vsnl.net.in
WEBSITE www.marudharhotels
.com
From December to March,
Welcomgroup pitches
luxurious tents inside the fort.
Welcomgroup also has a
mobile Royal Camp that visits
three Rajasthan fairs: Pushkar
(camels), Nagaur (cattle), and
Jaisalmer (desert culture).
[] 20 tents All major
cards

KHIMSAR FORT
$$
KHIMSAR
TEL 0141-382314
FAX 0141-381150
E-MAIL khimsar@jp1.net.in
WEBSITE www.khimsarfort.com
This beautifully renovated,
well-established, family-run
16th-century desert fort is
now part of Welcomgroup. A
large pool and lawns lie within
the massive bastioned walls.
Good for visits to Nagaur
Fort and the Jain temples at
Osian. Continental, Indian, and
Rajasthani cuisine served.
[] 50 [] 🏊 🏋️ All
major cards

NAWALGARH

ROOP NIWAS PALACE
$$
SHEKAWALI
TEL 01594-22006 OR
01594-24152
FAX 01594 23388
This quiet palace exudes
faded grandeur. Located on
the town's outskirts.
[] 35 P [] [] 🏊
 AE

OSIAN

FORT CHANWA
$
LUNI
TEL 0291-432460

Richly carved, 18th-century
desert fort, whose courtyards
and narrow stairs lead to
cleverly furnished little rooms.
Ideally situated for trips into
tribal areas.
 All major cards

RANAKPUR

MAHARANI BAGH ORCHARD
$$
SADRI
TEL 02934-85105
FAX 02934-85151
Custom-built traditional-style
rooms with deep verandas
are arranged among orchards
laid out in the 19th century
by the Jodhpur royals. The
restaurant makes a good stop
for lunch if you are visiting
Ranakpur.
[] 18 🏊 DC, V

RAWLA NARLAI
$
NARLAI
TEL 0291-510410
FAX 0291-63774
E-MAIL narlai@bigfoot.com
Charmingly refurbished
Jodhpur royal hunting lodge
situated in the Aravalli Hills.
[] 15 All major cards

RANTHAMBHOR

🏨 SAWAI MADHOPUR LODGE
$$$
SAWAI MADHOPUR
TEL 07462-23500
FAX 07462-20718
E-MAIL sawai.madhopur@
tajhotels.com
A 20-minute drive from
Ranthambhor National Park,
the Jaipur rulers' well-
maintained 1930s hunting
lodge is run by the Taj group;
sleep in a room or a tent.
🛏 22 including 6 tents 🖼
🖼 All major cards

🏨 VANYAVILAS
Oberoi group's sumptuous
Vanyavilas, a luxury jungle
camp resort, opens in 2002. It
will have state-of-the-art tents
with air-conditioning and more.

SAMODE

🏨 SAMODE PALACE & BAGH
$$$
SAMODE
TEL 0142-344123
FAX 0142-633370
E-MAIL jagdish@jpl.vsnl.net.in
Since they inherited the
disused palace, two brothers
meticulously restored its
elaborately painted rooms
and then renovated the
peaceful walled *bagh* (garden),
a 10-minutes' drive away, where
guests can stay in large tents.
🛏 44 plus 38 tents 🖼 at
both sites 🖼 All major
cards

SHEKHAWATI AREA

🏨 CASTLE MANDAWA
$$
MANDAWA
TEL 01592-23124
FAX 01592-23171
E-MAIL reservations@castel
mandawa.com
This large fort has been
transformed into a sociable,
entertaining, family-run hotel.
Delightful rooftop dining.
🛏 74 🖼 All major cards

🏨 PIRAMAL HAVELI
🍴 BAGAR
$
BAGAR
An especially elegant painted
haveli, sensitively refurbished
and well managed. Attractive
courtyards are enclosed by
colonial pillared corridors.
Traditional vegetarian cuisine
of the Marwaris is served.
Make reservations through
Neemrana Hotels (see p. 343).
🛏 18 🖼 All major cards

UDAIPUR

🏨 DEVIGARH FORT
🍴 $$$$$
DELWARA
TEL 02953-89211
FAX 02953-89357
E-MAIL reservations@
deviresorts.com
Just north of Eklingji,
this uncompromisingly
contemporary Indian hotel
is cleverly slotted into a
magnificent fort. Immaculate
craftsmanship throughout.
High terrace restaurant and
step-well style pool.
🛏 23 suites 🖼 🖼 🖼 All
major cards

🏨 LAKE PALACE HOTEL
$$$$
LAKE PICHOLA
TEL 0294-528800
FAX 0294-528700
E-MAIL lakepalace.udaipur@
tajhotels.com
This romantic island hotel,
reached by boat, was once the
maharana's summer palace.
Now much enlarged, with
some good recent renovation
and improved food. Managed
by the Taj group.
🛏 84 🖼 🖼 All major
cards

🏨 SHIKARHEDI
$$$
P. O. GOVERDHAN VILAS
TEL 0294-58300
FAX 0294-584841
Once the maharaja of
Udaipur's hunting lodge, the
grounds now support a
wildlife sanctuary and polo

pony stud farm. Quietly
situated away from town
center. Local wildlife can be
seen feeding in the lake and
monkeys play on the roof.
🖼 🖼 All major cards

🏨 SHIV NIWAS PALACE
🍴 $$$
CITY PALACE
TEL 0294-528016
FAX 0294-528006
E-MAIL lphm.hrh@axcess.net.in
Stunning palace refurbishment
that improves each year. The
rooms surround the large
central courtyard where
guests swim, relax, and eat
good food. This is the
centerpiece of the HRH hotel
group, which has three more
hotels in Udaipur alone
(Fateh Prakash, Dovecote,
and Shikarbadi). Good food at
all locations, plus delicious
Gujarati *thali* at their Garden
Restaurant next to the royal
car collection, and elegant tea
in the Durbar Hall.
🛏 34 🖼 None

🏨 UDAIVILAS
Oberoi group's lavish, new
hotel resort beside Pichola
Lake opens 2001.

🏨 KARNI FORT
$$
BAMBORA
TEL 0294-398283
E-MAIL karnihotels@salyam
.net.in
Immaculately renovated
Sisodia hilltop fort whose
rooms on various floors
overlook the spectacular
swimming pool and, beyond,
the village. Run by the
Welcomgroup, this makes a
good Udaipur-Mandu stop.
Make reservations at Karni
Bhawan, Jodhpur, tel 0291-
512101, fax 0291-512105.
🛏 32 🖼 🖼 AE, MC, V

🏨 SHIKARBADI
🍴 $$
GOVERDHAN VILAS,
AHMEDABAD RD.
TEL 0294-528008
FAX 0294-528006

Just a 15-minute drive from the city, this former Mewar hunting lodge has been converted into a comfortable hotel, with art deco style suites and lakeside chalets. Popular for its Mewari cuisine.
🛈 25 ⊠ ❄ 🅲 All major cards

🏨 CARAVANSERAI
$
14 LALGHAT
TEL 0294-4114103
FAX 0294-223177
On the banks of Lake Pichola and close to the City Palace, this historic *haveli* dates back to the mid-18th century. The rooftop restaurant overlooks the lake.
🛈 24 🅲 All major cards

🏨 JAGAT NIWAS PALACE
$
25 LALGHAT
LAKE PICHOLA
TEL 0294-420133
FAX 0294-422860
E-MAIL anything@jagatniwas
palace.com
Whitewashed *haveli* right beside the lake. The rooftop restaurant serves good food.
🛈 29 🅲 MC, V

🏨 TRIDENT
$
HARIDAS JI KI MAGRI, MULA TALATEL 0294-432200
FAX 0294-432211
E-MAIL sbhushan@trident
udp.com
This modest Oberoi hotel has a convenient lakeside city location. Rooms are adequately equipped and comfortable.
❄ 🔲 🅲 All major cards

GUJARAT

🏨 DABARGADH
$$
POSHINA
TEL 079-550 6590,
E-MAIL sheetal@gnahdl.globalnet
.ems.net.in

A small 17th-century Rajput fort in the heart of a village. Now an unpretentious family-run hotel. A useful hotel on the Rajasthan-Gujarat border between Udaipur and Ahmedabad.
🛈 10 🅲 All major cards

AHMEDABAD

🏨 HOLIDAY INN
$$$
KHANPUR RD.,
NEAR NEHRU BRIDGE,
KHANPUR
TEL 079-550 5505
FAX 079-550 5501
E-MAIL holidayinn@vsnl.com
Winner of Best of the Best Environmental Hotel 1999. Includes all the international modern conveniences expected, such as indoor swimming pool and complimentary breakfast.
🛈 63 ❄ 🔲 🅲 All major cards

🏨 TAJ RESIDENCY UMMED
$$$$
AIRPORT RD.,
HANSOL
TEL 079-286 4444
FAX 079-286 4454
EMAIL sofummed@wilnetonline
.net
Luxury hotel with decor inspired by Gujarat's textile tradition. Good Gujarati food in the Narmada restaurant.
🛈 85 ⊠ 🔲 🅲 All major cards

🏨 CAMA PARK PLAZA
$$
KHANPUR RD.
TEL 079-550 5281 OR
079-550 5289
FAX 079-550 5285
E-MAIL camahotel@vsnl.com
This long-established hotel, with garden terrace and outdoor pool, overlooks the Sabarmati River. Choice of two excellent restaurants. Western-style furnishing to a comfortable standard. Rooms in suites, each with private bathroom and sitting room.

🛈 49 ⊠ 🅲 All major cards

🏨 PALACE UTELIA
$$
9 GANDHI BAGH
TEL 079-644 5770 OR
079-656 9937
FAX 079-644 5770
EMAIL utelia@ad1.vsnl.net.in
Built at the turn of the 20th century in the Indo-Saracenic style with European influences, this amazing-looking hotel features domes, galleries, balconies, and porticoes. The quiet rural location is within easy reach of sights. Jeep safaris can be arranged from the hotel to Nalsarovar Bird Sanctuary or Velavadar National Park.
🛈 20 🅲 All major cards

🍴 KHYBER
$$
FORTUNE HOTEL LANDMARK,
ASHRAM RD.
TEL 079-755 2929
Good kebabs and panoramic views on the tenth floor.
🅲 All major cards

🍴 VISHALA
$$
SARKHEJ
Cleverly created cultural village setting for eating a delicious Gujarati *thali*, a whole meal on a platter distinctive for its vegetable dishes and sweetness.
🅲 All major cards

BHAVNAGAR

🏨 NILAMBAG PALACE
$$
NILAMBAG CIRCLE
TEL 0278-424241 OR
0278-429323
FAX 0278-428072
E-MAIL nilambag@varunnet.com
OR nilambag@ad1.vsnl.net.in
This grand, family-run, delicately carved stone building retains plenty of royal furnishings. Spacious lawns and gardens.
🛈 28 🅿 🅲 🔄 ⊠
🅲 All major cards

DAMAN

🏨 PRINCESS PARK
$

DEVKA BEACH
TEL 02638-54323
FAX 02638-50800
E-MAIL hpp@vapi.lsbss.net
The best beachfront hotel
in Daman.
ⓘ 25 ⊠ 🍴 All major
cards

DIU

🏨 APNA GUEST HOUSE
$

TEL 02876-52112
Modest guesthouse; some
rooms have sea views.
None

JAMNAGAR

🏨 THE NEW ARAM
$

NAND NIWAS,
PANDIT NEHRU MARG
TEL 0288-551701
FAX 0288-554957
A 1940s mansion with faded
period furnishings in large
rooms. Multi-cuisine
vegetarian garden restaurant.
ⓘ 28 All major cards

JASDEN & RAJKOT

🏨 HINGOLGADH CASTLE
$$

JASDEN
This low-lying hilltop castle
inside Hingolgadh Nature
Sanctuary is now a rustic,
rural hotel. Make reservations
at Saurashtra Safaris in Jasden.
ⓘ 7 None

JUNAGADH & SASAN GIR NATIONAL PARK

🏨 GIR LODGE
$

SASAN GIR
TEL 02877-85521
FAX 02877-85528
Good, no-frills hotel on the
edge of the park. Part of the
Taj group. Reservations
essential.
ⓘ 29 All major cards

MODHERA & PATAN

🏨 BALARAM PALACE RESORT
$$

CHITRASANI,
NEAR PALANPUR
TEL 079-6578412
FAX 079-6578412
E-MAIL bprhot@adl.vsnl.net.in
This grand, white, pavilioned
building was built as a royal
hunting lodge in the 1920s. It
has since been fully renovated
and is now in keeping with its
grand riverside location.
ⓘ 17 ⊠ 🍴 AE

SAURASHTRA

🏨 VADODARA
$$$

R C DUTT RD.,
VADODARA
TEL 0265-330033
FAX 0265-330055
E-MAIL vadora@welcomgroup
.com
A business person's hotel
reliably run by the Welcom-
group. Golf and horseback
riding can be arranged on
request.
ⓘ 163 ⊠ AE, MC, V

🏨 UTHELIA PALACE
$$

UTHELIA
TEL 02714-62222
FAX 07964-45770
E-MAIL sibal@adl vsnl.net.in
Family-run, small,
unpretentious 18th-century
hilltop palace close to Lothal.
ⓘ 14 All major cards

🏨 ORCHARD PALACE
$

PALACE ROAD,
GONDAL
TEL 079-6442019
FAX 079-6560962
E-MAIL nwsafaris@hotmail.com
Standing next to Huzoor
Palace amid extensive lawns
and gardens, the rooms retain
plenty of their regal character.
One suite is in a converted
railway saloon carriage
situated outside the hotel.
ⓘ 7 All major cards

🏨 RAJWANT PALACE RESORT
$

RAJPIPLA
TEL 02640-20071
E-MAIL ssibal@adl.vsnl.net.in
Stay in one palace, with
gardens, sports and its own
tribal museum, and you are
ideally located to visit several
others in town. The
adventurous can even take a
swim in the Narmada River.
⊠ All major cards

🏨 RIVERSIDE PALACE
$

PALACE ROAD, GONDAL
TEL 079-6302019 OR
079-6308031
FAX 079-6300962
E-MAIL sheetal@gnahd.globalnet
.ems.vsnl.net.in
Guests at this hotel enjoy free
access to both the City Palace
Museum and the royal vintage
car collection. Boat rides and
nature safaris can be
organized by hotel staff.
ⓘ 11 ⊠ All major
cards

🍴 KHANSA
$$

SAYAJI GUNJ
(OPPOSITE SURYA HOTEL)
Extremely good Gujarati thali.
If this is full, the restaurant of
the Surya Hotel (opposite) is
also good.

🍴 MARUTI
$$

NAND COMPLEX,
BEHIND RACE COURSE DEPOT
The distinctive pungent thali
of Kathiawad is served here in
a village ambience. The local
specialty, Undheu, is served on
Sundays.

🍴 MIRCH MASALA
$$

MEGHDHANUSH COMPLEX,
TRANSPECK CIRCLE
Themed along the lines of a
Punjabi dhabba, or roadside
restaurant. Serves good
tandoori dishes.

WANKANER & MORBI

🏨 OASIS HOUSE AND THE RESIDENCY
$
RANJIT VILAS PALACE
TEL 02828-20000
FAX 02828-20002
E-MAIL wankanerpalace@
planetace.com
Guests stay in the relatively simple outbuildings, with period furniture and an indoor art deco pool. You can visit the glorious Venetian-Gothic main palace.
🛈 24 🏊 🏊 🅢 None

MUMBAI & MAHARASHTRA
Mumbai (Bombay) has surprisingly few hotels, and room prices are high. However, restaurants abound inside and outside hotels so gourmands might consult *The Mid-Day Good Food Guide to Mumbai*. As Mumbai is a congested isthmus, location is everything.

MUMBAI

🏨 OBEROI
$$$$
NARIMAN POINT
TEL 022-202 5757
FAX 022-204 3133
E-MAIL akaul@oberoi-mumbai.com
Smaller and older than its sister hotel next door, and slightly more personalized. There is 24-hour butler service for all guests and a seriously good business center.
🛈 350 🏊 🐦 🅢 All major cards

🏨 OBEROI TOWERS
🍴 $$$$
NARIMAN POINT
TEL 022-202 4343
FAX 022-204 3282
E-MAIL devendra@oberoi-mumbai.com
This landmark tower on the Mumbai skyline is equipped with all modern conveniences. There is a superb business

center, an extensive upscale shopping center, and restaurants that include The Palms, a lavish all-day buffet.
🛈 650 🏊 🐦 🅢 All major cards

🏨 TAJ MAHAL HOTEL
🍴 $$$$
APOLLO BUNDER, COLABA
TEL 022-202 3366
FAX 022-287 2711
E-MAIL mahal.mumbai@tajhotels.com
One of the world's great hotels, the Old Wing was built in 1903 by Jamshtji Nusserwanji Tata and is the place to stay. Plenty of character, pleasant pool area, but tired with some sloppy service. Nine restaurants and bars include the Tanjore (Indian) and the Apollo Rooftop bar.
🛈 582 🏊 🐦 🅢 All major cards

🏨 TAJ PRESIDENT
$$$$
90 CUFFE PARADE
TEL 022-215 0808
FAX 022-215 1201
The informal Taj President is centrally located on Cuffe Parade.
🛈 317 🅢 🏊 🐦 🅢 All major cards

🏨 RITZ
$$$
5 JAMSEHDJI TATA RD.
TEL 022-282 0141
FAX 022-285 0494
Old hotel with character, in a good central position, just half a mile from the train station in the hub of the city's commercial district.
🛈 72 🅢 AE

🏨 GRAND
$$
17 SPROTT RD,
BALLARD ESTATE
TEL 022-261 3558
FAX 022-262 6581
Centrally located, established hotel, with rooms arranged around a central courtyard.
🛈 73 🅢 All major cards

PRICES

HOTELS
An indication of the cost of a double room without breakfast is given by **$** signs.
$$$$$	Over $280
$$$$	$160–$280
$$$	$100–$160
$$	$40–$100
$	Under $40

RESTAURANTS
An indication of the cost of a three-course dinner without drinks is given by $ signs.
$$$$$	Over $80
$$$$	$50–$80
$$$	$35–$50
$$	$20–$35
$	Under $20

🏨 YWCA INTERNATIONAL GUEST HOUSE
$
MADAME CAMA RD.,
COOPERAGE
TEL 022-202 5053
FAX 022-282 2057
Breakfast and one main meal included. Clean, no frills, excellent value. You should book several weeks in advance to be sure of a room here.
🅢 None

Airport hotels:
Convenient for some business areas, too.

🏨 LEELA KEMPINSKI
🍴 $$$$$
SAHAR, ANDHERI
TEL 022-691 1234
FAX 022-691 1212
E-MAIL leelarsv@theleela.com
WEBSITE www.theleela.com
Superdeluxe hotel with marble everywhere, serious restaurants (local dishes in the coffee shop) and good basement shops (imitation Italian leather goods, etc.). Great for killing a few hours between flights.
🛈 418 🏊 🐦 🅢 All major cards

HOTELS & RESTAURANTS

🏨 LE MERIDIEN MUMBAI
$$$$$
ASCOT CENTRE, SAHAR
AIRPORT RD.
TEL 022-838 0000
FAX022-838 0101
E-MAIL immumbai@vsnl.com
Maintains the upscale, quality
Meridien tradition.
🛏 170   🏊   🍽   🅰 All
major cards

🏨 ORCHID
$$$$
70-C NEHRU RD.,
VILE PARLE (EAST)
TEL 022-610 0707
FAX 022-610 0708
E-MAIL ohmu@orchidhotel.com
Close to the domestic air
terminal, the luxury Orchid
claims green credentials, too,
with water conservation and
energy saving, and recycling
strategies. Three restaurants
and a coffee shop.
🛏 167   🏊   🍽   🅰 All
major cards

RESTAURANTS
Mumbai is India's richest and
most international city, where
eating out is part of life for the
many wealthy. Almost all cuisines
are available but here are some
special ones.

🍴 PEARL OF THE ORIENT
$$$
AMBASSADOR HOTEL,
CHURCHGATE
A revolving rooftop
restaurant on the
Ambassador Hotel. Serves
Oriental dishes.

🍴 APOORVA
$$
MUMBAI SAMACHAR MARG,
NEAR HORNIMAN CIRCLE
Delicious Mangalorian food,
especially crab and shrimp.
Eating with your hands is
acceptable.

🍴 CHOWPATTY BEACH
$$
Try the special Mumbai *bhel-
puri* and *sev-puri* snacks.

🍴 KHYBER
145 MAHATMA GANDHI RD.
KALA GHODA,
BY RHYTHM HOUSE
TEL 022-267 3227
North Indian food, very
popular. Large capacity with
group and party facilities.

🍴 LING'S PAVILION
$$
19/21 K C COLLEGE HOSTEL
BUILDING, OFF COLABA
CAUSEWAY
Offshoot of the famous
Nanking Chinese restaurant.
Come here for seafood.

🍴 ONLY FISH
$$
TARDEO
Fish dishes from all around
India, popular with foreigners.

🍴 RAJDHANI
$$
SHEIKH MEMON ST,
OPPOSITE MANGALDAS
MARKET
Venture into the heart of the
city to sample dishes from
Rajasthan, Gujarat,
Maharashtra, and Kathiawad.

🍴 TRISHNA
$$
KALA GHODA,
BEHIND RHYTHM HOUSE
TEL 022-2672176
Popular with classy locals and
visitors. Excellent seafood.

🍴 VINTAGE
$$
MANDIK RD.
OFF COLABA CAUSEWAY
Known for rich royal
Hyderabadi dishes such as
stone-ghosth.

MAHARASHTRA

AURANGABAD

🏨 TAJ RESIDENCY
$$$
8/N-12 CIDCO
TEL 0240-381106
FAX 0240-381053

PRICES

HOTELS
An indication of the cost
of a double room without
breakfast is given by **$** signs.

$$$$$	Over $280
$$$$	$280– $160
$$$	$100–$160
$$	$40–$100
$	Under $40

RESTAURANTS
An indication of the cost of a
three-course dinner without
drinks is given by $ signs.

$$$$$	Over $80
$$$$	$50–$80
$$$	$35–$50
$$	$20–$35
$	Under $20

E-MAIL residency.aurangabad@
tajhotels.com
Perfect base for visiting Ajanta
and Ellora; big rooms with
verandas look onto splendid
garden and pool. Good food.
🛏 40   🏊   🍽   🅰 All major
cards

CHIPLUN

🏨 GATEWAY RIVERVIEW LODGE
$$
CHIPLUN
TEL 02356-72233
FAX 02356-72059
Renovated lodge brimful of
character, built around lush
terraced gardens and
excellent pool, with views
over the beautiful Vashishti
River Valley; delicious food.
Ideal stop on the Janjira–Goa
route; shame about the busy
road next to it.
🛏 37   🏊   🅰 All major
cards

KARLA, BHAJA, & BEDSA

🏨 DUKE'S RETREAT
$$
MUMBAI–PUNE RD.,
KHANDALA
TEL 022-261 8293

Established hotel with rooms and cottages overlooking beautiful lawn and splendid ravine. Reduced prices in the off-season.
🛈 62 🏊 🏋 🏧 All major cards

KOLHAPUR

🏨 SHALINI PALACE
$$
RANKALA, KOLHAPUR
TEL 0231-620401
FAX 0231-620407
Peaceful, atmospheric, and slightly neglected building, originally built for the Maharaja of Kolhapur in 1931. On the lakeside with lawns and attractive gardens.
🛈 41

MAHABALESHWAR

🏨 VALLEY VIEW RESORT
$$
NEAR MARKET
TEL 020-60066
FAX 022-888 1144
E-MAIL vvrbom@bom3.vsnl.net.in
Modern deluxe resort in this former hill station. Lovely views over the valley from most rooms and an attractive garden with landscaped lawns.
🛈 78 🏊 🏧 All major cards

🏨 BELMONT PARK HILL RESORT
$
WILSON POINT
TEL 022-415 3216
Small hotel with character; library, lawns and good Parsi food.
🛈 12 🏊 🏋 🏧 None

🏨 PANORAMA
$
28 M.G. RD.
TEL 02168-60404
FAX 02168-61234
Rooms in the hotel or in cottages in the grounds. Reduced prices in off-season.
🛈 11 🏊 🏧 None

MATHERAN

🏨 RUGBY
$
VITHALRAO KOTWAL RD.
TEL 02148-30291
FAX 02148-30252
Modest central hotel. Popular with Mumbai families seeking cool air in summer.
🛈 52 🏊 🏧 AE, MC, V

NASIK

🏨 TAJ RESIDENCY
$$
P-17, MIDC AMBAD,
MUMBAI–AGRA RD.
TEL 0253-384499
FAX 0253-382638
Executive rooms have the best views of the extensive gardens and hills; good food.
🛈 68 🏧 All major cards

PUNE

🏨 TAJ BLUE DIAMOND
$$$
11 KOREGAON RD.
TEL 020-612 5555
FAX 020-612 7755
E-MAIL bluediamond.pune@tajhotels.com
Pune's most established hotel, now renovated by the Taj group, stands in a leafy residential area.
🛈 109 🏊 🏋 🏧 All major cards

WEST COAST: GOA & KERALA
The hotel selection assumes you will probably be relaxing in this region and will want to be on or very close to a beach.

GOA
There is a well organized network of paying guest accommodations in traditional Goan homes; contact the Tourist Office, Patto, Panaji, tel 0832-224757.
The following selection of hotels are all either right on the beach or a few minutes' walk from it.

NORTH GOA

🏨 ALOR HOLIDAY RESORT APARTMENTS
$$
POIRAT, NAIKA VADDO, CALANGUTE
TEL 0832-22714 OR 0832-277220
E-MAIL alor@goatelcom.com
Two-roomed apartments with bathroom, kitchen, and balcony, set in a palm grove with restaurant and pool. Five-minute walk from Aguada Beach; ideal for independence and for long stays.
🛈 70 apartments 🏊 🏧 All major cards

🏨 ALFRAN GROUP
$$
TEL 0832-276936
FAX 0832-276266
E-MAIL alfran@giasbm01.vsnl.net.in.
With Dona Alcina as their delightful flagship hotel, this good value group has seven resorts in Goa, mostly around Calangute. All noted for their splendid lawns and gardens, friendly management, good pools, good barbecues with Goan food, and folk evenings.
🛈 40–185 🏊 🏧 All major cards

🏨 CASA DOMANI GUESTHOUSE
$$
CALANGUTE
Rooms have ceiling fans, no air conditioning, but guests benefit from personal Goan hospitality and have breakfast outside in the pretty yard; it's a seven-minute walk from Calangute waterfront village.
🛈 9 🏊 🏧 None

🏨 LAGUNA ANJUNA
$$
ANJUNA
TEL 0832-231999
FAX 0832-420213
Next to the beach, this beautiful, stylishly designed hotel follows the Goan style in its cottages. Splendid gardens.
🛈 22 cottages 🏊

PANAJI

🏨 CIDADE DE GOA
🍴 BEACH RESORT
$$
VAINGUINIM BEACH
TEL 0832-221133
FAX 0832-223303
E-MAIL hotel.cidade@sma
.sprintrpg.ems.vsnl.net.in
Charles Correa's fine design,
inspired by Goan architecture,
spreads through the gardens
strung around the private bay;
a small beach but no
peddlers. Built and run by the
Timblo family; relaxed
atmosphere, delicious food.
🛏 210 🛫 🍴 🚭 All
major cards

🏨 TAJ HOLIDAY VILLAGE
$$
SINQUERIM, BARDEZ
TEL 0832-276201
FAX 0832-276045
E-MAIL village.goa@tajhotels.com
Rooms arranged in Goa-style
bungalows scattered through
a mature garden immediately
behind the beachside
restaurants; informal
atmosphere. This is the
nicest of the Taj group's four
Goa hotels; next to and up
from the beach is their Fort
Aguada Beach Resort, with
superdeluxe Aguada
Hermitage above it, and Taj
Exotica, which opened in
2000, is in south Goa, at
Benaulim near Margao.
🛏 140 🛫 🍴 🚭 All
major cards

SOUTH GOA

Hotels here benefit from the
long and, so far, less crowded
beaches than in north Goa.

🏨 GOA RENAISSANCE
$$$
VARCA
TEL 0832-745200
FAX 0832-745225
E-MAIL rmda-goa@rml.sprintrpg
.ems.vsnl.net.in
Refurbished in 2000, this hotel
is now a deluxe resort with a
nine-hole golf course and
gardens down to the beach.

🛏 120 🛫 🍴 🚭 All
major cards

🏨 THE LEELA PALACE
GOA
$$$
MOBOR, CAVELOSSIM,
SALCETTE
TEL 0832-871234
FAX 0832-871352
E-MAIL info@leelapalace.com
Goa's southernmost upscale
hotel, the luxurious bungalows
and gardens set well back
from the beach; delightfully
quiet surrounding countryside. Find action up at Colva
and Margao.
🛏 137 🛫 🍴 🚭 All
major cards

🏨 MAJORDA BEACH
RESORT
$$
MAJORDA
TEL 0832-754871
FAX 0832-754342
E-MAIL mbr.goa@rma.sril.in
Lush gardens down to the
long beach; friendly staff
create a good atmosphere.
🛏 120 🛫 🍴 🚭 All
major cards

For a stop on the Goa
–Karnataka route, stay at Kali
River Camp (see Nagarhole,
p. 366).

RESTAURANTS
In addition to the hotels and the
delightful beach cafés, where a
plate of freshly grilled shrimp
makes a perfect light meal, Goa
has a large number of informal,
friendly, family-run restaurants
serving distinctive Goan dishes
such as *balcao* (shrimp with
ginger, garlic, and vinegar) and
caldiero (fish cooked with
coconut and coriander). Goa's
restaurants here tend to come
and go with the seasons, so it is
best to ask locally for
recommendations; or simply
walk outside your hotel and try
the first one you like the look
of—that way, you enter into
Goa's informal lifestyle.

COASTAL KARNATAKA

MANGALORE

🏨 MANJARUN
$$
OLD PORT RD., BUNDER,
MANGALORE
TEL 0824-420420
FAX 0824-420585
E-MAIL manjarun.mangalore@
tajhotels.com
In town, overlooking the sea
and the Nethravathi River; a
practical hotel stop with
rooms ranging from budget to
suites.
🛏 101 🛫 🍴 🚭 All
major cards

KERALA

THE BACKWATERS

🏨 COCONUT LAGOON
🍴 $$$
KUMARAKOM
TEL 0481-525834 OR
0481-525835
FAX 0481-524495
E-MAIL casino@vsnl.com
Reached by a boat from
Puthenangadi, this hotel's
guests have a choice of new
or old bungalows. Delicious
Kerala food overlooking
Vembanad Lake.
🛏 52 🛫 🍴 🚭 All major
cards

🏨 KETTUVALLOM
HOUSEBOATS
$$
KTDC, KUMARAKOM
TEL 0481-524258
FAX 0481-525862
E-MAIL ktdc@vsnl.com
Cruise through the
backwaters lounging in a
renovated country rice boat
and watching Kerala life. It is
worth going for one or two
nights and sleeping on board.
Meals are included in the
price.
🛏 Boats are 2 or 4 berth
🚭 All major cards

KUMARAKOM LAKE RESORT
$$
KUMARAKOM
TEL 0481-524900
FAX 0481-524987
E-MAIL klresort@vsnl.com
Part of the Golden Tulip hotel chain, this resort's old and new cottages are scattered over 10 acres of lawns, gardens, and canals. Good Kerala food served in an 18th-century mansion, serious Ayurvedic treatments in another.
[i] 22 cottages 🏊 💪 All major cards

SPICE VILLAGE
$$$
KUMILY–THEKADY RD., IDUKKI
TEL 0484-668421
FAX 0484-668001
E-MAIL casino@vsnl.com
Set in the Cardamom Hills just outside the Periyar Tiger Reserve, this is the ideal place to see southern India's nature and wildlife. Individual thatched dwellings offer comfort and privacy.
[i] 52 🏊 💪 All major cards

KOCHI (COCHIN) & ERNAKULUM

THE BRUNTON BOATYARD
$$$$
FORT COCHIN
TEL 0484-668421
FAX 0484-668001
E-MAIL casino@vsnl.com
The simple, contemporary design reminds you that this replaces a waterside industrial building; all the rooms have sea and delta views. Delicious seafood fresh daily and cooked to your taste.
[i] 26 🏊 All major cards

CASINO
$$
WILLINGDON ISLAND
KOCHI
TEL 0484-668421
FAX 0484-668001
E-MAIL casino@vsnl.com

Clean, comfortable and friendly, this hotel in a quiet setting of lawns and palm trees is ideally situated for exploring Kochi.
[i] 68 🏊 All major cards

MALABAR HOUSE
$$$
1/268, 1/269 PARADE RD., FORT COCHIN
TEL 0484-216666
FAX 0484-217777
E-MAIL malabarhouse@vsnl.com
Old Cochin mansion exquisitely renovated and furnished. Delicious food is served in two restaurants. The hotel has a good shop, and a stay in the rooftop suite is a special treat. Ayurvedic massage offered.
[i] 17 P 🏊 ❄ AE, MC, V

TAJ MALABAR
$$$
WILLINGDON ISLAND, KOCHI
TEL 0484-666811 OR 0484-668010
FAX 0484-668010
E-MAIL malabar.coching@tajhotels.com
Old wing rooms have character, new wing rooms have spectacular views over the harbor. The coffee shop's excellent Kerala dishes can be enjoyed by the waterside.
[i] 96 P 🏊 All major cards

KOZHIKODE (CALICUT)

TAJ RESIDENCY
$$
P. T. USHA RD.
TEL 0495-766371
FAX 0495-766448
E-MAIL residency.calicut@tajhotels.com
Practical hotel in fast-expanding Calicut; useful when traveling along the coast or down from inland Karnataka. The hotel has its own Ayurveda Center.
[i] 74 🏊 💪 All major cards

THE TREEHOUSES
$$
WYNAD
Guests stay in cottages and treehouses deep in the forests of the Western Ghats; a good stop between Kozhikode and Ooty or Mysore.
[i] 8 cottages and 3 treehouses 💳 No cards

MARARIKULAM

THE MARARI BEACH
$$$
ALLEPPEY
TEL 0484-668421
FAX 0484-668001
E-MAIL casino@vsnl.com
Thatched villas close to a vast expanse of beach make for a relaxing break. A buffet restaurant and more relaxed "beach shack" cater to all tastes, providing ethnic and international cuisine.
[i] 52 🏊 💪 All major cards

LAKSHADWEEP ISLANDS

BANGARAM ISLAND RESORT
$$$$$
BANGARAM ISLAND
TEL 0484-668421
FAX 0484-668001

❄ Air-conditioning 🏊 Indoor/🏖 Outdoor swimming pool 💪 Health club 💳 Credit cards   **KEY**

E-MAIL casino@vsnl.com
Reached by plane from Kochi to Agatti, then by boat or helicopter, this is the only island resort open to non-Indians. Guests staying in the simple but elegant hotel run by Kochi's Casino group can roam over 128 acres of uninhabited island and enjoy snorkeling and scuba diving under the sea. (As a modest alternative, non-Indians can take scuba diving courses on Kadmat Island.)
[i] 30 [☗] [⊗] All major cards

PERIYAR

[⌂] LAKE PALACE
$$$
PERIYAR NATIONAL PARK
TEL 04863-322023
FAX 04863-322282
TEL 0471-330031
Located on an island inside the park, ideal for bird-watching, painting, or just gazing at the lush forest and the odd elephant; game viewing by boat. Make reservations through KTDC, by Central Bus Station, Thampanoor.
[i] 6

[⌂] SHALIMAR SPICE GARDEN
$$$
MURUKKADY POST, THEKKADY
TEL 04863-22132
FAX 04863-23002
Italian-run elegant cottages in the vernacular style set amid fruit and spice trees; Ayurvedic treatments; the park is nearby.
[i] 12 rooms and cottages

VARKALA

[⌂] TAJ GARDEN RETREAT
$$
NEAR GOVERNMENT GUEST HOUSE, JANARDHANAPURAM
TEL 0472-603000
FAX 0472-602296
E-MAIL retreat.verkala@ tajhotels.com

Midway between Thiruvananthapuram and Kollam, this modern hotel overlooks its large pool and lawns and gardens that end at the beach; good food.
[i] 30 [☗] [⊗] All major cards

THIRUVNANTHA-PURAM (TRIVANDRUM) & KOVALAM

[⌂] SOMATHEERAM AYURVEDIC BEACH RESORT
$$
CHOWARA, SOUTH OF KOVALAM
TEL 0471-481601
FAX 0471-480600
E-MAIL soma@md2.vsnl.net.in
Cottages old and new, all in local styles and each with its own terrace, are scattered through the tropical gardens that reach down to the beach. Good Ayurvedic treatments, Yoga classes offered. The restaurant offers regional, Indian, Continental, and Chinese cuisine.
[i] 53 [P] [⊗] AE, MC

[⍾] SOUTH PARK
$$
M. G. RD., PALAYAM
TEL 0471-333333
FAX 0471-331861
E-MAIL hotel@vsnl.com
A good city hotel managed and fully renovated by the Welcomgroup. There is a comprehensive range of facilities and an attractive rooftop garden. The restaurant serves a wide variety of food, including interesting Kerala specialties.
[i] 83 [☗] [⊗] All major cards

[⌂] SURYA SAMUDRA
$$$
PULINKUDI, MULLUR
TEL 0471-480413
FAX 0471-481124
E-MAIL suryasamudra@vsnl.com
Established peaceful beach hotel, now run by Raphael

Hotels. Beautiful rustic cottages and an ingenious seawater pool, with steps down to the beach; good Ayurvedic treatments. Watch breathtaking sunsets over the Arabian Sea.
[i] 21 bungalows (26 rooms) [☗] [⊗] MC, V

THE DECCAN

ALAMPUR

[⌂] RAVIPRAKASH
$
RAILWAY STATION RD., KURNOOL
TEL 08518-21116
Simple hotel with lawns, a good base for the Alampur area.
[i] 46 [☗] [⊗] All major cards

ANANTAPUR

[⌂] SAPTHAGIRI
$
TEL 08554-20245
Very modest hotel, suitable for the intrepid travelers who visit this area.
[⊗] None

BADAMI

[⍾] BADAMI COURT
$$
STATION RD. BADAMI
TEL 08357-65230
FAX 08357-65207
Delightful hotel found along a tree-lined avenue that stretches from town. Delicious food.
[i] 27 [⊗] All major cards

BANGALORE

[⌂] THE OBEROI
$$$$
M. G. RD.
TEL 080-558 5858
FAX 080-558 5960
E-MAIL akaul@oberoiblr.com
This hotel is a rare achievement: a superdeluxe

guesthouse that manages to make both the business-person and the vacationer feel comfortable. Rooms surround lush central gardens. Good food.
🛏 160 ⬜ 🏋 🅰 All major cards

GATEWAY HOTEL
$$$
66 RESIDENCY RD.
TEL 080-558 4545
FAX 080-558 4030
E-MAIL gateway.bangalore@tajhotels.com
Useful Western-style hotel with the best restaurant in Bangalore. The Karavalli serves dishes from Goa, Mangalore, Kerala, and Karwar. The fish, chicken, and pork dishes are excellent; vegetarian dishes also offered
🛏 98 ⬜ 🅰 All major cards

LE MERIDIEN
$$$
28 SANKEY RD.
TEL 080-226 2233
FAX 080-226 7676
E-MAIL leme@vsnl.com
Responding to new IT wealth, Le Meridien brings its established international character to Bangalore.
🛏 196 ⬜ 🏋 🅰 All major cards

WINDSOR SHERATON & TOWERS
$$$
25 SANKEY RD.
TEL 080-226 9898
FAX 080-226 4941
E-MAIL guest@windsor.welcomgroup.co.in
Dazzlingly white Raj revival building with columns and porticoes. Accommodations are in houses with sumptuous rooms.
🛏 240 🅿 🔲 🔲 ⬜ 🏋 🅰 All major cards

VICTORIA
$
47-8 RESIDENCY RD.
TEL 080-558 4077
FAX 080-558 4945

Old, established, very central hotel with rooms open onto a spacious lawn, bringing back memories of the days of the Raj.
🅰 AE, MC, V

JUNGLE LODGES & RESORTS
$$$
SHRUNGAR SHOPPING CENTER, M.G. RD.
TEL 080-559 7021 OR 080-559 7024
FAX 080-558 6163
E-MAIL junglelodges@vsnl.com
A variety of adventure trips including white-water rafting, fishing, scuba diving, and wildlife viewing is available at several different resorts, including K. Gudi Camp in the B.R. Hills Wildlife Sanctuary and Devbagh Beach Resort. Accommodations are in log huts, tents, or tented cottages.
🅰 All major cards

MORE RESTAURANTS
Bangalore's lively and dynamic residents patronize the city's bars, clubs, and restaurants. Bars include Peco's, Nightwatchman, and the more sedate Polo Club. Southern Indian restaurants serving *thali* meals include Shilpa (on Lady Curzon Rd.), Haveli (off Brigade Rd.), Amravati (off Residency Rd.), and Nagarjuna (on Residency Rd.).

BIJAPUR

KSTDC MAURYA ADIL SHAHI
$
ANAND MAHAL RD.
TEL 08352-20943
Central and simple, with a courtyard garden. You can walk or take a pony and trap to the monuments.

BELUR & HALEBID

HOYSALA VILLAGE RESORT
$
HASSAN
TEL 08172-56065
FAX 08172-56794

Modern hotel with good staff. An ideal base for seeing the Hoysala temples.

HYDERABAD & SECUNDERABAD

ITC KAKATIYA SHERATON
$$$
BEGUMPET, HYDERABAD
TEL 040-331 0132
FAX 040-331 1045
E-MAIL kakatiiya@welcomgroup.com
Lavish, whitewashed, classical-style building with modern conveniences. The pool is built around a natural rock and has a built-in spa-bath. Good food.
🛏 189 ⬜ 🏋 🅰 All major cards

TAJ RESIDENCY
$$$
BANJARA HILLS, HYDERABAD
TEL 040-339 3939
FAX 040-339 2684
E-MAIL trhbcentre.hyd@tajhotels.com
Another gleaming white hotel serving the increasingly wealthy city of Hyderabad.
🛏 140 ⬜ 🅰 All major cards

🏨 TAJ BANJARA
🍽 $$$
ROAD NO. 1,
BANJARA HILLS
TEL 040-339 9999
FAX 040 339 2218
E-MAIL banjara.hyderabad@
tajhotels.com
A ten-minute drive from the
hub of the city in the elegant
Banjara Hills, this hotel is
attractively set overlooking
its own lake. The excellent
Dakhni restaurant is a
popular option, serving
authentic Hyderabadi and
Andhra cuisine.
🛏 18 🅿 📶 🚭 All
major cards

🏨 TAJ MAHAL
$
88 SARJINI DEVI RD.,
SECUNDERABAD
TEL 040-812105
Modest, established hotel
opened in 1949, with large
clean rooms. Good Andhra
food, but no bar.
🚭 All major cards

MORE RESTAURANTS
In addition to the hotel
restaurants, all of which are
good in this selection, the twin
cities have a number of
restaurants serving rich
Hyderabadi dishes such as
biryani, the spicy Andhra cuisine
of fish and mutton dishes, and
the Telegu Brahmin vegetarian
dosas, *idlis*, and *uttapams*.

KODAGU (COORG)

🏨 RAJDARSHAN
$
M. G. RD.,
MADIKERI
TEL 0872-29142
Simple but adequate base for
exploring this beautiful and
distinctive area.
🛏 26 🚭 All major cards

MALNAD

🏨 SAMMAN
$
SHIMOGA
TEL 08182-23319

Situated between Hassan and
Hospet, this hotel makes a
good base for visiting the
Malnad area.
🛏 23 🚭 No cards

MUDUMALAI NATIONAL PARK

🏨 BAMBOO BANKS FARM GUEST HOUSE
$
MASINAGUDI
TEL 0423-56222
Established guest house,
whose charming Parsee
owners provide their guests
with good food, pleasant
rooms, and a lawn with
garden.
🛏 6

MYSORE

🏨 LALITHA MAHAL PALACE
$$$
SIDHARTHA NAGAR
TEL 0821-571265
FAX 0821-571770
E-MAIL lmph@bgl.vsnl.net.in.
Spectacular extravaganza of a
palace built in 1931 for the
maharaja of Mysore's foreign,
meat-eating guests. It retains
the original billiards table.
Dining takes place in the
former ballroom.
🛏 72 🅿 📶 🚭 All major
cards

🏨 GREEN HOTEL
$
2270 VINOBA RD.,
JAYALAKSHMI PURAM
TEL 0821-512536
FAX 0821-516139
E-MAIL grenhotl@giasbg01
.vsnl.net.in
Filling part of pretty
Chittaranjan Palace on the
outskirts of town, the simple
rooms have charming local
furnishings, pretty gardens, and
delicious food. The hotel is
run according to strong
ecological principles.
🛏 31 🅿 📶 🚭 MC, V

NAGARHOLE NATIONAL PARK

🏨 KABINI RIVER LODGE
$$$
TEL/FAX 080-558 6163
The maharaja of Mysore's
hunting lodge and the
beautiful Kabini River are the
setting for a relaxed
atmosphere. Naturalists join
guests for riverside suppers
around a fire. Make
reservations in Bangalore,
through Jungle Lodges
& Resorts Ltd. (see p. 365)
🛏 14 plus 6 cottages 🚭 All
major cards

Jungle Lodges & Resorts runs
another camp, **Kali River
Camp** at Dandeli on the
Karnataka–Goa route, in the
thickly forested hills of the
Uttara Kannada area (see
p. 365 for more information.).

TIRUPATI

🏨 GUESTLINE
$
KARAKAMBADI RD.
TEL 08574-28800
FAX 08574-27774
Efficient, practical hotel
servicing pilgrims visiting the
temple at Tirumala.
🛏 110 🅿 📶 🚭 All
major cards

VIJAYANAGAR

🏨 MALLIGI TOURIST HOME
$
JAMBUNATH RD.,
HOSPET
TEL 08394-2201
FAX 08394-57038
From small beginnings, this
hotel has become an
institution with rooms of all
prices (the luxurious ones
are in a new wing). There
are also a garden restaurant,
café, and pool.
🛏 116 🅿 🚭 All major
cards

KEY 🏨 Hotel 🍽 Restaurant 🛏 No. of bedrooms 🅿 Parking 🕐 Closed 🛗 Elevator 🚭 Non-smoking

VIJAYAWADA

QUALITY INN DV MANOR
$
M. G. RD.
TEL 0866-474455
FAX 0866-483170
E-MAIL dvmanor@hotmail.com
Practical and pleasant base for visiting the Telugu heartland.
94 All major cards

VISHAKAPATNAM

TAJ RESIDENCY
$$
BEACH RD.
TEL 0891-567756
FAX 0891-564370
E-MAIL trhgm.viz@tajhotels.com
This dazzling and efficient hotel is quite a pleasant contrast from the surrounding rural area. It overlooks the Bay of Bengal.
94 All major cards

TAMIL NADU

CHENNAI (MADRAS)

If you want to base yourself by the sea for your exploration of Chennai and the surrounding area, see Mahabalipuram (Mamallapuram) below.

TAJ CONNEMARA
$$$
BINNY RD., OFF MOUNT RD.
TEL 044-852 0123
FAX 044-852 3361
E-MAIL tajcon@giasmd01.vsnl.in.
The Nawab of Wallajah's town house has been a spacious, superbly located hotel since the 1930s. It now has a courtyard pool and good food in two restaurants: Verandah, which serves a buffet lunch, and the outdoor Raintree (see p. 368), which serves Chettinad specialties.
150 All major cards

TAJ COROMANDEL
$$$
17 N. H. RD.
TEL 044-872827
FAX 044-825104
The Taj Group's specially built and more upscale Chennai hotel is ideal for business people, but lacks charm. Set in the business district, with easy access to shopping and entertainment. A number of restaurants offer a variety of dining options, including Southern Spice, featuring southern Indian specialties.
205 All major cards

WELCOMGROUP CHOLA SHERATON
$$$
CATHEDRAL RD.
TEL 044-8280101
FAX 044-8278779
E-MAIL chola@welcomgroup.com
Well-established and discreet, this hotel consists mostly of duplex-style suites with personal valet. Good food is provided at two restaurants, the rooftop Sagari (multicuisine) and the Peshwari (Northwest Frontier).
92 All major cards

THE GRAND ORIENT
$$
693 ANNA SALAI
TEL 044-852 4111
FAX 044-852 3412
E-MAIL empee.grand@orient.wiprobt.ems.vsnl.net.in.
Great central location, good value, and no frills. The restaurant offers a reasonable variety, including authentic southern Indian vegetarian dishes.
63 All major cards

NEW VICTORIA
$-$$
3 KENNET LANE, EGMORE
TEL 044-825 3638
FAX 044-825 0070
Modest hotel conveniently placed close to the station.

Rates are inclusive of a good breakfast.
50 All major cards

MORE RESTAURANTS
Chennai, a sophisticated coastal city, has plenty of restaurants that combine high levels of hygiene with delicious food. The vegetarian dishes and fresh seafood (shrimp, lobster, crab) make eating a rewarding experience. Try the hotels listed above, plus the restaurants listed below.

DAKSHIN
$$
PARK SHERATON & TOWERS
132 TTK RD.
TEL 044-499 4101
This restaurant, situated in the large and somewhat brash Welcomgroup Park Sheraton and Towers, serves a variety of southern Indian cuisines. It definitely merits a visit.
All major cards

ANNALAKSHI
$$
806 ANNA SALAI
TEL 044-852 5100
Reservations are essential at this popular vegetarian restaurant.

🍴 RAINTREE
$$
TAJ CONNEMARA,
BINNY RD., OFF MOUNT RD.
TEL 044-852 0123
This restaurant serves
distinctive and spicy dishes
that are part of the cuisine of
the Chettinad area.
🅢 All major cards

🍴 KARAIKUKI
$$
84 DR. RADHAKRISHNA RD.
Spicy Chettinad food.

🍴 PONNUSAMY
$$
ROYAPETTAH
A variety of dishes that draw
on traditional Chettinad
cooking for inspiration.

COIMBATORE

🏨 THE RESIDENCY
$$
AVANASHI ROD
TEL 0422-201234
FAX 0422-201414
E-MAIL rescbe@vsnl.com
Good business hotel, ideal
stop on the way up to, or
down from, Ooty.
🛈 135 🛌 🎦 🅢 All
major cards

COONOOR

🏨 TAJ GARDEN RETREAT
$$
CHURCH RD.,
UPPER COONOOR
TEL 0423-30021
FAX 0423-32775
E-MAIL retreat.coonoor@
tajhotels.com
Old sprawling house with
beautiful lawns and gardens.
Some rooms open onto their
own lawn. Fine views.
🛈 33 🅢 All major cards

KODAIKANAL

🏨 THE CARLTON
$$
LAKE RD.
TEL 04542-40056
FAX 04542-41170
E-MAIL carlton@vsnl.com

Enjoy the charms of a bygone
era at this hotel, which
overlooks the town's lake.
🛈 91 🎦 🅢 All major
cards

MADURAI

🏨 TAJ GARDEN RETREAT
$$$
PASUMALAI, TPK RD.
TEL 0452-601020
FAX 0452-604004
E-MAIL retreat.madurai@
tajhotels.com
Rambling 19th-century
mansion built for the local
manager of a British company.
Set in 62 acres of lush lawns
and gardens on Pasumalai Hill.
Find the pool tucked away,
well down the hillside.
🛈 50 🛌 🅢 All major
cards

🏨 PANDYAN
$$
RACE COURSE RD.
TEL 0452-537090
FAX 0452-533424
E-MAIL phl@pronet.xlweb.com
Practical hotel with shops and
a nice yard.
🛈 57 🅢 All major cards

MAHABALIPURAM (MAMALLAPURAM)

🏨 FISHERMAN'S COVE
$$
COVELONG BEACH
TEL 04114-44304
FAX 04114-44303
Perfect base for visiting
Mahabalipuram and Chennai,
and for exploring temples as
far afield as Kanchipuram. Set
right on the beach. Guests
usually favor the rustic
cottages—which afford peace,
privacy, and sea or garden
views. There is a romantic
beachside café. Avoid
weekend crowds.
🛈 50 plus 38 cottages 🛌
🅢 All major cards

🏨 GOLDEN SUN BEACH RESORT
$$
COVELONG RD.,

NEAR MAHABALIPURAM
TEL 04114-42245
FAX 04114-836247
Unpretentious waterfront
hotel, relaxing atmosphere,
and nice cottages. Good
Gujarati and local food.
🛈 20 plus 40 cottages 🛌
🎦 🅢 All major cards

🏨 IDEAL BEACH RESORT
$
COVELONG RD.,
NEAR MAHABALIPURAM
TEL 04114-42240
FAX 04114-42243
E-MAIL ideal@md2tvsnl.net.in
Simple waterfront hotel much
loved by discerning visitors to
India. Good seafood.
🛈 40 cottages 🛌 🅢 MC,
V

🏨 SILVERSANDS
$
COVELONG RD.,
NEAR MAHABALIPURAM
TEL 04114-42228
FAX 04114-42280
E-MAIL silver@silversandsindia
.com
Modest, beachside hotel
consisting of a wide range of
cottages, some with private
hammocks.
🛈 50 cottages 🅢 All major
cards

RAMESWARAM

🏨 HOTEL TAMIL NADU
$
TEL 04573-21277
FAX 04573-21070
Sufficient for the intrepid
traveler exploring this area.
🛈 10 🅢 None

THANJAVUR

🏨 PARISUTHAM
$$
CANAL RD.
TEL 04362-21601
FAX 04362-22318
Family-run downtown hotel
with friendly atmosphere,
simple but adequate rooms,
and a pleasant pool and lawn.
🛈 50 🛌 🅢 All major
cards

TIRUCHCHIRAPPALLI

🏨 SANGAM
🍴 $$
COLLECTOR'S OFFICE RD.
TEL 0431-414700 OR
0431-414480
FAX 0431-415779
E-MAIL hotelsangam@vsnl.com
WEBSITE www.hotelsangam.com
Practical hotel with pool and
excellent southern Indian *thali*
in the restaurant are a
welcome refuge after a day
of visiting temples.
🛈 56 🅿 ❄ 🏊 💪
🚗 All major cards

UDHAGAMANDALAM (OOTACAMUND, OOTY)

🏨 SAVOY HOTEL
$$$
SYLKS RD.
TEL 0423-444142
FAX 0423-443318
E-MAIL savoyna.oty@tajhotels
.com
Colonial hotel, opened in
1841 to provide facilities for
the British fleeing the heat,
now run by the Taj group.
Experience tea on the lawns
with views of the Nilgiri Hills,
and enjoy the wood fireplaces
in the cottages.
🛈 40 💪 🚗 All major
cards

EASTERN INDIA

ANDAMAN & NICOBAR ISLANDS

🏨 WELCOMGROUP BAY ISLAND
$$
MARINE HILL,
PORT BLAIR
TEL 03192-34101
FAX 03192-31555
E-MAIL wgbayisland@usa.net
Elegant hotel where the best
rooms have balconies
overlooking Phoenix Bay and
the sea. Delightful lawn and
gardens. Good food.
🛈 45 🏊 💪 🚗 MC, V

SINCLAIRS BAY VIEW
🏨 $$
ON THE COAST RD.,
TOWARD CORBYN'S CAVE
TEL 03192-33159
FAX 03192-31824
E-MAIL pressmanindia@
hotmail.com
Clifftop hotel, where the
balconies of the notably clean
rooms have grand sea views.
🛈 30 🏊 💪 🚗 All major
cards

BARGARH (for SAMBALPUR, ORISSA)

🏨 GANAPATHI
$
BARGARH
TEL 06646-31400
FAX 06646-30159
Simple but clean, this is a
good base for visiting both
the tribal area and the
weaving villages.
🚗 All major cards

BODH GAYA

🏨 BODH GAYA ASHOK
$$
NEXT TO THE MUSEUM
TEL 0631-400790
FAX 0631-400788
Traditional bungalow layout.
Ideally situated for walking to
the sites and for taking in the
museum's superb collection.
🛈 32 🅿 ❄ 24 🚗 AE,
MC, V

BHUBANESHWAR

🏨 OBEROI
$$$
CB-1 NAYAPALLI
TEL 0674-440890
FAX 0674-440898
Orissa's best hotel and a good
base. Centrally located in the
regional capital with lush
lawns and gardens.
🛈 70 🏊 🚗 All major
cards

🏨 SWOSTI
$$
103 JANPATH
TEL 0674-535771
FAX 0674-507524

Central, practical hotel near
state emporia for textile
shoppers; known for its good
food. Orissan dishes served if
ordered in advance.
🛈 60 🚗 All major cards

GOPALPUR-ON-SEA

🏨 OBEROI PALM BEACH
$$$$
DISTRICT GANJAM
TEL 0680-282021
FAX 0680-282300
E-MAIL pbeach@dte.vsnl.net.in
Charming, old-world
waterfront hotel with rooms
set around a courtyard and
along the garden facing the
sea. A peaceful location, with
local food, where you can
watch fishermen on beach.
🛈 20 🚗 All major cards

KOLKATA (CALCUTTA)

🏨 OBEROI GRAND
$$$
JAWAHARLAL NEHRU RD.
TEL 033-249 2323
FAX 033-249 3229
Built in the 1890s, this hotel
was bought in 1938 by
Mohan Singh Oberoi, founder
of the upscale Oberoi hotel
group. Today, this is its eastern
flagship. It is in a superb
location, is constantly
renovated, and successfully
mixes colonial character with
contemporary luxury.
🛈 218 🏊 💪 🚗 All
major cards

🏨 TAJ BENGAL
🍴 $$$
BELVEDERE RD.,
ALIPORE
TEL 033-223 3939
FAX 033-223 1766
E-MAIL bengal.cal@tajhotels.com
Just south of the Maidan, so
good for joggers. The interior
design is a mishmash of styles,
with a good Club floor where
suites have their own lawns.
The excellent restaurants
serve Chinese, French, and
rustic Indian cuisine.
🛈 250 🏊 💪 🚗 All
major cards

❄ Air-conditioning 🏊 Indoor/🏊 Outdoor swimming pool 💪 Health club 🚗 Credit cards **KEY**

HOTELS & RESTAURANTS

🏨 THE PARK
$$$
17 PARK ST.
TEL 033-249 7336
FAX 033-249 7343
Right in the center of town, this hotel has a good atmosphere and an informal garden restaurant much patronized by locals.
ℹ️ 149 ⬛ 📺 🚭 All major cards

🏨 PEERLESS INN
🍴 **$$**
12 JAWAHARLAL NEHRU RD.
TEL 033-228 0301
FAX 033-228 6650 OR
033-228 1270
E-MAIL peerinn@giascl01.vsnl.net.in
Next to the Oberoi Grand, this is a good value hotel, spotlessly clean, and home to Aaheli, Calcutta's best Bengali cuisine restaurant. Reservations essential.
ℹ️ 122 🅿️ 🛗 🚭 📺 🚭 All major cards

🏨 TOLLYGUNGE CLUB
$$
120 DESHAPRAN SASMAL RD.,
TEL 033-473 4749
Open to members and their friends (and a few well-connected travel agents), this 200-acre estate with its pools, tennis courts, golf course, other sports, and sedate informality is the perfect retreat after a day exploring one of the world's great cities. Rooms are simple.
ℹ️ 11 ⬛

MORE RESTAURANTS
Bengal's gentle cuisine, with delicately spiced fish (dahi maachh, malai shrimp) and rice is best eaten fresh, and thus it is mostly cooked at home. Only the famous Bengali sweetmeats (rossogolla, rasmalai, sondesh) are easily bought—K. C. Das on Esplanade Road is considered one of the best sources. To eat Bengali food, go to Peerless Inn (see above), Suruchi in Elliot Road, or Kewpies Kitchen on Elgin Lane (tel 033-475 9880).

LUCKNOW

🏨 TAJ RESIDENCY
🍴 **$$$**
GOMTI NAGAR
TEL 0522-393939
FAX 0522-392282
E-MAIL tmhgm.luc@tajgroup
.sprintrpg.ems.vsnl.net.in
Lavish and spacious custom-built colonial-style hotel set in extensive and beautiful formal gardens. The restaurants include the good Oudhyana (Avadh cuisine).
ℹ️ 110 ⬛ 🚭 All major cards

🏨 CLARKS AVADH
$$
MAHATMA GANDHI MARG
TEL 0522 216500
FAX 0522 220131
E-MAIL clarks.lko@sml.sprintrpg
.ems.vsnl.in
Well-established, downtown hotel. The hotel itself lacks character, but its Faluknama restaurant can, if asked in advance, produce good Avadh food.
⬛ 🚭 All major cards

MORE RESTAURANTS
The sophisticated culture of Uttar Pradesh's state capital is evident in its food—the rich and complex Avadh cuisine includes fine kebabs, romali rotis (handkerchief bread), and dum pukht (sealed and steam cooked meat and rice). Try it at the hotels (see above) and Nawabeen in Hotel Arif Castles. Kebabs and breads from stalls in the old market are delicious.

PATNA

🏨 MAURYA PATNA
$$
SOUTH GANDHI MAIDAN
TEL 0612-222061
FAX 0612-222069
E-MAIL maurya2@dte.vsnl.net.in
Efficient, central hotel. No frills.
ℹ️ 80 ⬛ 🚭 All major cards

PURI

🏨 MAYFAIR BEACH RESORT
$$
CHAKRATIRTHA RD.
TEL 06752-27800
FAX 06752-24242
E-MAIL mayfair1@dte.vsnl.net.in
Cottages, some with beautiful views, set amid plenty of greenery.
ℹ️ 34 cottages ⬛ 📺 🚭 AE, MC, V

RAJGIR

🏨 CENTAUR HOKKE
🍴 **$$$**
RAJGIR
TEL 06119-5254
FAX 06119-5231
Elegant, discreetly run Japanese hotel on the edge of town serving Buddhist pilgrims from the east. Mixture of Japanese and Western-style rooms, good Japanese food.
ℹ️ 26 🚭 All major cards

SHANTINIKETAN

🏨 CHHUTI HOLIDAY RESORT
🍴 **$**
CHARU PALLI, JAMBONI
TEL 03463-52692
Modest cottages somewhat in keeping with Shantiniketan's ideals. Good food.
🚭 All major cards

VARANASI (BENARES)

🏨 TAJ GANGES
$$$
NADESAR PALACE GROUNDS
TEL 0542-345100
FAX 0542-348067
E-MAIL ganges.varanasi@
tajhotels.com
This and Clark's, below, are, despite their price, disappointingly the best in town. A dependable stream of tourists and pilgrims fills this hotel. The staff has a laidback approach.
ℹ️ 130 ⬛ 🚭 All major cards

🏢 CLARK'S VARANASI

$$

THE MALL,
VARANASI CANTONMENT
TEL 0542-348501
FAX 0542-348186
E-MAIL clarksvns@satyam.net.in
Well-established, friendly hotel
with spacious rooms.
Centrally located, it also has
organized activities related to
the pilgrimage events at the
river.
🛈 133 🔁 🌊 🔗 AE, MC,
V

THE HIMALAYA

These hotels are useful bases
for trekking or exploring an
area. Several in the western
Himalaya are historic buildings
in beautiful settings. If you are
trekking, your travel agent
will arrange the modest
accommodations or tents.

WESTERN HIMALAYA

For hotels in Mussoorie,
Nainital, Rishikesh, and Shimla,
see p. 351.

ALMORA

🏢 MOUNTAIN RESORT

$

KHALI ESTATE
TEL 05962-22973
Stay in simple cottages or
bungalows at this resort
situated in the ancient cultural
capital of the Kumaun area.
All meals are provided.
🔗 All major cards

DALHOUSIE

🏢 AROMA & CLAIRE'S

$

COURT RD.
TEL 018982-2199
This rambling 1930s hillside
house retains plenty of hill
station atmosphere. From
here explore Dalhousie and
Chamba.
🔗 No cards

DEHRADUN

🏢 MADHUBAN

$

RAJPUR RD.
TEL 0135-749990 OR
0125-749995
FAX 0135 746496
E-MAIL hotelmadhuban@
sancharnet.in OR madhuban@nde
.vsnl.net.in
Winner of the Green Hotel
of the Year 2000, this makes
an excellent stop on the way
up to the hills. Good food.
🛈 42 plus 5 cottages 🍽
🔗 All major cards

KANGRA

🏢 JUDGES COURT

$$

PRAGPUR
TEL 01970-45035
FAX 01970-45335
E-MAIL eries@vsnl.com
A charming country mansion
built about 1900 for Justice Sir
Jai Lala and still redolent of its
colonial days. The hotel is set
in orchards overlooking the
Dhauladhar Mountains and is
next to Pragpur, India's first
heritage village. Now
managed by Welcomgroup.
🛈 10 🔗 AE, MC, V

🏢 TARAGARH PALACE

$$

TEL 01894-63034
FAX 01894-63523
Taragarh Palace was built high
in the foothills of the
Dhauladhar Mountains in the
1930s, and was later owned
by the Jammu & Kashmir royal
family. It retains its original
colonial decor and furnishings,
and is surrounded by stunning
countryside made up of forest
and tea gardens.
🛈 12 🌊 🔗 All major
cards

KAUSANI

🏢 AMAR HOLIDAY HOME

$

TEL 05969-84115
Modest, friendly, family-run
hotel with beautiful lawn and

PRICES

HOTELS
An indication of the cost
of a double room without
breakfast is given by **$** signs.
$$$$$	Over $280
$$$$	$160–$280
$$$	$100–$160
$$	$40–$100
$	Under $40

RESTAURANTS
An indication of the cost of a
three-course dinner without
drinks is given by $ signs.
$$$$$	Over $80
$$$$	$50–$80
$$$	$35–$50
$$	$20–$35
$	Under $20

views. This is a good base for
walks in the Kumaun.
🔗 No cards

MANALI

🏢 JOHN BANNON'S GUEST HOUSE

$$

THE MANALI ORCHARD
TEL 01902-52335
FAX 01902-52392
Small and personal place with
large, comfortable rooms and
great views down the valley.
Peacefully set in an orchard
about a five-minute walk
north of the main street.
🛈 12

EASTERN HIMALAYA

DARJILING

🏢 NEW ELGIN

🍽 $$

H. M. LAMA RD.
TEL 0354-54114
FAX 0354-54267
E-MAIL newelgin@cal.vsnl.net.in
Currently Darjiing's best hotel.
This is a comfortable and
well-maintained establishment,
with good food.
🛈 25 🔗 All major cards

HOTELS & RESTAURANTS

GANGTOK

🏨 NOR-KHILL
$$$
PALJOR STADIUM RD.
TEL 03592-23186
FAX 03592-23187
E-MAIL newelgin@cal.vsnl.net.in
Relatively luxurious former guesthouse of the much respected Chogyal rulers. It is unfortunately situated next to the stadium.
🚫 All major cards

KALIMPONG

🏨 KALIMPONG PARK
$$
RINKINGPONG RD.
TEL 03552-55304
FAX 03552-55982
E-MAIL parkotel@dte.vsnl.net.in
WEBSITE www.indiamart.com/kalimpongparkhotel
The former summer home of the maharaja of Dinajpur, with fine mountain views. Smoking is not permitted in the restaurant, which serves a variety of cuisines including local Nepalese and Tibetan dishes.
🛏 20 🅿 🚭 ⛵ 🍴
🚫 MC, V

🏨 KALIMPONG TOURIST LODGE (WBTDC)
$
MORGAN HOUSE
TEL 03552-55384
One of the best, established tourist lodges in the region, with plenty of character and fine views.
🛏 7 🚫 All major cards

NORTHEASTERN STATES

ARUNACHAL PRADESH

🏨 DONYI POLO ASHOK
$
ITANAGAR
TEL 0360-212626
FAX 0360-212611
Arunachal Pradesh's best hotel. Relatively good food.
🚫 All major cards

GUWHATI

🏨 TOURIST LODGE, GUWAHATI
$
BRAHMAPUTRA ASHOK
M. G. RD.
TEL 0361-541064
FAX 0361-540870
E-MAIL guwashok@indiatourism
.xeegan.xeemail.ems.vsnl.net.in
Modest hotel with an advantageous riverside setting.
🛏 50 🚫 All major cards

🍴 PARADISE
$
G. N. BORDOLOI RD.
CHANDMARI
TEL 0361-546904
There are curries and Chinese dishes here as well, but stay with the Assamese cooking and order a *thali*. You can have a meat or vegetarian option.
🚭

KAZIRANGA NATIONAL PARK

🏨 WILD GRASS RESORT
$
NEAR KOHORA
GOLAGHAT
TEL 03776-62011
Charming colonial-style lodge, extremely well run. The staff will arrange everything from picking you up at the airport to game drives, elephant rides, fishing trips, and rafting. A lodge is also located inside the park.
🛏 18 ⛵

🏨 PARADISE
$
SOLICITORS RD.
JOHAT
TEL 0376-321521
FAX 0376-323512
Modest base for seeing northern Assam.
🛏 31 🚫 All major cards

MANIPUR

🏨 IMPHAL
$
IMPHAL DIMAPUR RD.,

IMPHAL
TEL 03852-220459
FAX 03852-224354
Very simple hotel for travelers exploring Manipur.
🛏 60 🚫 No cards

MEGHALAYA

🏨 POLO TOWERS
$
OAKLAND RD.
POLO GROUNDS,
SHILLONG
TEL 0364-222340 OR
0364-222341
FAX 0364-220090
E-MAIL htp@vsnl.com
Practical and central, with good food.
🛏 50 🅿 ⬆ 🚫 AE, MC, V

MIZORAM

🏨 MOONLIGHT
$
BAWNGHAWN,
AIZWAL
TEL 0389-2647
Simple hotel, whose restaurant serves distinctive Mizo food—lentils, fish, bamboo shoots, and rice.
🚫 No credit cards

NAGALAND

🏨 JAPFU ASHOK
$
P. R. HILLS,
KOHIMA
TEL 0370-22721
Simple, with spacious rooms, this hotel is centrally situated in the town.
🛏 27 🚫 MC, V

TRIPURA

🏨 ROYAL GUEST HOUSE
$
PALACE COMPOUND,
WEST GATE,
AGARTALA
TEL 0381-225652
Modest yet comfortable and spacious, with good food.
🚫 No cards

SHOPPING IN INDIA

Take a tip from second-time visitors to India: Pack an extra hold-all bag in the bottom of your suitcase. This is for your inevitable shopping. Indian craftsmanship of almost every kind can be remarkable for its quality and originality, and prices are often lower than in other countries.

If you see something that is just what you want, buy it—if it is specifically local or particularly good, you may not see some thing similar again. If you have an idea of what you want to buy before you leave home, such as silk furnishing or dress fabrics, or a piece of jewelry to match an outfit, take color swatches with you as the Indian light can confuse the memory. Also, do some research on equivalent prices in your own country so you know when you are on to a bargain.

Shopping opportunities come in various forms: There are the government emporia, run by each state, often in dowdy concrete buildings. They stock high-quality crafts produced in that state and sell them at fixed prices. They have knowledgeable staff, accept credit cards, and will ship goods (after a bit of form-filling). You do not bargain.

Beware: Do not be seduced by private shops that pose as state-run emporia, giving themselves almost the same title, slipping in words such as "authorized" and "emporium"; they often stock shoddy goods at high prices or nice crafts at outrageous prices.

The hotel shops, unlike many in the West, are often extremely good and are even patronized by discerning locals. Their convenience and their long opening hours compensate for the slightly above average prices; bargaining is perfectly acceptable. Those selling fabric will usually offer a very fast tailoring service, too; if you are returning to a city, then there is time to order a garment and have a fitting to ensure it is precisely correct.
Finally, there are the markets. In

these you will probably have the most shopping fun, even if you only buy small items. A successful purchase demands your own judgement and your own sense of the right cost—remember, however hard you bargain the trader will always sell for more than cost price.

There are one or two high-priced items that need special care. A carpet is a big buy and, even in a reliable hotel shop, should be undertaken with extreme caution. It is wise to compare prices, to bargain hard and, if making a purchase, to sign the carpet on the back, measure it yourself, and take a picture of it. You should also have a full descriptive receipt. Then, when it arrives home, usually after about three months, you can be sure it is the one you chose.

As for the temptation of jewelry, apart from a few exceptions, stores in deluxe hotels are the safest places to buy big items. Modest buys, either loose or set, include garnets, topazes, amethysts, and black stars, all mined in India. Pearls, sorted and pierced in Hyderabad, are also a good value. A reputable jeweler should always be prepared to give you a certificate of authenticity and be prepared to buy back a piece you later decide you do not want.

The variety of India's fabrics is infinite and impossible to resist. Whether it is a woolen shawl, some Karnataka raw silk, or just some dazzlingly bright cotton from Jaipur's market, most people buy something. Silk and cotton are sold in sari lengths (which vary slightly around the country, so check) or by the meter. Here are some shopping ideas,

following the areas covered by the chapters of this book.

DELHI

Delhi is a shoppers' dream. The stores are conveniently close together, the staff usually excellent and efficient, and the stock is gleaned from all over India.

MARKETS
If you want to browse in bustling markets, head for Old Delhi (see pp. 64–67) and explore Kinari Bazar (see p. 66).

CRAFTS
For the best crafts shopping available in India, first get your eye attuned by visiting the National Crafts Museum (see p. 72), then go to two places in Connaught Place. One is the **Central Cottage Industries Emporium,** a multistory department store on Janpath, opposite the Imperial Hotel, that stocks quality crafts from each state; especially good for furnishing fabrics, home furnishings, and silk by the meter, and a safe place to buy a carpet. The other is the row of excellent individual state emporia that line one side of Baba Kharak Singh Marg. Arranged in three blocks, with a convenient café between blocks A and B for dazed shoppers, this is where you can focus in on, say, Varanasi silk at the Uttar Pradesh store called **Gangotri,** or *bidri* ware at the Andhra Pradesh store, called **Lepakshi.** If you forgot to buy your silk in Bangalore, you can do it here at **Cauvery,** the Karnataka store.

CONNAUGHT PLACE
You might want to explore Connaught Place itself with its mix of camera shops, clothes shops, restaurants, and several bazaars including **Shankar Market** (fabric, cheap tailors, wicker baskets) and **Palika Bazar** (underground market).

CLOTHES & JEWELRY

For a selection of contemporary goods, visit Santushti, a group of shops opposite Ashoka Hotel that includes a branch of the much-loved Jaipur shop, **Anokhi,** with comfortable cotton clothes for women at a fraction of their export price. The store also sells furnishings including quilts and table linens.

Other boutiques fill the lanes of Haus Khas and form a cluster at Marauli, near the Qutab Minar. A stroll around the art, antique, and jewelry shops of Sundar Nagar may lead you into buying art at the **Kumar Gallery** or a special piece of jewelry at **Bharany's,** a favorite with discerning locals. Most of the residential areas of ever expanding south Delhi have their own shopping areas.

AROUND DELHI

The best buy is at Agra, where the marble *pietra dura* (hard stone) inlay is almost as good as it is in the panels decorating the Taj Mahal, since the 5,000 or so craftsmen making it are descended from those who worked on the great building. Go to a good store, such as **Subhash Emporium** at 18/1 Gwalior Road, where you can see how it is done and study award-winning pieces. The **V.P. Handicraft Palace** at Fatehabad Road also has quality craftwork. The family who runs it descended from the original workers on the Taj Mahal, and these showrooms display their workmanship. You can purchase anything from an ornamental box to a huge table top made in marble inlaid with lapis lazuli, jasper, malachite, and cornelian. Weight is not a problem as a shipment of goods to anywhere in the world can be arranged.

But beware: Hawkers and even shopkeepers will try to sell inferior soapstone as marble. If you visit in February, the fair near the Taj Mahal parking garage is well worth visiting to buy quality crafts direct from craftsmen from all over India.

RAJASTHAN & GUJARAT

These two states are a joy for those interested in folk crafts, bright colors, and bold fabrics (see pp. 144–45). Throughout the area you can find tie-dye fabrics, mirror-work appliqué, and heavy tapestry. Cottons, not silks, predominate; and colors are bold blues, saffron, pinks, and reds. Jewelry is equally bold, especially the big silver bangles for wrists and ankles, and the heavy silver earrings.

JAIPUR

At Jaipur, you find the best block prints at **Anokhi,** but leave time to explore **Johari Bazar** (silver, cloth), **Badi Chopra** (bangles, sandals) and **Gopalji ka Bazar** (gemstones). **Soma of Jaipur** specializes in soft furnishings and women's clothes.

JODHPUR

Jodhpur has lacquer wooden boxes, beautiful puppets, and the best tie-dye fabrics.

AHMEDABAD

In Ahmedabad you can feast on Gujarat's rich tradition of high-quality weaving, hand-block print-ing, and tie-dye fabrics. Indeed, the choice of fabrics ranges from fine cotton crepe to one of the great achievements of Indian weaving, the *patola* sari of Rajkot. The **Art Book Center,** Madalapur (tel 079-658 2130 or 079-640 7361, fax 079-630 6376), near the Jain Temple, is an outstanding source of books on Indian art, textiles, and architecture. **Honeycomb International,** in the basement of the Cama Hotel, has a collection of antique textiles, woven, embroidered, and appliqued, as well as less expensive modern pieces. High quality, but well worth the price. Gujarat is also known for its highly decorative carved and lacquered furniture, its brass and wood chests, and toys. The good state emporium, **Gujari,** is on Ashram Road.

In Patan on Patolawala Street you will find **Vinayak K. Salvi,** master weavers of double *ikat* (patola). They specialize in the weaving of hand-dyed silk from Patar in northern Gujarat. The use of traditional skills to weave elaborate patterns is reflected in the prices—starting around $4,500 for a sari length. Even if you cannot afford to buy, admire the skill needed to produce these pieces. At **Khatri Mohammadbhai Siddikbhai & Co.** in Dhamadka, traditional hand-blocked printing and dyeing using natural colors is used to produce shawls, tablecloths, throws, bedcovers, and cushion covers.

MUMBAI & MAHARASHTRA

To shop well in Mumbai needs more skill than in Delhi, and a good knowledge of the city. Eschewing the bourgeois lifestyle that encourages India's craftsmen, Mumbai looks toward Rome and Hollywood for fashion inspiration. If your hotel is downtown, check out the in-hotel shops of the Taj Mahal and Oberoi. Two blocks behind the Taj Mahal is Colaba, a splendid street lined with shops selling excellent leather goods, suits, shirts, and shoes, with a row of stalls in front of them managed by witty hawkers selling copies of everything from Nike to Armani.

If you're passing through Mumbai and spending a few hours at the **Leela Kempinski Hotel,** do not miss the in-house leather shops whose locally made handbags, jackets, and briefcases are of startling similarity to those sold in Italy.

WEST COAST

South of Mumbai, shopping is unexciting apart from the bags of delicious fresh cashew nuts sold everywhere.

KOCHI

Jewtown has spice shops and a bookshop, while in the Fort area the **Malabar House Hotel**'s shop is an inspiration. Across the water in Ernakulum, a booming economy means the main high street, M.G. Road, has well-stocked jewelry shops and excellent silk shops at the north end whose saris include the traditional cream-colored Kerala one with its refined gold stripe. **Kairali,** the state emporium, and **Saurabhi,** the handicrafts emporium, are also here, stocking carved rosewood, masks, and other Kathakali props.

THE DECCAN

BANGALORE

Bangalore is the center of Karnataka's state-run silk industry (see p. 229), so prices are especially good. You can choose the color, weight, and texture—smooth, raw, stone-washed, chiffon, or crepe. A cluster of silk shops on Commercial Street includes the reliable **Deepam,** but you should shop around among them. This street, M.G. Road, and Brigade Road form the hub of fashionable and easy shopping.

Shops here sell ready-made clothes and traditional Karnataka goods such as sandalwood, ivory, brass, rosewood inlay, and Lambani jewelry. Visit **Cinnamon** at 11 Walton Road for top-quality clothes and jewelry. **Cotton World** in the Barton Centre, M.G. Road, sells Western-style shirts, blouses, trousers, and shorts at bargain prices.

For "Modern Indian" go to **FabIndia** at 54, 17th Main, 2nd Block. This house converted into a shop is filled with stylish Indian clothing, crafts, rugs, and much more, including excellent *kurtas, salwar kameez,* jackets, and waistcoats. A wide range of shoes and sandals are stocked at **Lord's Shoes,** 189 Brigade Road. Fine arts and crafts are sold at **Artworks,** 10/2 O'Shaughnessy Road, above Canara Bank in Langford Town.

HYDERABAD

In Hyderabad, shopping is not easy, although there are some great buys if you are prepared to look hard. Go to **Char Minar** for pearls of every size and color. In the Abids area, find southern Indian silks at **Meena Bazaar** and **Pochampally Silks and Sarees,** both on Tilak Road; here, too, are glass and studded bangles and traditional bidri ware (black metal inlaid with silver).

TAMIL NADU

This is the state to find top-quality hand-woven silk. It is tempting to buy in Kanchipuram, but prices are high and you may have little time to browse.

CHENNAI

This is the best large city for shopping in southern India. On Mount Road find the state emporium, **Poompuhar,** and a branch of **Central Cottage Industries Emporium** (see p. 373), the **Khadi** shop, and various other state emporia. A branch of **FabIndia** for home furnishings is nearby on Woods Road. Visit **Handloom House** on Rattan Bazaar, and **Rasi Silk Emporium** on Anna Salai. **Spencer & Co.,** on the same street, sell local pickles, Chettinad spices, fresh tea, and other specialties. **Vummidi Bangaru Jewellers** stock distinctive southern Indian jewelry.

EASTERN INDIA

This area of India has some wonderful markets that, while not as colorful as Rajasthan's, are full of spirit.

KOLKATA

In Kolkata, **New Market** has acquired the status of a monument, and the shops around it mix practicality with fashion. For traditional Bengali goods rarely found outside the state, go to **Ananda** on Russell Street; for boutiques, try **Ritu's** on Park Street. **Handloom House** and **Bengali Handloom,** in the CIT Complex, Dhakshinapan, sell fabrics. The state emporium, **Monapali,** is on Loudon Street, and **Central Cottage Industries Emporium** is on J. L. Nehru Road.

BHUBANESHWAR

In Orissa, find delicate silver jewelry, sculpture, basketry, appliqué work, metal figurines, and outstanding fabrics, such as ikat weaves in the Bhubaneshwar shops. **Utkalika,** in Market Building on Rajpath, is the state emporium; several fabric shops nearby include Orissa state **Handloom Development Corporation.**

VARANASI

Varanasi is famous for its rich brocade silks, known as Barnasi brocade, found on the tiny lane off the silk market (see p. 307). Explore the nearby brass market, too. See the fine chikan work (white embroidery on fine muslin) sold at **UP Handlooms** in the Hazratganj area.

THE HIMALAYA

India's hills are for relaxing or hiking in, not for shopping. Local woolen shawls and walking sticks are good buys. Pilgrimage centers sell Ganga water.

ACTIVITIES & ENTERTAINMENT

Most people visit India to see its outstanding historic monuments, its superb scenery, and its fascinating lifestyle. Some visitors may like to spend at least part of their time there taking part in India's two most popular activities: trekking and visiting wildlife sanctuaries and national parks. But India can also offer you plenty of other activities and entertainment to add to your sight-seeing. Why not a round of golf in the cool of the morning? Or a visit to a festival performance of dance-drama in the evening?

PERFORMING ARTS

Many artistic performances in India are connected more or less directly to its religions. Although there is plenty going on, it is not always easy to find. Your first stop in a town should be the tourist office where staff are usually very good; some offices even have a printed list of one-off events and festivals (see also the section on Festivals pp. 379–82)—a religious festival may well draw top stars in classical music or dance. Tourist offices can book tickets, which are usually modestly priced and readily available; most Indian people do not like to book up their time in advance in the way Western people do. The local English edition of national newspapers such as *The Times of India*, *The Hindustan Times*, *The Indian Express*, or *The Hindu* also list the day's events. Delhi, Mumbai, Bangalore, Chennai, and Kolkata each have their own local events magazines, usually given away free in hotels.

You may expect quality dance, dance-drama, and music to be performed in custom-built halls such as those in Delhi or the Bharat Bhawan in Bhopal. But many top performances are given outside, by or in temples, in ruins, at shrines, in forts or beneath modest awnings— Delhi's major Ram Lila spectacle is performed on a temporary platform rigged up outside the Red Fort; Chennai's musicians sometimes perform in backstreet gardens. The one place top artists do not

like to perform is hotels. Kathakali shows (see p. 207) are a special event in Kerala. The Kalamandalam Academy performs at the Kerala Kathakali Center, Kochi Aquatic Club, River Road, and Fort Cochin waterfront.

SPORTS & RECREATION

Not only are there plenty of sports in India, they are serviced to a degree rare in the West. Hikers and trekkers have their equipment carried for them, horseback riders have their horses prepared for them, fishermen even have the bait put on the hook for them. In Goa you can enjoy most water sports, while in the lower Himalaya you can ski and river raft.

GOLFING

Golfers are especially well served in India, the first country outside Britain to lay golf courses. The Royal Calcutta Golf Club was founded in 1829. At most clubs visitors are welcome and given temporary membership, and can rent equipment. Spectacularly beautiful courses include **Shillong** with its wooded dells, **Delhi** with its Mogul remains, and **Gulmarg** with a mountain backdrop.

HORSEBACK RIDING

Riders are increasingly well catered for in India, especially at Udaipur and other Rajasthan cities. There are imaginative and well-run expeditions, or you can simply arrange an individual ride when you arrive at your hotel.

The adventurous could try a camel ride in a desert area such as Rajasthan. Your hotel or the local tourist office will have details of reliable operators.

SCUBA DIVING

Scuba diving is popular in the Andaman Islands and in Goa. Equipment can be hired from local dive centers, who also run courses from beginners' level to advanced.

SPECTATOR SPORTS

Indians love to bet, and horse-racing is a favorite source of inspiration. Much of the horse training in India is centered around Bangalore. Here and at Mumbai, Mysore, and Kolkata there are very pretty courses that make an afternoon at the races great fun. So, too, is a polo match. You are most likely to find the latter on a weekend at either Delhi or Jaipur polo grounds.

Cricket, however, is the national obsession. You do not have to understand very much about it; simply enjoy the gentle rhythm of the game. Americans might like to think of it as the ancestor of baseball: Two batsmen take it in turns to defend one of the "wickets" (wooden frames of three uprights and two crosspieces) from the bowlers of the opposing side. The batsman's aim is to score runs, either by running between the wickets while the ball is out in the field, or by hitting the ball to the boundary (four runs) or over it (six runs). The bowler's aim is to knock down the wicket or to cause the batsman to hit the ball into the air where it can be caught by one of the fielding side—that batsman is then "out" and another takes his place. When ten men from one side are all out, the other side bats and the first side fields.

All over India you will see kids putting bat to ball anywhere they can—inside a mosque, on a road, in a field of sugarcane, on a railway siding—even sharing valuable space with another team and having players field for two teams simultaneously.

Other spectator sports are soccer, and field hockey—at which Indians have been champions for decades.

SWIMMING & OTHER WATER SPORTS

Hotels provide some facilities. Many have swimming pools, but these may be closed when there is a big local function using the adjoining terrace. If a pool is important to you, check its availability. Most hotels allow non-guests to use their pools for a small fee (around 550 rupees).

There are long stretches of delightful beaches along India's coasts; Goa in particular is known for its beach resorts. If you are intending to swim in the sea, check carefully for a possible undertow and check that the lifeguard is on the beach when you swim. In areas with few tourists, be sure not to wear a scanty bikini or locals will be upset; put a T-shirt over your usual outfit, and do not go topless.

TENNIS

Some hotels have tennis courts, although their conditions vary, and supply balls and rackets, but keen players should bring their own equipment. Other hotel facilities might include table tennis, badminton, and mini-golf. If the hotel does not have the sports facility you want, the management can usually arrange for you to use a local club.

TREKKING

Trekking can mean a rugged 14-day high-altitude expedition in the Himalaya with a guide and porters or a day hike in the Nilgiri Hills guided by information from the local tourist office.

The toughness of the trek you choose and your own fitness determine the preparation you need to make; age is no barrier. However, if you keep below 11,000 feet (3,360 m) you should need little preparation if you are reasonably fit. In the Himalaya a trek can be a gentle hike with porters and ponies, a climb with just a Sherpa (mountain guide), or a rigorous expedition into the high mountains. Confident and experienced trekkers can arrange a route and porters for themselves, but it is always wise to consult the local tourist office, which will have knowledge of local conditions. Alternatively let the tourist office arrange the trek for you. They should be able to provide an English-speaking leader who will hire porters, deal with problems, and may even be able to tell you something about the history of the area, and about the wildlife that you see on your trek.

For most people it is best to go in a group, organized by a specialist trekking company. This will be more expensive, but such companies have experience of what suits most foreign visitors and have all the necessary back-up should anything go wrong. There are plenty of such companies in India as well as in the U.S. and the U.K. (see below).

It is important that you check precisely what your route entails and do not challenge yourself too much. Ensure you have all your inoculations; mountain air and water may feel healthy but they can carry the same diseases; and do take malaria prophylactics, even if you are above the transmission cut-off height of 6,500 feet (2,000 m) for most of your trip. As for packing, the less and the lighter the better. Use the expertise of a good mountaineering store to buy all your specialist items, from rucksack to water bottle and boots. Once on your trek, a good Sherpa will ensure you pause to acclimatize as you

climb, and will never push you too far. Remember that the Himalaya trekking season can be short and tip generously as your porter may only have a few earning months a year. Your company will advise what is appropriate.

Specialist trekking companies

India
Himalayan Journeys
P.O. Box 15, The Mall, Manali 175131 Himachal Pradesh; tel 01902-52365 or 01902-53355; fax 01902-53065; e-mail himjourn@del3.vsnl.net.in; website www.himalayanjourneys india.com

Clipper Holidays
Suite 406 Regency Enclave, 4 Magrath Rd., Bangalore; tel 080-559 9032 or 080-559 2023; fax 080-559 9833 e-mail clipper@bangalore.wipro .net.in

Corbett Trails India
114 Siddharth Enclave, New Delhi 110014; tel 011-691 4308 or 011-684 6857; fax 011-981 0064 322; e-mail info@corbett-trails.com; website www. corbett-trails.com

Crystal Holidays
B601, Ansal Chambers 1, 3 Bhikaji Cama Place, New Delhi 110066; tel 011-618 6909 or 011-618 2772 or 011-616 1252 or 011-616 3107; fax 011-618 6122; e-mail trekking@crystal holidays.com; website www .indiamart.com/crystalholidays

United States
Geographic Expeditions
2627 Lombard St., San Francisco, CA 94123; tel 415/922-0448; fax 415/346-5535; e-mail info@geoex.com; website geoex.com

Abercrombie & Kent
1520 Kensington Rd., Oak Brook, IL 60529; tel 630/954-2944; fax 630/954-3324; e-mail info@abercrombiekent.com

website www.abercrombiekent
.com

Concordia Expeditions Inc.,
P.O. Box 4159, Buena Vista, CO
81211; tel 719/395-9191; fax
719/395-4868; e-mail info@
concordiaexpeditions.com;
website www.concordia
expeditions.com

United Kingdom
Abercrombie & Kent
Sloane Square House, Holbein
Place, London SW1W 8NS; tel
020-7730 9600; fax 020-7730
9376; e-mail info@abercrombie
kent.co.uk

Explore Worldwide
1 Frederick St., Aldershot, Hants
GU11 1LQ; tel 01252-760 100;
fax 01252-760 001; website
www.explore.co.uk

Guerba Expeditions Ltd.
Wessex House, 40 Station Rd.,
Westbury, Wilts BA13 3JN; tel
01373-826611; fax 01373-
858351; e-mail info@guerba
.demon.co.uk; website
www.guerba.com

WILDLIFE SANCTUARIES & NATIONAL PARKS

A stay in one of India's many
wildlife sanctuaries or national
parks may be a highlight of your
visit. It is a chance to relax, catch
up on your diary, and learn from
the usually well informed guides
something about the geography,
wildlife, and nature of the
extraordinary country you have
come to visit. You may arrive
thinking only of seeing a tiger,
but a successful visit is much
more than this.

Park accommodations can be
good, although this is not always
the case. For a fixed price it
usually includes your room and
washing facilities, your meals,
early morning and afternoon tea,
jeep, elephant and boat rides
with naturalists as guides (you
are not usually allowed to walk
in the parks unescorted), and

extra nature walks, wildlife films,
or talks. Beware of temperature
extremes: chilly at dawn and
dusk in winter, blisteringly hot at
noon in summer.

Best viewing is from March to
June, the pre-monsoon period
when the animals have less
choice of water holes. Do not
wear brightly colored clothing;
wear a hat, take good binoculars,
a camera; and 400 or 800 ASA
film; use a cushion or back-
pillow for rides in jeeps. Take
great notice of your guide's
safety instructions. Tipping on
departure is important (100
rupees a day per person for the
camp staff and naturalist, 50
rupees for the driver).

Useful contacts include:

**Indian Adventures Wildlife
Resorts**
257 S.V. Rd., Bandra (W),
Mumbai 400050, India; tel 022-
640 8742; fax 022-645 8401;
e-mail iawr@vsnl.com; website
www.indianadventures.com

Wild Grass
Barua Bhavan, 107 M.C. Rd.,
Uzan Bazar, Guwahati 781001;
tel 0351-546827; fax 0361-
630465; e-mail wildgrass@gwl
.dot.net.in

FESTIVALS IN INDIA

Traveling through India, you will almost certainly bump into a festival. It may be a small village celebration with the temple deity dressed up and enthroned in a field surrounded by drummers, pipers, a small fair, and some cows with brightly painted horns. It may be a wedding procession, with dancing through the town's back-streets to the accompaniment of a brass band and fancy chandeliers powered by a mobile generator. It may be an arts festival, such as the Bharata Natyam dance season in Chennai. Or you may happen to be in the right place at the right time for one of the great Hindu festivals, such as Durga Puja in Kolkata or Diwali in Rajasthan. Whatever it is, Indian people will welcome you joining them.

Fortunately, many of the most spectacular festivals are held during the cooler winter months when visitors tend to time their India trips. Here is a tiny selection of month-by-month suggestions for especially colorful festivals to look out for. The state where the festival is held (or, for nationwide festivals, the best place to witness each) is given after the name, if relevant; the specific date is given if there is one. Since many festival dates are determined by the lunar calendar, even some of the major festivals can vary their dates from year to year. Other festivals may be arranged with little warning, such as the elephant ones in Kerala. You should check for major dates with the Government of India Tourist Office before you leave home, and then check at local tourist offices to see what is going on as you move around India. Also, beware that apart from major festivals as Republic Day, when everything closes across the country, such things as closures of local forts or museums at festival times are often unpredictable, so be flexible.

JANUARY

Feast of the **Reis Magos** or Three Kings, Goa, January 6. Elaborate processions at Cansaulim, Chandor, and Reis Magos churches.

Elephant March, Kerala. Over 100 caparisoned elephants

parade from Trissur to Thiruvananthapuram over three days, during which snake boat races are held at Alappuzha. The spectacular fourth day finale involves many otherwise hard-to-see regional Kerala dances and displays of Kalariphayat (local martial arts).

Pongal, Tamil Nadu, mid-January.
This is the celebration of the rice harvest, and is southern India's most important festival. It is at its most colorful in Tamil Nadu where four days of celebrations start with houses and bullocks being scrubbed and painted, and women drawing *kolams* (elaborate rice patterns) outside their doors. On Pongal, the first dish of newly harvested rice is boiled up with sugarcane and turmeric—according to tradition the more the boiling mixture froths and spills over the pot, the better the next harvest will be. The next day, the bullocks, with their long horns newly painted, are garlanded and raced through the villages by young men.

Delhi Rose Show, Delhi.
An impressive show with serious judges and proud winners, held against the backdrop of Safdarjang's grand tomb.

Kite Festival, northern India, mid-January.
Flimsy, brightly colored paper kites are flown by people of all ages. Kite battles are staged from the rooftops, and for these the kite strings are coated with

crushed glass and gum to turn them into lethal weapons for their handlers to use against their opponents' kites.

Lori, Punjab, mid-January.
Music and dancing to celebrate the height of winter.

Republic Day, nationwide, January 26.
India's principle national holiday celebrates the inauguration of the Republic of India and the adoption of its constitution in 1950. Celebrations are most dramatic in New Delhi, where the President's bodyguard leads a spectacular morning-long public parade of state floats, dancers, camels, elephants, and military equipment. Tickets are on sale at travel agencies, tourist offices, and hotel bell desks. All the events are televised country-wide. Each evening during the week, Rastrapati Bhawan (see p. 86) is illuminated and, once the visiting foreign dignitaries have left Delhi, its spectacular Mughal Gardens are open to the public for about six weeks.

Folk Dance Festival, Delhi, January 27–28.
The capital's public halls are filled with performances of colorful and fascinating dances from all over India.

Beating the Retreat, Delhi, January 29.
A brief but impressive ceremony held at sunset at the bottom of Raisina Hill. Massed bands parade, camels stand at attention on the ramparts, and the Last Post is sounded by a lone trumpet from one high pavilion as the north star comes out. Fireworks then burst into the sky. This, like the Republic Day celebrations, is televised. A few tickets are on sale.

JANUARY–FEBRUARY

Teepam, Madurai.
Known as the Floating Festival, this celebrates the birthday of

the 17th-century ruler, Tirumala Nayak. Temple deities are dressed up in silk, garlands, and jewelry, and paraded to the city's large tank. Here, they are put on barges that are pulled through the water, accompanied by plenty of music and chanting.

Desert Festival, Jaisalmer. First held in 1979, this is a good chance to see some camel polo and races, and some traditional Rajasthani dance, music, and crafts.

Nagaur Fair, Nagaur, near Jodhpur. This is one of India's biggest livestock fairs, and now augments its traditional trading with dance and entertainment for visitors.

Ulsavom, Ernakulam. The 8-day festival at Shiva Temple includes an elephant procession, dance, and music.

FEBRUARY

Tansen Music Festival, Delhi. There are, in fact, two festivals honoring this great musician who was part of the Mogul emperor Akbar's court; the other is held at his home city, Gwalior, in December (see p. 382). Tansen helped to develop and elaborate the stately *dhrupad* form of Hindustani classical vocal and instrumental music, as well as the particular *Gwalior gharana* form of singing. At both festivals, some of India's greatest musicians play for several days and nights.

Dhrupad Music Festival, Delhi and Varanasi. A chance to hear top musicians who have mastered northern India's demanding and complex classical music. Look out for other classical music and dance arts festivals in Delhi this month.

Delhi Flower Show, Delhi. Spectacular blooms of all colors and sizes, from marigolds to gladiolis and chrysanthemums,

are on show at Purana Qila. Around this time, the fiercely competitive gardens created on Delhi's many roundabouts are judged and signs indicate the proud winners.

FEBRUARY–MARCH

Shivratri, nationwide. Devotees of Shiva spend the whole night worshiping their deity, and major Shiva temples are alive with puja, music, bell ringing, processions, and chanting. Good places to witness this include Chidambaram, Khajuraho (which holds a 10-day-long fair), Mandi, Ramaswaram, Udaipur (and Eklingji), and Varanasi.

Holi, Rajasthan and Mathura. Although this festival is to an extent celebrated across India, Rajasthan is the place to experience it. The festival marks the arrival of spring and the triumph of good over evil. Homes are cleaned, and bonfires sizzle with unwanted possessions. On Holi eve, the first dish of lentils is singed in the communal bonfire, then eaten ceremoniously at home. On the day of Holi itself, social rules are suspended until noon while men and women flirt, dance through the streets, and play holi by squirting pink water at one another and throwing handfuls of pink, red, and mauve powder. Children, elders, and visitors join in the state-wide party—but be sure to wear old clothes. At Mathura and its surrounding villages—associated with Krishna—the celebrations are equally intense and include plays acting out Krishna's life.

Carnival, Goa. For the four days before Lent, this informal, open-air fancy dress party focuses on a different city each day: Panaji, Margao, Mapusa, and Vasco. Everyone is welcome to join in the celebrations with the processions, dancing, bands,

barbecues, and floats that fill city and village streets and continue as all-night beach parties.

MARCH

Khajuraho Dance Festival, Kajuraho. Each evening for a week, top dancers perform India's classical dances such as Kathak in front of the illuminated western group of temples (see pp. 112–113).

MARCH–APRIL

Gangaur, Udaipur. Rajasthan's important spring festival, celebrated about two weeks after Holi and best seen at Udaipur. Gauri (a name sometimes used for Shiva's wife, Parvati) is the goddess of abundance and fertility. Women pray in temples to painted images of her, asking for bliss and faithfulness in marriage. Then, dressed in yellow, they parade these images down to Lake Pichola to give them a ceremonial bath, singing all the way. The same festival is celebrated in Bengal and Orissa, where it is called Doljatra.

Mahvir Jayanti, Gujarat. Jains remember Mahavira, the 24th Tirthankara and founder of their religion, with special pilgrimages to sacred sites such as Palitana. Celebrations also occur at Ranakpur and Shravanabelagola.

Lent Procession, Goa. The Procession of All Saints of the Franciscan Third Order is held on the Monday after Palm Sunday at St Andrew's Church, Velha. Over 20 figures of saints are paraded round the streets on decorated floats, a tradition begun in the 17th century.

Hindu New Year, nationwide, April 13. An official public holiday, with local fairs.

APRIL–MAY

Minakshi Kalyanam, Madurai.
The vast and warrenlike Minakshi temple is thronged with the faithful, who spend ten days celebrating the marriage of Minakshi (a name for Parvati) to Shiva. It ends with a great procession of deities on a huge *rath.* More impressive and inclusive than the similar and better known Puri festival.

Baisakhi, northern India.
This spring festival is celebrated with particular fervor in the hills, with dancing among the almond blossom of the orchards and in the green wheat fields of the Punjab. There Sikhs also celebrate Guru Gobind Singh's forming of the faithful into Khalso (the pure one) in 1689.

MAY–JUNE

Buddha Purnima, Bodh Gaya.
Celebrated on full moon night at all sacred Buddhist sites, to remember Buddha's birth, enlightenment, and attainment of Nirvana. This is a particularly intense experience at Bodh Gaya, where Buddha received enlightenment.

JUNE–JULY

Hemis Setchu, Leh.
Crowds of locals dressed in their traditional garments watch the two-day pageant that includes wonderful *chaam* dances performed with crashing cymbals and thundering drums, and lamas dressed in silk and ghoulish masks performing mime dance-dramas from Buddhist mythology. The festival ends with a symbolic triumph of Buddhism over ignorance. Every 12 years (next time 2004) the *gompa's* prize *thanka* (painted scroll) is unwound and hung across the entire facade of the building.

JULY–AUGUST

Teej, Rajasthan.
If you have suffered from the pre-monsoon heat and humidity of Rajasthan, you will empathize with locals who celebrate the onset of the monsoon with singing, dancing, and playing on garlanded swings. The women wear striped green veils. The moment also remembers the reunion of Shiva and Parvati, and at Jaipur caparisoned elephants escort Parvati's image and crowds of faithful worshippers from her parents' symbolic home to her husband's.

AUGUST

Independence Day,
nationwide.
This is a public holiday across the country in remembrance of the midnight hour on August 14–15 when Viceroy Lord Mountbatten handed over power to Jawaharlal Nehru and independent India was born. In Delhi each year, the prime minister makes a televised speech from the ramparts of the Red Fort, and Rastrapati Bhavan is illuminated.

AUGUST–SEPTEMBER

Janmashtami, Vrindaban.
Celebrations of Krishna's birthday are best seen in the villages associated with his mythical, flirtatious, and eventful youth, particularly in Vrindaban, just south of Mathura. Here, temple festivities include the lyrical *ras lila* dances which are performed in circles just as they appear in miniature paintings, where Krishna is pictured with his consort, Radha.

Onam, Kottayam.
Kerala's harvest festival and new year are rolled into one for a celebration that lasts for a week leading up to full-moon day. Amid the feasting and dancing, its highlight is the series of snake boat races held on the backwaters, especially those at Kottayam. Fiercely competitive teams of up to 100 members each row their long, narrow, dug-out boats. The men sing and shout war cries while their fast paddling is kept in time by a man pounding a wooden pole.

SEPTEMBER

Ganpati, Mumbai.
The elephant-headed god of good fortune and prosperity is eminently suited to money-making Mumbai, where his festival brings the city to a standstill. More than 6,000 gaudily painted clay images are made annually, the large ones for factories who display them on top of lorries. Ten days of celebration begin with *pujas* performed to smaller images in homes and on street corners. On full-moon day, citizens parade their idols down to Chowpatty beach, which is already adorned with multi-colored Ganesh sand-sculptures, amid much dancing, singing, and throwing of pink powder. Finally, the people give up the images to the water and watch them bob out to sea and disintegrate.

SEPTEMBER–OCTOBER

Dussehra, nationwide.
A countrywide celebration of good over evil, which is particularly elaborate in certain cities. In the north, celebrations focus on Rama's defeat of the demon Ravana to save his wife Sita. In Delhi, classical and contemporary plays, dance, and music fill every hall; special nightly play cycles recount the *Ramayana;* and in Old Delhi there are processions and spectacular open-air *Ramayana* shows. In Varanasi, a month of nightly Ram Lila plays and music, each in a different venue, ends with a huge procession and continuous temple readings of

the epic. In Kolkata, where the festival is called Durga Puja, celebrations take over the city for three weeks and focus on Durga, destroyer of evil: Here huge, brightly painted and tinsel-decorated images, made throughout the year, are set up in the streets, and Bengalis visit them on nightly promenades, enjoying plenty of dance, music, and theater until the final day when the images are taken through the decorated streets down to the Hooghly and immersed in the water. At Mysore, this festival is called Dassera and focuses on Chamundeswari's triumph over the demon Mahishasura: Ten days of medieval pageantry and classical and folk dance and drama end with a sumptuous procession and fireworks.

OCTOBER–NOVEMBER

Diwali, nationwide.
This nationwide festival is best seen in the north of the country. About four weeks after Dussehra, Diwali celebrates the return of Rama with his rescued wife, Sita, to his capital city, Ayodhya. Tiny terra-cotta oil lamps symbolically light the way for the couple while also welcoming Lakshmi, goddess of wealth, to the new Hindu financial year (not to be confused with the Hindu New Year on April 13), ending with late night fireworks. This is a time for families to come together, for giving boxes of sweetmeats, and for going to special cultural events.

NOVEMBER

Sonepur Fair, Patna.
Held just outside the city on the banks of the Ganga, this centuries-old, month-long fair claims to be the world's largest agricultural fair. India's longest station platform allows for trainloads of livestock to be transported here. Starting on full

moon day, this is the place to see cows, horses, parrots, goats, and often more than a hundred elephants traded. All kinds of agricultural seeds, plants, and equipment are also sold.

Nanak Jayanti, Amritsar.
The birthday of Guru Nanak, founder of the Sikh religion, is celebrated by Sikhs, especially at the Golden Temple in their holy city, Amritsar.

Desert Festival, Bikaner.
This Rajasthan city's desert festival is more modest and less crowded than that in Jaisalmer during February.

NOVEMBER–DECEMBER

Pushkar Cattle Fair, Pushkar.
This was once just a cattle fair, full of natural interest and charm. It is now almost drowned by tourists and their requisite shopping opportunities.

DECEMBER

Tansen Music Festival, Gwalior.
See February (p. 380).

DECEMBER–JANUARY

Chennai Dance and Arts Festival, Chennai.
Four weeks of nightly performances by the country's top classical musicians and dancers, often in deceptively informal settings of simple white awnings in backstreets. A superb opportunity if you are touring southern Indian temples, since the music and dance you see now was developed in the temples and originally only performed in them. Tickets can be bought at the tourist office on arrival at the city.

Kumbh Mela
This great religious cleansing festival is held every three years in one of four places

consecutively: Allahabad, Nasik, Ujjain, and Haridwar—it is at Nasik in 2004. According to legend, each of these cities is located where a drop of nectar was spilled by Vishnu, thus allowing the devout to cross from this world into that of the gods. Literally millions of Hindu pilgrims and holy men gather for their holy bath, stimulating the arrival of fairs, stalls, and entertainers. Foreign visitors are beginning to take a keen interest in the Kumbh Mela, but facilities are simple and hygiene not always good.

Mohini Alankaram, Tiruchchirappalli.
The huge, rambling Sri Ranganathaswamy Temple fills with the faithful, temple elephants, and worship of all sorts for this festival. Two other festivals are also held here at around the same time: Vaikunta Ekadasi and the Car Festival.

MUSLIM FESTIVALS

Muslim festivals move right around the year and are celebrated with feasts, fairs, fine literature, and jollity. The best places to witness them are the old Muslim centers such as Lucknow, Old Delhi, Hyderabad, and Ahmedabad. The principal ones are:

Id-ul-Fitr (also called **Ramzan-Id**)
Celebrates the end of 30 days of fasting during Ramadan.

Id-ul-Zuhar (also called **Bakr-Id**)
Commemorates Abraham's attempted sacrifice of Ishmail.

Muharram
Lasting for ten days, this commemorates the martyrdom of Mohammed's grandson, Imam Hussain, and is best seen at Lucknow where *tazias* (replicas of Hussain's tomb) are paraded by mourning men, accompanied by drummers.

GLOSSARY

English is the connecting language of India, and used by the travel industry, hotel staff, shops, guides and, usually, drivers. You do not need a phrase book for Hindi, the predominant language of northern India, nor for the languages of other areas; even if you go right off the beaten track you are likely to have a guide or driver who will translate. However, it is useful to know the meanings of some everyday words, some words to do with India's religions, and some unfamiliar uses of English words. Words to do with food can be found at the front of the book on p. 24.

A
adivasi tribal person
agarbati incense
ahimsa non-violence
apsaras heavenly nymphs who seduce men and escort gods
arak liquor distilled from coconuts or rice
ashram spiritual retreat; center for yoga and meditation
auto-rickshaw two-seater scooter-powered taxi
avatar incarnation of a god, especially Vishnu
ayurveda ancient system of medicine
ayyanar large terra-cotta images of deities

B
baba term of respect for old man
bagh garden
baksheesh bribe to get service; tip to reward service; gift to beggar
Balarama brother of god Krishna
baoli (or *vav*) stepped water well, often elaborately decorated
bandhana tie-dye craft
banyan huge fig tree, often with drooping lateral roots
bazar market, market-place
beedi small, hand-rolled cigarette
betel leaf or nut that is an ingredient of paan
Bhagavad Gita Song of the Lord, see p. 76
Bhagavata Purana Hindu epic, see p. 76
bhakti emotional religious devotion
bharata natyam classical dance of Tamil Nadu
bhavan house
Bhumi earth goddess
bindi (bindu) fashion decoration on a woman's forehead
bodhi enlightenment; pipal tree, see p. 58
Bodhisattva Buddhist saint who shows others the way
Brahma Creator of the universe; head of the Trimurti (Hindu Trinity) of Brahma, Vishnu and Shiva; Saraswati is his consort/daughter; Hamsa, the goose, is his vehicle
brahman highest Hindu caste group, the teachers and priests, see p. 54
Buddha The Enlightened One, see p. 58
burqa body-covering garment worn by orthodox Muslim women

C
cantonment military area of a town
caste broad Hindu social status at birth; see also p. 29
cenotaph tomb
chaat snack
chair tea
chaitya Buddhist shrine
chappals sandals
char bagh garden divided into four symmetrical parts
charpoi string bed with wooden-frame
chhatri tomb, mausoleum, cenotaph, domed pavilion
choli blouse worn with sari
chorten see *stupa*
chowk crossroads; courtyard
chowkidar watchman, caretaker
coolie porter, laborer
crore 10 million
curd yogurt, also called *dahi*

D
dargah Muslim saint's tomb
darshan for Hindus, the merit-winning glimpse of a deity
deepastambha lamp tower
deva god
devi goddess

dhabba roadside café
dhal pulses, especially lentils
dharma religious and social duty (Hindu); Buddha's teachings (Bhuddist)
dhobi laundry
dhoti white cloth worn by men
dhurrie flat weave rug
dikpalas guardians of the four directions, often sculptures at temple doorways
diwan chief minister
diwan-i-am public audience hall
diwan-i-khas private audience hall
dowry agreed marriage gifts from bride's family to groom's family
Dravidian culture of Southern India, derived from Dravidadesh, the former name for Tamil Nadu
dupatta Muslim woman's veil
durbar government meeting/hall
Durga malevolent aspect of the goddess Parvati

E
emporium shop, often large and selling local crafts

F
feni an alcoholic drink made in Goa by distilling coconut or cashew fruit
fresco a method of painting using colors ground in water, laid on the wall or ceiling while the plaster is still wet

G
gadi throne
gandharvas Indra's heavenly musicians
Ganesh elephant-headed god of learning and good fortune, son of Shiva and Parvati
garbha griha womb of a Hindu temple
garh fort (see also *kot, qila*)
Garuda eagle or mythical sunbird, vehicle of Vishnu
ghaghra skirt
ghat step; stepped mountains
ghazal Urdu song
ghee clarified butter
godown warehouse
gompa monastery
gopi young cowgirls who play with Krishna
gopura temple gateway with tapering tower

guru teacher, mentor

gurudwara Sikh place of worship

gymkhana social club with good sports facilities

H

haj Muslim pilgrimage to Mecca

haldi turmeric

Hanuman the monkey god, Rama's ally in the *Ramayana*

Hanti Panchika's (q.v.) consort

harijans children of God, Gandhi's word for untouchables; see p. 29

haveli courtyard house (mansion)

Hinayana Lesser Vehicle, the Buddhist sect that spread to Sri Lanka, Burma, and Thailand

hookah cooling water pipe for smoking tobacco

howdah elaborate elephant saddle

I

imam Muslim teacher/leader

Indra god of rain and thunder

ITDC India Tourism Development Corporation

J

jali pierced screen

Jangha body of a Hindu temple

jatakas tales about Buddha's life and teachings

-ji name suffix to show respect

jihad justified holy war for Muslims

jina Jain tirthankara/saint

johar mass self-immolation by women after war defeat

K

Kali fearsome goddess of destruction, an aspect of Parvati

kailasha mountain abode of the gods

karma idea that deeds in previous existences determine one's status at rebirth

kasti wrestling

Kartikeya god of war, son of Shiva and Parvati, also known as Skanda or Subramanya

katcha no good, opposite of pukka

kathak classical dance of N. India

kathakali dance-drama of Kerala

khadi hand-spun and woven cotton

kolam a ritual pattern created using colored rice flour

kot fort (see also *garh, qila*)

Krishna blue-skinned human incarnation of Vishnu

kshatriya warrior caste, see p. 29

kumkum red mark on forehead worn by married women

kurta man's loose-fitting shirt

L

lakh 100,000

Lakshmi goddess of wealth and good fortune, consort of Vishnu

lingam Shiva's phallic emblem symbolizing energy

lunghi similar to dhoti, often colored

M

machan watchtower (hide) in a wildlife park

madrasa Islamic school, often in mosque

Mahabharata Hindu epic, see p. 76

mahal palace

maharaja great king

maharani great queen

Mahatma great soul; epithet of Gandhi

Mahayana Great Vehicle, the Buddhist sect that spread to China, Japan, and Tibet

mahout elephant keeper/driver

maidan large open space

makara aquatic monster, often symbol of sea god or of River Ganga

mala garland

mandala religious diagram

mandapa hall, porch

mandir temple

mantra sacred verse

marg road

masala mixture, as in spices for cooking

masala dosa rice pancake stuffed with vegetables

masjid mosque

mela festival

memsahib term of respect for Western woman

mendhi henna

mihrab prayer niche of a mosque, with *qibla* (indicator) for the direction of Mecca

mimbar mosque's pulpit

minaret tower the faithful are called to prayer from a mosque's minaret

mithuna amorous couple, as in temple sculpture

moksha blissful release from rebirth

monsoon rainy season, see p. 20

mudra hand gestures in rituals, dance, and art (Hindu, Jain); teachings of Buddha (Buddhist)

muezzin man calling Muslims to prayer

muggu colored rice flour

mullah Muslim teacher/scholar

N

naga snake

nala mountain stream, gorge

namaste word of respectful greeting

natak dance

natya drama

nawab Muslim prince

nirvana blissful state when personal identity is extinguished

O

om symbol for the origin of all things

P

paan betel (q.v.) nut and sweet/sour condiments wrapped in a leaf and chewed as a digestive

padma lotus

paise 100th of a rupee

pajama man's baggy trousers

palanquin covered couch carried by servants (litter)

palo decorated end of a sari

Panchika guardian of the earth's treasures (Buddhist)

parikrama ritual walk clockwise round a temple/shrine

Parsee Zoroastrian (see p. 60)

Parvati goddess of peace and beauty, symbol of female energy, malevolent aspects include Devi, Kali, and Durga; consort of Shiva

pietra dura patterned stone inlay

pilo head veil

pol gate

prasad food offered in a temple, blessed, then shared by devotees

puja worship

pukka correct

Puranas ancient myths and legends, see p. 76

purdah the practice of women living separately from men, and covering their heads with veils in public

Q

qawwali devotional songs of Muslim *Sufis* (q.v., see p. 60)

qila fort; other words for fort include *garh, kot*

R

ragamala series of music themes, poems or art iconography related to a specific mood, each called a raga or ragini

raj rule The Raj was British imperial rule 1858–1947

raja ruler, king

Rajput kshatriya sub-caste that dominated north and west India

Rama incarnation of the god Vishnu, hero of the *Ramayana*; brother of Bharata and Lakshmana; his wife is Sita

Ramayana Hindu epic, see p. 76

rangoli geometric pattern of rice powder

rath chariot for parading temple deities

S

sadhu Hindu holy man free from caste or family ties

sagar lake, ocean

sahib term of respect for a man

salwar kameez baggy trousers and long shirt worn by women

samadhi site of Hindu saint's death or burial

samsara the spirit's movement across the generations enduring a cycle of rebirths, whose liberation is nirvana or moksha

sangam academy

sangeet music

sannyasi homeless ascetic; final stage of a Hindu's life

sarai inn, originally on the trade routes

Saraswati goddess of knowledge, music, arts; daughter or consort of Brahma

sari length of fabric worn by women

Sat truth, the Sikh idea of God

revealed through the gurus

sati a widow's honorable self-immolation, often on her husband's funeral pyre

satya truth

satyagraha grasping truth; Gandhi's campaign of non-violent protest

scheduled castes official name for untouchables (q.v.)

sepoy Indian soldier in European service

serai medieval equivalent of a motel

Seven Sacred Cities Varanasi, Haridwar, Ujjain, Mathura, Ayodhya, Dwarka, and Kanchipuram are sacred pilgrimage centers for Hindus

Shaivite worshiper of Shiva

shakti life force

shastra Hindu treatise

Sherpas Nepalese people renowned as high-altitude mountaineers

Shesha serpent on whom Vishnu reclines on the Cosmic Ocean

shikar hunting

shikara tapering temple tower

Shiva (Siva) The Auspicious, third member of the Hindu Trinity, symbol of destructive and creative energy, manifested in Nataraj (Lord of the Dance), etc.; consort Parvati, sons Ganesh and Kartikeya; vehicle Nandi the bull; emblem the lingam

Sita wife of Rama

shri title of respect

shudra laborer caste (see p. 29)

singh lion

stupa Buddhist funerary mound signifying Buddha's presence

Surya god of the sun; Arjuna, symbol of dawn, is his charioteer

swami title of holy man

swaraj self-rule, Gandhi's word for independence

T

tandoor clay oven

tank water reservoir, artificial lake

tazia multi-colored tinsel, silver or brass replicas of Hussain's tomb, paraded at the Muslim festival of Muharram

tempera a method of painting on

plaster or chalk with powder colors mixed with the yolk or white of egg, often used on internal walls

thangka scroll painting

tilak red dot priest puts on the forehead during worship

Tirthankara ford-makers, the 24 Jain saints and teachers

thali platter, usually used for vegetarian meals

tiffin light meal

tiffin can lunch box

tulsi basil

U

uba dando straight rod

untouchable lowest strata of Hindu society; see also *harijan* (q.v.) and p. 30

urs Muslim saint's festival

V

vahana deity's vehicle

Vaishnavite worshiper of Vishnu

vaishya merchant caste, see p. 29

vav see *baoli*

vedas Hindus' sacred early texts

vihara Buddhist or Jain monastery

vimana principle temple or central shrine of a Hindu temple; tower above temple

Vishnu The Preserver, second member of the Hindu Trinity; symbol of preservation to maintain the balance of the universe; incarnations include Rama and Krishna; consort Lakshmi; vehicle Garuda

W

wallah fellow, e.g. dhobi-wallah

wazir chief minister

Y

yatra pilgrimage

yoga psycho-physical discipline involving the practice of meditation, exercise positions, and breathing control to achieve spiritual peace

yoni symbol of the female sexual organ, often depicted in a temple as a circular shape surrounding a central lingam (q.v.)

Z

zenana women's quarters

ILLUSTRATIONS CREDITS

Abbreviations for terms appearing below: (t) top; (b) bottom; (l) left; (r) right; (c) center

Cover (tl), Images Colour Library. (tr), Gettyone/Stone. (bl), Photographer's Library. (br), Images Colour Library. Spine, Eye Ubiquitous.
1, Wolfgang Kaehler Photography. 2/3, Andrea Booher/Gettyone/Stone. 4, Catherine Karnow. 9, Steve McCurry/National Geographic Society. 11, J. McNally/National Geographic Society. 12/13, J. McNally/National Geographic Society. 14/15, Steve McCurry/National Geographic Society. 16/17, Steve McCurry/National Geographic Society. 18/19, Aspect Picture Library. 21, R. Ian Lloyd Productions. 22/23, Steve McCurry/National Geographic Society. 25, Bennett Dean/Eye Ubiquitous. 27, David Cumming/Eye Ubiquitous. 28/29, Steve McCurry/National Geographic Society. 31, Bury Peerless. 33, Bury Peerless. 34/35, Wolfgang Kaehler Photography. 36, Maxine Cass. 37, Bury Peerless. 38, Wolfgang Kaehler Photography. 41, Trip & Art Directors Photo Library. 43, Gettyone/Stone. 44/45, Mary Evans Picture Library. 47, By Courtesy of the National Portrait Gallery, London. 48/49, Royal Photographic Society, London. 50, Hulton Getty Picture Collection Ltd. 50/51, Steve McCurry/National Geographic Society. 52, Steve McCurry/National Geographic Society. 53, Raghu Rai/Magnum Photos. 55, Steve Jones/Axiom. 56/57, Steve McCurry/National Geographic Society. 58, Trip & Art Directors Photo Library. 59, Steve McCurry/National Geographic Society. 61, Dinodia Picture Agency/Images of India. 62, AA Photo Library/D. Corrance. 64/65, Peter Sanders Photography. 66, Mecky Fögeling. 67, Christine Osborne Pictures/MEP. 68, Mecky Fögeling. 69t, Steve McCurry/National Geographic Society. 69b, Jeremy Horner/Gettyone/Stone. 70, Wolfgang Kaehler Photography. 70/71, Peter Sanders Photography. 72, C. Wormald/Trip & Art Directors Photo Library. 73, AA Photo Library/D. Corrance. 74, Christine Osborne Pictures/MEP. 76/77, AA Photo Library/D. Corrance. 77l, Rex Features. 77r, Rex Features. 78, T. Bognar/Trip & Art Directors Photo Library. 80, Maxine Cass. 81, Hutchison Library. 82, Bury Peerless. 83t, Gerald Cubitt. 83b, Superstock Ltd. 84/85, Peter Sanders Photography. 85, AA Photo Library/D. Corrance. 86, Victoria & Albert Museum, London/Bridgeman Art Library. 87, National Museum of India, New Delhi, India/ Bridgeman Art Library. 88, Rene Burri/Magnum Photos. 89t, Rene Burri/Magnum Photos. 89c, F. Good/Trip & Art Directors Photo Library. 89b, David Forman/Eye Ubiquitous. 90/91, Elk Photo.

92, Images Colour Library. 93, Bennett Dean/Eye Ubiquitous. 94, Eye Ubiquitous. 96/97, Wolfgang Kaehler Photography. 98, AA Photo Library/D. Corrance. 99, Robert Holmes. 100/101, Steve McCurry/National Geographic Society. 102l, David Cumming/Eye Ubiquitous. 102r, Raghu-Rai/Magnum Photos. 103l, AA Photo Library/D. Corrance. 103r, Robert Holmes. 104, Terry Harris. 105t, Terry Harris. 105b, Wolfgang Kaehler Photography. 106, Gerald Cubitt. 107, M. Powles/Eye Ubiquitous. 108, Hutchison Library. 109, Steve McCurry/Magnum Photos. 110, Robert Harding Picture Library. 111, Robert Harding Picture Library. 112/113, Dinodia Picture Agency/Images of India. 113, Trip & Art Directors Photo Library. 114, Hutchison Library. 115, Hutchison Library. 116, Trip & Art Directors Photo Library. 117, Dinodia Picture Agency/Images of India. 118/119, Wolfgang Kaehler Photography. 120, Dinodia Picture Agency/Images of India. 122/123, Bennett Dean/Eye Ubiquitous. 123, H. Rogers/Trip & Art Directors Photo Library. 124, Elk Photo. 124/125, Elk Photo. 126, Gerald Cubitt. 127, Hutchison Library. 128, Robert Holmes. 129, Hutchison Library. 130/131, Superstock Ltd. 131, Elk Photo. 132, AA Photo Library/D. Corrance. 133, AA Photo Library/D. Corrance. 134, David Sanger. 135t, Eye Ubiquitous. 135b, Gettyone/Stone. 136, Axiom. 137t, Hutchison Library. 137b, Trip & Art Directors Photo Library. 138, AA Photo Library/D. Corrance. 139, AA Photo Library/D. Corrance. 141, Steve McCurry/National Geographic Society. 142, AA Photo Library/D. Corrance. 143, Trip & Art Directors Photo Library. 144, Eye Ubiquitous. 145t, Eye Ubiquitous. 145c, Eye Ubiquitous. 145b, Hutchison Library. 146/147, Trip & Art Directors Photo Library. 147, Trip & Art Directors Photo Library. 148, Trip & Art Directors Photo Library. 149, Trip & Art Directors Photo Library. 150, Dinodia/Trip & Art Directors Photo Library. 151, Hulton Getty Collection Ltd. 152/153, Trip & Art Directors Photo Library. 153, Bennett Dean/Eye Ubiquitous. 154/155, Trip & Art Directors Photo Library. 156, Gerald Cubitt. 157, Hutchison Library. 159, Catherine Karnow. 160/161, Catherine Karnow. 162, Catherine Karnow. 163, D. Constantine/Axiom. 164/165, Catherine Karnow. 166/167, Catherine Karnow. 168, Christine Pemberton/Hutchison Library. 169, Hutchison Library. 170/171, Hutchison Library. 171, Hutchison Library. 172, Travel Ink. 173, Robert Leon. 174, Powerstock Zefa Picture Library. 175, R. Francis/Hutchison Library. 176/177, Bury Peerless. 177, D. Shaw/Axiom. 178, Eye Ubiquitous. 179, Jean-Louis Nou/AKG, London. 180, Bury Peerless. 181, Bibliotheque National, Paris, France/Bridgeman Art Library. 182, R. Burri/Magnum Photos. 183t, Robert Leon. 183b, Robert Leon. 184, Robert Leon. 185, Robert Leon. 186, H. Rogers/Trip & Art Directors Photo Library. 187, Robert Leon.

188, Robert Leon. 189, Terry Harris. 190, Axiom. 192/193, Aspect Picture Library. 194, Aspect Picture Library. 195, Christine Osborne Pictures/MEP. 196, Christine Osborne Pictures/MEP. 197, Christine Osborne Pictures/MEP. 198, Trip & Art Directors Photo Library. 199, Terry Harris. 200/201, S. Jones/Axiom. 201, Trip & Art Directors Photo Library. 202, Terry Harris. 203, Terry Harris. 204, Christine Osborne Pictures/MEP. 205bl, Christine Osborne Pictures/MEP. 205br, Trip & Art Directors Photo Library. 205t, Robert Leon. 206, Bury Peerless. 207, Barbara Lloyd. 208, Wolfgang Kaehler Photography. 210, Hutchison Library. 211, Aspect Picture Library. 212, David Sanger. 213, Aspect Picture Library. 214, John Isaac/Still Pictures. 215t, Christine Osborne Pictures/MEP. 215bl, Harry Gryaert/Magnum Photos. 215br, Bennett Dean/Eye Ubiquitous. 216, Terry Harris. 217, Terry Harris. 219, Leon Schadeberg/Eye Ubiquitous. 220, Barbara Lloyd. 221, Aspect Picture Library. 223t, Trip & Art Directors Photo Library. 223b, Travel Ink. 224/225, Axiom. 226, Sarah Errington/Hutchison Library. 227, Hutchison Library. 228, Axiom. 229t, Hutchison Library. 229b, James Davis Worldwide. 230, Nicholas Sumner. 231, Travel Ink. 232, Eye Ubiquitous. 233, Trip & Art Directors Photo Library. 234, Hutchison Library. 235, C. Caldicot/Axiom. 236/237, Aspect Picture Library. 238, Barbara Lloyd. 238/239, Michael Freeman. 240, Barbara Lloyd. 241, Eye Ubiquitous. 242, Tim Beddow/Hutchison Library. 245, Joerg Boetheling/Still Pictures. 247, Barbara Lloyd. 248, Hutchison Library. 249, Trip & Art Directors Photo Library. 251, Bury Peerless. 253, Barbara Lloyd. 254, Eye Ubiquitous. 256, Trip & Art Directors Photo Library. 257, Trip & Art Directors Photo Library. 258, Hutchison Library. 260, Barbara Lloyd. 261, Bury Peerless. 262, Trip & Art Directors Photo Library. 263t, Bury Peerless. 263b, Hutchison Library. 264, Bury Peerless. 266, Eye Ubiquitous. 267, Eye Ubiquitous. 268, Bury Peerless. 269, Trip & Art Directors Photo Library. 270/271, Trip & Art Directors Photo Library. 271, Hutchison Library. 272/273, Barbara Lloyd. 274, Eye Ubiquitous. 277, David Sanger. 278/279, Hutchison Library. 279, Hutchison Library. 281, Hutchison Library. 283, F. Good/Trip & Art Directors Photo Library. 285, Eye Ubiquitous. 287, Paul Harris Photography. 288/289, Paul Harris Photography. 291, Hutchison Library. 292, T. O'Brien/Trip & Art Directors Photo Library. 293, James Davis Worldwide. 294, Hutchison Library. 295, Eye Ubiquitous. 296, Trip & Art Directors Photo Library. 297tl, Elk Photo. 297tr, Paul Harris Photography. 297b, F. Good/Trip & Art Directors Photo Library. 298/299, Photo Resource Hawaii, Inc. 300/301, Michael Freeman. 302/303, Hutchison Library. 304, Francis Bacon/Axiom. 305t, Dinodia/Trip & Art Directors Photo Library. 305bl, R. Rai/Magnum Photos. 305br, Ray

The world's largest nonprofit scientific and educational organization, the National Geographic Society was founded in 1888 "for the increase and diffusion of geographic knowledge." Since then it has supported scientific exploration and spread information to its more than nine million members worldwide.

The National Geographic Society educates and inspires millions every day through magazines, books, television programs, videos, maps and atlases, research grants, the National Geography Bee, teacher workshops, and innovative classroom materials.

The Society is supported through membership dues, charitable gifts, and income from the sale of its educational products. Members receive NATIONAL GEOGRAPHIC magazine—the Society's official journal—discounts on Society products, and other benefits.

For more information about the National Geographic Society, its educational programs, publications, or how to support its work, call 1-800-NGS-LINE (647-5463), or write to: National Geographic Society, 1145 17th Street, N.W., Washington, D.C. 20036 U.S.A.

Printed in the U.S.A.

Published by the National Geographic Society
John M. Fahey, Jr., *President and Chief Executive Officer*
Gilbert M. Grosvenor, *Chairman of the Board*
Nina D. Hoffman, *Executive Vice President,*
President, Books and School Publishing
Elizabeth L. Newhouse, *Director of Travel Publishing*
Barbara A. Noe, *Senior Editor and Project Manager*
Cinda Rose, *Art Director*
Carl Mehler, *Director of Maps*
Joseph F. Ochlak, *Map Coordinator*
Gary Colbert, *Production Director*
Richard S. Wain, *Production Project Manager*
Lise Sajewski, *Editorial Consultant*
Caroline Hickey, *Senior Researcher*
Lawrence Porges, *Editorial Coordinator*
Verena Phipps, *Contributor*

Edited and designed by AA Publishing (a trading name of Automobile Association Developments Limited, whose registered office is Norfolk House, Priestley Road, Basingstoke, Hampshire, England RG24 9NY. Registered number: 1878835).
Virginia Langer, *Project Manager*
David Austin, *Senior Art Editor*
Victoria Barber, *Senior Editor*
Inna Nogeste, *Senior Cartographic Editor*
Richard Firth, *Production Director*
Steve Gilchrist, *Prepress Production Controller*
Cartography by AA Cartographic Production
Maps © 2001. Based upon Survey of India maps with the permission of the Surveyor General of India
Picture Research by Zooid Pictures Ltd., & Carol Walker, AA Picture Library
Area maps drawn by Chris Orr Associates, Southampton, England
Cutaway illustrations drawn by Maltings Partnership, Derby, England

ISSN 1536-8637

Printed and bound by R.R. Donnelley & Sons, Willard, Ohio.
Color separations by Leo Reprographic Ltd., Hong Kong
Cover separations by L.C. Repro, Aldermaston, U.K.
Cover printed by Miken Inc., Cheektowaga, New York.

Visit the society's Web site at http://www.nationalgeographic.com

The information in this book has been carefully checked and to the best of our knowledge is accurate. However, details are subject to change, and the National Geographic Society cannot be responsible for such changes, or for errors or omissions. Assessments of sites, hotels, and restaurants are based on the author's subjective opinions, which do not necessarily reflect the publisher's opinion. The publisher cannot be responsible for any consequences arising from the use of this book.

NATIONAL GEOGRAPHIC
TRAVELER

A Century of Travel Expertise in Every Guide

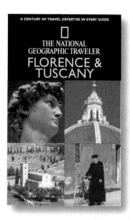

- **Arizona** ISBN: 0-7922-7899-2
- **Australia** ISBN: 0-7922-7431-8
- **Boston & Environs** ISBN: 0-7922-7926-3
- **California** ISBN: 0-7922-7564-0
- **Canada** ISBN: 0-7922-7427-X
- **The Caribbean** ISBN: 0-7922-7434-2
- **China** ISBN: 0-7922-7921-2
- **Costa Rica** ISBN: 0-7922-7946-8
- **Egypt** ISBN: 0-7922-7896-8
- **Florence & Tuscany** ISBN: 0-7922-7924-7
- **Florida** ISBN: 0-7922-7432-6
- **France** ISBN: 0-7922-7426-1
- **Great Britain** ISBN: 0-7922-7425-3
- **Greece** ISBN: 0-7922-7923-9
- **Hawaii** ISBN: 0-7922-7944-1
- **India** ISBN: 0-7922-7898-4
- **Italy** ISBN: 0-7922-7562-4
- **Japan** ISBN: 0-7922-7563-2
- **London** ISBN: 0-7922-7428-8
- **Los Angeles** ISBN: 0-7922-7947-6
- **Mexico** ISBN: 0-7922-7897-6
- **Miami and the Keys** ISBN: 0-7922-7433-4
- **New Orleans** ISBN: 0-7922-7948-4
- **New York** ISBN: 0-7922-7430-X
- **Paris** ISBN: 0-7922-7429-6
- **Rome** ISBN: 0-7922-7566-7
- **San Francisco** ISBN: 0-7922-7565-9
- **Spain** ISBN: 0-7922-7922-0
- **Sydney** ISBN: 0-7922-7435-0
- **Thailand** ISBN: 0-7922-7943-3
- **Venice** ISBN: 0-7922-7917-4

AVAILABLE WHEREVER BOOKS ARE SOLD